Seyyed Hossein Nasr

KNOWLEDGE

AND THE

SACRED

THE GIFFORD LECTURES, 1981

CROSSROAD · NEW YORK

1981
The Crossroad Publishing Company
575 Lexington Avenue, New York, NY 10022

Library of Congress Cataloging in Publication Data

Nasr, Seyyed Hossein.
Knowledge and the sacred.

(Gifford lectures; 1981)
Includes bibliographical references and index.
Contents: Knowledge and its desacralization—What
is tradition?—The rediscovery of the sacred: the
revival of tradition—[etc.]
1. Knowledge, Theory of (Religion) I. Title.
II. Series.
BL51.N316   291.2   81-12453
ISBN 0-8245-0095-4   AACR2

Contents

يا مريم عليك السلام ۔۔۔ بسم الله الرحمن الرحيم

Yā Maryam[u] 'alayka'l-salām
Bismi'Llāh al-raḥmān al-raḥīm

Preface

Since the Gifford Lectures were first delivered at the University of Edinburgh in 1889, they have been associated with the names of some of the most celebrated theologians, philosophers, and scientists of Europe and America, and have resulted in books which have wielded extensive influence in the modern world. Moreover, most of these works have been associated with specifically modern ideas which have characterized the Western world since the Renaissance and which have been also spreading into the East since the last century. When, therefore, some four years ago we were invited to deliver these prestigious lectures, it marked for us not only a singular honor but also an occasion to present the traditional perspective of the millennial civilizations of the Orient where we first received and accepted the invitation to deliver them. Being the first Muslim and in fact the first Oriental to have the occasion to deliver the Gifford Lectures since their inception at the University of Edinburgh nearly a century ago, we felt it our duty to present to the Western audience not a secondhand version of certain modern ideas or *isms* in pseudo-Oriental dress as happens so often these days, but in conformity with the world view which is our own, to expound some aspect of that truth which lies at the heart of the Oriental traditions and in fact of all tradition as such whether it be of the East or the West.

In the Orient knowledge has always been related to the sacred and to spiritual perfection. To know has meant ultimately to be transformed by the very process of knowing, as the Western tradition was also to assert over the ages before it was eclipsed by the postmedieval secularization and humanism that forced the separation of knowing from being and intelligence from the sacred. The Oriental sage has always embodied spiritual perfection; intelligence has been seen ultimately as a sacrament, and knowledge has been irrevocably related to the sacred and its actualization in the being of the knower. And this relation continues wherever and whenever tradition still survives despite all the vicissitudes of the modern world.

During the past two centuries, countless Western students of the Orient have been, whether intentionally or unintentionally, instrumental in the process of the secularization of the East through the destruction of its traditions by interpreting its sacred teachings through historicism, evolutionism, scientism, and the many other means whereby the sacred is reduced to the profane. The study of the East by the majority of those so-called orientalists who have been themselves influenced by the various waves of secularism in the West, far from being simply a harmless, objective exercise in scholarship, has played no small role in the transformation of the subject of their studies. Moreover, these scholarly efforts have hardly been carried out through either love for the subject or charity, despite many notable and honorable exceptions which have been labors of love and which have produced valuable studies of various aspects of Oriental civilization. Most modern scholarly works concerned with the East are in fact the fruit of a secularized reason analyzing and studying traditions of a sacred character.

In the present study our aim has been in a sense the reverse of this process. It has been to aid in the resuscitation of the sacred quality of knowledge and the revival of the veritable intellectual tradition of the West with the aid of the still living traditions of the Orient where knowledge has never become divorced from the sacred. Our aim has been to deal first of all with an aspect of the truth as such which resides in the very nature of intelligence and secondarily with the revival of the sapiential perspective in the West, without which no civilization worthy of the name can survive. If in the process we have been severely critical of many aspects of things Western, our view has not been based on disdain and hatred or a kind of "occidentalism" which would simply reverse the role of a certain type of orientalism that has studied the Orient with the hope of transforming its sacred patterns of life, if not totally destroying all that has characterized the Orient as such over the ages. In criticizing what from the traditional point of view is pure and simple error, we have also tried to defend the millennial tradition of the West itself and to bring to light once again that perennial wisdom, or *sophia perennis*, which is both perennial and universal and which is neither exclusively Eastern nor Western.

When the invitation to deliver the Gifford Lectures first reached us, we were living in the shades of the southern slopes of the majestic Alborz Mountains. Little did we imagine then that the text of the lectures themselves would be written not in the proximity of those exalted peaks but in sight of the green forests and blue seas of the eastern coast of the United States. But man lives in the spirit and not in space and time so that despite all the unbelievable dislocations and turmoil in our personal life during this period, including the loss of our library and the preliminary notes for this work, what appears in the following pages has grown out of the seed originally conceived when we accepted to deliver the lectures and represents a continuity of thought with the intellectual genesis of this work even if the material and human conditions altered markedly during the period of the realization of its original idea.

Since this work seeks to be at once metaphysical and based on scholarship, it consists of a text upon which the actually delivered lectures were based as well as extensive footnotes which both complement the text and serve as a guide for further research for those who are attracted to the arguments and theses presented in the text. Upon delivering the lectures in the stately capital of Scotland during the spring when the city of Edinburgh blooms with flowers of great beauty, we became convinced even more than before of the necessity of these rather extensive footnotes. The lively reaction of the audience and many meetings with its members after the lectures brought to light the keen interest displayed by many of them in pursuing the arguments presented in this work despite the fact that its point of view is that of tradition and different from most of what has been the concern of most of the other Gifford lecturers over the years.

In preparing this work we are indebted most of all to all of our traditional masters in both East and West who over the years have guided us to the fountainhead of sacred knowledge. We wish to express our gratitude especially to Frithjof Schuon whose unparalleled exposition of traditional teachings is reflected, albeit imperfectly, upon many of the pages which follow. We also wish to thank Miss Kathleen O'Brien who aided us in many ways in preparing the manuscript for publication.

CHAPTER ONE

Knowledge and Its Desacralization

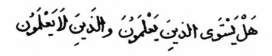

Are those who know and those who do not know equal?

Quran

Why standest Thou afar off, O Lord? *Why* hidest Thou
Thyself in times of trouble?

Psalms

In the beginning Reality was at once being, knowledge, and bliss
(the *sat, chit,* and *ānanda*[1] of the Hindu tradition or *qudrah, ḥikmah,*
and *raḥmah* which are among the Names of Allah in Islam) and in that
"now" which is the ever-present "in the beginning," knowledge
continues to possess a profound relation with that principial and
primordial Reality which *is* the Sacred and the source of all that is
sacred. Through the downward flow of the river of time and the
multiple refractions and reflections of Reality upon the myriad mirrors of both macrocosmic and microcosmic manifestation, knowledge has become separated from being and the bliss or ecstasy which
characterizes the union of knowledge and being. Knowledge has
become nearly completely externalized and desacralized, especially
among those segments of the human race which have become transformed by the process of modernization, and that bliss which is the
fruit of union with the One and an aspect of the perfume of the sacred
has become well-nigh unattainable and beyond the grasp of the vast
majority of those who walk upon the earth. But the root and essence
of knowledge continues to be inseparable from the sacred for the very
substance of knowledge is the knowledge of that reality which is the
Supreme Substance, the Sacred as such, compared to which all levels

of existence and all forms of the manifold are but accidents.[2] Intelligence, which is the instrument of knowledge within man, is endowed with the possibility of knowing the Absolute. It is like a ray which emanates from and returns to the Absolute and its miraculous functioning is itself the best proof of that Reality which is at once absolute and infinite.

In paradise man had tasted of the fruit of the Tree of Life which symbolizes unitive knowledge.[3] But he was also to taste of the Tree of Good and Evil and to come to see things as externalized, in a state of otherness and separation. The vision of duality blinded him to the primordial knowledge which lies at the heart of his intelligence. But precisely because this unitive vision resides at the center of his being as well as lying at the root of his intelligence, knowledge continues to be a means of access to the Sacred and sacred knowledge remains as the supreme path of union with that Reality wherein knowledge, being and bliss are united. Despite the tasting of the fruit of the Tree of Good and Evil and all the subsequent falls of man recorded in different manners by the various religions of the world, knowledge remains potentially the supreme way to gain access to the Sacred, and intelligence a ray which pierces the density and coagulation of cosmic manifestation and which, in its actualized state, is none other than the Divine Light itself as it is reflected in man and, in fact, in all things in different manners and modes.

It is, however, human intelligence which, despite the fall and all the resulting impediments and obstacles existing within the human soul which prevent intelligence from functioning fully in most instances, remains the central theophany of this Divine Light and the direct means of access to that Original Reality which "was" at once the source of cosmic reality "at the beginning" and is the origin of all things in this eternal "now," in this moment that always is and never becomes, the "now" which is the ever-recurring "in the beginning."[4]

Today modern man has lost the sense of wonder, which results from his loss of the sense of the sacred, to such a degree that he is hardly aware how miraculous is the mystery of intelligence, of human subjectivity as well as the power of objectivity and the possibility of knowing objectively. Man is oblivious to the mystery that he can turn inwardly upon the infinite world within himself and also objectivize the world outside, to possess inner, subjective knowledge as well as knowledge of a totally objective order. Man is endowed with this precious gift of intelligence which allows him to know the Ultimate Reality as the Transcendent, the Beyond and the objective world as a distinct reality on its own level, and the Ultimate Reality as the Immanent, as the Supreme Self underlying all the veils of subjectivity and the many "selves" or layers of consciousness within him. Knowledge can attain the Sacred both beyond the subject which knows and at the heart of this very subject, for finally that Ultimate Reality which *is* the Sacred as such is both the knower and the known, inner consciousness and outer reality, the pure immanent Subject and the Transcendent Object, the Infinite Self and Absolute Being which does not exclude Beyond Being. Despite the layers of the dross of forgetfulness that have covered the "eye of the heart" or the seat of intelligence, as a result of man's long journey in time, which is none other than the history of forgetfulness with occasional reversals of the downward flow through divine intervention in the cosmic and historical process, human intelligence continues to be endowed with this miraculous gift of knowledge of the inward and the outward, and human consciousness continues to be blessed with the possibility of contemplating the Reality which is completely other and yet none other than the very heart of the self, the Self of oneself.

Consciousness is itself proof of the primacy of the Spirit or Divine Consciousness of which human consciousness is a reflection and echo. The very natural propensity of the human intelligence to regard the Spirit as having primacy over the material and of consciousness as being on a higher level of reality than even the largest material object in the universe is itself proof of the primacy of the substance of knowledge over that which it knows, for the raison d'être of intelligence is to know reality objectively, totally, and adequately[5] according to the famous principle of adequation of the medieval Scholastics.[6] Human consciousness or subjectivity which makes knowledge possible is itself proof that the Spirit is the Substance compared to which all material manifestation, even what appears as the most substantial, is but an accident. It is in the nature and destiny of man to know and ultimately to know the Absolute and the Infinite through an intelligence which is total and objective and which is inseparable from the Sacred that is at once its origin and end.

Man is, of course, from a certain point of view the rational being defined by the philosophers, but the rational faculty which is at once an extension and reflection of the Intellect can become a luciferian force and instrument if divorced from the Intellect and revelation which alone bestow upon knowledge its numinous quality and sacred content. Therefore, rather than defining him only as a "rational animal," one can define man in a more principial manner as a being endowed with a total intelligence centered upon the Absolute and created to know the Absolute. To be human is to know and also to transcend oneself. To know means therefore ultimately to know the Supreme Substance which is at once the source of all that comprises the objective world and the Supreme Self which shines at the center of human consciousness and which is related to intelligence as the sun is related to its rays. Despite the partial loss and eclipse of this properly speaking intellectual faculty and its replacement by reason, the roots of knowledge remain sunk in the ground of the Sacred and sacred knowledge continues to be at the heart of the concern of man for the sacred. It is not possible in fact to rediscover the sacred without discovering once again the sacred quality of principial knowledge. Moreover, this process can be facilitated by tracing the trajectory which knowledge followed in its fall from being the fruit of the Tree of Life to becoming limited to the realm of profane knowledge, which in its expansion and even totalitarianism only hastens man's fall from the state of wholeness and the abode of grace, resulting finally in the desacralization of all of human life to an ever greater degree. To reinstate man to his position of humanity cannot occur without the rediscovery of the basic function of intelligence as the means of access to that which is central and essential, to the Reality from which issues all religion and all wisdom but also the nonsapiential modes of perfection such as the way of good works and love.

The reduction of the Intellect to reason and the limitation of intelligence to cunning and cleverness in the modern world not only caused sacred knowledge to become inaccessible and to some even meaningless, but it also destroyed that natural theology which in the Christian context represented at least a reflection of knowledge of a sacred order, of the wisdom or *sapientia* which was the central means of spiritual perfection and deliverance. Natural theology which was originally *sapientia* as understood by Plato in the *Republic* and *Laws*,[7] and which was later relegated by Saint Augustine and other Christian authorities to an inferior but nevertheless valuable form of knowledge of things divine, was completely banished from the citadel of both science and faith as the process of the desacralization of knowledge and the reduction of reason to a purely human and "this-worldly" instrument of perception reached its terminal point with the last phases of development of modern Western philosophy. To reinstate the supernaturally natural function of intelligence, to wed reason (*ratio*) to the Intellect (*intellectus*) once again, and to rediscover the possibility of attaining to sacred knowledge include therefore also a return to the appreciation of the importance of natural theology on its own level, which is of a lower order than what could be called *scientia sacra*, but which has nevertheless been of much importance in the traditional intellectual landscape of the Western world.

The eclipse of natural theology has also been accompanied by the casting into oblivion of the essentially sacred character of both logical and mathematical laws which are aspects of Being itself and, one might say, the "ontology of the human microcosm."[8] What is the origin of this logical and mathematical certitude in the human mind and why do these laws correspond to aspects of objective reality? The origin is none other than the Divine Intellect whose reflection on the human plane constitutes the certitude, coherence, and order of logical and mathematical laws and which is, at the same time, the source of that objective order and harmony which the human mind is able to study through these laws. Logical laws, in contrast to subjective limitations and individual idiosyncracies associated with the lucife-rian tendencies of rationalism, are rooted in the Divine[9] and possess an ontological reality. They, as well as principial knowledge tradition-ally associated with wisdom, are essentially of a sacred character whatever certain antirational theologians, anxious to prevent ratio-nalism from overrunning the citadel of faith, may claim. As a result of the loss of the sapiential perspective in modern times and the desa-cralization of knowledge, however, not only has natural theology been cast aside as irrelevant but logic and mathematics have been so divorced from concern with the sacred that they have come to be used as the primary tools for the secularization and profanation of the very act and process of knowing. Many a theologian has taken a defensive position before the achievements of the mathematical sciences, un-aware that in the certitude which the propagators of such sciences claim lies a reflection of that Intellect[10] which is the grand path to the Sacred and which itself is of a sacred nature, the Intellect without whose reflection there would be no logical and mathematical laws and all operations of the mind would be reduced to sheer arbitrariness.

The depleting of knowledge of its sacred character and the creation of a "profane" science which is then used to study even the most sacred doctrines and forms at the heart of religion have led to a forgetting of the primacy of the sapiential dimension within various traditions and the neglect of the traditional doctrine of man which has envisaged him as a being possessing the possibility of knowing things in principle and the principles of all things leading finally to the knowledge of Ultimate Reality. In fact, the sapiential perspective has been so forgotten and the claims of rationalism, which reduces man's intellectual faculty to only the extroverted and analytical function of the mind that then turns against the very foundations of religion, so emphasized, that many a religiously sensitive person in the West has been led to take refuge in faith alone, leaving belief or doctrinal creed to the mercy of ever-changing paradigms or theories caught in the process of relativization and constant transformation.[11] Without in any way denying the central role of faith and the crucial significance of revelation to actualize the possibilities inherent within the microcosmic intellect, a point to which, in fact, we shall turn later in this work, it must be remembered that in the sapiential perspective faith itself is inseparable from knowledge so that not only does the Anselmian dictum *credo ut intelligam* hold true from a certain perspective but that one can also assert *intelligo ut credam* which does not mean to reason first but to "intellect" or use the intellectual faculty of which the rational is only a reflection and extension.

Moreover, the basic teachings of the religions which are both the background and the goal of faith contain in one way or another the sapiential perspective which views knowledge as ultimately related to the Divine Intellect and the Origin of all that is sacred. Even a rapid glance at the different living traditions of mankind proves the validity of this assertion. In Hinduism, that oldest of religions and the only echo of the "primordial religion" to survive to this day, the sacred texts which serve as the origin of the whole tradition, namely the Vedas, are related to knowledge. Etymologically *veda* and *vedānta* derive from the root *vid* which means "seeing" and "knowing" and which is related to the Latin *videre* "to see" and the Greek *oida* "to know."[12] The Upanishads which are hymns of the primordial soul of man yearning for the Absolute mean literally "near-sitting," which the master of Hindu gnosis[13] Śankara explains as that *science* or *knowledge* of Brahma which "sets to rest" or destroys what appears as the world along with the ignorance which is its root. The cause of all separation, division, otherness, and ultimately suffering is ignorance (*avidyā*) and the cure knowledge. The heart of the tradition is supreme knowledge (*jñāna*),[14] while the various "schools" usually called philosophy, the *darśanas*, are literally so many perspectives or points of view. The Hindu tradition, without of course neglecting love and action, places the sacred character of knowledge at the heart of its perspective and sees in the innate power of man to discern between *Ātman* and *māyā* the key to deliverance. Hinduism addresses itself to that element in man which is already divine and which man can come to realize only by knowing him-Self. The Sacred lies at the heart of man and is attainable most directly through knowledge which pierces the veils of *māyā* to reach the Supernal Sun which alone is. In this tradition where the knowledge of God should properly be called autology rather than theology,[15] the function of knowledge as the royal path toward the Sacred and the ultimately sacred character of all authentic knowledge is demonstrated with blinding clarity over and over again in its sacred scripture and is even reflected in the meaning of the names of the sacred texts which serve as the foundations for the whole tradition.

Although Buddhism belongs to a very different perspective than Hinduism and, in fact, began as a rebellion against many Brahmanical doctrines and practices, it joins Hinduism in emphasizing the primacy of knowledge. The supreme experience of the Buddha was illumination which implies knowledge. The beginning of Buddhism is *Boddhisattvayāna* which means "birth of awareness that all things are void." At the heart of Buddhism, therefore, lies knowledge that was to lead later to the elaborate metaphysics of the Void which is the foundation of the whole of Buddhism and which was championed by Nāgārjuna.[16] Also all the virtues of the Bodhisattva, the *pāramitās*, culminate in wisdom or *prajñā*. They all contribute to the dawning of this knowledge which liberates and which lies as a possibility within the being of all humans. The Buddha image itself reflects inward knowledge and that contemplation of the Void which is the gate through which inner peace flows and inundates even external manifestation while, from another point of view, this contemplation serves as the support and "seat" for supreme knowledge.[17] One can hardly conceive of Buddhism without becoming immediately aware of the central role of knowledge, although of course the way of love and mercy could not be absent from such a major religion as can be seen in Amidhism and the figure of the Avalokiteśvara or Kwan Yin itself.

As far as the Chinese tradition is concerned, here again in both Confucianism and Taoism the role of knowledge as the central means for the attainment of perfection reigns supreme. This is to be seen especially in Taoism where the perfect man is seen as one who *knows* the Tao and lives according to this knowledge which means also that he lives according to his own "nature."[18] As Chuang-Tzŭ says,

> The man of virtue . . . can see where all is dark. He can hear where all is still. In the darkness he alone can see light. In the stillness he alone can detect harmony.[19]

It is the principial or sacred knowledge which allows the sage to "see God everywhere," to observe harmony where others see discord, and to see light where others are blinded by darkness. The man of knowledge goes beyond himself to reach Heaven and through this process the Tao of his own self which is none other than the sacred ground of his own being, the original "darkness" which is not dark because of the lack of light but because of the excess of luminosity, like the sacred dark grotto of medieval tales from which flows the spring of life.

> The divine man rides upon the glory of the sky where his form can no longer be discerned. This is called absorption into light. He fulfils his destiny. He acts in accordance with his nature. He is at one with God and man. For him all affairs cease to exist, and all things revert to their original state. This is called envelopment in darkness.[20]

Turning to Western Asia, we discern the same concern for knowledge as the key to the attainment of the sacred and the doctrine that the substance of knowledge itself is sacred in Zoroastrianism and other Iranian religions such as Manichaeism which bases the whole of religion on the goal of freeing, through asceticism and knowledge, the particles of light scattered through the cosmos as a result of the sacrifice of the primordial man.[21] Besides mystical tales of the quest of the gnostic after knowledge which abound in Mazdaean literature, the whole of Mazdaean angelology is based on the doctrine of illumination of the soul by various agencies of the Divine Intellect. All religious rites are an aid in creating a closer link between man and the angelic world, and man's felicity resides in union with his celestial and angelic counterpart, the *Fravarti*.[22] The religious life and all contact with the sacred are dominated by angelic forces which are elements of light whose function it is to illuminate and to guide. Concern with knowledge of the sacred and sacred knowledge is at the heart of Zoroastrianism while the more philosophical Mazdaean religious texts such as the *Dēnkard* have dealt in greater detail with the question of knowledge, thereby developing more fully the doctrine of innate and acquired wisdom and their complementarity and wedding which leads to the attainment of sacred knowledge.[23]

Nor is this concern in any way absent from the Abrahamic traditions although because of the desacralization of the instrument of knowing itself in modern times, modern interpretations of Judaism and Christianity have tended to neglect, belittle, or even negate the sapiential dimensions of these religions. This process has even taken place to some degree in the case of Islam which is based completely on the primacy of knowledge and whose message is one concerning the nature of Reality.

In Judaism the significance of *hokhmah* or wisdom can hardly be overemphasized even in the legal dimension of the religion which is naturally concerned more with correct action than with knowledge. In Genesis (3:22) knowledge is considered as an essential attribute belonging to God alone, and the wisdom writings emphasize praying to the "Lord of Wisdom." The Jewish people accepted the Proverbs, Job, and Ecclesiastes as books of wisdom to which the Christians later added the Psalms and the Song of Songs. In the Jewish wisdom literature although wisdom belonged to God, it was also a divine gift to man and accessible to those willing to submit to the discipline of the traditional teaching methods consisting of instruction (*musar*) and persuasion ('*eṣah*). This means that Judaism considered the attainment of wisdom or sacred knowledge as a possibility for the human intellect if man were to accept the necessary discipline which such an undertaking required. This doctrine was to be elaborated by later Jewish philosophers, Kabbalists, and Hasidim in an elaborate fashion, but the roots of all their expositions are to be found in the Bible itself where, in the three books of Job, the Proverbs, and Ecclesiastes, the term *hokhmah* (later translated as *sophia*) appears nearly a hundred times.[24] Long before these later elaborations were to appear, the *maskilim* of the Qumran community were considered as recipients and dispensers of sacred knowledge of the Divine Mysteries like the *pneumatikoi* mentioned by Saint Paul.

The Jews also believed that the Torah itself was the embodiment of wisdom and some works like the Wisdom of Ben Sira identified the Torah with the preexistent wisdom of God while the Kabbalists considered the primordial Torah to be the *Hokhmah* which is the second of the *Sephiroth*. The whole Kabbalistic perspective is based on the possibility for the inner man to attain sacred knowledge and the human mind to be opened to the illumination of the spiritual world through which it can become sanctified and united with its principle.[25]

The famous Chabad Chassidus text, the *Liqquṭei Amarim* [*Tanya*], says, "Every soul consists of *nefesh, ruaḥ* and *neshamah* [the three traditional elements of the soul]. Nevertheless, the root of every *nefesh, ruaḥ* and *neshamah,* from the highest of all ranks to the lowest that is embodied within the illiterate, and the most worthless, all derive, as it were, from the Supreme Mind which is the Supernal Wisdom (*Hokhmah Ilaʿah*)."[26] The same text continues,

> In like manner does the *neshamah* of man, including the quality
> of *ruaḥ* and *nefesh,* naturally desire and yearn to separate itself
> and depart from the body in order to unite with its origin and
> source in God, the fountain-head of all life, blessed be He.[27]

This propensity to unite with the One is "its will and desire by nature," and "this nature stems from the faculty of *hokhmah* found in the soul, wherein abides the light of the blessed *En Sof*."[28]

No more explicit expression of the presence of the spark of divine knowledge in the very substance of the soul of man and the attainment of the sacred through this very supernaturally natural faculty of intellection within man could be found in a tradition which, although based on the idea of a sacred people and a divine law promulgated by God for this people, possessed from the beginning a revelation in which the primacy of wisdom was certainly not forgotten. This doctrine was, however, emphasized sometimes openly as in the Proverbs and sometimes symbolically and esoterically as in the Song of Songs where the verses "Let him kiss me with the kiss of his mouth: for thy love *is* better than wine" and "I *am* black, but comely. . . ." certainly refer to esoteric or sapiential knowledge (to Sophia identified later with the Virgin Mary) and its transmission, although other meanings are not excluded. In the day of profane knowledge certainly sacred wisdom appears as dark, and it is through the mouth that the Name of God is uttered, the Name whose invocation is the key to the treasury of all wisdom, the Name which contains within itself that sacred knowledge whose realization is accompanied by that supreme ecstasy of which the ecstasy of the kiss of the earthly beloved is but a pale reflection.[29]

As for Islam, which like Judaism remains in its formal structure within the mold of Abrahamic spirituality, the message of the revelation revolves around the pole of knowledge and the revelation addresses man as an intelligence capable of distinguishing between the real and the unreal and of knowing the Absolute.[30] Although the earthly container of this message, that is the Semitic Arab mentality, has bestowed upon certain manifestations of this religion an element of emotional fervor, impetuosity, and a character of inspirationalism which on the theological plane have appeared as an "antiintellectual" voluntarism associated with the Ash'arites, the content of the Islamic message remains wed to the sapiential perspective and the primacy of knowledge. The testimony of the faith *Lā ilāha illa'Llāh* (There is no divinity but the Divine) is a statement concerning knowledge, not sentiments or the will. It contains the quintessence of metaphysical knowledge concerning the Principle and its manifestation. The Prophet of Islam has said, "Say *Lā ilāha illa'Llāh* and be delivered" referring directly to the sacramental quality of principial knowledge. The traditional names used by the sacred scripture of Islam are all related to knowledge: *al-qurʾān* "recitation," *al-furqān* "discernment," and *umm al-kitāb* "the mother of books." The Quran itself refers in practically every chapter to the importance of intellection and knowledge, and the very first verses revealed relate to recitation (*iqraʾ*) which implies knowledge and to science (*ʿilm*—hence *taʿlīm*, to teach-*ʿallama*, taught),

> *Recite* [iqraʾ]: *In the name of thy Lord who createth,*
> *Createth man from a clot.*
> *Recite: And thy Lord is the Most Bounteous,*
> *Who teacheth* [ʿallama] *by the pen,*
> *Teacheth man that which he knew not.*
> [XCVI; 1-5, Pickthall translation, slightly modified]

Even the etymology of the Arabic word for Islamic jurisprudence (*fiqh*) is related to intellection or knowing. In Islam and the civilization which it created there was a veritable celebration of knowledge[31] all of whose forms were, in one way or another, related to the sacred extending in a hierarchy from an "empirical" and rational mode of knowing to that highest form of knowledge (*al-maʿrifah* or *ʿirfān*) which is the unitive knowledge of God not by man as an individual but by the divine center of human intelligence which, at the level of gnosis, becomes the subject as well as object of knowledge. That is why the gnostic or illuminated sage is called *al-ʿārif biʾLlāh*, the "gnostic who knows through or by God" and not only the gnostic who knows God. The Arabic word for intellect *al-ʿaql* is related to the word "to bind," for it is that which binds man to his Origin; etymologically it could be compared to religion itself, for in this case *religio* is also what binds and relates man to God. Even the Arabic word for poetry (*al-shiʿr*) is related to the root meaning consciousness and knowledge rather than making as is the case with *poiēsis*. The Islamic tradition presents blinding evidence of the ultimately sacred character of knowledge and the centrality of the sapiental perspective in the spiritual life, a perspective which remains faithful to and aware of the saving function of knowledge and the nature of intelligence as a precious gift from God which, once actualized by revelation, becomes the most important means of gaining access to the Sacred, intelligence being itself ultimately of a sacred character.

Before turning to the Christian tradition which is of special concern in this study because of the rise of a purely secular concept of knowledge within a civilization which was Christian, a word must be said about the Greek tradition. Usually this tradition is seen today either from the point of view of modern rationalism or of the mainstream of early Christianity which, having to save a whole humanity from the excesses of rationalism and naturalism, emphasized more the contrast between Greek wisdom as knowledge of a this-worldly nature and love and redemption associated with and issuing from the grace of Christ and his incarnation in human history. A reevaluation of the meaning of the Greek *sophia* and *philo-sophia* as sacred knowledge in contrast to the sophistic and skeptical forms of rationalism during the later life of Greek civilization and religion will be carried out later, as will the Christian appreciation of this aspect of the Greek legacy. Here suffice it to say that the Orphic-Dionysian dimension of the Greek tradition, which was to become crystallized later in the Pythagorean-Platonic school, and also Hermeticism, which resulted from the wedding between certain aspects of the Egyptian and the Greek traditions, must be studied as sacred knowledge much like the metaphysical doctrines of Hinduism, and not only as profane philosophy.[32] These forms of wisdom are related to the Greek religious tradition and should be viewed as such and not only in opposition to "revealed truth."[33] In the more universal sense of "revelation," they are in fact the fruit of revelation, that is, a knowledge which derives not from a purely human agent but from the Divine Intellect, as in fact they were viewed by the long tradition of Islamic, Jewish, and Christian philosophy before modern times. There is an aspect of Greek philosophy which is *sapientia* without whose appreciation one cannot understand those sapiential schools within Christianity and even Judaism which were based on a unity above and beyond the current dichotomy between so-called Greek "intellectualism" and Hebrew "inspirationalism." A major problem in the rediscovery of the sacred root of knowledge and knowledge of the sacred is the type of interpretation of Greek philosophy which has dominated the mainstream of Western thought in modern times and which has caused an eclipse of the sapiential quality of certain aspects of the Greek intellectual heritage and obliterated the real nature of the content and meaning of the message of many Christian and Jewish sages who are simply excused away as being "Neoplatonic," as if this term would somehow magically annul the inner significance of doctrines of a sapiential character.

As far as the Christian tradition is concerned, it is often referred to as a way of love; especially in modern times its sapiential dimension is, for the most part, forsaken as if it were simply an alien intrusion into a purely ethical religious message based on divine and human love and the central element of faith. To be sure, Christianity *is* more than anything else a way of love; but being a total and integral religion, it could not be completely divorced from the way of knowledge and sapience. That is why the Johannine "In the beginning was the Word" was interpreted for centuries as an affirmation of the primacy of the Logos as source of both revelation and knowledge before the surgical knife of so-called higher criticism, itself the product of a purely secularized reason, anathemized the particular sapiential Gospel of John into a gradual accretion of statements influenced by alien modes of thought somewhat removed from the message and meaning of the "original" historical Christ. Moreover, the Christian tradition, in accepting the Old Testament as part of its sacred scripture, not only inherited the Hebrew wisdom tradition but even emphasized certain books of the Bible as source of wisdom even beyond what is found in the Judaic tradition.

In the Proverbs, chapter 8, Wisdom personified speaks in a famous passage as follows:

> I wisdom dwell with prudence, and find out knowledge of witty inventions . . . I lead in the way of righteousness, in the midst of the paths of judgment: that I may cause those that love me to inherit substance: and I will fill their treasures. The Lord possessed me in the beginning of his way, before his works of old. I was set up from everlasting, from the beginning, or ever the earth was. When *there were* no depths, I was brought forth; where *there were* no fountains abounding with water . . . While as yet he had not made the earth, nor the fields, nor the highest part of the dust of the world. When he prepared the heavens, I *was* there: when he set a compass upon the face of the depth: when he established the clouds above: when he strengthened the fountains of the deep: . . . Then I was by him, *as* one brought up *with him:* and I was daily *his* delight, rejoicing always before him; . . . Now therefore harken unto me, O ye children: for blessed *are they that* keep my ways.[34]

The Christians meditated upon this and similar passages as the revealed sources of a sapiential path leading to the knowledge of God and *theosis.* As late as the last century even a philosopher such as Schelling was to call this passage "a breeze from a sacred morning dawn." In early ante-Nicene Christianity charity itself was considered by a figure such as Saint Maximus the Confessor as "a good disposition of the soul which makes it prefer the knowledge of God above all things," as well as the bliss inhering in this knowledge and the love of God as the source of the illumination of knowledge.[35] Also the earlier forms of Christology emphasized the role of Christ in illuminating the human mind and bestowing divine knowledge upon the qualified.[36]

The early Christians, moreover, viewed Sophia as an almost "divine being" unto herself, a "complement" to the Trinity. The Orthodox revered her especially and built perhaps the most beautiful sacred structure of early Christianity, the Hagia Sophia, in her honor. Sophia appeared in the vision of saints and illuminated them with knowledge. She often manifested herself as a woman of celestial beauty and was identified by many sages and saints with the Virgin Mary in the same way that among some of the Muslim sages wisdom appeared as a beautiful celestial figure identified with Fāṭimah, the daughter of the Prophet, and a "second Mary" within the more specific context of the Islamic tradition. For Christians wisdom was at once related to the Son, to the Christ figure itself, and to the feminine principle which was inseparable from the inviolable purity and beauty of the Virgin. One should not forget that that supreme poet of Christian spirituality, Dante, who was so profoundly devoted to the Virgin, was guided in *Paradiso* by a woman, by Beatrice, who symbolizes the feminine figure of Sophia, without this fact detracting in any way from the role of Christ as dispenser and also embodiment of wisdom. In Christianity as in other traditions there is complementarity of the active and passive, or masculine and feminine elements, in wisdom as well as in love.

Returning to the origins of the Christian tradition, we must remember that the emphasis upon the sapiential dimension of Christianity is to be seen in Saint Paul himself who saw Christ as the new Torah identified with Divine Wisdom. The letters of Saint Paul contain references to the possessors of sacred knowledge, the *pneumatikoi*, who speak the wisdom (*sophia*) of God and who possess inner knowledge (*gnosis*), *sophia* and *gnosis* being "pneumatic" gifts imparted to the pneumatics by God. Although modern scholars have debated extensively about the meaning in 1 Corinthians (12:8) of "a word of wisdom . . . and a word of knowledge,"[37] even profane methods based only on historical and philological evidence, and ignoring the oral tradition, have not been able to prove a Greek or some other kind of foreign origin for the Pauline doctrine of divine knowledge.[38] There is a gnosis in these texts of a definitely Christian origin not to be confused with second-century gnosticism of a sectarian nature, for as Saint Paul asserted, sacred knowledge is one of Christ's most precious gifts, to be sought earnestly by those qualified to receive and to transmit it. Had there not been such a Christian gnosis, the Christian tradition would have been able to integrate Greek wisdom and adopt Graeco-Alexandrian metaphysical formulations for the expression of its own teachings.

The nearly two thousand years of Christian history were to be witness, despite all obstacles, to the survival of this sapiential dimension of the Christian tradition as well as its gradual eclipse, this latter process leading to the secularization of the concept of knowledge itself. To trace the history of this long tradition from the early Church Fathers to recent times would require a separate study of monumental proportions. Here is suffices to refer briefly to some of the representatives of the sapiential perspectives within the Christian tradition, figures who considered it possible for man to attain the knowledge of the sacred and who saw the root of knowledge itself as being sunk in the soil of the sacred and the holy. To reassert and rediscover the sacramental quality of knowledge in the contemporary West, it is certainly helpful to recall this long-neglected dimension of the Christian tradition, a dimension which is either cast aside and deliberately ignored in the more easily accessible works on Western intellectual life or, when mentioned in such sources, treated in such a way as to reduce it to a harmless borrowing, of interest only for the history of thought. Of course, there is little wonder in the observation of such a spectacle for only the like can know the like. How can a mind totally depleted of the sense of the sacred grasp the significance of the sacred as sacred?

The sapiential current in Christian spirituality, distinct from what came to be known as gnosticism, is found among many of the major figures of early Christianity such as Saint Gregory of Nyssa and Gregory of Nazianzus as well as the early desert fathers and the community which produced the Nag Hammadi texts. But it is especially strong among the Alexandrian fathers whose writings are a fountainhead of Christian gnosis and who stress the central role of sacred knowledge and knowledge of the sacred in the attainment of sanctity. Among them none is more important than Clement of Alexandria (140–c.220) who saw Christianity as a way to wisdom.[39] In his teachings Christ is identified with the Universal Intellect which God has also placed at the center of the cosmos and in the heart of man.[40] Clement, who spent much of his life in Alexandria, was well acquainted with Greek wisdom which he did not oppose to Christianity but which he considered to have issued from the same Intellect to which the Christians had full access through Christ. For him true philosophy was not a "profane knowledge" to be opposed to Christian faith but a knowledge of an ultimately sacred character derived from the Intellect which God had revealed in Christ and through sacred Scripture. The true sage, the person who has attained sacred knowledge, is he who has first become pure and achieved moral perfection,[41] and subsequently become a "true gnostic."[42] Concerning such a person, "one can no longer say that he has science or possesses gnosis, but he is science and gnosis."[43]

As far as the possibility of an actual initiatic path within Christianity based on knowledge is concerned, the case of Clement presents evidence of unusual interest, for Clement did not only possess sacred knowledge, but writes that he received it from a human dispenser of such knowledge. While in Alexandria, he met a master named Pantaenus who, according to Clement, "deposited pure gnosis" in the spirits of men and who had in turn received it from those who had transmitted the esoteric knowledge handed down to them orally and secretly by the apostles and ultimately by Christ himself. Through this regular chain of transmission of a "divine wisdom," Clement had received that gnosis which implied knowledge of God and the angelic world, science of the spiritual significance of sacred Scripture, and the attainment of total certitude. Clement was in turn to become a spiritual master as revealed by such works as the *Protrepticus* and *Stromateis*, which are treatises of spiritual guidance, as well as the resumé of his *Hypotypsis* as summarized by Photius. But it is significant, as far as the later history of the Christian tradition and the place of gnosis in it is concerned, that he was not canonized as a saint and that the regularity of transmission of sacred knowledge did not continue for long, although Clement did train Origen, another of the important figures of early Christianity who was concerned with sapience and the role of knowledge in gaining access to the sacred.

Like Clement, Origen (185–253 or 254) was well acquainted with Greek philosophy which he studied in Alexandria.[44] In fact, his teacher was the mysterious Ammonias Saccas, the teacher of Plotinus, and the philosophical education of Origen paralleled closely that of Plotinus who represents the most universal and central expression of the esoteric and metaphysical aspects of Greek wisdom. As for Clement so for Origen, Christianity itself was "philosophy" in the sense of wisdom, and Greek philosophy a depository of that sacred knowledge which was to be found in its fullness in the Christian message. Origen, in a sense, continued the teachings of Clement as far as the relation between Christianity and philosophy was concerned, although emphasizing more the importance of asceticism.

The central depository of sacred knowledge for Origen is sacred

Scripture which nourishes the soul of man and provides for his need to know. But Scripture is not only the literal text. Like man, sacred Scripture is composed of body, soul, and spirit or the literal, moral, and sapiential or spiritual dimensions.[45] Not all readers can understand the inner meaning present in the text, but even those who cannot grasp this wisdom are aware that there *is* some kind of message hidden in the Book of God.[46] Origen relates sacred knowledge directly to sacred Scripture and believes that it is the function of spiritual beings to discover this inner meaning of revealed truth and to use their intelligence in the contemplation of spiritual realities. The spiritual life of man is none other than the gradual development of the power of the soul to grasp the spiritual intelligence of Scripture which, like Christ himself, feeds the soul.

It is the presence of the Logos in the heart of man and at the root of his intelligence that makes it possible for man to grasp the inner meaning of sacred Scripture and to become illuminated by this knowledge. The Logos is the illuminator of souls,[47] the light which makes intellectual vision possible. In fact, the Logos which exists *in divinis* is the root of intelligence in man and is the intermediary through which man receives sacred knowledge.[48] In as much as the Logos is the origin of human intelligence and the source of the human instrument of knowledge, knowledge of the sacred is the ultimate ground of knowledge as such, as well as its goal.

As one of the outstanding representatives of those who composed sapiential commentaries upon the Bible, Origen wrote extensive spiritual and esoteric commentaries upon various parts of both the Old and the New Testaments, wherein he sought to reveal the sacred knowledge which a person whose intellect is already sanctified and illuminated by the Logos can grasp. In Origen there is that harmonious wedding between a sacramental conception of knowledge and study of sacred Scripture, which became rather rare in later phases of Christian history with the result that hermeneutics, as the science of penetration into the *inner* meaning of sacred Scripture on the basis of a veritable *scientia sacra* and with the aid of an intelligence which is already illuminated by the Word or Logos, became reduced to the desacralization of the Holy Book itself by a mentality which had lost the sense of the sacred. Origen's perspective is, therefore, an especially precious one if the meaning of the sapiential perspective in the Christian tradition is to be understood in conjunction with the central reality of a revealed book. Origen's commentaries include many direct allusions to the esoteric nature of scriptural passages and the sacred knowledge which they convey to those capable of grasping their message. For example, concerning the already cited verse from the Song of Songs, "Let him kiss me with the kiss of his mouth" (which is also of paramount importance in Jewish esoterism), Origen writes,

> But when she has begun to discern for herself what was obscure, to unravel what was untangled, to unfold what was involved, to interpret parables and riddles and the sayings of the wise along the lines of her own expert thinking, then let her believe that she has now received the kisses of the Spouse Himself, that is, the Word of God.[49]

Here again, the "kiss of his mouth" is seen as none other than the transmission of inner knowledge through that organ which is endowed with the power to invoke His Name and to utter His Word.

Although the crystallization of Western Christianity in the various credal and theological formulations tended to emphasize the fall of man and his sinfulness and to outline a type of Christology which did not bring into focus the role of Christ as the source of knowledge and the illuminator of the human mind but rather as the savior of man from his sins, the significance of knowledge as a means of attaining the sacred was not completely forgotten. Even Saint Augustine, whose anthropology was rather pessimistic and who limited the nature of man to a fallen creature immersed in sin, nevertheless accepted the innate power of the intellect as given by God to man to receive divine illumination.[50] To think the truth, according to Saint Augustine, man needs the illumination which proceeds from God.[51] Augustine, therefore, despite his emphasis upon faith as the key to salvation, preserves the essentially sacramental function of intelligence, even if it is envisaged in a somewhat more indirect manner. In him one does not encounter the same antithesis between knowledge and faith that was to characterize much of later Western Christian thought.

The sapiential dimension in Christianity was to find one of its most eloquent and profound expositors in that mysterious figure, Dionysius the Areopagite, whom an Indian metaphysician of the stature of A. K. Coomaraswamy was to call the greatest of all Europeans with the possible exception of Dante. This sage, who traced his lineage to Saint Paul and whose writings are considered by modern scholars as belonging to the fifth and sixth centuries, appears more as an intellectual function than an individual. Translated into Latin by Hilduin and later by Scotus Erigena, Dionysius was to influence not only the Christian sapiential tradition through Erigena himself, the Victorine mystics, and the German theosophers but also Christian art.[52] The two hierarchies to which Dionysius was to devote two of his works, namely the celestial or angelic order and the ecclesiastical, are themselves related to degrees of the sacred (*taxis hiera*) and of science *epistēmē*. For him sacramental action leading to *theosis* or divinization of the being of man is inseparable from progress in knowledge which, finally, in union reaches that "unknowing" of the Ultimate Reality, that, although possessing many names, is "Nameless" (*anonymous*). In Dionysius is to be found the root of that sapiential perspective which based its method on "unknowing" but which in reality is knowledge as rooted in the Sacred in its highest sense and leading to the Sacred, the "unknowing" being the dissolution of all limited and separative knowledge, of all vision of the periphery that would blur the Center which is the Sacred as such.

The detailed exposition of the important elements of the teachings of Dionysius, as they bear upon the destiny of the sapiential tradition within Christianity, was to come in the ninth century in the work of his Latin translator, John the Scot or Scotus Erigena, who was born in Ireland and who wrote his major opus *De divisione naturae* (*Periphyseon* in its Greek title) between 864 and 866.[53] In this majestic statement of Christian gnosis, long neglected and even feared because of its later association with Albigensian and Cathari circles, is to be found a clear statement of the central role and function of knowledge as rooted in the sacred and as the means of gaining access to it. The Erigenian statement remains of singular importance in the sapiential dimension of the Christian tradition despite all the attempts to reduce it to a simple Neoplatonist or pantheist position, as if the import of any truth could be destroyed by simply characterizing it by a currently pejorative or harmless title.[54]

Erigena was devoutly Christian but also one who saw at the heart of Christianity a sacred knowledge or wisdom which for him was none other than authentic philosophy. "True religion is true philosophy," Erigena would assert.[55] In wisdom philosophy and religion become united, and wisdom is a virtue common to man and angel.[56] The source of this wisdom lies in Christ in whom is to be found not only the divine Scripture but even the liberal arts which are an image of Christ and which reflect his wisdom.[57]

As would be expected, Erigenian teachings emphasize the role of the Logos not only as the origin of revealed truth but as the source of sacred knowledge here and now. The *erat* of *in principio erat verbum* is interpreted by Erigena as *est* or "is," for not only "In the beginning *was* the Word" but also "In the beginning," which as stated above is none other than the present "now," *is* the Word. Although the Logos is ever present man, however, has become separated from God and as a result divine knowledge is no longer immediately available to man. The men of this age can no longer "speak to God" and see things *in divinis* as did Adam in paradise or as did men in the Golden Age. Yet, this light remains accessible through Scripture and nature, the two grand books of divine knowledge and it can become available to man even now, if he would and could only benefit from the grace of the Light of God which resides within the very substance of man.[58] In a manner more typical of Greek theology which emphasizes the presence of the Light of God in nature than of Western theology which focuses upon the presence of God in history, Erigena saw in the book of nature the means of discovering that sacred knowledge which lies within the very substance of the human microcosm.[59]

According to Erigena, human perfection and the quest for the attainment of sacred knowledge, which is in fact the end and final goal of this perfection, begins with the awareness of the human mind that all causes come from God. After this stage, *scientia* becomes transformed into *sapientia*, and the soul of man becomes illuminated by God who, in fact, contemplates Himself in those whom He has illumined.[60] This illumination in turn enables man to realize that the very essence of things is God's knowledge of them[61] and that there is a reciprocity and, finally, identity between knowing and being. The intellect becomes transformed into what it knows, the highest object of that knowledge being God. But the knowledge of the Divinity is not immediately accessible to man in his present state. Before the fall man possessed knowledge of everything *in divinis*, in an inward manner as reflected in and reflecting God. But after the fall his knowledge became externalized. To regain that sacred knowledge, the soul must pass through the eight stages consisting of the earthly body passing into vital motion, vital motion into senses, sense into reason, reason into soul, soul into knowledge, knowledge into wisdom, and finally the supernatural passage (*occasus*) of the purified soul into God.[62]

The final goal is *theosis*, the attainment through gnosis comprised of the stages of *ephesis, erōs,* and *agapē* of that Reality which neither creates nor is created. The human intellect can reach this goal which is the knowledge of God through the rediscovery of its own essence. This rediscovery in turn cannot be achieved save through that "negative way" which is a "cosmolytic" process that reverses the cosmogonic one. Intelligence is already a gift of God (*datum*) which, through special grace (*dotum*), is able to reach *theosis*, the very goal of human existence and the very substance of intelligence itself.[63]

Although singularly neglected, Erigena's doctrines were nevertheless to influence such major figures as Richard and Hugo of Saint Victor, Raymond Lull, and later Nicholas of Cusa. But he was not at the center of the arena of European intellectual life which, after a period of intense debate on the relation between faith and reason, turned toward the formation of those major theological syntheses associated with the names of Saint Bonaventure, Saint Thomas, and Duns Scotus. These masters developed languages and systems of discourse which are perfectly adequate for the exposition of traditional metaphysics, and all were aware of the sapiential dimension of the spiritual life—Saint Bonaventure having developed a theology which rests upon the primacy of contemplation and Saint Thomas having left his pen for contemplative silence which crowns his vast theological and metaphysical edifice. Yet, these syntheses, especially the Thomistic one, tended to become overrationalistic in imprisoning intuitions of a metaphysical order in syllogistic categories which were to hide, more than reveal, their properly speaking intellectual rather than purely rational character. In fact, the purely sapiential aspect of medieval Christianity is reflected perhaps more directly in the medieval cathedrals and that central epiphany of Christian spirituality, the *Divine Comedy* of Dante, itself a literary cathedral, than in the theological syntheses which, while containing Christian Sophia, also tended to veil it. These theologies, therefore, although belonging in a certain sense to the sapiential dimension of the Christian tradition, characterize the crucial intermediate stages of the process whereby knowledge became desacralized and philosophy gradually divorced from wisdom, despite the very synthesis in which such elements were wed together by the powerful mind and pen of a figure such as Saint Thomas.[64]

The great medieval theologians were men of both faith and knowledge and cannot be blamed for the reaction of reason against faith which was to follow soon after their syntheses saw the light of day. Yet, the philosophical agnosticism which was to surface in Europe within two centuries after Saint Thomas himself could not have come about had the intellectual life of Christianity remained impregnated by gnosis; had not the reality of knowledge as *theosis* become transformed into the question of using rational knowledge to preserve faith from being corroded or weakened by the attacks of rationalism; and had not the type of intellectuality characterized by Saint Thomas's contemporary, Meister Eckhart, remained more or less peripheral as far as the main line of development of theology and philosophy in Christian Europe was concerned.

The most powerful and majestic expression of Christian gnosis in the medieval period is in fact associated with Meister Eckhart. His teachings have attracted a great deal of attention during the past few decades in a Western world in search of some doctrine of Western origin which would correspond to the grand metaphysical teachings of the Orient that are now becoming increasingly better known in the West. More and more the German sage is becoming for many the authority par excellence of Christian gnosis.[65]

For Eckhart the root of the intellect is grounded in the Divinity, for the intellect is *increatus et increabilis*; in fact, God is first and foremost *intelligere* and only secondarily *esse*. There exists within the soul of man a spark which Eckhart calls *Seelenfünklein*.[66] This spark is the seat of consciousness through which man can reach knowledge of the Divinity or the *Grund*. The soul has access to levels of knowledge leading from sensual to "abstract" forms and, finally, the "spark" which is both the heart or root of intelligence and the means whereby God is known. This possibility lies in the nature of intelligence itself, although there is need of grace for this knowledge to be actualized *per speculum et in lumine*.[67] For Eckhart, the eye with which man sees God is the eye with which God sees man. And this eye is none other than that supernal intellect or intelligence which relates man to the sacred in a direct manner and which enables knowledge to become the central means of access to the sacred. There is no more explicit formulation of the sacramental nature of intelligence and of knowing in Western Christianity than that of Meister Eckhart who, thanks to the functioning of the *Fünklein* at the center of his own soul, was able to present one of the most remarkable expositions of that *scientia sacra* which is and has always been the heart of traditional knowledge in both East and West.

Although the Renaissance marked the beginning of the process of the radical secularization of man and knowledge, resulting in the humanism which characterizes this epoch, there is nevertheless a definite reassertion, at this time, of the sapiential perspective—this being almost as a cosmic reaction to the rapid disappearance of the traditional world view in the West. From the efforts of Gemistus Plethon and especially Marsiglio Ficino there grew a new appreciation of Graeco-Alexandrian wisdom in its Pythagorean, Platonic, Neoplatonic, and Hermetic forms, although much of this appreciation took place outside the framework of the dominant tradition in the West which was Christianity. But there were also specifically Christian forms of gnosis such as Christian Hermeticism, doctrines of illumination which such figures as Francesco Patrizzi called *Cognitio matutina,* and Christian Kabbala of a definitely sapiential nature. The Renaissance was also witness to one of the most outstanding masters of Christian sapiential doctrines, namely, Nicholas of Cusa. He expounded a traditional metaphysics of remarkable profundity based on an essentially gnostic perspective, although emphasizing again the process of unknowing and the doctrine of "ignorance" at the very moment when the newly discovered humanism, which was ignorance of another kind, was about to dominate the European scene.[68]

Nicholas of Cusa (1401–1464), who was a cosmologist, physicist, and mathematician as well as metaphysician and theologian, felt obliged to "dissolve" and "undo" the excessively confining and rationalistic categories in which late medieval theology had dealt with the Divine, before being able to expound metaphysics.[69] He was also forced to take into consideration the effect of the nominalism which preceded him without his falling into the pitfall of doubt and nihilism. Although nominalism was definitely a major factor in destroying the basis of certitude upon which the earlier medieval philosophy had rested,[70] more recent research has tried to point to its positive features as a theology which sought after divine immediacy.[71] Be that as it may, Cusa had to remove the conceptual limitations placed upon the notion of the Godhead which were attacked by various forms of rationalism, theological and otherwise, in order to be able to expound a knowledge of a truly gnostic and metaphysical order, following at the same time upon the wake of the earlier pre-Scholastic Christian masters such as Dionysius and the members of the Victorine school. Cusa therefore emphasized that "the highest wisdom consists in this, to know . . . how that which is unattainable may be reached or attained unattainably."[72] Cusa explains in the following lines what he means by knowledge as ignorance in commenting upon the saying of Solomon that "the wisdom and the locality of understanding lie hidden from the eyes of all the living":

> . . . we may be compared to owls trying to look at the sun; but since the natural desire in us for knowledge is not without a purpose, its immediate object is our own ignorance. Nothing could be more beneficial for even the most zealous searcher for knowledge than his being in fact most learned in that very ignorance which is peculiarly his own; and the better a man will have known his own ignorance, the greater his learning will be.[73]

This *docta ignorantia* is, however, directed toward that partial form of knowledge which would seek to replace sacred knowledge as such. It applies to reason not to the intellect which *can know* the *coincidentia oppositorum*. Cusa in fact distinguishes rigorously between the power of knowing identified as *ars coincidentiarum* and that relative and desacralized knowledge which, according to him, is no more than conjecture and which he identifies as *ars conjecturarum*.[74] Man's ignorance which parades as knowledge and which Cusa's learned ignorance seeks to cure belongs to man's fall. Otherwise, Cusa, like the Christian sages before him, believes in Divine Wisdom which is accessible to man and which is identified with the Divine Word. This knowledge cannot, however, be attained except through being experienced and tasted. It is *sapientia* according to the etymological sense of the term (from the Latin *sapere* meaning "to taste").[75] Certainly the Cusanian ignorance does not lead to agnosticism or nihilism or to the denial of sacred knowledge. On the contrary, it is a means of opening a path for the ray of gnosis to shine upon a space already darkened by excessively rationalistic categories which seemed to negate the very possibility of unitive knowledge and which were leading to skepticism and even nihilism. That is why, while emphasizing the importance of the process of "unknowing" and the realization that our so-called positive knowledge is ignorance, he confirms the reality and centrality of that wisdom with respect to which all limited and limiting knowledge *is* ignorance.[76] There is no doubt that the teachings of Nicholas of Cusa which in a sense crown the school based on "unknowing" or "ignorance" represent a major stand of the sapiential dimension of the Christian tradition.[77]

The century which followed Cusa and which was to lead to the modern period, properly speaking, was marked by the major event of the rise of Protestantism with its opposition to the Scholastic syntheses of the Middle Ages as well as the types of mysticism associated with Catholicism. There is no doubt that the later growth of Protestantism was not unconnected to the process of the secularization of knowledge, but it is also certain that the teachings of, at least, Luther possessed certain aspects which are closely related to the sapiential dimension of Christianity. Needless to say, Luther emphasized faith above everything else as Catholicism has emphasized love. But in the same way that Christian love is, or at least can be, related to knowledge through union which is the goal of both love and knowledge, so is faith related to knowledge through the fact that without some knowledge there cannot be faith, for were there no knowledge one could have faith in just anything and the object of faith would not matter.

In any case, Lutheran spirituality, with all of its emphasis upon faith and negation of Catholic theology and the Christian sapiential tradition as interpreted by the medieval Christian sages, nevertheless allowed the possibility of a mysticism of an essentially sapiential nature.[78] It is known that there were many Lutheran Hermeticists and Rosicrucians—the coat of arms of Luther himself having been the cross and the rose. The evangelical movement begun by Luther included such figures as Sebastian Franck, Paracelsus, V. Weigel, Jacob Boehme, G. Arnold, G. Gichtel, F. C. Oetinger, and many other theosophers, mystics, and spiritual alchemists and created a climate of a kind of "Abrahamic quality" in which the wedding between faith and knowledge was a definite possibility. The whole phenomenon of the existence of a theosophy, which in its traditional sense is none other than sacred knowledge, in the bosom of Lutheranism is a matter of great significance as far as the question of the presence of a sapiential tradition in the West is concerned.[79] Even some of the music associated with the Lutheran movement is of a contemplative quality in conformity with the sapiential perspective.[80] Therefore, although the breakup of the unity of the Christian church during the Renaissance played a crucial role in the secularization of the Western world, a spirituality based upon sacred knowledge and knowledge of the sacred continued to survive even within the Lutheran tradition with all its emphasis upon faith at the expense of everything else.

With Jacob Boehme (1575–1624), who wrote that as a child he was loved by the Divine Sophia, the sapiential dimension of the Christian tradition reaches one of its peaks in recent history.[81] Boehme was an avid reader of the Bible upon which he wrote a commentary in his *Mysterium Magnum* in 1623, just before his death. Moreover, he considered himself to have been illuminated by the Divine Sophia and enabled to penetrate into the inner meaning of the sacred text by virtue of inner illumination (*innere Erleuchtungen*). All that he wrote and said was from the point of view of this *sapientia* received from both sacred Scripture and inner illumination, or the objective and subjective modes of revelation.

Boehme sees man not only as the fallen being depicted in most works of Christian theology but also as a creature in whom there is still an element which is unaffected by the fall and which yearns for the Infinite and the Eternal since it comes from that Divine Ground which is both Infinite and Eternal.[82] It is the state of purity and innocence which he calls *Tempratur*. Likewise, there is an aspect of creation which is still pure and paradisal, unaffected by that force of evil which is personified in Satan, the aspect which Boehme calls "the holy or paradisal element" (*heiliges* or *paradiesische Elemente*). But this element remains inaccessible to most men except those who remain aware of their own paradisal and primordial nature which seeks wisdom and the Eternal spontaneously and naturally. This search for the Eternal is related to the possibility of attaining perfect knowledge of God not only in Himself but also in both nature and the human soul.[83] The mission of man in this world is in fact the attainment of this knowledge with the aid of which he is able to decipher the various "signatures," the sum of which comprise the universe.[84]

While in paradise, man possessed the "natural language" which was at once the language of paradise and the essential knowledge of all things. The root of both human language and knowledge was identical with the sacred or quintessential knowledge of creation itself. But consequent upon the fall he lost the knowledge of this language, at least in that part of his being which is identified with the consequences of the fall. Yet, this primordial knowledge of a sacred order remains in the depth of man's being, in that very aspect of his being which is still in the state of paradisal innocence.[85]

This doctrine of language is closely associated with the role and function which Boehme accords to intelligence as the instrument for the attainment of knowledge of the sacred, an intelligence which becomes operative only upon man's receiving inner illumination. Boehme also reasserts the primary significance of wisdom or Sophia as the "fullness of God's Universe"[86] and an ontological reality of blinding splendor which is the means of access to the Divine Presence in a universe dominated by the sapiential perspective.

At the end of the Renaissance and in the face of seventeenth-century rationalism, another branch of the tree of the Christian sapiential tradition was to grow on the other side of the European continent in England where the so-called school of Cambridge Platonists, whom Coleridge called Plotinists, saw the light of day. There such figures as Benjamin Whichcote, Ralph Cudworth, Henry More, and John Smith were to express important elements of traditional wisdom especially as it concerned knowledge of the "intermediate world," the *mundus imaginalis*,[87] which More, one of the foremost members of this school, calls *spissitudo spiritualis*. As far as sacred knowledge is concerned, this school was also important in emphasizing the possibility of a knowledge which is immediate like that of the senses but not sensuous in the usual meaning of this term, thereby negating the epistomological dualism of Cartesian origin which was so important in the secularization of knowledge in the seventeenth century and also the empiricism which was becoming prevalent in England. John Smith, in fact, speaks of "spiritual sensation" meaning thereby immediate, concrete knowledge of the sacred as against the "abstract" knowledge which the philosophy of that period posited against the "concrete" seen only as that which is related to external, sensual knowledge.[88] He also reasserts the traditional doctrine of sacred knowledge being attainable not through the mind but the heart once it is purified and the "eye of the heart," as the Sufis would call it, opened.[89] Through the purification of the heart, according to John Smith and quoting Plotinus, "Contemplative man knits his own center unto the center of Divine Being."[90] The school of Cambridge Platonism represents a precious restatement of certain aspects of sapience in a northern European climate, influenced in the religious sphere by the kind of voluntarism associated with Calvin and, more particularly, in an England which was turning nearly completely in the direction of an empiricism in which the sanctifying function of intellection possessed no meaning at all. It is worthwhile to remember that, despite what was to occur later both philosophically and theologically, the influence of this school, as well as other forms of traditional doctrines, remained to some degree alive in England, although at the periphery of the main arena of philosophical and what today is called intellectual activity.

Although the influence of Boehme was to be felt far and wide, ranging from French and German theosophers and esoterists to Russian contemplatives, perhaps the most artistically powerful expression of purely sapiential teachings deeply influenced by him are to be found in those hymns of Christian gnosis which compromise the *Cherubic Wanderer* (*Der Cherubische Wandersmann*) of Angelus Silesius (1624–1677), which are also among the most remarkable works of German literature.[91] This collection, so close in both form and content to Sufi poetry, is based upon the central theme of return to God through knowledge. The path of the wanderer is none other than the path of knowledge;[92] it is the *al-maʿrifah* of Islam or *jñāna* of Hinduism and very much in accord with works of such nature whether they be in Arabic and Persian or Sanskrit.[93]

For Silesius, man is the mirror in which God reflects Himself, His other "self."

> *I am God's other self. He findeth but in me*
> *That which resembleth him eternally.*[94]

This function man fulfills through sacred knowledge which is none other than wisdom.

> *Eternal Wisdom builds:*
> *I shall the palace be*
> *When I in wisdom rest*
> *And Wisdom rests in me.*[95]

To attain this knowledge man must brush aside all accidents and return to his center and essence which *is* pure consciousness and knowledge, the eternal essence which survives all change and becoming.

Man should essential be;
For, when this world is gone
All accident is past
The essence still lives on.[96]

Moreover, the attainment of this center which means also the opening of the "eye of the heart" and the vision of God is not to be postponed to the posthumous state. The beatific vision must be attained here and now through that spiritual death which makes of the gnostic "a dead man walking" even in this life. The beatific vision belongs to the eternal now which opens unto the Infinite at this very present moment.

"In good time we shall see
God and his light," ye say.
Fools! Ye shall never see
What ye see not today![97]

It is the function of man to know God here and now through the knowledge which comes from God Himself. The grandeur of man and what places him even above the angels is this possibility of unitive knowledge through which he becomes the "bride" of God and attains beatific union.

The angels are in bliss.
But better is man's life
For no one of their kind
Can ever be God's wife.[98]

Despite the ever-tightening circle of rationalism and empiricism the sapiential tradition expounded by Boehme and Silesius continued to survive on the margin of European intellectual life, while the center of the stage became occupied to an even greater degree by those who prided themselves in being enlightened while denying to the mind all possibility of illumination by the inner Intellect. As a matter of fact, during the eighteenth century the teachings of such masters as Boehme were revived in opposition to the so-called enlightenment by those who sought to combat the stifling influence of the new all-encompassing rationalism. As a result, one can observe alongside the well-known philosophers of the Enlightenment or the *Aufklärung,* the appearance of illuminism on the Continent and an attempt made from several quarters to stem the tide of rationalism, empiricism, mechanism, secularism of science and the cosmos, and other prevalent ideas and *isms* of the day through recourse to various types of esoteric teachings.[99]

In France and Germany numerous figures appeared whose significance is only now being realized and who are gradually being brought out of oblivion resulting from almost systematic neglect by later academic scholarship. In France itself, which was the citadel of the new rationalism associated with Descartes and Wolf, the eighteenth century was witness to Martines de Pasqually, reviver of certain of the traditional sciences and a Christian and Freemason at the same time; Claude Saint-Martin, master of French prose and reviver of Boehme in France; Joseph de Maistre, at once a Catholic and Freemason who saw Christianity as an initiatic path; Fabre d'Olivet, a student of ancient languages and wisdom and resuscitator of Pythagoreanism in which there was much interest at that time; and Höné Wronski, of Polish origin but residing in France, like Fabre d'Olivet attracted especially to traditional mathematical doctrines and what has been called "arithmasophy."

In Germany there was even greater activity in the resuscitation and continuation of esoteric and theosophic teachings centering around the works and thought of Boehme. There was Friedrich Oetinger, initiated into the Kabbala, who left Malebranche to study Boehme and who sought to synthesize the teachings of Boehme and Lurian Kabbala; Jakob Obereit who opposed esoteric knowledge to the skepticism of the *Aufklärung* and wrote against many of the theses of Kant; Karl von Eckartshausen, scientist and theosopher who sought to overcome the opposition created by Kant between phenomena and noumena and to unite all levels of knowledge, and numerous other figures.[100] Boehmian doctrines even influenced well-known literary and philosophical figures such as Novalis, whose fiancée, Sophie von Kühn, who died as a youth, was identified by the poet with Sophia; and Friedrich Schelling, the celebrated philosopher, who in his later works, such as the *Ages of the World,* was influenced by earlier German theosophers, especially Boehme.

In northern Europe the enigmatic figure of Swedenborg, both scientist and visionary, was to cast much influence in England as well as in Scandinavia and to propagate certain theosophic theses especially in relation to the "spiritual body" (*Geistleiblichkeit*) which were to lead to the founding of a new Protestant church and which contained a strong polemical aspect.[101] In England itself, although the influence of Boehme was less marked than in continental Europe, there were a few figures like John Hutchinson who were deeply immersed in Boehmian teachings. But perhaps the most notable figure who should be mentioned in this connection is Sir Isaac Newton. The father of classical physics not only composed the *Principia* which, despite the wishes of its author, had such a major role to play in the secularization of the world and in propagating scientific rationalism but also wrote the *Observations upon the Prophecies of Daniel* and works on alchemy[102] and is considered by some scholars to have been a follower of Boehme.[103] But as can be gauged from the study of such figures, the influence of earlier masters of wisdom no longer amounted to a continuation of a total and complete knowledge of a sacred character but a partial and segmented one.

It is of interest to note in passing that the sapiential teachings of the remarkable German cobbler were also to influence certain figures in Russia which was now turning toward the West. Ivan Lopouchine, who was both a Freemason and attracted to the Hesychast tradition within Orthodox Christianity, was related to esoteric circles in France and Germany, while Alexander Labzine translated Boehme into Russian. Although the Orthodox world has possessed a rich tradition concerning Sophia, which we cannot treat in this survey concerned mainly with the West, it is of much interest to note that many of the followers of sapiential teachings in the Occident were interested in bringing Western Christianity closer to Orthodoxy and that the most notable influence of Boehme in modern times has been on such Russian figures as P. Florensky, V. Soloviev, and S. Boulgakov.

Of particular interest among the later representatives of the sapiential perspective in Europe is Franz von Baader (1765–1841), perhaps the last gnostic and theosopher in the West in the full sense of these terms before the segmentation and obcuring of the sapiential tradition in the nineteenth century, the figure whom A. W. Schlegel called *Boehmius redivivus* and who, besides reconfirming Boehmian theosophy, sought without success to bring the Catholic and Orthodox churches closer together on the foundation of a common sapiential spirituality. Von Baader was at first a student of medicine, mineralogy, and even engineering but later turned to the study of philosophy and metaphysics.[104] He opposed the main theses of modern European philosophy of his day, including both the *cogito* of Descartes and the "agnosticism" of Kant,[105] and sought to bestow once again upon knowledge its sacramental quality. He asserted that, since God is reflected in all things, all knowledge is in a sense the knowledge of some aspect of the Divinity and has a sacred quality.[106] Attracted deeply to the study of nature, he considered his early philosophy as natural wisdom (*Naturweisheit*) which was to lead directly to the theosophy he was to develop later in life. In fact, in accordance with the sapiential perspective he did not make an absolute distinction between the natural and supernatural and saw in nature a reflection of the sacred which the official theology had confined strictly to the supernatural realm.

Von Baader emphasized the sapiential aspect of both religious practice and thought. Like Boehme, he identified Sophia with the Virgin Mary to whom he was especially devoted. He also spoke of wisdom as the "image of the Father" and emphasized the sacramental character of knowledge. For him all authentic knowledge led ultimately to God, and he did not fail to point to the positive function of reason and logic as channels through which the light of the Intellect shines upon the human state and which can lead man to the precinct of sacred knowledge.[107] Yet, despite his influence upon the rise of neo-Scholasticism, his voice as a spokesman for the sapiential perspective was a lonely one in the spiritual wilderness of the nineteenth century. Although there were a few figures here and there such as Antonio Rosmini in Italy, who wrote the *Theosophia* in the nineteenth century[108] upon the wake of and in a perspective akin to von Baader's works, the main arena of European thought was now reaping the fruit of the secularization of knowledge in the form of the antirationalistic philosophies which soon began to deny even to reason the possibility of attaining some degree of knowledge and certitude. As for sapiential teachings, what remained of them became more and more of a fragmentary nature, separated from the grace of the living Christian tradition, an "esoterism" which was properly speaking an "occultism" and a knowledge which, although originally of a sacred character, had become a body without a soul. It was the cadaver of sacred knowledge depleted of sacred presence and confined mostly to the cosmological rather than the purely metaphysical level. As for Christian mysticism, it had become nearly completely emptied of intellectual and metaphysical content, becoming a passive way of love which, although precious from the general religious point of view, could not stem the tide of the total desacralization of knowledge any more than could the existing occultisms, some of which possessed partial knowledge of traditional doctrines while others were impregnated with antitraditional forces which stood opposed to all that the sacred signifies. But to understand why such a phenomenon took place in the West, it is necessary to return to the earlier centuries of European history and to trace the process by which knowledge became gradually desacralized.

The process of desacralization of knowledge in the Occident begins already with the ancient Greeks among whom the first instance of the rise of an antitraditional society is to be seen in this cycle of human history. The loss of the symbolist spirit already decried by Plato, the emptying of the cosmos of its sacred content in the Olympian religion leading to Ionian natural philosophy, the rise of rationalism as independent of intellection, and many other important transformations mark this process of desacralization. The Greek tradition, instead of developing various intellectual perspectives like the *darśanas* of Hinduism, was witness to the rise of Sophism, Epicurianism, Pyrrhonism, the New Academy, and many other schools based on rationalism or skepticism which eclipsed almost totally the sacramental function of knowledge and reduced knowledge to either ratiocination or simple mental acrobatics, thus making it necessary to distinguish between knowledge and wisdom,[109] as well as bringing about the reaction against Greek philosophy as a whole which was to come with Christianity. What the post-Renaissance came to call the "Greek miracle" is, from the traditional point of view, a miracle in reverse because it substituted reason for the intellect and sensuous knowledge for inner illumination.[110]

There was, however, a veritable Greek miracle in the appearance in Greece of those sapiential doctrines and systematic metaphysics deriving from the Orphic and Dionysian mysteries. These were associated with such figures as Pythagoras, Empedocles, Plato, the Neoplatonists, especially Plotinus and Proclus, and even Aristotle, all of whom provided doctrines of a veritable metaphysical nature, although Aristotle hid intellection in a syllogistic mode and in a sense forms the link between metaphysics and philosophy in its later sense.[111] Certain Muslims have called Plato a prophet and he, as well as figures such as Pythagoras and Plotinus, must be considered as metaphysicians and seers like the *ṛṣis* of India rather than as profane philosophers. Their doctrines are based on the Intellect which illuminates rather than on simple ratiocination. With them knowledge is still impregnated with its sacred quality and is the means of attainment of *theosis*. These sages are gnostics whose teachings were to provide providentially the doctrinal language for many of the sapiential schools of Islam, Judaism, and Christianity. The rediscovery of the sacred character of knowledge today would lead, almost before anything else, to a rediscovery of Greek wisdom, of Plato, Plotinus, and other Graeco-Alexandrian sages and writings such as Hermeticism, not as simply human philosophy but as sacred doctrines of divine inspiration to be compared much more with the Hindu *darśanas* than with philosophical schools as they are currently understood. The belief of Muslim philosophers that the Greek philosophers had learned their doctrines from the prophets, especially Solomon, and that "philosophy derives from the niche of prophecy,"[112] if not verifiable historically, nevertheless contains a profound truth, namely, the relation of this wisdom to the sacred and its origin in revelation, even if this revelation cannot be confined in the strictly Abrahamic sense to a particular figure or prophet.

Christianity expanded in a world already suffering from a rationalism and naturalism which had stifled the spirit and hardened the heart as the seat of intelligence, dividing reason from its ontological root. It therefore had to present itself as a way of love which had to sweep aside completely all the "ways of knowing" that lay before it, not distinguishing in its general theological formulations between intellection and ratiocination and preferring quite rightly a true theology and a false cosmology to a false theology and a true cosmology.[113] In trying to overcome the prevalent danger of cosmolatry, Christianity, in its widely accepted theological formulations, not only drew an excessively tight boundary between the supernatural and the natural, leading to an impoverished view of nature, but also caused the eclipse of the supernaturally natural function of the Intellect. In the dialogue between the Hellenist and the Christian in which both sides presented an aspect of the truth and in which Christianity triumphed, from a certain point of view, precisely because it was a new dispensation from Heaven destined to save a whole world from the loss of religious faith, the sapiential dimension of Greek wisdom was criticized and dismissed along with skepticism and rationalism.[114] All knowledge appeared to a large number of Christian theologians as "pride of intelligence" and a climate was created which, from early days, was not completely favorable to the sapiential perspective. Although as described earlier, Christian gnosis existed from the beginning and continued through the centuries, the role and function of the Intellect was never considered as central as in certain other traditions such as Hinduism and Islam. As a result, the mainstream of Christian theology, especially after the early centuries, insisted upon the *credo ut intelligam*, a formula later identified with Saint Anselm, while limiting the function of intellection to that of a handmaid of faith rather than the means of sanctification, which of course would not exclude the element of faith. What the prevalent medieval Christian theology did exclude was the ecstatic or "rhapsodic intellect";[115] the ecstasy resulting from intellection was dismissed as a possibility and disdained religiously along with sexual ecstasy whose spiritual significance was left outside of the perspective of the official theology and which found its exposition in Christian Hermetic writings as well as in the Kabbala.

As far as the early centuries are concerned, it must be remembered that in the *Acts of the Stone and the Twelve Apostles* belonging to the Nag Hammadi collection, which contains the oldest form of Christology, Christ is described as the *Christos Angelos,* at once messenger and angel.[116] He is the celestial figure, the angel-man, the celestial archetype of the human soul who, like the *Fravarti* of Zoroastrianism, illuminates the soul and the mind and bestows upon it knowledge of a sacred order. There is moreover a direct relation between this Christology and alchemical and mineral symbolism and direct reference to the pearl which is also found in the "Hymn of the Soul" in the Acts of Thomas. The pearl is the universal symbol of the gnosis which purifies, sanctifies, and delivers, the pearl which Christ instructed his followers not to cast before swine. Throughout these early documents one finds constant reference to a type of Christology which emphasizes the gnostic character of both Christ himself as the bestower of wisdom and of his message as containing an inner significance of a gnostic and esoteric nature. To overcome the danger of various kinds of schisms associated with gnosticism, an official Christology was formulated which hid to some extent this aspect of the

Christ nature and thereby relegated the sapiential dimension of Christianity to a more marginal and secondary function, without of course obliterating or destroying it altogether.

A further eclipse of the sapiential dimension and the secularization of knowledge was to come in the twelfth and thirteenth centuries with the spread of Aristotelianism and Averroism in the West and their wedding with various forms of Christian theology, especially those schools which followed upon the wake of Saint Thomas. Until this period Augustianism had still preserved the primacy of illumination in the act of knowledge, whereas Saint Thomas, trying to preserve the primacy of Scripture, denied the possibility of the illumination of the mind by the Intellect and considered all knowledge as having a sensuous origin. Despite the imposing theology created by Saint Thomas, his adoption of Aristotelian categories for the expression of Christian doctrines and emphasis upon the sensual origin of knowledge played a role in the further desacralization of knowledge, although Saint Thomas himself did not accept the separation of faith and reason which he in fact sought to harmonize.[117] But the harmony of faith and reason is one thing and the sanctifying function of knowledge another. Had Thomism continued to be interpreted by a Meister Eckhart, the intellectual destiny of the West would have been very different. But as it happened, the excessively positive categories of theology (or kataphatic theology) combined with a dimming of intellectual intuition, which caused the very meaning of realism to be soon forgotten, led to the nominalism that marked the swan song of medieval Christianity and destroyed the harmony which had been established between reason and faith in a world dominated by the sacred.

Thomism was certainly religious philosophy at its highest level and Christian theology in a most mature and all-embracing form. But it was not the pure *sapientia* based on the direct illumination of reason by the Intellect, although even in this respect it provided a perfectly suitable language and a world view which could lead to a purely sapiential vision of things as one can in fact observe in Dante. But the excessive emphasis upon reason at the expense of the Intellect in Scholasticism combined with the destruction or disappearance of the Order of the Temple, the *fedeli d'amore,* and other depositories of Christian esoteric and gnostic teachings certainly helped to create an atmosphere which was more conducive to the rise of rationalism and the eclipse of a perspective of a truly intellectual nature. In the intellectual life of a religious civilization such as that of Christianity or Islam or for that matter in the Jewish tradition, one can detect three and not just two major schools or ways of thinking: philosophy, theology, and gnosis or metaphysics (or theosophy) in its traditional sense. Saint Thomas was a great philosopher and certainly an outstanding theologian. But even if he himself may have also been a Christian gnostic when he put his pen down and chose silence, his works provided the West more with traditional philosophy and theology than with the kind of sapiential doctrines based directly on the sanctifying function of the Intellect. In any case, men who criticize Saint Thomas today are, for the most part, not those who are of such lofty intellectual realization and metaphysical insight that they must simply move beyond the confines of Thomistic categories but are usually those who simply fail to comprehend what Saint Thomas is saying. A true gnostic would be the first to realize the immense importance of Thomism, as in Islam figures like Suhrawardī and Mullā Ṣadrā, who based their epistemology on the sacramental function of knowledge and its illumination by the Intellect, were the first to point to the importance of Muslim Peripatetics (*mashshāʾīs*) whose perspective was in many respects close to that of Saint Thomas and whom the Angelic Doctor quotes so often.

To understand the process of the gradual desacralization of knowledge in the West the role of the teachings of Ibn Sīnā and Ibn Rushd in the Latin world are of some importance.[118] Avicennian philosophy which was to serve in the Islamic world as the basis for the restatement of the sacramental function of knowledge and intellection by Suhrawardī and many later sages reached the West in only a truncated version and under a much more rationalistic garb.[119] But even what did reach the West and led to what has been called Latin Avicennism[120] never enjoyed the same popularity or influence as the more rationalistic Latin Averroism. Furthermore, even in the case of Ibn Rushd (Averroes), who was much more rationalistic than Ibn Sīnā and did not emphasize illumination of the mind by the angel as did the latter, there is no doubt that again the Latin Averroes is more of a secularized and rationalistic philosopher than the original Ibn Rushd when read in Arabic. The study of the destiny of these two masters of Islamic philosophy in the Islamic and Christian worlds reveals to what extent the West was moving toward a more rationalistic interpretation of this philosophic school while the Islamic world was moving in the other direction to reaffirm the primacy of intellection over ratiocination. The appearance of Suhrawardī and the school of illumination (*al-ishrāq*) testifies to a new assertion of the sacred quality of knowledge and the ultimately "illuminative" character of all knowledge in the Islamic intellectual universe.[121]

In the Occident, however, it was not the doctrine of illumination of a Suhrawardī which came to the fore but the nominalism which reacted against the positive theology of the thirteenth century. Although as already mentioned, a certain aspect of nominalism was instrumental in preparing the ground for the type of apophatic and mystical theology identified with Nicholas of Cusa, the movement as a whole marked the final phase of cutting reason off from certitude. It thereby created a philosophical agnosticism which even in the world of faith implied an impoverishment of the power of reason and the function of knowing as related to the sacred, causing a vacuum which had dire consequences for the Christian world. Although religious faith was still too strong to permit an open type of agnostic rationalism which was to appear during later centuries, nominalism, in combination with certain other forces, helped to eclipse the type of sacred knowledge which every religion needs if it is to be total and complete and able to cater to the mental and intellectual needs of all of its followers. The result was the attempt on the part of certain Christians of an intellectual bent to seek outside of Christianity for answers to quench their thirst for causality and the explanation of the nature of things, answers which in many cases only esoterism and veritable metaphysics can supply. This quest in turn led to the breakup of the homogeneous and integral Christian world view which had dominated the Middle Ages. Men then sought certitude and a firm foundation for knowledge on another basis and level; hence the establishment of modern philosophy, properly speaking, with Descartes.[122]

During the Renaissance there was certainly a quest for primordial wisdom, for lost knowledge, for a new foundation for certitude. Gemistus Plethon whose influence was deeply felt in the Italian Renaissance had spoken of Plato and Zoroaster as fathers of a sacred Sophia, while Ficino set about to revive the whole corpus of Platonic wisdom and translate it into Latin. There was renewed interest in Hermeticism and even the ancient Oriental mysteries, but despite figures such as Ficino and Cusa, much of the search for sacred knowledge was in reality being carried out outside of the mainstream of the Christian tradition in forms which were "pagan" in the theological sense of the term. The subject studied was sacred knowledge but the mind which set out to carry out this study was in many cases being affected to an ever greater degree by an individualism and humanism which could not but result in the total rationalism that soon followed. Although there was a great deal of interest in Orphism and the *Orphica,* which, like the *Hermetica,*[123] was widespread during the Renaissance, the "Orphic Christ" who was such an important figure of the Latin literature of the earlier period[124] ceased to be a central influence as in days gone by. One could say that Orpheus went one way and Christ another. Ancient wisdom based on the doctrine of the sanctity of the Intellect began to appear independent of the living tradition of the West which was Christianity. And since only a living tradition can convey and bestow the quality of the sacred in an operative manner, the very process of resuscitation of ancient wisdom had, to a large extent, the result of further weakening what remained of the traditional Christian intellectuality. As a result, despite the presence of groups and circles which possessed authentic knowledge of a sacred character, groups such as the Rosicrucians, the Kabbalists, the Hermeticists, and the school of Paracelsus, the revival of ancient wisdom during the Renaissance and even later and the opposition of most followers of this "newly found" wisdom to Scholasticism did not result in the integration of Scholasticism into a higher sapiential perspective within Christianity,[125] but in the destruction of Scholasticism from "below" leading to the nearly complete secularization of knowledge in the main currents of European philosophy in the seventeenth century. The profusion of teachings of an esoteric and sapiential nature during the Renaissance, much of which in fact was an externalization and profanation of what had been known and preserved secretly during the Middle Ages, did not lead to the reestablishment of the sapiential dimension at the heart of the Christian tradition but to a further breakup of the Christian intellectual world and the secularization of reason resulting in the more or less radical separation of philosophy from theology, reason from faith, and mysticism from gnosis, which has characterized the main current of Western intellectual history since the Renaissance.

Since man is by nature a being in quest of certainty, the philosophical agnosticism following the nominalist attack against medieval philosophy had to be overcome in one way or another. This feat was in fact achieved, as far as later European history is concerned, not by the revival of the ancient wisdom during the Renaissance, which in reality contained all the necessary teachings if only their true nature had been fully understood, but through recourse to the radical individualism and rationalism which mark modern European philosophy as such. Descartes has been quite rightly called the father of modern philosophy for it is he more than his contemporaries, Spinoza and Leibniz, who epitomizes what lies at the heart of modern philosophy and even modern science, namely, the reduction of knowledge to the functioning of the individual reason cut off from the Intellect, in both its microcosmic and macrocosmic aspects.

In seeking a new basis for certain knowledge Descartes appealed neither to the Intellect as it functions in the heart of man and as the source of reason nor to revelation, but to the individual consciousness of the thinking subject. The famous *cogito* could possibly have referred to the primacy of the subject over the object in the sense that the Vedantists consider *Ātman* to be the primary reality compared to which all externalized existence and objectivization is *māyā*. The *cogito ergo sum* in fact contains a profound metaphysical significance if understood in this Vedantic sense. But in saying "I think, therefore I am," Descartes was not referring to the divine I who some seven centuries before Descartes had uttered through the mouth of Manṣūr al-Ḥallāj,[126] "I am the Truth" (*ana᾽ l-Ḥaqq*), the Divine Self which alone *can* say I. It was Descartes's individual, and therefore from the gnostic point of view "illusory" self, which was placing its experience and consciousness of thinking as the foundation of all epistemology and ontology and the source of certitude. Even being was subordinated to it and considered a consequence of it, hence the *ergo*. Even if he did begin with the act of thinking, Descartes could have concluded with *est* rather than *sum*, asserting that my thinking and consciousness are themselves proofs that God is, not that "I" as individual am.[127] Had he done so, he would have joined a particular perspective of traditional philosophy and preserved the central role of ontology in philosophy.

As it was, he made the thinking of the individual ego the center of reality and the criterion of all knowledge, turning philosophy into pure rationalism and shifting the main concern of European philosophy from ontology to epistemology. Henceforth, knowledge, even if it were to extend to the farthest galaxies, was rooted in the *cogito*. The knowing subject was bound to the realm of reason and separated from both the Intellect and revelation, neither of which were henceforth considered as possible sources of knowledge of an objective order. Knowing thus became depleted of its sacred content to the extent that anything that partakes of reality *can* become divorced from the sacred which is ultimately inseparable from reality, the Ultimate Reality being the Sacred as such. But to the mentality of those who were caught in the web of the newly established rationalism, this most intelligent way of being unintelligent, knowledge and science were henceforth totally separated from the sacred even if the sacred were to be accepted as possessing a reality. To this mentality the very concept of a *scientia sacra* appeared as a contradiction in terms and, in fact, it still appears as either contradictory or meaningless not only to those who either consciously or unconsciously follow the rationalism inherent in Cartesian epistemology but also to those who have rebelled against this rationalism from below with the kinds of irrationalism which characterize so much of modern thought.

After the seventeenth century, there was but a single step to Humean doubt and the Kantian "agnostic" position which in a characteristically subjective fashion denied to the intellect the possibility of knowing the essence of things, as if to say that since my rational faculties cannot know the noumena, reason as such is incapable of such knowledge, and since my reason is not illuminated by the Intellect which would permit me to know the noumena through intellectual intuition, no one else can possess such an intellectual faculty either.

In the case of both Descartes and Kant, however, the functioning of reason as such is at least still accepted and the knowledge that it can attain is considered to have an immutability which characterizes that which is of an intellectual order. Although these philosophers did not recognize the ultimately sacred character of the very categories of logic which enables man to know even on the level of ordinary logic, they still preserved a vision of permanence and immutability of logical categories which, despite their own unawareness of its real nature, is seen from the metaphysical point of view as a reflection of the sacred, which is in fact the permanent and the eternal in itself and in its reflections into the domains of change and becoming.

In the unfolding of this process of secularization, however, even this reflection was to disappear with those nineteenth-century philosophies such as Hegelianism and Marxism which based reality upon dialectical becoming and change itself and transformed an immutable vision of things into a constantly changing one, whether this process was taken as being spiritual or material. Hegel has been, of course, interpreted in many ways, and his complicated thoughts allow interpretations ranging all the way from those of conservative theologians in nineteenth-century Germany to agnostic leftists. But what characterizes the whole dialectical thought process in its nineteenth-century development, and in contrast to many traditional philosophies of change, is not its concern with becoming or process but the reduction of reality to the temporal process, of being to becoming, of the immutable categories of logic, not to mention metaphysics, to everchanging thought processes. This loss of the sense of permanence in schools of philosophy standing in the mainstream of modern Western thought marks, along with the crass positivism of an Auguste Comte, a more advanced phase of not only the desacralization of knowledge but also of the loss of the sense of the sacred which characterizes modern, but not necessarily contemporary, man as such. All that follows, either in the form of irrational philosophies reacting against Hegelianism or various later forms of positivism or analytical philosophy, carry out the final phases of the program to destroy completely the sacred quality of knowledge by either totally separating religion and the quest for the sacred from rationality and logic or by depleting both language and thought processes, that are of course related to language, from any significance of a metaphysical order which may still lurk in some recess from days when man's concern with knowledge was inseparable from his attachment to and quest for the sacred.[128] The result has been the creation of philosophies which, from the traditional point of view, could only be called monstrous and which can only be characterized as what the German scholar H. Türck has called "misosophy," that is, the hatred rather than love of wisdom and which others have considered as "antiphilosophy."[129]

Since only the like can know the like, the secularized reason which became the sole instrument of knowing in modern times could not but leave its mark and effect upon everything that it studied. All subjects studied by a secularized instrument of knowledge came out to be depleted and devoid of the quality of the sacred. The profane point of view could only observe a profane world in which the sacred did not play a role. The quest of the typically modern man has been in fact to "kill the gods" wherever he has been able to find them and to banish the sacred from a world which has been rapidly woven into a new pattern drawn from the strands issuing from a secularized mentality.

The effect of desacralized knowledge was to appear first of all in the domain of thought itself. In contrast to the Christian Platonists and Aristotelians, Renaissance Hermeticists like Ficino, who sought to revive Hermetic gnosis to which Pico della Mirandola was to add a Christianized version of the Kabbala,[130] or even certain later theosophers and esoterists, most of those who have studied such subjects in the modern world have failed to distinguish between a sacred wisdom based upon intellection and profane philosophy. The grandeur of metaphysical doctrines has been reduced to the triviality of profane thought, the conceptual category of "thought" like "culture" being itself a modern invention which one is forced to use in contemporary discourse. The most sublime form of wisdom has been transformed into simple historical borrowing, Neoplatonism, as mentioned already, playing the role of the ideal historical tag with which one could destroy the significance of the most profound sapiential doctrines. It has been and still is simply sufficient to call something Neoplatonic influence to reduce it, spiritually speaking, to insignificance. And if that has not been possible, then terms such as pantheistic, animistic, naturalistic, monistic, and even mystical in the sense of ambiguous have been and still are employed to characterize doctrines whose significance one wishes to destroy or ignore. Plato, Plotinus, and Proclus are presented as simple philosophers as if they were professors of philosophy in some nearby university; and those among Christians who had adopted their metaphysical formulations as people who went astray from "pure" Christianity and therefore fell under the influence of Greek thought. How different is the appreciation of Pythagoras, Plato, or even Aristotle in al-Fārābī and even in the works of Thomas Taylor or K. S. Guthrie than among those for whom all philosophy is the fruit of a reason divorced from its roots and depleted of the sense of the sacred. The rediscovery of tradition and the reconfirmation of the sacred quality of knowledge would make possible not only the reappraisal of the whole of philosophy and the reevaluation of Greek wisdom and philosophy, but also enable contemporary man to understand the significance of the providential role played by this philosophy in the three monotheistic religions which were spread throughout the Mediterranean world and Europe following the demise of Graeco-Roman civilization. The reevaluation of the Greek intellectual heritage in the light of tradition is one of the most important tasks which must be achieved in the contemporary world, a task which if carried out fully would affect profoundly the present state of the study of not only philosophy but also theology and even comparative religion.

The secularization of the cosmos was also related to the secularization of reason. Although there are numerous intellectual and historical causes for the desacralization of the cosmos,[131] the reduction of the knowing mind or the subject of the Cartesian *cogito* to the purely rationalistic level was certainly one of the main ones. It is not accidental that the mechanization of the cosmos and the emptying of the substance of the world of its sacred quality took place at the same time as the desacralization of knowledge and the final divorce between the reason which "knows" scientifically from the world of faith on the one hand, and the Intellect which knows principially and essentially on the other. Some have even attributed the spiritual chaos of modern times to this mechanization of the world in seventeenth-century science.[132] It is of singular interest to note that nearly all those philosophers and theologians who were opposed to the reduction of knowledge to only the level of reason also opposed the mechanistic conception of the world,[133] and that those, such as the followers of Boehme in Germany, who sought to continue his teachings based on the illumination of the mind by the Intellect were also the foremost proponents of the *Naturphilosophie* which opposed violently the mechanistic point of view.[134] In any case there is little doubt that the desacralization of knowledge was related directly to the desacralization of the cosmos.

Nor was history and the temporal process spared the fate which befell the cosmos. Reason cut off from its root in the permanent could not but reduce reality to process, time to pure quantity, and history to a process without a transcendent entelechy and, at the same time, the mother and progenitor of all that the modern mentality considered as reality. Time rather than eternity became the source of all things. Ideas, rather than being considered as true or false in themselves, were relegated completely to the domain of historical change and considered significant only as historical events. A historicism was born which resulted in the same kind of desacralization of history and the temporal process itself that one finds in philosophy and science. Although many contemporary critics have realized the poverty of historicism[135] and sought to envisage the historical process from other points of view, historicism has continued to survive as a prevailing mode of thought in a world where, for many people, reason remains divorced from the twin source of permanence, namely, the Intellect and revelation, and all permanence is reduced to becoming. Both the destruction of the qualitative aspect of time and the reduction of all realities to their reflection upon the stream of becoming are the result of the turning away of man's mental faculties from his immutable Center to the fluctuating periphery of his existence. Cut off from the heart which is the seat of the Intellect, reason could not but become engrossed in transience and change which then began to usurp the role and function of the permanent. In reducing the Absolute to the relative and the permanent to the changing, the profane point of view also depleted the relative and the changing of the sacred quality which they possess on their own level.

Since formulated knowledge is inseparable from language, the desacralization of knowledge could not but affect the use of language. If European languages have become less and less symbolic and ever more unidimensional, losing much of the inward sense of classical languages, it is because they have been associated with thought patterns of a unidimensional character. The antimetaphysical bias of much of modern philosophy is reflected in the attempt made to divest language of all metaphysical significance, a process which, however, is impossible to achieve completely because language like the cosmos is of an ultimately divine origin and cannot be divorced totally from the metaphysical significance embedded in its very roots and structures. Nevertheless, already in the seventeenth century the rise of rationalism and the mechanization of the world began to affect European languages almost immediately in the direction of secularization. Galileo still accepted the traditional idea that nature is a great book to be deciphered,[136] but for him the language of this book was no longer the sacred language of Saint Bonaventure, Dante, or the Kabbalists, associated with symbolic and anagogical meaning, but mathematics understood in its purely quantitative and not Pythagorean sense.[137] Kepler also thought that "quantity was the mode of God's expression" in the universe (*Dico quantitatum Deo propositam*),[138] although in contrast to Galileo he never lost sight of the symbolic and qualitative aspect of mathematics, itself associated with the Pythogorean philosophy of harmony and the symbolism of numbers and geometric forms to which he was in fact deeply devoted.

Henceforth, many European philosophers even tried to create a language based upon mathematics, and in the case of Mersenne upon music. It was in fact this movement that underlaid the symbolic logic of Leibniz who sought to connect thought to calculation whereas in the traditional perspective it is thought and language which are inseparable from each other. In many traditional sources *logos* and *ragione* (discourse) are interconnected and in certain contexts refer to the same thing.

Be that as it may, the secularization of language and the attempt to substitute pure quantity for the symbolic significance of language in the reading of the cosmic text also reflected upon the language of sacred Scripture itself, which until now had been considered as a gift from God and which had been connected by certain Catholic and also Protestant theologians with the book of nature. But now that human language had become degraded and mathematics considered as the proper language of nature, the language of sacred Scripture began to appear as "more the slipshod invention of illiterate man than the gift of omniscient God."[139] The link between divine language and human language broke down,[140] leaving the latter to undergo the successive "falls" or stages of secularization which have resulted in the various forms of bastardization of languages today and also, on another level, to the sacrifice of the liturgical art connected with Latin in favor of vernacular languages which have already moved a long way from their sacred prototypes and become only too familiar as the everyday languages of an already secularized world filled with experiences of triviality. There is an almost one to one correspondence between the depleting of knowledge of its sacred content and the desacralization of the language associated with it; and also vice versa the attempt to elevate language once again to its symbolic and anagogical level whenever there has been a revival or reconfirmation of sacred knowledge or *scientia sacra* which would then seek to have itself expressed in the language available, but also appropriate, to it.[141]

Finally, the process of desacralization of knowledge has reached the citadel of the sacred itself, that is, religion. As a result of the final step taken by Hegel to reduce the whole process of knowledge to a dialectic inseparable from change and becoming, the world of faith began to appear as something totally separated by a chasm from the ground upon which "thinking" men stood. The reaction to Hegel was Kierkegaard, and from him grew both existential theology and existential philosophy whether theistic or atheistic. For such figures as Jaspers, Marcel, and even Heidegger there is despair in man's attempt to understand and make sense of reality so that he must make a leap in order to make sense of things. In theology likewise the thought of Karl Barth requires a leap into "the upper story of faith."[142] Theology ceases to have contact with either the world of nature or human history.[143] The unifying vision which related knowledge to love and faith, religion to science, and theology to all the departments of intellectual concern is finally completely lost, leaving a world of compartmentalization where there is no wholeness because holiness has ceased to be of central concern, or is at best reduced to sentimentality. In such a world those with spiritual and intellectual perspicacity sought, outside of the confines of this ambience, to rediscover their traditional roots and the total functioning of the intelligence which would once again bestow upon knowledge its sacramental function and enable men to reintegrate their lives upon the basis of this unifying principle, which is inseparable from both love and faith. For others, for whom such a criticism of the modern world and rediscovery of the sacred was not possible but who, at the same time, could not be lulled to sleep before the impoverished intellectual and spiritual landscape which was presented to them as modern life, there was only lament and despair which, in fact, characterizes so much of modern literature and which the gifted Welsh poet Dylan Thomas was to epitomize in the poem that was also to become his elegy:

> *Too proud to die, broken and blind he died*
> *The darkest way, and did not turn away,*
> *A cold kind man brave in his narrow pride*
> *Being innocent, he dreaded that he died*
> *Hating his God, but what he was was plain.*
> *An old kind man brave in his burning pride.*

But because God *is* both merciful and just, the light of the Intellect could not be completely eclipsed nor could this despair be the final hymn of contemporary man.

NOTES

1. The Hindu expression *Sat-Chit-Ānanda* is one of the Names of God. *Sat-Chit-Ānanda* is usually translated as "Being-Consciousness-Bliss," but the most "essential" translation—the one that makes most clear the metaphysical meaning of these terms— is "Object-Subject-Union." At the highest level this ternary may also be expressed as "Known-Knower-Knowledge" or "Beloved-Lover-Love." This ternary also has an operative or spiritual meaning related to invocatory prayer, such as the Prayer of Jesus (Christianity), *japa* (Hinduism), and *dhikr* (Islam). Here it takes the form of "Invoked-Invoker-Invocation" (in Islamic terms *madhkūr-dhākir-dhikr*).

2. "The substance of knowledge is Knowledge of the Substance; that is, the substance of human intelligence, in its most deeply real function, is the perception of the Divine Substance." "Atmā-Māyā," *Studies in Comparative Religion*, Summer 1973, p. 130.

3. Gen. 2:17 and 3:24.

St. Bonaventure describes man in the state of unitive knowledge as follows, "In the initial state of creation, man was made fit for the quiet of contemplation, and therefore *God placed him in a paradise of delights* (Gen. 2:15). But turning from the true light to changeable good, man was bent over by his own fault, and the entire human race by original sin, which infected human nature in two ways: the mind with ignorance and the flesh with concupiscence. As a result, man, blinded and bent over, sits in darkness and does not see the light of heaven unless grace with justice come to his aid against concupiscence and unless knowledge with wisdom come to his aid against ignorance." *Bonaventure, The Soul's Journey into God*, trans. and introd. by E. Cousins, New York, 1978, p. 62.

4. The Muslim sages, when discussing metaphysical subjects, especially if they concern the nature of God, state that it was so as so and then add, often abruptly, *al-ān kamā kān* ("And it is now as it was then."), confirming the identity of the present "now" with that "then" or moment "in the beginning" which was the origin of things in time yet stood itself outside of time.

5. "Ce qui est naturel à la conscience humaine prouve *ipso facto* sa vérité essentielle, la raison d'être de l'intelligence étant l'adéquation au réel." F. Schuon, "Conséquences découlant du mystère de la subjectivité," *Sophia Perennis* 4/1 (Spring 1978): 12; also in the author's *Du Divin à l'humain* (in press).

6. The well-known Scholastic principle is *adaequatio rei et intellectus* which St. Thomas comments upon in his saying, "knowledge comes about in so far as the object known is within the knower."

7. Plato used *theologia* as the highest form of philosophy which was to know the Supreme Good through the intellect. St. Augustine adopted the term *theologica naturalis* in his *De civitas Dei*, basing himself on M. Terentius Varro's distinction between natural theology and ideas related to myths and the state. From Augustinian teachings there issued the distinction between revealed and natural theology which Scholasticism treated as a branch of philosophy. See W. Jaeger, *The Theology of the Greek Thinkers*, Oxford, 1947, pp. 1–5. It is significant to note that with the radical secularization of reason and the process of knowing natural theology was discarded, to be resuscitated in the last few years along with the rise of interest in the more traditional conception of reason in its relation to both the Intellect and revelation.

8. "Les lois de la logique sont sacrées,—comme aussi celles des mathématiques,—car elles relèvent essentiellement de l'ontologie, qu'elles appliquent à un domaine particulier: la logique est l'ontologie de ce microcosme qu'est la raison humaine." F. Schuon, "Pas de droit sacré à l'absurdité," *Études Traditionnelles* 79/460 (Avril–Mai–Juin 1978): 59.

9. "Nous ajouterons—et c'est même ce qui import le plus—que les lois de la logique se trouvent enracinées dans la nature divine, c'est-à-dire qu'elles manifestent, dans l'esprit humain, des rapports ontologiques; la délimitation même de la logique est

extrinsèquement chose logique, sans quoi elle est arbitraire. Que la logique soit in-opérante en l'absence des données objectives indispensables et des qualifications subjectives, non moins nécessaires, c'est l'evidence même, et c'est ce qui réduit à néant les constructions lucifériennes des rationalistes, et aussi, sur un tout autre plan, certains spéculations sentimentales et expéditives des théologiens." F. Schuon, "L' enigme de l'Epiclèse," *Études Traditionnelles* 79/459 (Jan.–Feb.–Mar. 1978): 7; also in the author's *Christianisme/Islam—Visions d'oeucuménisme ésotérique* (in press).

10. Schuon, "Pas de droit sacré à l'absurdité," p. 52.

11. See, for example, W. C. Smith, *Faith and Belief*, Princeton, 1979, where a sharp distinction is made between faith and belief in the modern sense of the word as it is shorn of all elements of doctrinal certitude and separated from a knowledge which is rooted in the Divine. The author quite rightly distinguishes between the meaning of belief as certain knowledge in the traditional context and its reduction to conjecture and knowledge mixed with doubt in the modern world.

12. See R. Guénon, *Man and His Becoming According to the Vedanta*, trans. R. C. Nicholson, London, 1945, p. 14.

13. In this study gnosis is always used in the sense of sapiential knowledge or wisdom, as the knowledge which unifies and sanctifies and not in a sectarian sense as related to gnosticism or in a narrow theological sense as employed by certain early Christian authors who contrasted it with *sophia*.

14. The term *jñāna* implies principial knowledge which leads to deliverance and is related etymologically to gnosis, the root *gn* or *kn* meaning knowledge in various Indo-European languages including English.

15. See A. K. Coomaraswamy, *Hinduism and Buddhism*, New York, 1943.

16. See T. R. V. Murti, *The Central Philosophy of Buddhism*, London, 1955; E. Conze, *Buddhist Thought in India*, London, 1964; F. I. Stcherbatsky, *The Conception of Buddhist Nirvāna*, New York, 1973; and K. Venkata Ramanan, *Nāgārjuna's Siddha-Nāgārjuna's Philosophy as presented in the Mahā-prajñā pāramitā-sāstra*, Rutland, Vt., 1966.

17. "If one considers the canonical image of the Buddha, the following observation can be made: . . . if he is the supreme Knowledge, the lotus will be contemplation, with all the virtues that are implied in it." F. Schuon, *In the Tracks of Buddhism*, trans. M. Pallis, London, 1968, p. 157.

18. This "nature" could be interpreted in the Islamic tradition as *al-fitrah* or the primordial nature which is the nature possessed by man when he lived in the proximity of the Tree of Life and ate the fruit of unitive knowledge or wisdom and which he still carries at the center of his being.

19. H. A. Giles, *Chuang-Tzǔ—Taoist Philosopher and Chinese Mystic*, London, 1961, p. 119.

20. Ibid., p. 127. This is the Chinese manner of stating that knowledge of principles allows man to see things *in divinis* and finally return to the Divine Origin of all things himself. This theme is also developed in many chapters of the *Tao-Te Ching*, concerning the perfect man who is characterized by knowledge of principles which is of course always combined with virtue. See C. Elorduy, *Lao-Tse—La Gnosis Taoista del Tao Te Ching*, Ona, Burgos, 1961, esp. "El hombre perfecto," pp. 53–58.

The apparent opposition of Lao-Tze to wisdom is to ostentatious "wisdom" and not knowledge as such as the verses of chap. 33, "He who knows men has wisdom—He who is self-knowing is enlightened," bear out. Lao-Tze also emphasizes the "primor-dial nature" of man, the "uncarved block," and the importance of "unknowing" to reach that state. For example, the verses of chap. 81 (trans. G. Feng and J. English, in *Lao-Tsu: Tao Te Ching*, New York, 1972),

> Those who know are not learned,
> Those who are learned do not know.

Here learning means the assembling of facts and worldly knowledge to which princi-pial knowing is contrasted. That is why (ibid., chap. 48)

In the pursuit of learning, every day something is acquired.
In the pursuit of Tao, every day something is dropped.

The "something dropped" refers to the process which is also called "unknowing" and which is central in reaching sacred knowledge as certain of the most important sapiential schools in the West, to which we shall turn shortly, have emphasized.

21. On Manichaean gnosis see N. C. Puech, *Le Manichéisme: son fondateur, sa doctrine,* Paris, 1949.

22. On this doctrine and Zoroastrian angelology in general see A. V. W. Jackson, *Zoroastrian Studies,* New York, 1928; R. C. Zaehner, *Zurvan, A Zoroastrian Dilemma,* Oxford, 1955; G. Widengren, *The Great Vohu Manah and the Apostle of God: Studies in Iranian and Manichaean Religion,* Leipzig, 1945; idem, *Die Religionen Irans,* Stuttgart, 1965; M. Molé, *Culte, mythe et cosmologie dans l'Iran ancien; le problème zoroastrien et la tradition mazdéenne,* Paris, 1963; H. S. Nyberg, *Die Religionen des alten Iran,* Leipzig, 1938; and many of the works of Corbin including his *En Islam iranien,* 4 vols., Paris, 1971–72; and *Celestial Body and Spiritual Earth, from Mazdean Iran to Shi'ite Iran,* trans. N. Pearson, Princeton, 1977.

23. "There are many kinds of masculinity and femininity. Masculinity and femininity are ever thus: innate wisdom and acquired wisdom. Acquired wisdom occupies the place of the masculine, and innate wisdom occupies the place of the feminine. . . . Innate wisdom without acquired wisdom is like a female without a male, who does not conceive and does not bear fruit. A man who possesses acquired wisdom, but whose innate wisdom is not perfect, is like a female who is not receptive to a male." *Aturpāt-i Ēmētān, The Wisdom of the Sasanian Sages (Dēnkard VI),* trans. S. Shaked, Boulder, 1979, p. 103.

24. See G. von Rad, *Wisdom in Israel,* London, 1972.

25. See L. Schaya, *The Universal Meaning of the Kabbalah,* trans. N. Pearson, London, 1971.

26. *Liqqutei Amarim [Tanya]* by Rabbi Schneur Zalman of Liadi, trans. N. Mindel, Brooklyn, N.Y., 1965, pp. 26–27.

27. Ibid., p. 113.

28. Ibid., pp. 113–14.

29. Jewish esoterism also speaks in an erotic language when discussing the three *Sefiroth, Chachma, Binah, Da'ath,* together abbreviated as *Chabad,* which are wisdom, understanding, and knowledge in both the principial, Divine Order and in the human microcosm considered in its totality. *Chachma* is considered as the father, *Binah* as the mother, and the *Da'ath* as the son born of their union. (*Da'ath* also means sexual union, indicating the symbolic relation between the ecstasy of sexual union and gnosis).

"*Chachma* is called *Abba* (Father), and *Binah* is called *Imma* (Mother). Metaphorically speaking, the seed of *Abba* is implanted in the womb of *Imma,* and there the rudimentary plant of the seed is developed, expanded, externalised, and informed. *Da'ath* is called *Ben* (Son), i.e., the offspring of this union of *Chachma* and *Binah.*" Rabbi Jacob Immanuel Sebochet, *Introduction to the English Translation of IGERETH HAKODESH,* Brooklyn, N.Y., 1968, p. 35.

30. F. Schuon, *Understanding Islam,* trans. D. M. Matheson, London, 1963, chap. 1; and S. H. Nasr, *Ideals and Realities in Islam,* London, 1980, chap. 1. We have dealt extensively with the Islamic conception of knowledge and the central role of intelligence as the means of access to the Divinity in many of our other writings including *Science and Civilization in Islam,* Cambridge, Mass., 1968; and *An Introduction to Islamic Cosmological Doctrines,* London-Boulder, 1978.

31. See F. Rosenthal, *Knowledge Triumphant: The Concept of Knowledge in Medieval Islam,* Leiden, 1970, where this theme is treated from a scholarly rather than a metaphysical point of view but with much worthwhile documentation. Rosenthal, looking as a historian upon the meaning of knowledge in the Islamic perspective as reflected in the sayings of the Prophet, writes, "In the Prophet's view of the world, 'knowledge' which in its totality is a matter of deepest concern to him consists of two principal parts. There is human knowledge, that is, a secular knowledge of an elementary or more

advanced character and a religious human knowledge; the latter constitutes the highest development of knowledge attainable to man. . . . But in addition to human knowledge both secular and religious, there also exists a divine knowledge. It is basically identical with human knowledge, still, it is somehow of a higher order both quantitatively and qualitatively. The most important features of these aspects of knowledge are felt and respected by the Prophet as interlocking and interdependent." Ibid., p. 31.

On the Islamic conception of knowledge see also ʿAbd al-Halīm Mahmūd, "Islam and Knowledge," *Al-Azhar Academy of Islamic Research: First Conference of the Academy of Islamic Research,* Cairo, 1971, pp. 407–53.

32. The relation between Greek and Hindu wisdom as compared and studied by such a figure as A. K. Coomaraswamy is principial and not merely historical even if certain historical links may have existed between them as asserted by many recent authors such as J. W. Sedlar, *India and the Greek World,* Totowa, N.J., 1980.

33. There are exceptional studies of much value which have remained fully aware of the link between Greek philosophy and various dimensions of Greek religion. See, for example, F. Cornford, *Principium sapientiae: the Origins of Greek Philosophical Thought,* Cambridge, 1952; idem, *From Religion to Philosophy: a Study in the Origins of Western Speculation,* New York, 1957; and idem, *The Unwritten Philosophy and Other Essays,* Cambridge, 1967.

34. V. 12 on from the King James Version.

35. Quoted by F. Schuon in *Spiritual Perspectives and Human Facts,* trans. D. M. Matheson, London, 1953, p. 153.

"If the life of the spirit is the illumination of knowledge and if it is love of God which produces this illumination, then it is right to say: there is nothing higher than love of God." St. Maximus the Confessor, *Centuries of Charity.* And "Holy knowledge draws the purified spirit, even as the magnet, by a natural force it possesses, draws iron." Evagrius of Ponticum, *Centuries of Charity* (both cited from Schuon, *Spiritual Perspectives and Human Facts,* p. 153). The chap. "Love and Knowledge" in *Spiritual Perspectives and Human Facts* contains the essence of the meaning of the way of knowledge or the sapiential path in Christian spirituality as well as in other traditions.

36. There is no doubt that certain forms of Christology rejected by Western Christianity during later centuries in order to combat various types of theological heresy, had a profound metaphysical significance when interpreted not only theologically and literally but metaphysically and symbolically. See F. Schuon, *Logic and Transcendence,* trans. P. N. Townsend, New York, 1975, esp. pp. 96ff.

37. See A. Feuillet, *Le Christ sagesse de Dieu,* Paris, 1966; and E. E. Ellis, *Prophecy and Hermeneutic in Early Christianity,* Grand Rapids, 1978, esp. pp. 45ff.

38. See, for example, J. Dupont, *La Connaissance religieuse dans les Epitres de Saint Paul,* Paris, 1960.

39. On Clement and his gnostic doctrines see T. Camelot, *Foi et gnose. Introduction à l'étude de la connaissance mystique chez Clément d'Alexandrie,* Paris, 1945; J. Daniélou, *Histoire des doctrines chrétiennes avant Nicée. t. II: Message evangélique et culture hellénistique aux IIᵉ et IIIᵉ siècles,* Paris, 1961; J. Munck, *Untersuchungen über Klemens von Alexandria,* Copenhagen/Stuttgart, 1933; E. F. Osborn, *The Philosophy of Clement of Alexandria,* Cambridge, 1954; and W. Völker, *Der wahre Gnostiker Clemens Alexandrianus,* Berlin, 1952. In this as in other similar instances in this book, the bibliographical references do not mean to be exhaustive but are simply a guide for those who wish to pursue further study of the figure in question. Needless to say, there is a vast literature on Clement, much of which is indicated in the bibliographies contained in the scholarly works cited above.

40. Of course Intellect is used in this context and in fact throughout this work in its original sense of *intellectus* or *nous* and as distinct from reason or *ratio* which is its reflection.

41. "He who is already *pure in heart,* not because of the commandments, but for the sake of knowledge by itself,—that man *is a friend of God." Clement of Alexandria. Miscellanies Book VII,* introd., translation and notes by F. J. A. Hort, London, 1902, p. 31.

42. "It is our business then to prove that the gnostic alone is holy and pious, worshipping the true God as befits him; and the worship which befits God includes both loving God and being loved by him. To the gnostic every kind of pre-eminence seems honourable in proportion to its worth. In the world of sense rulers and parents and elders generally are to be honoured; in matters of teaching, the most ancient philosophy and the earliest prophecy; in the spiritual world, that which is elder in origin, the Son, the beginning and first-fruit of all existing things, himself timeless and without beginning; from whom the gnostic believes that he receives the knowledge of the ultimate cause, the Father of the universe, the earliest and most beneficent of all existences, no longer reported by word of mouth, but worshipped and adored, as is his due, with silent worship and holy awe; who was manifested indeed by the Lord so far as it was possible for the learners to understand, but apprehended by those whom the Lord has elected for knowledge, those, says the apostle, who have their senses exercised." Library of Christian Classics, vol. II, *Alexandrian Christianity*, selected and trans. J. E. L. Oulton and H. Chadwick, London, 1954.

43. *Stromateis* IV.6.

44. On Origen see W. R. Inge, *Origen*, London, 1946; M. Harl, *Origène et la fonction révélatrice du verbe incarné*, Paris, 1958; H. de Lubac, *Histoire et Esprit, l'intelligence de l'Écriture d'après Origène*, Paris, 1950; R. A. Greer (ed.), *Origen*, New York, 1979; J. Oulton and H. Chadwick, *Alexandrian Christianity; Selected Translations of Clement and Origen*, Philadelphia, 1954; H. Urs von Balthasar, *Geist und Feuer. Ein Aufbau aus seinen Schriften*, Salzburg, 1951; and E. R. Redepenning, *Origenes. Eine Darstellung seines Lebens und seiner Lehre*, 2 vols., Bonn, 1966.

45. "Thus, just as a human being is said to be made up of body, soul and spirit, so also is the Sacred Scripture, which has been granted by God's gracious dispensation for man's salvation." From *First Principles*, book 4, cited in Greer, op. cit., p. 182.

46. "And if anyone reads the revelations made to John, how can he fail to be amazed at how great an obscurity of ineffable mysteries is present here? It is evident that even those who cannot understand what lies hidden in them nevertheless understand that something lies hidden. And indeed, the letters of the apostles, which do seem to some clearer, are they not filled with profound ideas that through them, as through some small opening, the brightness of an immense light seems to be poured forth for those who can understand the meaning of divine wisdom?" Ibid., p. 181.

47. See de Lubac, op. cit. Origen devotes much of his *First Principles* to the question of the Logos in its relation to the attainment of knowledge by man. ". . . das Christliche Leben sich für Origenes als eine fortschneitende Läuterung und darauffolgende Erkenntnis formt." H. Koch, *Pronoia und Paideusis*, Berlin and Leipzig, 1932, p. 84. Koch gives an analysis of Origen's "theory of knowledge" in pp. 49–62 of this work.

48. "Le *logos* est présent, en l'homme, chez qui il est l'intelligence. Parce qu'il se trouve à la fois en Dieu et en l'homme, comme en deux extrémités, il peut les relier et il le fait, d'autant mieux qu'il est également entre les deux, comme un intermédiaire de connaissance. Il joue le rôle que joue la lumière pour la vision des objets: la lumière rend l'objet lumineux et elle permet à l'oeil de voir, elle est lumière de l'objet et lumière du sujet, intermédiaire de vision. De la même façon, le *logos* est à la fois intelligibilité de Dieu et l'agent d'intellection de l'homme, médiateur de connaissance." Harl, op. cit., p. 94.

49. Origen, *The Song of Songs—Commentary and Homilies*, trans. and annotated by R. P. Lawson, London, 1957, p. 61.

50. "In as much as man is endowed with an intellect, he is by nature a being illumined by God." E. Gilson, *The Christian Philosophy of Saint Augustine*, New York, 1960, p. 80.

51. "Thus God does not take the place of our intellect when we think the truth. His illumination is needed only to make our intellects capable of thinking the truth, and this by virtue of a natural order of things expressly established by Him." Ibid., p. 79. This quotation also shows that already in Augustinian epistemology the sacred character of knowledge is perceived in a somewhat more indirect manner than what we find in the "gnostic" perspective of the Alexandrian fathers.

52. In describing the sapiential dimension in Christianity one could practically confine oneself to Dionysius alone, seeing how important his teachings were. But from the point of view of this cursory study it suffices to emphasize the significance of his well-known doctrines whose development can be seen in Erigena, Eckhart, Cusa, and so many other later Western masters of sapience.

On Dionysius, so unjustly referred to as pseudo-Dionysius as if to detract from the significance of his works through such an appellation, see M. de Gandillac (ed.), *Oeuvres complètes du pseudo-Denys d'Aréopagite*, Paris, 1943; R. Roques, *Structures théologiques de la gnose à Richard de Saint-Victor*, Paris, 1962; idem, *L'Univers dionysien. Structure hiérarchique du monde selon le pseudo-Denys*, Paris, 1954; W. Voelker, *Kontemplation und Ekstase bei Pseudo-Dionysius Ar.*, Wiesbaden, 1954; and A. M. Greeley, *Ecstasy: A Way of Knowing*, Englewood Cliffs, N.J., 1974.

53. There is a great amount of literature on Erigena in various European languages. See, for example, R. Roques, *Libres sentiers vers l'Erigénisme*, Rome, 1975; G. Allegro, *G. Scoto Eriugena—Antrolopogia*, Rome, 1976, esp. "Intelletto umano et intelletto angelico," pp. 62ff.; idem, *G. Scoto Eriugena, Fede e ragione*, Rome, 1974; J. J. O'Meara and L. Bieler (eds.), *The Mind of Erigena*, Dublin, 1973; E. Jeanneau (trans.), *Jean Scot, Homelie sur le prologue de Jean*, Paris, 1969, which shows the degree of devotion of Erigena to John whom he almost divinizes as being "superhuman"; G. Kaldenbach, *Die Kosmologie des Johannes Scottus Erigena*, Munich, 1963; G. Bonafede, *Scoto Eriugena*, Palermo, 1969; C. Albanese, *Il Pensiero di Giovanni Eriugena*, Messina, 1929; H. Bett, *Johannes Scotus Erigena, A Study in Medieval Philosophy*, Cambridge, 1925; A. Gardner, *Studies in John The Scot*, New York, 1900; M. S. Taillandier, *Scot Erigène et la philosophie scholastique*, Strasbourg-Paris, 1843; and T. Gregory, *Giovanni Scoto Eriugena, Tre studi*, Florence, 1963.

54. See, for example, W. Seul, *Die Gotteserkenntnis bei Johannes Skotus Eriugena*, Bonn, 1932; and A. Schneider, *Die Erkenntnislehre des Johannes Erigena*, Berlin and Leipzig, 1923, both of which give a rather rationalistic interpretation of Erigena reducing Erigena's doctrines to a "harmless" Neoplatonist influence. Later studies have emphasized his Christian character somewhat more but nevertheless still fail for the most part to see in him a crystallization of something essential to the sapiential dimension of Christianity.

55. "Spesso ci si è cruduti costretti a doner scegliere una posizione di fronte alla celebre riduzione, o identificazione, che Scoto compie fra 'vera religio' e 'vera philosophia'." Allegro, *G. Scoto Eriugena, Fede e ragione*, p. 63.

56. "C'est la sagesse, la sapience, qui est cette vertu commune à l'homme et à l'ange; c'est elle qui donne à l'esprit la pure contemplation, et lui fait apercevoir l'Éternel, l'Immuable." Taillandier, op. cit., p. 84.

57. "All the natural (liberal arts) concur in signifying Christ in a symbolic manner, (these arts) in whose limits is included the totality of Divine Scripture." *Expositiones super ierarchiam caelestiam sancti Dionysii*, ed. H. J. Floss in *Patrologia Latina* 122, I, 140A. Erigena states that in the same way that *nous* is an image of God, *artes* is an image of Christ. See Roques, *Libres sentiers*, p. 62.

58. "When [our reason] possesses the presence of the Word of God, it knows the intelligible realities and God Himself, but not by its own means, rather by grace of the Divine Light that is infused in him." Jeanneau (trans.), op. cit., p. 266.

59. See Allegro, *G. Scoto Eriugena, Fede e ragione*, "Il mondo come teofania," pp. 285ff. This relation between the sapiential perspective and interest in the study of nature as the theater of divine activity is to be seen throughout the whole sapiential tradition in the West and is one of the very few principles in which all of the Western esoteric schools of later centuries, even those whose knowledge remains partial, are in accord.

60. "Et puisque Dieu se crée dans sa manifestation, celle-ci *se crée elle-même* sous la motion divine en exprimant Dieu et elle-même. Dieu passe du Rien au Tout en suscitant les causes primordiales et l'esprit. Indivisiblement, l'esprit créé tire de cette nuit illuminatrice le déploiement qui le fait esprit, c'est-à-dire conscience du tout et de soi-même. Il y a une *noophanie* à l'interieur de la théophanie. Si bien qu'on peut dire à la fois que Dieu se pense dans les esprits qu'il illumine et que cette pensée est leur auto-

réalisation." J. Trouillard, "Erigène et la théophanie créatrice," in O'Meara and Bieler (eds.), op. cit., p. 99.
  61. Following the dictum of Dionysius, *Cognito earum, quae sunt, ea quae sunt, est.*
  62. See Bett, op. cit., p. 86.
  63. See R. Roques, "Remarques sur la signification de Jean Scot Erigène," in *Miscellanea A. Combes*, Rome, 1967.
  64. There is no doubt that both St. Bonaventure and St. Thomas were metaphysicians, properly speaking, as well as theologians as can be seen when they are treated metaphysically and not only theologically by a figure such as A. K. Coomaraswamy. But the fact remains that their purely sapiential teachings (esp. that of St. Thomas) became more or less veiled in a theology which, although of great value, also helped create an intellectual climate in which gnosis appeared to be of less direct concern and in fact less and less accessible to the extent that during the Renaissance many figures had to search outside the prevalent Christian theological orthodoxy for the kind of wisdom or gnosis which had been more accessible within the Western Christian tradition during earlier centuries of Christian history. It seems that for St. Thomas reason impregnated and supported by faith was of greater consequence than intelligence in its sacramental function. St. Thomas was certainly not opposed to intellection although he did not consider in a central manner the role and function of the intelligence as a sacrament because of his adoption of Aristotelianism which counters a penetrating and interiorizing intelligence with an exteriorized and exteriorizing will.
  "In the case of the Stagirite, the intelligence is penetrating but the tendency of the will is exteriorizing, in conformity moreover with the cosmolatry of the majority of the Greeks; it is this that enabled Saint Thomas to support the religious thesis regarding the 'natural' character of the intelligence, so called because it is neither revealed nor sacramental, and the reduction of intelligence to reason illuminated by faith, the latter alone being granted the right to be 'supernatural'." F. Schuon, *Logic and Transcendence*, pp. 174–75.
  As for St. Bonaventure he remains closer to the Augustinian position emphasizing illumination and that "cotuition," to use his own terminology, which for him is the sixth and crowning stage of the journey of the mind to God even beyond the realm of the contemplation of God as Being to the Divine Darkness. See St. Bonaventure, *The Mind's Journey to God—Itinerarium Mentis in Deum*, trans. L. S. Cunningham, Chicago, 1975.
  In any case, any complete study of Christian sapiential teachings would have to include certainly the theology of St. Bonaventure and also those of St. Thomas, Duns Scotus, and others which this more cursory survey has to leave aside. Another reason for our passing rapidly over medieval theology is the fact that these schools are well-known in comparison with the more directly gnostic teachings.
  65. On Eckhart's doctrine of knowledge as related to the sacred see E. Heinrich, *Verklärung und Erlösung im Vedânta, bei Meister Eckhart und bei Schelling*, Munich, 1961, esp. "Von der Verklärung und von der Einung mit der Gottheit," pp. 80ff.; J. Kopper, *Die Metaphysik Meister Eckharts*, Saarbrücken, 1955, esp. pp. 73–121; J. Hammerich, *Über das Wesen der Götterung bei Meister Eckhart*, Speyer, 1939; H. Schlötermann, "Logos und Ratio, Die platonische Kontinuität in der deutschen Philosophie des Meister Eckhart," in *Zeitschrift für philosophische Forschung* 3 (1949): 219–39; O. Spann, "Meister Eckharts mystische Erkenntnislehre," in *Zeitschrift für philosophische Forschung* 3 (1949): 339–55; G. Stephenson, *Gottheit und Gott in der spekulativen Mystik Meister Eckharts*, Bonn, 1954, esp. pp. 73–96; V. Lossky, *Théologie négative et connaissance de Dieu chez Maître Eckhart*, Paris, 1960; J. M. Clark, *Meister Eckhart. An Introduction to the Study of His Works*, New York, 1957; E. Soudek, *Meister Eckhart*, Stuttgart, 1973; C. Clark, *The Great Human Mystics*, Oxford, 1949; V. Brandstätter and E. Sulek, *Meister Eckharts mystische Philosophie*, Graz, 1974; and F. Brunner, *Maître Eckhart, introduction, suivi de textes traduits pour la premier fois du latin en français*, Paris, 1969, which contains an exceptional treatment of Meister Eckhart from the point of view of traditional metaphysics or the *scientia sacra* with which we shall deal later.

The extent of recent interest in Eckhart can be gauged from the number of current works on the master such as C. F. Kelley, *Meister Eckhart on Divine Knowledge*, New Haven, 1977; R. Shurmann, *Meister Eckhart: Mystic & Philosopher*, Bloomington, Indiana, 1978; M. C. Walshe, *Meister Eckhart: Sermons and Treatises*, London, 1980; and many new translations or editions of older translations such as the well-known one by F. Pfeiffer as well as numerous comparative studies which involve him and different masters of Oriental wisdom. An incomparable and masterly work of this kind is A. K. Coomaraswamy, *The Transformation of Nature in Art*, which contains an exposition of the metaphysics of art of Meister Eckhart and the traditional doctrines issuing from Hinduism.

66. St. Thomas had used this term in Latin (*scintilla animae*) before Eckhart, but this concept plays a more central role in Eckhart esp. as far as epistemology is concerned.

67. See V. Lossky, op. cit., p. 180, where one can find a masterly analysis of many Eckhartian theses.

68. E. Cassirer, who was one of the major influences in the revival of interest in Cusa, in fact believed that Cusa tried to create a third way or school beside the Scholastic and humanist schools which were combating each other during the Renaissance. See Cassirer, *Individuum und Kosmos in der Philosophie der Renaissance*, Leipzig, 1927.

69. On Cusa see, E. Van Steenberghe, *Le Cardinal Nicholas de Cues*, Paris, 1920; H. Bett, *Nicholas of Cusa*, London, 1932, esp. chap. 5 where his theory of knowledge is discussed but somewhat rationalistically; P. de Gandillac, *La Philosophie de Nicholas de Cues*, Paris, 1941; A. Bonetti, *La ricerca metafisica nel pensiero de Nicolo Cusano*, Bresca, 1973; N. Herold, *Menschliche Perspektive und Wahrheit*, Munster, 1975; A. Bruntrup, *Konnen und Sein*, Munich, 1973; G. Schneider, *Gott-das Nichtandere, Untersuchunger zum metaphysichen Grunde bei Nickolaus von Kues*, Munster, 1970; K. Jacobi, *Die Methode der Cusanischen Philosophie*, Munich, 1969; N. Henke, *Der Abbildbegriff in der Erkenntnislehre des Nickolaus von Kues*, Munster, 1967; and A. Lubke, *Nikolaus von Kues, Kirchenfurst zwischen Mittelalter und Neuzeit*, Munich, 1968.

70. See E. Gilson, *The Unity of Philosophical Experience*, New York, 1937.

71. See, for example, H. Oberman, "The Theology of Nominalism," *Harvard Theological Review* 53 (1960): 47–79.

72. J. P. Dolan (ed.), *Unity and Reform—Selected Writings of Nicholas of Cusa*, Chicago, 1962, p. 105.

73. Ibid., pp. 8–9.

74. This is treated extensively by de Gandillac in his work cited in n. 69 above.

75. "Just as any knowledge of the taste of something we have never tasted is quite empty until we do taste it, so the taste of this wisdom cannot be acquired by hearsay but by one's actually touching it with his internal sense, and then he will bear witness not of what he has heard but what he has experimentally tasted in himself." From *De sapientia*, quoted in Dolan, op. cit., pp. 111–12.

76. "Wisdom is the infinite and never failing food of life upon which our spirit lives eternally since it is not able to love anything other than wisdom and truth. Every intellect seeks after being and its being is living; its living is to understand; its understanding is nurtured on wisdom and truth. Thus it is that the understanding that does not taste clear wisdom is like an eye in the darkness. It is an eye but it does not see because it is not in light. And because it lacks a delectable life which for it consists in seeing, it is in pain and torment and this is death rather than life. So too, the intellect that turns to anything other than the food of eternal wisdom will find itself outside of life, bound up in the darkness of ignorance, rather dead than alive. This is the interminable torment, to have an intellect and never to understand. For it is only the eternal wisdom in which every intellect can understand." Dolan, op. cit., pp. 108–9.

77. See A. Conrad, "La docte ignorance cusaine," *Etudes Traditionnelles* 78/458 (Oct.–Dec. 1977): 164–71.

78. See F. Schuon, "Le problème de l'evangélisme," in his *Christianisme/Islam*, chap. 3.

79. It is of interest to note that this theosophy survived during the past four centuries almost exclusively in Lutheran areas or those influenced by Lutheranism. The German Lutheran mystic Tersteegen in fact distinguishes clearly between Christian mystics and theosophers, claiming all theosophers to be mystics but not all mystics to be theosophers "whose spirit has explored the depths of the Divinity under Divine guidance and whose spirit has known such marvels thanks to an infallible vision." From his *Kurzer Bericht von der Mystik* quoted by Schuon (ibid.).

80. The work of J. S. Bach is a perfect example of this type of music in which the deepest yearning of the European soul for the sacred seems to have taken refuge in an age when the other art forms had become so depleted of the sense of the sacred. Even the *Coffee Cantata* of Bach is of a more religious character than many a modern setting of the Psalms to music. A work like the *B Minor Mass* has an archetectonic structure impregnated with a powerful piety and sense of the sacred which make it very akin and conformable to the sapiential perspective. On the metaphysics of musical polyphony and counterpoint in which Bach was a peerless master see M. Pallis, "Metaphysics of Musical Harmony," in his *A Buddhist Spectrum*, London, 1980, pp. 121ff.

81. "Pour Böhme, la Sagesse est une Vierge éternelle, symbole de Dieu, reflet du Ternaire, image dans laquelle ou par laquelle le Seigneur s'exprime en dévoilant la richesse infinie de la virtualité. Dans le miroir de la Sagesse la volonté divine trace le plan, la figure de son action créatrice. Elle 'imagine' dans ce miroir, acte qui représente l'acte magique par excellence. Ainsi s'accomplit le mystère d'exprimer, de traduire, dans des images finies la pensée infinie de Dieu." A. Faivre, *L'Ésotérisme au XVIIIᵉ siècle en France et en Allemagne,* Paris, 1973, p. 38.

On Boehme see A. Koyré, *La Philosophie de Jacob Boehme*, Paris, 1929; E. Benz, "Über die Leiblichkeit des Geistigen zur Theologie der Leiblichkeit bei Jacob Böhme," in S. H. Nasr (ed.), *Mélanges offerts à Henry Corbin,* Paris-Tehran, 1977, pp. 451–520; Benz, *Der Vollkommene Mensch nach Jacob Boehme,* Stuttgart, 1937; *Revue Hermès,* (ed. J. Masui) 3 (1964–65), containing articles on Boehme; R. M. Jones, *Spiritual Reformers in the 16th and 17th Centuries,* London, 1914, chaps. 9–11; H. T. Martensen, *Jacob Boehme: His Life and Teaching,* trans. T. Rhys Evans, London, 1885; H. Tesch, *Vom Dreifachen Leben,* Bietigheim/Württ., 1971; G. Wehr, *Jakob Böhme in Selbstzeugnissen und Bilddokumenten,* Hamburg, 1971; V. Weiss, *Die Gnosis Jakob Böhmes,* Zurich, 1955; V. Hans Grunsky, *Jacob Boehme,* Stuttgart, 1956; H. H. Brinton, *The Mystic Will,* New York, 1930; and A. J. Penny, *Studies in Jacob Böhme,* London, 1912.

82. Boehme deals with this theme esp. in chap. 14 of his *De signatura rerum*.

83. According to A. Koyré, the desire for the Eternal is "aussi le gage de la possibilité d'atteindre à une connaissance parfaite de Dieu, et de le connaitre à la fois dans la nature par laquelle il s'exprime et dans l'âme ou il habite, virtuellement au moins." Koyré, *La Philosophie de Jacob Boehme*, p. 454.

84. This is the specifically Baaderian interpretation of Boehme, but certainly implicit in his writings.

85. Boehme treats this question in his *Mysterium Magnum* chap. XXXV, 60. The idea of a "natural language" of a sacred character can also be found in other sapiential works of the period such as *Confessio Fraternitatis der Hochlöblichen Bruderschaft von Rosenkreutz.* See Koyré, op. cit., p. 457, n. 4.

86. "When God recognizes and views Himself with holy delight, He apprehends not only Himself, but also all His contents—the 'fullness' of His universe. This fullness, which is best thought of as a universe of ideas, streaming forth in multiplicity from the Father, is gathered by the Son into intellectual unity, and is shaped by the Spirit into a world of ideas, distinct from God, and yet inseparable from Him. We have here what Boehme calls *wisdom*." H. L. Martensen, *Jacob Boehme,* trans. T. Rhys Evans, new ed. and notes by S. Hobhouse, London, 1949, p. 106.

87. On the Cambridge Platonists see J. Tulloch, *Rational Theology and Christian Philosophy in England in the Seventeenth Century,* 2 vols., London and Edinburgh, 1872; E. A. Burtt, *The Metaphysical Foundations of Modern Physical Science,* London, 1925; F. J. Powicke, *The Cambridge Platonists,* London, 1926; E. Cassirer, *The Platonic Renaissance in*

England, trans. J. P. Pettegrove, Edinburgh, 1953; C. E. Raven, *Natural Religion and Christian Theology*, Cambridge, 1953; S. Hutin, *Henry More, Essai sur les doctrines théosophiques chez les Platoniciens de Cambridge*, Hildensheim, 1966, which treats this school more from a, properly speaking, sapiential rather than merely philosophical and rational point of view; and J. A. Passmore, *Ralph Cudworth*, Cambridge, 1951, where an extensive bibliography of earlier works is provided.

On the theme of Henry More's *spissitudo spiritualis* in comparison with doctrines developed by his Muslim contemporary Ṣadr al-Dīn Shīrāzī see H. Corbin, *En Islam iranien*, vol. 4, p. 158. See also the "prélude à la deuxième édition" of Corbin's *Corps Spirituel et terre céleste—de l'iran mazdéen à l'iran shî'ite*, Paris, 1979.

88. "Were I indeed to define *Divinity*, I should rather call it a *Divine life*, than a *Divine science;* it being something rather to be understood by a *Spiritual sensation*, than by any *Verbal description.*" John Smith, "A Praefatory Discourse concerning the True Way or Method of Attaining to Divine Knowledge," in E. T. Campagnac, *The Cambridge Platonists*, Oxford, 1961, p. 80.

It is interesting to note that despite his insistence on the primacy of Divine Knowledge, John Smith accepted Cartesian mechanism—distinguishing "science" from "wisdom"—and opposed Cudworth and More on this central issue demonstrating not only differences of view which existed among the Cambridge Platonists but also the partial character of the traditional knowledge which this school possessed and expounded. On the differences among the Cambridge Platonists, esp. concerning Descartes who had been read by all of them, see J. E. Saveson, "Differing Reactions to Descartes Among the Cambridge Platonists," *Journal of the History of Ideas* 21/4 (Oct.–Dec. 1960): 560–67.

89. "Divinity indeed is a true Efflux from the Eternal light, which, like the Sunbeams, does not only enlighten, but heat and enliven; and therefore our Saviour hath in his *Beatitudes* connext Purity of heart with the Beatifical Vision." Campagnac, op. cit., p. 80.

90. Campagnac, op. cit., p. 96.

91. On Angelus Silesius (Johannes Scheffler) see J. Baruzi, *Création religieuse et pensée contemplative, 2ᵉ part.: Angelus Silesius*, Paris, 1951; E. Suzini, *Le Pélerin Chérubique*, 2 vols., Paris, 1964; G. Ellinger, *Angelus Silesius. Ein Lebensbild*, Munich, 1927; H. Plard, *La Mystique d'Angelus Silesius*, Paris, 1943; Von Willibald Köhler, *Angelus Silesius (Johannes Scheffler)*, Munich, 1929; J. Trautmann, *Von wesentlichem Leben: Eine Auswahl aus dem Cherubinischen Wandersmann des Angelus Silesius*, Hamburg, 1946; J. L. Sammons, *Angelus Silesius*, New York, 1967; and G. Rossmann, *Das königliche Leben: Besinnung auf Angelus Silesius*, Zurich, 1956.

92. "Il s'agit, dans son livre, d'un retour à Dieu, et d'abord par la connaissance. C'est le sens du titre, devenu le sien à partir de la seconde édition (1675); *Der Cherubische Wandermann*, où sont réunies l'idée d'une marche vers Dieu, et la connaissance, ou plus exactement, la sagesse comme principe de cette marche." H. Plard, *La Mystique d'Angelus Silesius*, Paris, 1943.

93. How remarkably close is the verse of Silesius,

> *Stirb, ehe du noch stirbst, damit du nichte darfst sterben*
> *Wenn du nun sterben sollst; sonst möchtest du verderben.*

> *Die now before thou diest; that thou mayst not die*
> *When thou shalt die, else shalt thou die eternally.*

to the verses of Jalāl al-Dīn Rūmī

روبمیرای خواجه قبل از مردنت   تا نباشد زحمت جان دادنت

آنچنان مرگی که در نزری روی   نی چنان مرگی که در گوری روی

O man go die before thou diest
So that thou shalt not have to suffer death when thou shalt die.
Such a death that thou wilst enter unto light
Not a death through which thou wilst enter unto the grave.

These and other amazingly similar utterances of Silesius and Sufi poets point not to historical borrowings but common archetypes. They indicate similar types of spirituality within the members of the Abrahamic family of religions.

94. J. Bilger, *Alexandrines, Translated from the Cherubischer Wandermann of Angelus Silesius 1657*, North Montpelier, N.Y., 1944, p. 33.

95. Angelus Silesius, *The Cherubic Wanderer*, selections trans. W. Trask, New York, 1953, p. 27.

96. Angelus Silesius, *A Selection from the Rhymes of a German Mystic*, trans. P. Carus, Chicago, 1909, p. 163.

97. Silesius, *The Cherubic Wanderer*, p. 60.

98. Silesius, *A Selection*, p. 152. This rather jarring anthropomorphic imagery must of course be understood in its esoteric and symbolic sense, signifying both union and ecstasy which characterize the state of the intellect when it attains knowledge of the sacred at its highest level.

99. It is certainly paradoxical that the eighteenth century which, along with the period that was to follow, must be characterized as the age of darkness from the sapiential point of view should be identified with "light," this age being known as the Enlightenment, *l'âge des lumières, illuminismo,* or *Aufklärung* in various European languages. If in a hypothetical situation an Oriental sage such as Śankara or Ibn ʿArabī were to review the later history of Western thought, perhaps few facts would amaze him more than seeing men like Diderot and Condorcet called "enlightened." He would also be surprised that some (but of course not all) of those figures who were called *les frères illuminés* and who belonged to various "esoteric" and "occultist" groups were opposed to theism not from the point of view of the Advaita or the "transcendent unity of being" (*waḥdat al-wujūd*), which "comprehends" the theistic position, but from the perspective of a deism which was practically agnostic if not outright atheistic. See E. Zolla, "Che Cosa Potrebbe Essere un Nuova Illuminismo" in his *Che Cos'è la Tradizione*, Milan, 1971.

It is, however, important to note also that careful studies carried out only recently have shown that there were a large number of figures in the eighteenth century who, although belonging to this period in time, stood opposed to the rationalism of the age. This group embraced many figures ranging all the way from real gnostics and theosophers who possessed authentic esoteric knowledge to different kinds of occultists who were to be the forerunners of the better known occultist groups of the late nineteenth and early twentieth centuries. No one in recent years has done as much as A. Faivre to make better known the teachings of these marginal but important figures of the eighteenth and early nineteenth century. See his *L'Ésotérisme au XVIIIᵉ siècle en France et en Allemagne*, Paris, 1973; *Kirchberger et l'illuminisme du XVIIIᵉ siècle*, The Hague, 1966; *Epochen der Naturmystik: Hermetische Tradition im wissenschaftlichen Forschritt*, Berlin, 1977; and "De Saint-Martin à Baader, le 'Magikon' de Kleuker," in *Revue d'Etudes Germaniques*, April–June 1968, pp. 161–90. See also R. Le Forestier, *La Franc-Maçonnerie occultiste au XVIIIᵉ siècle et l'Ordre des Elus-Coens*, Paris, 1928; idem, *La Franc-Maçonnerie occultiste et templière aux XVIIIᵉ et XIXᵉ siècles*, Paris, 1970; E. Benz, *Adam, der Mythus von Urmenschen*, Munich, 1955; "L'illuminisme au XVIIIᵉ siècle," ed. R. Amadou, in *Les Cahiers de la Tour Saint-Jacques*, Paris, 1960; and H. Schneider, *Quest for Mysteries*, Ithaca, N.Y., 1947.

100. See A. Faivre, *Eckartshausen et la théosophie chrétienne*, Paris, 1969. Eckartshausen was not only influential in Russia but even left his effect upon such more recent occultists as Eliphas Lévi and Papus.

101. There is a vast literature on Swedenborg. See, for example, E. Benz, *Swedenborg, Naturforscher und Seher*, Munich, 1948; and H. Corbin, "Herméneutique spirituelle comparée (I. Swedenborg—II.) Gnose ismaëlienne," in *Eranos-Jahrbuch* 33 (1964):

71–176, where an interesting morphological study is made of Swedenborg's hermeneutics and that of certain Ismāʿīlī exegetes who sought to reveal the inner significance of the Quran.

102. On Newton and alchemy see B. Dobbs, *The Foundations of Newton's Alchemy; or, "The Hunting of the Greene Lyon,"* Cambridge, 1976. Although the interest of the author is more scholarly and historical than philosophical and metaphysical, she has provided in this study much material on Newton's alchemy not available before including a list of Newton's considerable alchemical writings in Appendix A, pp. 235–48.

On Newton's alchemy see also P. M. Rattansi, "Newton's Alchemical Studies," in A. Debus (ed.), *Science, Medicine and Society in the Renaissance. Essays to Honor Walter Pagel,* 2 vols., New York, 1972, II, pp. 167–82.

103. Concerning Newton's profound interest in Boehme see S. Hutin, *Les Disciples anglais de Jacob Böhme,* Paris, 1960; also K. R. Popp, *Jakob Böhme und Isaac Newton,* Leipzig, 1935. The thesis that Boehme has influenced Newton has been refuted by H. McLachlan, *Sir Isaac Newton: Theological Manuscripts,* Liverpool, 1950, pp. 20–21, on the basis of lack of any substantial extracts from Boehme's writings in Newton's theological works. His view has also been espoused by Dobbs in op. cit., pp. 9–10. On the general philosophical level of the meaning of alchemy, however, one can see a relation between them and the thesis of S. Hutin and others who claim a link between Boehme and Newton cannot be totally refuted through the lack of either citations of names or quotations of texts or even the fact that Newton had another side very different from Boehme.

104. It is remarkable how little of the writings of this important figure is available in the English language. On von Baader see H. Fischer-Barnicol (ed.), *Franz von Baader vom Sinn der Gesellschaft,* Köln, 1966; M. Pulver, *Schriften Franz von Baaders,* Leipzig, 1921; E. Susini, *Franz von Baader et le romantisme mystique,* 3 vols., Paris, 1942; J. Glaassen, *Franz von Baaders Leben und theosophische Ideen,* 2 vols., Stuttgart, 1886.

105. See E. Klamroth, *Die Weltanschauung Franz von Baaders in ihrem Gegensatz zu Kant,* Berlin, 1965. To Descartes's *cogito ergo sum,* von Baader was to answer *cogitor, ergo cogito et sum* ("I am thought [by God], therefore I think and I am"), placing God's knowledge of man as the source of both his being and intelligence. See F. Schuon, *Logic and Transcendence,* p. 44. For von Baader knowledge does not begin with *cogito* but with God's knowledge of us.

106. This doctrine is found especially in his two major works *Fermenta cognitionis* and *Spekulative Dogmatik.*

Von Baader also considered religion as a sacred science and sacred science as religion. For him religion should be based on knowledge of a sacred character and not only sentiments. Likewise, science should be ultimately rooted in the Divine Intellect which would make of it religion in the vastest sense of this term. "Baader affirme que la religion doit devenir une science, et la science une religion; qu'il faut savoir pour croire, croire pour savoir." A. Faivre, *L'Esotérisme au XVIIIᵉ siècle,* p. 113.

107. See Susini, op. cit., esp. vols. 2–3, pp. 225ff.

108. The influence of Rossmini was to continue in Italy until recent times among such Catholic thinkers as F. Sciacca, but he is hardly known in the English-speaking world and remains like von Baader and similar philosophers a peripheral figure in a world where philosophy became reduced to rationalism and finally irrationalism.

109. The root of knowledge is of course the same as the Sanskrit *jñāna* as well as the Greek *gnosis* which mean both knowledge and sapiential wisdom. The distinction made in later Greek thought and also by the church fathers between *gnosis* and *epistēmē* already marks the separation of knowledge from its sacred source. Otherwise *knowledge* in English or *Erkenntnis* in German containing the root *kn* should also reflect the meaning of *gnosis* as *jñāna* does in Sanskrit, a root which implies at once knowledge and coming into being as the word *genesis* implies.

110. "Le 'miracle grec', c'est en fait la substitution de la raison à l'Intellect, du fait au Principe, du phénomène à l'Idée, de l'accident à la Substance, de la forme à l'Essence, de l'homme à Dieu, et cela dans l'art aussi bien que dans la pensée." F. Schuon, *Le Soufisme voile et quintessence,* Paris, 1980, p. 106.

111. "Le véritable miracle grec, si miracle il y a,—et dans ce cas il serait apparenté au 'miracle hindou',—c'est la métaphysique doctrinale et la logique méthodique, providentiellement utilisées par les Sémites monothéistes." Ibid., p. 106.

112. See S. H. Nasr, *Three Muslim Sages*, Albany, N.Y., 1975, chaps. 1 and 2.

113. On the issues involved in this "dialogue" see F. Schuon, "Dialogue between Hellenists and Christians," in *Light on the Ancient Worlds*, trans. Lord Northbourne, London, 1965, pp. 58–71.

114. Of course Hellenism triumphed in another dimension by surviving as a doctrinal language and way of thinking and looking upon the world at the heart of Christianity itself.

"Like most inter-traditional polemics, the dialogue in which Hellenism and Christianity were in opposition was to a great extent unreal. The fact that each was right on a certain plane—or in a particular 'spiritual dimension'—resulted in each emerging as victor in its own way: Christianity by imposing itself on the whole Western world, and Hellenism by surviving in the heart of Christianity and conferring on Christian intellectuality an indelible imprint." Ibid., p. 58.

It would be worthwhile to note that, while Western Christianity opposed so strongly what it considered as Greek "paganism," in Western Asia in certain Christian circles during early centuries of Christian history such figures as Socrates were considered as pre-Christian saints.

115. We owe this term to Th. Roszak. See his *Where the Wasteland Ends*, New York, 1972.

116. See J. Robinson (ed.), *The Nag Hammadi Library*, New York, 1977, "Acts of Peter and the Twelve Apostles," pp. 265ff.; also H. Corbin, "L'Orient des pélerins abrahamiques," in *Les Pelerins de l'orient et les vagabonds de l'occident, Cahiers de l'Université Saint-Jean de Jérusalem*, no. 4, Paris, 1978, p. 76; and Corbin, "La necessité de l'angélologie," in *Cahiers de l'hermétisme*, Paris, 1978, chap. 4, II.

117. For his views on this crucial question see E. Gilson, *Reason and Revelation in the Middle Ages*, New York, 1938.

118. S. H. Nasr, *An Introduction to Islamic Cosmological Doctrines*, pp. 185ff.

It is interesting that neo-Thomist European scholars of Islamic thought such as L. Gardet have posed the question as to whether Ibn Sīnā's thought is Islamic philosophy or just Greek philosophy in an Islamic dress, while a scholar such as Corbin, who was so devoted to the sapiential school of the West including the Renaissance Protestant mystics, insists upon not only the importance of Ibn Sīnā as an Islamic philosopher for Islamic thought itself but the sapiential and gnostic teachings of Suhrawardī and Mullā Sadrā. Despite our deep respect for such scholars as Gardet, who precisely because of their Thomism are able to understand many important aspects of Islam which simply secularist or agnostic scholars have neglected and ignored, on this particular issue we agree totally with the views of Corbin. Anyone who, in fact, knows later Islamic thought well and who also comprehends the purely metaphysical perspective cannot but be led to a similar if not identical conclusion as we see in the writings of T. Izutsu who has also made many important studies of later Islamic philosophy and gnosis. See Corbin in collaboration with S. H. Nasr and O. Yahya, *Histoire de la philosophie islamique*, vol. 1, Paris, 1964; the prologomena of Corbin to Sadr al-Dīn Shīrāzī, *Le Livre des pénétrations métaphysiques*, Paris-Tehran, 1964; and T. Izutsu, *The Concept and Reality of Existence*, Tokyo, 1971.

119. See H. Corbin, *Avicenna and the Visionary Recital*, trans. W. Trask, Dallas, 1980.

120. On Latin Avicennism and Latin Averroism see R. de Vaux, "La première entrée d'Averroës chez les Latins," *Revue des Sciences Philosophiques et Théologiques* 22 (1933): 193–245; de Vaux, *Notes et textes sur l'Avicennisme latin aux confins des XIIe–XIIIe siècles*, Paris, 1934; M. T. d'Alverny, *Avicenna nella storia della cultura medioevale*, Rome, 1957; d'Alverny, "Les traductions latines d'Ibn Sīnā et leur diffusion au Moyen Âge," *Millénaire d'Avicenne. Congrès de Bagdad*, Baghdad, 1952, pp. 59–79; d'Alverny, "Avicenna Latinus," *Archives d'Histoire, Doctrinale du Moyen-Âge* 28 (1961): 281–316; 29 (1962): 271–33; 30 (1963): 221–72, 31 (1964): 271–86; 32 (1965): 257–302; M. Bouyges, "Attention à Averroista'," *Revue du Moyen Âge Latin* 4 (1948): 173–76; E. Gilson, *History of Christian*

Philosophy in the Middle Ages, New York, 1935; and F. Van Steenberghen, *Siger de Brabant d'après ses oeuvres inédites,* 2 vols., Louvain, 1931–42.

121. See Nasr, *Three Muslim Sages.*

122. This process has been admirably treated by E. Gilson in his *Unity of Philosophical Experience,* although Gilson in conformity with his Thomistic perspective does not point to the significance of the loss of the sapiential or gnostic dimension in the destruction of Thomism itself. For in the absence of the availability of that type of knowledge which is immediate and sanctifying, even the imposing edifice of Thomism, which leads to the courtyard of the Divine Presence but not the beatific union itself, was finally criticized and rejected. Also had the intellectual intuition of men not become dimmed, the realist-nominalist debate would not have even taken place and a situation would perhaps have developed not dissimilar to what is found in India and also the Islamic world where positions similar to nominalism have existed but only at the margin of the traditional spectrum whose center has always been occupied by doctrines of a *jñāni* or *ʿirfānī* nature.

123. See D. P. Walker, *The Ancient Theology, Studies in Christian Platonism from the Fifteenth to the Eighteenth Century,* London, 1972.

124. On the integration of various figures of Greek wisdom such as Apollo and Orpheus which marks the integration of ancient wisdom into the Christian tradition and its literature see E. R. Curtius, *European Literature and the Latin Middle Ages,* trans. W. R. Trask, New York, 1953. Perhaps the last European literary figure for whom the Orpheus-Christ figure was still a reality was the seventeenth-century Spanish playwright Calderón, the author of *El Divino Orfeo,* for whom "Christ is the divine Orpheus. His lyre is the wood of the Cross." Curtius, op. cit., p. 244. Calderón viewed Greek wisdom as a second Old Testament and wrote in his *Autos sacramentales:*

> la voz de la Escritura
> Divina en los Profetas
> Y humana en los poetas

But like the Spanish philosophers of his day, he did not stand in the mainstream of European culture.

Likewise, in Shakespeare who represents the continuation of tradition in Elizabethan England there remains an awareness of the inner relationship between Greek wisdom and Christianity, although he too stood opposed to the prevalent tendencies of his day. "For Shakespeare and for Dante, just as for the ancient priests and priestesses at Delphi, Apollo is not the god of light but the Light of God." M. Lings, *Shakespeare in the Light of Sacred Art,* London, 1966, p. 17.

125. As Suhrawardī, Quṭbal-Dīn Shīrāzī, and later Mullā Ṣadrā were to do for Peripatetic philosophy in Islam.

126. The celebrated Sufi of the fourth/eleventh century who was put to death in Baghdad for uttering esoteric sayings (theophonic utterances called *shath* in Arabic) and who is considered as one of the great masters of Islamic gnosis. His life and teachings have been treated amply by L. Massignon in his classical work, *La Passion d'al-Hallāj,* 2nd ed., 4 vols., Paris, 1975; this work has been translated in its entirety into English by H. Mason and is to appear shortly.

127. "Metaphysics prescinds from the animistic proposition of Descartes, *Cogito ergo sum,* to say, *Cogito ergo Est;* and to the question, *Quid est?* answers that this is an improper question, because its subject is not a what amongst others but the whatness of them all and of all that they are not." A. K. Coomaraswamy, *The Bugbear of Literacy,* London, 1947, p. 124; enlarged edition, London, 1980.

128. Certain forms of analytical philosophy have rendered, relatively speaking, a positive service in clarifying the language of philosophical discourse which had in fact become ambiguous in modern times but not in traditional schools where philosophical language, let us say in Arabic, Hebrew, or Latin, is as precise as that of modern science and not like modern philosophy. But this clarification of language is not the only task

achieved by analytical philosophy and positivism in general whose much more devastating effect has been the trivialization of philosophy and its goals, causing many an intelligent seeker after *philo-sophy* to search for it in disciplines which do not bear such a name in contemporary academic circles.

129. "Academic philosophy as such, including Anglo-Saxon philosophy, is today almost entirely anti-philosophy." F. A. Schaeffer, *The God Who is There*, Downers Grove, Ill., 1977, p. 28.

130. See F. Yates, *The Occult Philosophy in the Elizabethan Age*, London and Boston, 1979.

131. We have dealt extensively with this issue in our *Man and Nature*, London, 1976; see also Roszak, *Where the Wasteland Ends* and his *Unfinished Animal*, New York, 1975.

132. Referring to critics of modern science E. J. Dijkterhuis, who has done extensive research and provides a detailed account of how the process of mechanization of the world took place, writes, "They are inclined to look upon the domination of the mind by the mechanistic conception as one of the main causes of the spiritual chaos into which the twentieth-century world has, in spite of all its technological progress, fallen." Dijkterhuis, *The Mechanization of the World*, trans. C. Dikshoorn, Oxford, 1961, pp. 1–2. This process has also been dealt with by many historians of science of the Renaissance and seventeenth century such as A. Koyré, G. Di Santillana, and I. B. Cohen.

133. For an example of reactions against the new astronomy which served as a basis for the mechanistic world view among such figures as Oetinger and Swedenborg see E. Benz, "Der kopernikanische Schock und seine theologische Auswirkung," in *Eranos Jahrbuch* 44 (1975): 15–60; also *Cahiers de l'Université de St. Jean de Jérusalem*, vol. 5, Paris, 1979.

134. Goethe and Herder who championed the cause of both integral knowledge and *Naturphilosophie* were among those who opposed the mechanized conception of the world and who reasserted the idea of the interrelatedness of the parts of nature into a living whole which accords with traditional teachings. Goethe writes, "Die Natur, so mannigfaltig sie erscheint, ist doch immer ein Eins, eine Einheit, und so muss, wenn sie teilweise manifestiert, alles übrige Grundlage dienen, dieses in dem übrigen Zusammenhang haben." Quoted in R. D. Gray, *Goethe, The Alchemist*, Cambridge, 1952, p. 6. See also H. B. Nisbet, *Goethe and the Scientific Tradition*, London, 1972, p. 20.

135. The popular work of K. Popper, *The Poverty of Historicism*, Boston, 1957, is one of the best known of these criticisms by a famous contemporary philosopher of science.

Modern phenomenology has also reacted against historicism and produced alternative ways and methods of studying religion, philosophy, art, etc., and has produced notable results when wed to the traditional perspective. Otherwise, it has led to a kind of sterile study of structures divorced from both the sense of the sacred and the history of various traditions as sacred history. Nevertheless, there lies at the heart of the intuition which led to phenomenology an awareness of the "poverty of historicism" and the recollection of the richness of the permanent structures and modes which one observes even in the phenomenal world and which reflect aspects of the permanent as such.

136. He refers to the idea of nature as a great book at the beginning of his *Dialogue Concerning the Two Chief World Systems—Ptolemaic and Copernican*.

137. "Philosophy is written in this grand book, the universe, which stands continually open to our gaze. But the book cannot be understood unless one first learns to comprehend the language and read the letters in which it is composed. It is written in the language of mathematics and its characters are triangles, circles, and other geometric figures without which it is humanly impossible to understand a single word of it." From the *Assayer* in *Discoveries and Opinions of Galileo*, trans. Stillman Drake, New York, 1957, pp. 237–38. Quoted in M. De Grazia, "Secularization of Language in the 17th century," *Journal of the History of Ideas* 41/2 (April–June 1980).

There is little evidence of Galileo showing direct interest in Pythagoreanism although his father was keenly interested in Pythagorean teachings.

138. Kepler develops this idea in several of his works including the *Mysterium Cosmographicum*.

139. De Grazia, op. cit., p. 326.

140. "In the seventeenth century, the traditional connection between human and divine language broke down. God's language was no longer considered primarily verbal; human words ceased to be related both in kind and quality to the divine Word." Ibid., p. 319.

This process was without doubt facilitated in the West because Christianity, in contrast to Judaism and Islam, did not possess a sacred language, Latin being, properly speaking, a liturgical language and not sacred as are Arabic and Hebrew for Islam and Judaism.

141. The same process has had to take place in the revival of traditional doctrines today to which we shall refer in the following chapters.

The whole question of the relationship between the process of the desacralization of knowledge and language in the modern world deserves a separate, detailed study to which we can allude here only in passing. The process of the desacralization of the traditional languages of the Orient in the face of the secularization of thought in the East today affords a living example of what occurred in the West over a period of some five centuries.

142. One might of course say that this radical departure from the realm of reason and taking refuge in faith alone are because "modern rationalism does its work against faith with silent violence, like an odorless gas." K. Stern, *The Flight from Woman*, New York, 1965, p. 300. But the question is why should a Christian theologian accept the limitation of reason imposed by rationalism if not because of the loss of the sapiential perspective which has always seen in reason not the poison gas to kill religion but a complement to faith since both are related to the Divine Intellect. The fact that such types of theology appear indicates that the depleting of the faculty of knowing of the sacred by modern Western philosophy and science has been finally accepted by the theologians themselves, some of whom then carry it out to a much more radical stage than do many contemporary scientists in quest of the rediscovery of the sacred.

143. Speaking of Barth, Schaeffer writes, "He has been followed by many more, men like Reinhold Niebuhr, Paul Tillich, Bishop John Robinson, Alan Richardson, and all the new theologians. They may differ in details, but their struggle is the same—it is the struggle of modern man who has given up a unified field of knowledge. As far as the theologians are concerned, they have separated religious truth from contact with science on the one hand and history on the other. Their new system is not open to verification, it must simply be believed." Schaeffer, op. cit., p. 54.

The case of Teilhard de Chardin presents, from the traditional point of view, a new dimension of theological subversion with which we shall deal later.

CHAPTER TWO

What Is Tradition?

By adhering to the Tao of the past
You will master the existence of the present.
Tao Te-Ching

I do not create; I only tell of the past.
Confucius

T he term *tradition* has been used profusely in the previous chapter. It is now necessary to define it as completely as possible in order to avoid misunderstanding about a concept which lies at the heart of our concern for the meaning of the sacred in its relation to knowledge. The usage of the term *tradition* in the sense understood in the present study came to the fore in Western civilization at the moment of the final phase of the desacralization of both knowledge and the world which surrounded modern man. The rediscovery of tradition constituted a kind of cosmic compensation, a gift from the Divine Empyrean whose mercy made possible, at the moment when all seemed to be lost, the reassertion of the Truth which constitutes the very heart and essence of tradition. The formulation of the traditional point of view was a response of the Sacred, which is both the alpha and the omega of human existence, to the elegy of doom of modern man lost in a world depleted of the sacred and therefore, of meaning.

> For though all seem lost, yet All is found
> In the Last who is the First. Faithful pageant,
> Not amiss is thy mime, for manifest in thee
> Omega is an archway where Alpha stands framed,
> The First who comes Last, for likewise art thou
> The season of seeds, O season of fruits.[1]

"The First who comes Last," the reassertion at this late hour of human history of tradition which itself is both of a primordial character and possesses continuity over the ages, made possible once again access to that Truth by which human beings have lived during most—or rather nearly all—of their terrestrial history. This Truth had to be stated anew and reformulated in the name of tradition precisely because of the nearly total eclipse and loss of that reality which has constituted the matrix of life of normal humanity over the ages. The usage of the term and recourse to the concept of tradition as found in the contemporary world are themselves, in a sense, an anomaly made necessary by the anomaly which constitutes the modern world as such.[2]

Various languages before modern times did not use a term corresponding exactly to tradition, by which this premodern humanity itself is characterized by those who accept the traditional point of view. Premodern man was too deeply immersed in the world created by tradition to have the need of having this concept defined in an exclusive manner. He was like the baby fish who, according to a Sufi parable, went one day to their mother and asked to have explained to them the nature of water about which they had heard so much, but which they had never seen nor had had defined and described for them. The mother answered that she would be glad to reveal the nature of water for them provided they would first find something other than water. In the same way, normal humanities lived in worlds so impregnated with what we now call tradition that they had no sense of a separate concept called tradition as it has been necessary to define and formulate in the modern world. They had an awareness of revelation, of wisdom, of the sacred and also knew of periods of decadence of their civilization and culture, but they had had no experience of a totally secularized and antitraditional world which would necessitate the definition and formulation of tradition as has been the case today. In a sense the formulation of the traditional point of view and the reassertion of the total traditional perspective, which is like the recapitulation of all the truths manifested in the present cycle of human history, could not have come but at the twilight of the Dark Age which marks at once an end and the eve preceding a new morning of splendor. Only the end of a cycle of manifestation makes possible the recapitulation of the whole of the cycle and the creation of a synthesis which then serves as the seed for a new cycle.[3]

The concept of tradition had to be brought forth and traditional teachings expressed in their totality; and this is exactly what has taken place during this late stage of human history. But the traditional writings are far from being widely known in the modern world. In fact had the writings of those who belong to the traditional point of view become well-known, it would hardly have been necessary to redefine here and now the meaning of tradition to which so many pages, articles, and even books have been devoted.[4] One of the remarkable aspects of the intellectual life of this century, however, is precisely the neglect of this point of view in circles whose official function it is to be concerned with questions of an intellectual order. Whether this neglect is deliberate or accidental is not our concern here. Whatever the cause might be, the result is that some sixty or seventy years after the appearance of works of a traditional character in the West, tradition is still misunderstood in most circles and confused with custom, habit, inherited patterns of thought, and the like. Hence, the necessity of delving once again into its meaning despite all that has been written on the subject.

As far as traditional languages are concerned, they do not possess, for reasons already mentioned, a term corresponding exactly to tradition. There are such fundamental terms as the Hindu and Buddhist *dharma*, the Islamic *al-dīn*, the Taoist *Tao*, and the like which are inextricably related to the meaning of the term *tradition*, but not identical with it, although of course the worlds or civilizations created by Hinduism, Buddhism, Taoism, Judaism, Christianity, Islam, or for that matter any other authentic religion, is a traditional world. Each of these religions is also the heart or origin of the tradition which extends the priciples of the religion to different domains. Nor does tradition mean exactly *traditio* as this term is used in Catholicism, although it does embrace the idea of transmission of a doctrine and practices of an inspired and ultimately revealed nature implied by *traditio*. In fact, the word *tradition* is related etymologically to transmission and contains within the scope of its meaning the idea of the transmission of knowledge, practice, techniques, laws, forms, and many other elements of both an oral and written nature. Tradition is like a living presence which leaves its imprint but is not reducible to that imprint. What it transmits might appear as words written upon parchment but it may also be truths engraved upon the souls of men, and as subtle as the breath or even the glance of the eye through which certain teachings are transmitted.

Tradition as used in its technical sense in this work, as in all our other writings, means truths or principles of a divine origin revealed or unveiled to mankind and, in fact, a whole cosmic sector through various figures envisaged as messengers, prophets, *avatāras,* the Logos or other transmitting agencies, along with all the ramifications and applications of these principles in different realms including law and social structure, art, symbolism, the sciences, and embracing of course Supreme Knowledge along with the means for its attainment.

In its more universal sense tradition can be considered to include the principles which bind man to Heaven, and therefore religion, while from another point of view religion can be considered in its essential sense as those principles which are revealed by Heaven and which bind man to his Origin. In this case, tradition can be considered in a more restricted sense as the application of these principles. Tradition implies truths of a supraindividual character rooted in the nature of reality as such for as it has been said, "Tradition is not a childish and outmoded mythology but a science that is terribly real."[5] Tradition, like religion, is at once truth and presence. It concerns the subject which knows and the object which is known. It comes from the Source from which everything originates and to which everything returns. It thus embraces all things like the "Breath of the Compassionate" which, according to the Sufis, is the very root of existence itself. Tradition is inextricably related to revelation and religion, to the sacred, to the notion of orthodoxy, to authority, to the continuity and regularity of transmission of the truth, to the exoteric and the esoteric as well as to the spiritual life, science and the arts. The colors and nuances of its meaning become in fact clearer once its relation to each of these and other pertinent concepts and categories is elucidated.

During the past few decades for many attracted to the call of tradition, the meaning of tradition has become related more than anything else to that perennial wisdom which lies at the heart of every religion and which is none other than the Sophia whose possession the sapiential perspective in the West as well as the Orient has considered as the crowning achievement of human life. This eternal wisdom from which the idea of tradition cannot be divorced and which constitutes one of the main components of the concept of tradition is none other than the *sophia perennis* of the Western tradition, which the Hindus call the *sanatāna dharma*[6] and the Muslims *al-ḥikmat al-khālidah* (or *jāvīdān khirad* in Persian).[7]

In one sense, *sanatāna dharma* or *sophia perennis* is related to the Primordial Tradition[8] and therefore to the Origin of human existence.

But this view should not in any way detract from or destroy the authenticity of the later messages from Heaven in the form of various revelations, each of which begins with *an* origin which is *the* Origin and which marks the beginning of a tradition that is at once *the* Primordial Tradition and its adaptation to a particular humanity, the adaptation being a Divine Possibility manifested on the human plane. The attraction of Renaissance man for the quest of origins and the "Primordial Tradition" that caused Ficino to put aside the translation of Plato for the *Corpus Hermeticum,* which was then considered as more ancient and primordial, an attraction which also became part of the world view and *Zeitgeist* of the nineteenth century,[9] has caused much confusion in the question of the meaning of "Primordial Tradition" in its relation to various religions. Each tradition and Tradition as such are related in depth to the perennial wisdom or Sophia, provided this link is not considered only temporally and not as a cause for the rejection of those other messages from Heaven which constitute the different religions and which are, of course, inwardly related to the Primordial Tradition without being simply its historical and temporal continuity. The spiritual genius and particularity of each tradition cannot be neglected in the name of the ever present wisdom which lies at the heart of each and every celestial descent.

A. K. Coomaraswamy, one of the foremost expositors of traditional doctrines in the contemporary period, translated *sanatāna dharma* as *philosophia perennis* to which he added the adjective *universalis.* Under his influence many have identified tradition with the perennial philosophy to which it is profoundly related.[10] But the term *philosophia perennis* or its English translation is somewhat problematic in itself and needs to be defined before tradition can be better understood with reference to it. Contrary to Huxley's assertion, the term *philosophia perennis* was not employed first by Leibniz who did quote it in a well-known letter to Remond written in 1714.[11] Rather, the term was probably employed for the first time by Agostino Steuco (1497-1548), the Renaissance philosopher and theologian who was an Augustinian. Although the term has been identified with many different schools including Scholasticism, especially of the Thomistic school,[12] and Platonism in general, these are more recent associations, whereas for Steuco it was identified with a perennial wisdom embracing both philosophy and theology and not related to just one school of wisdom or thought.

The work of Steuco *De perenni philosophia* was influenced by Ficino,

Pico, and even Nicolas of Cusa, especially the *De pace fidei* which speaks of harmony between various religions. Steuco, who knew Arabic and other Semitic languages and was librarian of the Vatican Library where he had access to the "wisdom of the ages" as far as this was possible in the Occident at that time, followed the ideas of these earlier figures concerning the presence of an ancient wisdom which had existed from the dawn of history. Ficino did not speak of *philosophia perennis* but he did allude often to the *philosophia priscorium* or *prisca theologia*, which can be translated as ancient or venerable philosophy and theology. Following Gemisthus Plethon, the Byzantine philosopher, who wrote of this ancient wisdom and emphasized the role of Zoroaster as the master of this ancient knowledge of a sacred order, Ficino emphasized the significance of the *Hermetic Corpus* and the *Chaldaean Oracles* which he considered to have been composed by Zoroaster as the origins of this primordial wisdom. He believed that true philosophy originated with Plato who was heir to this wisdom,[13] and true theology with Christianity. This true philosophy, *vera philosophia*, was for him the same as religion and true religion the same as this philosophy. For Ficino, as for so many Christian Platonists, Plato had known the Pentateuch and was a "Greek-speaking Moses," the Plato whom Steuco called *divinus Plato* in the same way that many Muslim sages had given him the title *Aflāṭūn al-ilāhī*, the "Divine Plato."[14] Ficino, in a way, reformulated the views of Gemisthus Plethon concerning the perennity of true wisdom.[15] Ficino's compatriot Pico della Mirandola was to add to the sources of the *philosophia priscorium*, the Quran, Islamic philosophy, and the Kabbala along with the non-Christian and especially Graeco-Egyptian sources considered by Ficino, although he followed the perspective of Ficino and emphasized the idea of the continuity of a wisdom which is essentially one throughout various civilizations and periods of history.

Steuco's *philosophia perennis* was none other than this *philosophia priscorium* but under a new appellation.[16] Steuco asserted that wisdom was originally of divine origin, a sacred knowledge handed by God to Adam which, for most human beings, was gradually forgotten and turned into a dream surviving only and most fully in the *prisca theologia*. This true religion or philosophy, whose goal is *theosis* and attainment of sacred knowledge, has existed from the beginning of human history and is attainable through either the historical expressions of this truth in various traditions or by intellectual intuition and "philosophical" contemplation.

Although severely attacked from many quarters for expressing such ideas so opposed to both the prevalent humanism of the Renaissance and the rather exoteric and sectarian interpretations of Christianity prevalent at that time, the term used by Steuco continued to survive and became celebrated through its use by Leibniz who did have a certain degree of sympathy with traditional ideas. But interestingly enough, it is only in the twentieth century that the term has gained wide popularity. If perennial or ancient wisdom is in fact understood as Plethon, Ficino, and Steuco understood it, then it is related to the idea of tradition and can even be employed as a translation for *sanātāna dharma*, provided the term *philosophia* is not understood only in a theoretical manner but embraces realization as well.[17] Tradition contains the sense of a truth which is both of divine origin and perpetuated throughout a major cycle of human history through both transmission and renewal of the message by means of revelation. It also implies an inner truth which lies at the heart of different sacred forms and which is unique since Truth is one. In both senses, tradition is closely related to the *philosophia perennis* if this term is understood as the Sophia which has always been and will always be and which is perpetuated by means of both transmission horizontally and renewal vertically through contact with that reality that was "at the beginning" and is here and now.[18]

Before leaving the subject of *philosophia perennis*, it seems appropriate to turn for a moment to the destiny of this idea in the Islamic tradition where its relation to sacred knowledge and its meaning as a perennial truth revived within each revelation is quite evident and more emphasized than in the Christian tradition. Islam sees the doctrine of unity (*al-tawhīd*) not only as the essence of its own message but as the heart of every religion. Revelation for Islam means the assertion of *al-tawhīd* and all religions are seen as so many repetitions in different climes and languages of the doctrine of unity. Moreover, wherever the doctrine of unity is to be found, it is considered to be of divine origin. Therefore, Muslims did not distinguish between religion and paganism but between those who accepted unity and those who denied or ignored it. For them the sages of antiquity such as Pythagoras and Plato were "unitarians" (*muwahhidūn*) who expressed the truth which lies at the heart of all religions.[19] They, therefore, belonged to the Islamic universe and were not considered as alien to it.

The Islamic intellectual tradition in both its gnostic (*ma'rifah* or *'irfān*) and philosophical and theosophical (*falsafah-ḥikmah*)[20] aspects saw the source of this unique truth which is the "Religion of the Truth" (*dīn al-ḥaqq*) in the teachings of the ancient prophets going back to Adam and considered the prophet Idrīs, whom it identified with Hermes, as the "father of philosophers" (*Abu'l-ḥukamā'*).[21] Many Sufis called not only Plato "divine" but also associated Pythagoras, Empedocles, with whom an important corpus which influenced certain schools of Sufism is associated, and others with the primordial wisdom associated with prophecy. Even early Peripatetic (*mashshā'ī*) philosophers such as al-Fārābī saw a relation between philosophy and prophecy and revelation. Later figures such as Suhrawardī expanded this perspective to include the tradition of pre-Islamic Persia.[22] Suhrawardī spoke often of *al-ḥikmat al-laduniyyah* or Divine Wisdom (literally the wisdom which is near God) in terms almost identical with what Sophia and also *philosophia perennis* mean traditionally, including its aspect of realization.[23] A later Islamic figure, the eighth/fourteenth (Islamic/Christian) century gnostic and theologian Sayyid Ḥaydar Āmulī, made no reservations in pointing to the correspondence existing between the "Muḥammadan" pleroma of seventy-two stars of the Islamic universe and the seventy-two stars of the pleroma comprised of those sages who had preserved their primordial nature but belong to a world outside of the specifically Islamic one.

Ṣadr al-Dīn Shīrāzī identified true knowledge with a perennial wisdom which has existed since the beginning of human history.[25] The Islamic conception of the universality of revelation went hand in hand with the idea of a primordial truth which has always existed and will always exist, a truth without history. The Arabic *al-dīn*, which is perhaps the most suitable word to translate the term tradition, is inseparable from the idea of permanent and perpetual wisdom, the *sophia perennis* which can also be identified with the *philosophia perennis* as understood by such a figure as Coomaraswamy.

To understand better the meaning of tradition, it is also necessary to discuss somewhat more fully its relation to religion. If tradition is related etymologically and conceptually to transmission, religion in turn implies in its root meaning, "binding" (from the Latin *religare*).[26]

As already mentioned, it is what binds man to God and at the same time men to each other as members of a sacred community or people, or what Islam calls an *ummah*. Understood in this sense, religion can be considered as the origin of tradition, as the heavenly beginning which through revelation manifests certain principles and truths whose applications then comprise tradition. But, as indicated before, the plenary meaning of tradition includes this origin as well as its ramifications and deployment. In this sense, tradition is a more general concept embracing religion, as the Arabic term *al-dīn* means at once tradition and religion in its most universal sense, while religion as used in its widest sense is understood by some to include the application of its revealed principles and its later historical unfolding, so that it would in turn embrace what we mean by tradition although the traditional point of view is not identical with the religious as a result of the intrusion of modernism and antitraditional forces into the realm of religion itself.

Moreover, the limited meaning that the term religion has gained in European languages has caused certain of the traditional authors such as Guénon to limit this term only to the Western religions especially in their exoteric expressions distinguishing them from Hinduism, Taoism, and the like which they call tradition rather than religion. But there is no limitation in principle in the term religion and no reason to exclude Hinduism from the category of religion if this latter term is understood as that which binds man to the Origin through a message, revelation, or manifestation which comes from the Ultimate Reality.

The limitation of religion to its most outward aspects in the recent history of the West has also caused such terms as religious art or religious literature to become so depleted of the sense of the sacred and removed from tradition considered as the application of principles of a transcendent order, that what is currently called religious art, literature, etc., in many cases is nontraditional or even antitraditional in character. It has, therefore, become necessary to distinguish traditional from religious in such contexts. But once the term religion is resuscitated to mean that which descends from the Source in those objective manifestations of the Logos called revelation in the Abrahamic religions or *avatāric* descent in Hinduism, then it can be seen as the heart of that total and all-embracing order which is tradition. Of course, this understanding of religion in all its amplitude and universality is possible only when the traditional point of view is revived and reality is viewed from the perspective of the traditional and the sacred, and not the profane.

To discuss the relation of tradition to religion requires of necessity delving into the problem of the plurality of religions. The multiplicity of religious forms implies the multiplicity of traditions, while one also speaks of the Primordial Tradition or Tradition as such in the same way that there is one *sophia perennis* but many religions in which it is to be found in different forms. One is thus confronted of necessity with the basic question of Tradition and traditions, a question about which much has been written and which has been the cause of so much misunderstanding. From a certain point of view there is but one Tradition, the Primordial Tradition, which always *is*. It is the single truth which is at once the heart and origin of all truths. All traditions are earthly manifestations of celestial archetypes related ultimately to the immutable archetype of the Primordial Tradition in the same way that all revelations are related to the Logos or the Word which was at the beginning and which is at once an aspect of the Universal Logos and the Universal Logos as such.[27]

Yet, each tradition is based on a direct message from Heaven and is not just the result of the historical continuity of the Primordial Tradition. A prophet or *avatār* owes nothing to anyone save what he receives from the Origin. In the modern world certain occultist and pseudo-"esoteric" circles claiming to be traditional have spoken of an actual depository of the Primordial Tradition on the earth, often identifying the locus with some region of Middle Asia and even claiming contact with representatives of the center.[28] Streams of aspirants have wandered into the mountains of the Hindu Kush or the Himalayas in quest of such a center and a whole science fiction has been created around a sacred geography which has been interpreted in a literal rather than a symbolic fashion. From the traditional point of view the reality of the Primordial Tradition and the "Supreme Center" is strongly confirmed, but this affirmation does not in any way decrease or destroy the authenticity or complete originality of each religion and tradition which conforms to a particular archetype and represents a direct manifestation from the Origin, marking a rupture of the horizontal and temporal dimension by the vertical and the transcendent. There is both Tradition and the traditions without one contradicting the other. To speak of Tradition does not mean to reject the celestial origin of any of the authentic religions and traditions but to confirm the sacred in each "original" message from Heaven,[29] while remaining aware of that Primordial Tradition which is confirmed by each tradition in not only its doctrines and symbols but also through the preservation of a "presence" which is inseparable from the sacred.

The traditional perspective is in fact so closely wed to the sense of the sacred that it is necessary to say something about the sacred itself and to try to "define" its meaning. In a sense, the sacred, like truth, reality, or being, is too principial and elemental to delimit in the logical manner of defining a universal by means of genus and specific difference. The sacred resides in the nature of reality itself, and normal humanity has a sense for the sacred just as it has for reality which one distinguishes naturally from the unreal.[30] But the condition of modern man is such that even this natural sense has become nearly forgotten, causing the need to provide a "definition" of the sacred. It is of much interest to note that attempts such as those of R. Otto to relate the sacred to the irrational have attracted the greatest deal of interest during this century. This fact implies that the relation of intellectual truth or knowledge to the sacred has been ignored precisely because of the depleting of knowledge of its sacred content. Moreover, in a secularized world the sacred has come to be viewed from the perspective of the profane world for which the sacred is then the totally other.[31] This point of view is perfectly understandable for most men do live in a world of forgetfulness in which the remembrance of God is wholly "other"; they live in a world of indifference and pettiness in which the grandeur of the sacred represents a radical "otherness." But what is exceptional in the modern world is that the sapiential perspective, which lives in the sacred and sees the profane in terms of the sacred and which had always been a living presence within normal civilizations, has become so forgotten that the view of the sacred as completely alien to what appears as "normal" human life has become the only view, if the sacred is accepted as a possibility at all. To the extent that the reality of the sacred is accepted at least in religious circles, it is connected with the power of God rather than His wisdom.

Perhaps the most direct way of approaching the meaning of the sacred is to relate it to the Immutable, to that Reality which is both the Unmoved Mover and the Eternal. That Reality which is immutable and eternal is the Sacred as such, and the manifestation of this Reality in the stream of becoming and the matrix of time is that which possesses the quality of sacredness. A sacred object or sacred sound is an object or a sound which bears the imprint of the Eternal and the Immutable in that physical reality which comprises outwardly the object or the sound. Man's sense of the sacred is none other than his sense for the Immutable and the Eternal, his nostalgia for what he really *is*, for he carries the sacred within the substance of his own being and most of all within his intelligence which was created to know the Immutable and contemplate the Eternal.

The Sacred as such is the source of Tradition and what is traditional is inseparable from the sacred. He who has no sense of the sacred cannot perceive the traditional perspective, and traditional man is never separated from the sense of the sacred. Nevertheless, the sacred is more like the blood which flows in the arteries and veins of tradition, an aroma which pervades the whole of a traditional civilization.[32] Tradition extends the presence of the sacred into a whole world, creating a civilization in which the sense of the sacred is ubiquitous. The function of a traditional civilization may be said to be nothing other than creating a world dominated by the sacred in which man is saved from the terror of the nihilism and skepticism which accompanies the loss of the sacred dimension of existence and the destruction of the sacred character of knowledge.

The all-embracing nature of tradition is made possible by the presence within each integral tradition, and going back to the religion which lies at the origin of the tradition, of not one but several dimensions, levels of meaning or types of teaching corresponding to the different types of spiritual and intellectual capabilities and needs of the humanity chosen as the earthly vehicle of the tradition in question. Although these dimensions or levels are multiple in number and many traditions speak of seven or forty or some other symbolic number of levels, they can be reduced at the first stage to the two basic dimensions of the exoteric and the esoteric: the first, concerning that aspect of the message from Heaven which governs the whole of the life of a traditional humanity; the other, the spiritual and intellectual needs of those who seek God or the Ultimate Reality here and now. In Judaism and Islam the two dimensions of the tradition as the Talmudic and Kabbalistic or the *Sharī'ah* and the *Ṭarīqah* are clearly delineated, although even in those cases there are intermediary regions and a spectrum which is far from being abruptly separated.[33] As for Christianity, although it is essentially an eso-exoterism with a less well-defined esoteric dimension than the other two Abrahamic traditions, it too did possess at the beginning a distinctly esoteric message which has manifested itself in various ways during the later history of Christianity.[34]

Although the Indian and Far Eastern worlds have different traditional structures from the Abrahamic ones, there are nevertheless such realities as the Law of Manu complementing Advaita Vedanta, Confucianism complementing Taoism, and the Theravada and Mahayana schools of Buddhism which correspond in their own context to the exoteric-esoteric dimensions of tradition. Although our concern in this study is with sacred knowledge and therefore more with the esoteric dimension which is related more directly to sacred knowledge, it is important to emphasize the significance of the exoteric dimension and its necessity for an integral, living tradition. This point is particularly important to mention in the light of the pretensions of so many pseudoesoteric groups today which claim themselves to be beyond the need of the exoteric in contrast to the greatest sages of days gone by who amidst the most exalted utterances concerning spiritual realization remained faithful to the forms and exoteric teachings of their religions, the rare exceptions being only those which prove the rule.[35]

Esoterism is that inward dimension of tradition which addresses the inner man, *ho esō anthrōpos* of Saint Paul. It is hidden because of its very nature and accessible to only the few because in this stage of human history only the few remain aware of the inner dimensions of their nature; the rest live on the periphery of the circle of their own existence, oblivious to the Center which is connected by the esoteric dimension of tradition to the circumference or periphery.[36] The esoteric is the radius which provides the means of going from the circumference to the Center, but it is not available to all because not everyone is willing or qualified to undertake the journey to the Center in this life. To follow the exoteric dimension of religion, however, is to remain on the circumference and hence in a world which has a center, and to remain qualified to carry out the journey to the Center in the afterlife, the beatific vision being only a posthumous possibility from the exoteric point of view.

The authentically esoteric is always contained within a total and integral tradition. It is only in the modern West, and possibly during the decadence of the late antiquity, that esoteric teachings have become divorced from the tradition within whose matrix the esoteric is veritably the esoteric. As a result of this phenomenon, which as far as the modern world is concerned goes back to the eighteenth century, the esoteric has been made to appear, for the most part, as being opposed to the Christian tradition, while what has survived of the Christian tradition has in most instances disdained the very idea of the esoteric in the same way that gnosis or sacred knowledge has been left out of consideration in the exposition of the message of most Christian churches in recent times. Because of its detachment from a living tradition, this so-called esoterism has usually degenerated into an inoperative or even harmful occultism and the shell of sacred knowledge has remained but become depleted of the sacred. What has paraded for the most part as esoterism in the modern world has become divorced from the sense of the sacred in complete contrast to genuine esoterism as understood traditionally, which is by nature concerned with the sacred and is the means par excellence of gaining access to the sacred in that here and now which is the reflection of the Immutable and the Eternal.[37]

Whether considered in its exoteric or esoteric aspect, tradition implies orthodoxy and is inseparable from it. If there is such a thing as truth, then there is also error and norms which allow man to distinguish between them. Orthodoxy in its most universal sense is none other than the truth in itself and as related to the formal homogeneity of a particular traditional universe. The loss of the multidimensional character of religion and its reduction to a single level have also caused the narrowing of the sense of orthodoxy in such a manner that the esoteric and the mystical have often been castigated as unorthodox. Orthodoxy has become identified with simple conformity and has gained an almost pejorative sense among those concerned with intellectuality, and many who unknowingly thirst for orthodoxy in its most universal sense have claimed themselves as heterodox vis-à-vis a narrowly formulated and conceived orthodoxy which has left no living space for the liberating flight of the sanctified intellect. The narrowing of the meaning of the term orthodoxy is, in fact, not unconnected with the loss of the original meaning of intellectuality and its reduction to rationalism. Otherwise intellectuality in its authentic sense cannot but be related to orthodoxy.[38]

If orthodoxy is understood in its universal sense as the quality of the truth in the context of a particular spiritual and religious universe as well as the truth as such, then it must be interpreted on different levels like tradition itself. There are certain doctrines which are extrinsically heterodox vis-à-vis a particular traditional universe but intrinsically orthodox. An example would be Christianity as viewed from Judaism and Buddhism from the point of view of Hinduism. Even within a single tradition, a particular esoteric school may appear as unorthodox from the point of view of the exoteric dimension or even from the perspective of another esoteric school of that same tradition, as seen in certain schools of Japanese Buddhism. In all these cases the concept of orthodoxy is of capital importance in judging the character of the teachings involved from the traditional point of view and is almost synonymous with the traditional as far as conformity to the truth is concerned. There is no possibility of tradition without orthodoxy nor of orthodoxy outside of tradition. Moreover, both are exclusive of all those imitations, aberrations, and deviations of a purely human or sometimes subhuman origin, which either claim openly to stand outside of the traditions or imply such departures from the traditional universe as to make impossible the gaining of access to the doctrines, practices, and spiritual presence which alone enable man to go beyond his limited self and to reach the entelechy which is his raison d'être. In any case, a tree is judged by the fruit it bears and this principle is nowhere more applicable than in the judgment of what is orthodox and what departs or deviates from orthodoxy at all levels of man's religious life, including not only law and morality but also and especially the domain of knowledge and intellectuality. The full attainment of sacred knowledge, including its realized aspect, is as much related to the key concept of tradition as to orthodoxy; and it is not possible to understand the significance of tradition without an appreciation of its relation to orthodoxy understood in its most universal sense.[39]

To speak of the truth and of orthodoxy in the traditional context is also to speak of authority and the transmission of truth. Who or what determines religious truth and guarantees the purity, regularity, and perpetuity of a tradition? This is a key question to which all traditions have addressed themselves in different ways. Moreover, they have provided answers which guarantee the authenticity of the tradition without their having recourse to simply one solution. There are traditions which have a *magisterium* and others a sacred community which itself guarantees the purity and continuity of the message.[40]

Some have emphasized the continuity of a sacerdotal function and others of a chain of transmission through teachers whose qualifications have been determined and defined by the tradition in question. Sometimes even within a single tradition several means have been used, but in all cases traditional authority remains inseparable from the meaning of tradition itself. There are those who are authorities in traditional matters and there are those who are not; there are those who know and those who do not. Individualism in any case does not and cannot play a role in the transmission and interpretation of that which is by definition suprahuman, even if an extensive field is left for human elaboration and interpretation. Intellectual and spiritual authority is inseparable from that reality which is tradition and authentic traditional writings always possess an innate quality of authority.

Likewise, tradition implies the regularity of transmission of all of its aspects ranging from legal and ethical rulings and precepts to esoteric knowledge. Different means of transmission including oral transmission, initiation, transfer of power, techniques, and knowledge from master to disciple, and the perpetuation of a particular spiritual perfume and sacred presence are all related to and inseparable from that reality which is tradition. To live in the traditional world is to breathe in a universe in which man is related to a reality beyond himself from which he receives those principles, truths, forms, attitudes, and other elements which determine the very texture of human existence. And this reception is made possible through that transmission which brings the reality of tradition to the lives of the members of each generation according to their capacities and destiny and guarantees the perpetuation of this reality without the corruption which characterizes all that is affected by the withering influence of time and becoming.

The all-embracing nature of tradition is also a trait which needs to be emphasized. In a civilization characterized as traditional, nothing lies outside the realm of tradition. There is no domain of reality which has a right to existence outside the traditional principles and their applications. Tradition therefore concerns not only knowledge but also love and works. It is the source of the law which governs society even in cases where the law is not derived directly from the revelation.[41] It is the foundation of ethics. In fact, ethics has no meaning outside the cadre established by the tradition. It also sets the principles and norms for the political aspect of the life of society, and political authority is related to that of the spiritual although the relation between the two is far from being uniform in different traditions.[42] Likewise, tradition determines the structure of society applying immutable principles to the social order, resulting in structures outwardly as different as the Hindu caste system and the Islamic "democracy of married monks," as some have characterized theocratic Islamic society, in which there is nevertheless an equality before God and the Divine Law, but of course not in the quantitative modern sense.[43]

Tradition also governs the domains of art and science, with which we shall deal in later chapters, and is especially concerned with principial knowledge or that supreme science which is metaphysics and which has been often confounded in the West with philosophy. Our concern being knowledge in its relation to the sacred rather than all aspects of tradition, it is necessary to pause here to distinguish between the kinds of knowledge which exist in a traditional civilization. Besides the various cosmological sciences, there are, as already noted, three modes of knowing dealing with principles which one can distinguish in a traditional world, especially those governed by one of the Abrahamic religions: these three being philosophy, theology, and gnosis, or in a certain context theosophy. The modern world distinguishes only two modes or disciplines: philosophy and theology rather than the three existing in the traditional world of not only Christianity but also Islam and Judaism.

In the Islamic tradition after several centuries during which the various perspectives were formed, a situation developed which demonstrates fully the role and function of philosophy, theology, and metaphysics or gnosis in a traditional context. There were schools such as that of the Peripatetics (*mashshāʾī*) which could be called philosophical in the traditional sense. There were schools of theology (*kalām*) such as that of the Muʿtazilites, the Ashʿarites, the Maturidites, the Ismāʿīlīs, and the Twelve-Imam Shīʿites. Then there was gnosis or metaphysics associated with various schools of Sufism. As far as the eastern Islamic world was concerned, there also gradually developed a school associated with Suhrawardī and his school of illumination (*al-ishrāq*) which was both philosophical and gnostic and which should be called, properly speaking, theosophical,[44] while in the western lands of Islam, contemporary with this development, philosophy ceased to exist as a distinct discipline becoming wed to theology on the one hand and gnosis on the other. Likewise, medieval Judaism could distinguish between the same three kinds of intellectual perspectives represented by such figures as Judas Halévy, Maimonides, Ibn Gabirol, and Luria. Needless to say, in medieval Christianity one could also distinguish between the theology of a Saint Bernard, the philosophy of an Albertus Magnus, and the gnosis of a Meister Eckhart, not to speak of a Roger Bacon or Raymond Lull, who correspond more to the school of *ishrāq* of Suhrawardī than anything else if a comparison is to be made with the Islamic tradition.[45]

All three disciplines have a role and function to play in the intellectual life of a traditional world. There is an aspect of "philosophy" which is necessary for the exposition of certain theological and gnostic ideas as there are elements of theology and gnosis which are present in every authentic expression of philosophy worthy of the name. One can, in fact, say that every great philosopher is also to some extent theologian and metaphysician, in the sense of gnostic, as every great theologian is to some extent philosopher and gnostic and every gnostic to some degree philosopher and theologian as found in the case of an Ibn ʿArabī or Meister Eckhart.[46]

Although, due to the complete depletion of what passes, in the modern world, as philosophy of traditional truth and the sacred, traditional authors such as A. K. Coomaraswamy and F. Schuon and especially R. Guénon have attacked philosophy severely in order to clear the ground for the presentation of metaphysics and to prevent any distortions or deviations which might be caused by the confusion between profane philosophy and sacred knowledge,[47] there is no doubt that there is such a thing as traditional philosophy or philosophy in the traditional context.[48] Despite all the depreciation that the term philosophy has suffered in the modern world, still something of the Pythagorean and Platonic conception of philosophy resonates through it. It is possible to resuscitate the meaning of this discipline and its function provided the sacred character of knowledge is established once again. In any case, the traditional intellectual world implies the presence of different dimensions and perspectives, including what in the Western tradition would be called not only theology and philosophy but also gnosis and theosophy.[49] The disappearance of gnosis from the mainstream of modern Western thought could not but result in the trivialization of the meaning of philosophy, the diluting of the substance of theology and finally the appearance of that type of inversion of traditional knowledge which has paraded as "theosophy" during the past century.

Although the essence of tradition is present eternally *in divinis,* its historical manifestation can either disappear completely from the earthly plane or become partly inaccessible or "lost." Not every tradition is a living one. The Egyptian tradition, for example, which is one of the most remarkable known to man, cannot be practiced or lived although its art forms, symbols, and even a certain presence of a psychological rather than spiritual kind belonging to it survive. That spiritual life, which invigorated and animated the earthly body of the tradition, left for the abode of the origin of all religions and the tradition cannot be said to be alive as can, let us say, Hinduism or Islam. There are also certain traditions which are only partially accessible or "alive" in the sense that only certain of their dimensions or teachings are available. In this case there is always the possibility of a rejuvenation and regeneration of what has been lost or forgotten, provided the roots and channels of transmission of the tradition remain intact. Likewise the civilizations created by various traditions can become weakened, decay, or die without the religion and certain aspects of the tradition which gave birth to the civilization in question decaying or dying. Such is in fact the case of the traditional civilizations of Asia today which have decayed in different degrees while the traditions which gave birth to them remain alive.

As for traditional symbols, since they have their root in the archetypal world of the Spirit, it is possible to have them resuscitated provided there is a living tradition which can absorb symbols, images, and even doctrines of another traditional world, this absorption implying much more than mere historical borrowing.[50] In any case, symbols and ideas of nonliving or alien traditions cannot be legitimately adopted or absorbed into another world which is not itself traditional, as so many attempt to do in the modern world. He who attempts to carry out such a process independent of tradition is doing nothing less than usurping the function of a prophet or the figure whom the Muslims call the Mahdī and the Hindus the Chakravartin. The adoption of any element from another tradition must follow the laws and principles which determine the mode of existence of the tradition which is adopting the elements in question. Otherwise, the adoption of elements of an even originally traditional character can result in the diffusion of forces of dissolution which can cause great harm or even destruction to an already living tradition not to speak of organizations of purely human origin playing with forces far beyond their ken of understanding or power of control.[51]

This and numerous other dangers, obstacles, and precipices which face modern man who has decided to live by bread alone have forced those who have sought to resuscitate the traditional point of view in the modern world to express their categorical opposition to modernism, which they do not at all identify with the contemporary world as such but with that revolt against Heaven which began in the Renaissance in the West and which has now invaded nearly the whole globe. At other times, it would have been possible to speak of what constitutes tradition without discussing forces of secularism but such a possibility does not exist in a world already influenced and, from the traditional point of view, contaminated by modernism. To speak of tradition is to be concerned with the truth and therefore error, and to be faced with the necessity of evaluating the modern world in the light of those truths which comprise the very principles of tradition. The unrelenting opposition of traditional authors to modernism issues first and foremost from their dedication to traditional truth and then from compassion and charity toward a humanity entangled in a world woven of the threads of half-truths and errors.

Today the criticism against the modern world and modernism has become commonplace, ranging from works of poets to analyses of even sociologists.[52] But the opposition of tradition to modernism, which is total and complete as far as principles are concerned, does not derive from the observation of facts and phenomena or the diagnosis of the symptoms of the malady. It is based upon a study of the causes which have brought about the illness. Tradition is opposed to modernism because it considers the premises upon which modernism is based to be wrong and false in principle.[53] It does not neglect the fact that some element of a particular modern philosophical system may be true or some modern institution may possess a positive feature or be good. In fact, complete falsehood or evil could not exist since every mode of existence implies some element of that truth and goodness which in their purity belong to the Source of all existence.

What tradition criticizes in the modern world is the total world view, the premises, the foundations which, from its point of view, are false so that any good which appears in this world is accidental rather than essential. One could say that the traditional worlds were essentially good and accidentally evil, and the modern world essentially evil and accidentally good. Tradition is therefore opposed in principle to modernism. It wishes to slay the modern world[54] in order to create a normal one. Its goal is not to destroy what is positive but to remove that veil of ignorance which allows the illusory to appear as real, the negative as positive and the false as true. Tradition is not opposed to all that exists in the world today and, in fact, refuses to equate all that exists today with modernism. After all, although this age is given such epithets as the space age or the atomic age because man has traveled to the moon or split the atom, through the same logic it could just as well have been called the age of monks, because monks do still exist along with astronauts. The fact that this age is not called the age of monasticism but of space is itself the fruit of the modernistic point of view which equates modernism with the contemporary world, whereas tradition distinguishes sharply between the two, seeking to destroy modernism not in order to destroy contemporary man but to save him from continuing upon a path whose end could not but be perdition and destruction. From this point of view the history of Western man during the past five centuries is an anomaly in the long history of the human race in both East and West. In opposing modernism in principle and in a categorical manner, those who follow the traditional point of view wish only to enable Western man to join the rest of the human race.[55]

The emphasis upon the East or the Orient by contemporary traditional authors is in fact due to the historic situation in which modernism and rebellion against tradition arose in the West. Otherwise tradition embraces both East and West for it is derived from none other than that "Blessed Olive Tree" or central axis of cosmic existence to which the Quran refers stating that it is neither of the East nor of the West.[56] It is true that during this century those who have spoken of tradition have emphasized the three major spiritual universes of the East comprising the Far East, India, and the Islamic world with their own distinct features as well as their points of interpenetration. It is also true that some have even thought that traditional civilization simply means Oriental civilization. But even during this century since a work such as *East and West* of R. Guénon was written, a great deal has changed in Asia itself giving further reason for not identifying tradition with a geographic Orient alone, although more of what is traditional still survives in the geographic East than in the West and these terms have not lost their geographic sense completely.[57]

As the tragic history of these decades unfolds, however, it becomes more and more necessary to identify tradition with that East or Orient which belongs to sacred geography and which is symbolic rather than literal. The Orient is the source of light, the point where dawn breaks and where the sun rises casting its light upon the horizons, removing darkness and bringing forth the warmth which vivifies. The Orient is the Origin as well as the point toward which we turn in our journey in life, the point without which there would be no orientation, without which life would become disarray and chaos and our journey a meandering in the labyrinth of what the Buddhists call *samsāric* existence. Tradition is identified with this Orient. It, too, issues from the Origin and provides orientation for human life. It provides a knowledge which is at once Oriental and illuminating, a knowledge which is combined with love as the light of the sun is combined with heat, a knowledge which issues from the Precinct of the Sacred and which leads to the Sacred.

To the extent that the shadows of the land of the setting sun cover the living space of the human species and the geographical Orient becomes ravaged by various forms of modernism, to that extent the Orient becomes a pole carried within the heart and soul of human beings wherever they might be. To the extent that the physical Orient ceases to be, at least outwardly, the land of tradition as it has been over the millennia,[58] to that extent tradition spreads once again into the Occident and even into the "Far West" preparing the ground symbolically for that day when "the Sun shall rise in the West." To identify tradition with the Orient today is to identify it with that Orient which is the place of the rising Sun of our own being, the point which is at once the center and origin of man, the center which both illuminates and sanctifies and without which human existence on both the individual and collective levels becomes like a circle without center, a world deprived of the enlightening and vivifying luminosity of the rising Sun.

NOTES

1. From the poem "Autumn" of M. Lings, one of the leading contemporary traditional writers who is also a poet, in his *The Heralds and Other Poems*, London, 1970, p. 26.

2. As one of the foremost of the contemporary traditional masters has asserted, the exposition of traditional doctrines in their totality is necessary today because "one irregularity deserves another."

3. On the microcosmic level traditional eschatologies teach that at the moment of death the whole life of a human being is recapitulated in a nutshell before him. He is then judged accordingly and enters a posthumous state in accordance with his state of being and of course the Divine Mercy whose dimensions are imponderable. The same principle exists on the macrocosmic level and as it involves the life of humanity as such with of course all the differences which the shift from the individual to the collective level implies.

4. The earliest works of R. Guénon, one of the foremost expositors of the traditional perspective in the modern West, contain many passages on the meaning of tradition. See "What is Meant by Tradition," in his *Introduction to the Study of Hindu Doctrines*, trans. M. Pallis, London, 1945, pp. 87–89; and "De l'infaillibilité traditionnelle," in id., *Aperçus sur l'initiation*, Paris, 1946, pp. 282–88. Likewise, A. K. Coomaraswamy and F. Schuon have written numerous pages and passages on the concept of tradition itself. See, for example, Coomaraswamy, *The Bugbear of Literacy*, esp. chaps. 4 and 5; and F. Schuon, *Spiritual Perspectives and Human Facts*, pt. 1; idem, *Light on the Ancient Worlds*, chaps. 1 and 2; idem, "Fatalité et progrès," *Études Traditionnelles*, no. 261 (July–August 1947): 183–89; and idem, "L'Impossible convergence," *Études Traditionnelles*, no. 402–3(September–October 1967): 145–49. See also E. Zolla, *Ché cos' è la tradizione?*, esp. pt. 2, "La Tradizione Eterna," which deals with tradition from a more literary point of view; and idem, "What is Tradition?," in the volume dedicated to A. K. Coomaraswamy and edited by R. Fernando (in press). Tradition has also been used with a similar but more limited meaning than intended in this work by certain Catholic authors such as J. Pieper, *Überlieferung-Begriff und Anspruch*, Munich, 1970, while other Catholic figures to whom we shall turn later have embraced the traditional idea fully.

5. F. Schuon, *Understanding Islam*.

6. *Sanātāna dharma* cannot be translated exactly, although *sophia perennis* is perhaps the closest to it since *sanātāna* means perennity (that is, perpetuity throughout a cycle of human existence and not eternity) and *dharma*, the principle of conservation of beings, each being having its own *dharma* to which it must conform and which is its law. But *dharma* also concerns a whole humanity in the sense of *Mānava-dharma* and in that case is related to the sacred knowledge or Sophia which is at the heart of the law governing over a human cycle. In that sense *sanātāna dharma* corresponds to *sophia perennis* esp. if the realized and not only the theoretical dimension of Sophia is taken into consideration. In its plenary meaning *sanātāna dharma* is primordial tradition itself as it has subsisted and will continue to subsist throughout the present cycle of humanity. See R. Guénon, "Sanātāna Dharma," in his *Études sur l'Hindouisme*, Paris, 1968, pp. 105–6.

7. This is in fact the title of a well-known work by Ibn Miskawayh (Muskūyah) which contains metaphysical and ethical aphorisms and sayings by Islamic and pre-Islamic sages. See the A. Badawi edition *al-Hikmat al-khālidah: Jāwīdān khirad*, Cairo, 1952. This work discusses the thought and writings of many sages and philosophers, including those from ancient Persia, India, and the Mediterranean world (Rūm). On this work see the Introduction of M. Arkoun to T. M. Shushtarī's Persian translation of Ibn Miskawayh, *Jāvīdān khirad*, Tehran, 1976, pp. 1–24.

8. The primordial tradition is none other than what Islam refers to as *al-dīn al-hanīf* to which the Quran refers in many different contexts but usually in relation to the Prophet Abraham who is usually referred to as *hanīf*; for example, "Nay but, (we follow) the religion of Abraham, the upright (*hanīfan*), and he was not of the idolators" (II; 135–Pickthall translation). See also verses Ill; 67 and 95–VI; 79 and 161–XVI; 120–and XVII; 31.

9. See M. Eliade, "The Quest for the 'Origins of Religion'," *History of Religions* 4/1 (Summer 1964): 154–69.

10. The well-known work of A. Huxley, *Perennial Philosophy*, New York, 1945, is one of the works which has sought to demonstrate the existence and to present the content

of this enduring and perennial wisdom through selections of sayings drawn from various traditions, but the work remains incomplete in many ways and its perspective is not traditional. The first work which carried out in full the suggestion of Coomaraswamy in assembling a vast compendium of traditional knowledge in order to show the remarkable perennity and universality of wisdom is the sadly neglected work of W. N. Perry, *A Treasury of Traditional Wisdom*, London and New York, 1971, which is a key work for the understanding of what traditional authors mean by perennial philosophy.

11. After stating in this letter that truth is more extensive than has been thought before and that its trace is found among the ancients he says, "et ce serait en effect perennis quaedam Philosophia." C. J. Gerhardt (ed.), *Die philosophischen Schriften von Gottfried Wilhelm Leibnitz*, Berlin, 1875–90, vol. 3, p. 625. Quoted also in C. Schmitt, "Perennial Philosophy: Steuco to Leibniz," *Journal of the History of Ideas* 27 (1966): 506. This article (pp. 505–32 of the cited volume) traces the history of the usage of the term *philosophia perennis* with special attention paid to its Renaissance background in Ficino and other early Renaissance figures. See also J. Collins, "The Problem of a Perennial Philosophy," in his *Three Paths in Philosophy*, Chicago, 1962, pp. 255–79.

12. The identification of the "perennial philosophy" with Thomism or Scholasticism in general is a twentieth-century phenomenon, while in the Renaissance the Scholastics in general opposed the theses of Steuco.

13. Specifically heir to Zoroaster, Hermes, Orpheus, Aglaophemus (the teacher of Pythagoras), and Pythagoras.

14. This term is found among both Islamic philosophers like al-Fārābī and certain Sufis.

15. On the views of Ficino see the various works of R. Klibansky, E. Cassirer, and P. O. Kristeller on the Renaissance, esp. Kristeller's *Studies in Renaissance Thought and Letters*, Rome, 1956; and idem, *Il pensiero filosofico di Marsilio Ficino*, Florence, 1953.

16. This fact is shown clearly by Schmitt in his already cited article which demonstrates that although the term *philosophia perennis* is of Renaissance origin, the idea even in Western intellectual life is of a medieval and ultimately ancient Greek origin.

17. Referring to *religio perennis* Schuon writes, "These words recall the *philosophia perennis* of Steuchus Eugubin (sixteenth century) and of the neo-scholastics; but the word 'philosophia' suggests rightly or wrongly a mental elaboration rather than wisdom, and therefore does not convey exactly the intended sense." *Light on the Ancient Worlds*, p. 143.

18. "'*Philosophia perennis*' is generally understood as referring to that metaphysical truth which has no beginning, and which remains the same in all expressions of wisdom. Perhaps it would here be better or more prudent to speak of a '*Sophia perennis*'. . . .

"With *Sophia perennis*, it is a question of the following: there are truths innate in the human Spirit, which nevertheless in a sense lie buried in the depth of the 'Heart'—in the pure Intellect—and are accessible only to the one who is spiritually contemplative; and these are the fundamental metaphysical truths. Access to them is possessed by the 'gnostic', 'pneumatic' or 'theosopher',—in the original and not the sectarian meaning of these terms,—and access to them was also possessed by the 'philosophers' in the real and still innocent sense of the word: for example, Pythagoras, Plato and to a large extent also Aristotle." Schuon, "*Sophia perennis*": *Studies in Comparative Religion*, trans. W. Stoddart, (in press). See also Schuon, *Wissende, Verschwiegene. Ein geweihte Hinführung zur Esoterik*, Herderbücherei Initiative 42, Munich, 1981, pp. 23–28; and idem, the introduction and first chapter, "Prémisses épistémologiques," in his *Sur les traces de la religion pérenne* (in press).

19. We have dealt with this theme in many of our writings. See, for example, our *An Introduction to Islamic Cosmological Doctrines*, pp. 37ff.

20. *Falsafah* and *hikmah* can be translated as both philosophy and theosophy depending on how these terms are understood in English and in what context the Arabic terms are employed.

21. On the figure of Hermes in Islamic thought see L. Massignon, "Inventaire de la littérature hermétique arabe," in A. Nock and A. J. Festugière, *La Révélation d'Hermès Trismégiste,* 1, Paris, 1949, app. 3; S. H. Nasr, "Hermes and Hermetic Writings in the Islamic World," in *Islamic Life and Thought,* London, 1981, pp. 102ff; F. Sezgin, *Geschichte der Arabischen Schrifttums,* Leiden, 1970 on, with references to Hermes on many different pages, for example, vol. 3, 1970, pp. 170–71, vol. 4, 1971, pp. 139–269; and the article "Hirmis" by M. Plesser in the *New Encyclopaedia of Islam.*

22. The emphasis upon pre-Islamic Persia as well as Greece as the home of the "perennial philosophy" is also found in Ibn Miskawayh and Abu'l Hasan al-ʿĀmirī although not to the same extent as Suhrawardī who considered himself the resurrector of the wisdom of the ancient Persians. See Nasr, *Three Muslim Sages,* chap. 2; and H. Corbin, *En Islam iranien,* vol. 2.

23. Suhrawardī also refers to this wisdom as *al-hikmat al-ʿatīqah* (the ancient wisdom) which is exactly the same as the Latin *philosophia priscorum.* Whether there is a historical link or simply the repetition of the same truth and even terminology in twelfth-century Persia and Renaissance Italy cannot be answered until more study is made of the dissemination of the teachings of Suhrawardī in the West. See S. H. Nasr, "The Spread of the Illuminationist School of Suhrawardī," in *La Persia nel Medioevo,* Rome, 1971, pp. 255–65.

24. Sayyid Haydar Âmolî, *Le texte des textes (Naṣṣ al-Noṣûṣ), commentaire des "Fosûṣ al-hikam" d'Ibn Arabî. Les prolégomènes,* ed. by H. Corbin and O. Yahya, Tehran-Paris, 1975, §865. The author has provided elaborate diagrams which are like *mandalas* based on the vision of the intelligible world containing the names of various spiritual and intellectual figures, both Islamic and pre-Islamic. These diagrams have been analyzed by Corbin in his, "La paradoxe du monothéisme," *Eranos-Jahrbuch,* 1976, pp. 77ff. Concerning the "extraordinary interest" of these diagrams depicting the sages in the spiritual firmament Corbin writes, "[Cet intérêt] est dans la correspondance instituée pour les deux *diagrammes* 21 et 22 entre la totalité mohammadienne groupé autour de la famille ou du temple des Imams immaculés (*Ahl al-bayt*) et la totalité des religions groupés autour des hommes dont la nature foncière originelle a été préservée (*fiṭra salîma*). La *fiṭra salîma,* c'est la nature humaine, l'*Imago Dei,* telle qu'elle est 'sortie des mains' du Créateur, sans avoir jamais été détruite." Ibid., pp. 98–99.

25. The masterpiece of Ṣadr al-Dīn Shīrāzī, *al-Ḥikmat al-mutaʿāliyah fī'l-asfār al-arbaʿah,* is not only a *summa* of Islamic philosophy and theosophy but also a major source for the history of Islamic thought as well as the pre-Islamic ideas which Muslim philosophers and theologians encountered. In almost every discussion Mullā Ṣadrā turns to ancient philosophies as well as Islamic ones and takes the point of view of the *philosophia perennis* for granted. The same point of view is to be seen in his other works such as *Hudūth al-ʿālam.* See S. H. Nasr, *Ṣadr al-Dīn Shīrāzī and His Transcendent Theosophy,* London, 1978; and idem, "Mullā Ṣadrā as a Source for the History of Muslim Philosophy," *Islamic Studies* 3/3 (Sept. 1964): 309–14.

26. "*Religio* is that which 'binds' (*religat*) man to Heaven and engages his whole being; as for the word '*traditio*', it is related to a more outward and sometimes fragmentary reality, besides suggesting a retrospective outlook. At its birth a religion 'binds' men to Heaven from the moment of its first revelation, but it does not become a 'tradition', or admit more than one 'tradition', till two or three generations later." Schuon, *Light on the Ancient Worlds,* p. 144.

27. The multiplicity of religious forms in the light of unitary and sacred knowledge shall be dealt with in chap. 9 of this work.

28. The book of R. Guénon, *Le Roi du monde,* Paris, 1927, has itself given rise to many such speculations by people of such tendencies.

29. Strictly speaking, only that which comes from the Origin can be original. That is precisely how the traditional perspective views originality in contrast to the antitraditional view for which originality is divorced from both the truth and sacred presence and therefore from all that comprises religion or tradition as such.

30. This distinction is so fundamental that even those sophists who try to disprove

the reality of the real nevertheless live and act upon the basis of the intuition of the distinction between the real and the unreal.

31. It is this idea of the sacred as wholly other that was developed by R. Otto in his well-known work The Idea of the Holy, trans. J. Harvey, New York, 1958, pp. 12ff., and which has attracted so much attention among scholars of religion during recent decades.

32. For example, all sacred art is traditional art but not all traditional art is sacred art. The latter comprises that aspect of traditional art which deals directly with the symbols, images, rites, and objects dealing with the religion which lies at the heart of the tradition in question. We shall treat this question more fully in chap. 8 dealing with sacred art.

33. On these dimensions in Islam see S. H. Nasr, Ideals and Realities of Islam; as for exoterism and esoterism in general see F. Schuon, The Transcendent Unity of Religions, trans. P. Townsend, New York, 1975, chaps. 2 and 3.

34. "We have put forward the view that the process of dogmatic enunciation during the first centuries was one of successive Initiation, or in a word, that there existed an exoterism and an esoterism in the Christian religion. Historians may not like it, but one finds incontestable traces of the lex arcani at the origin of our religion." P. Vuillaud, Études d'ésotérisme catholique, quoted in Schuon, Transcendent Unity, p. 142.

35. It is often forgotten that a Śankara who was the supreme jñāni in Hinduism composed hymns to Śiva and that a Ḥāfiẓ or Rūmī who spoke constantly of casting aside forms (ṣūrah) in favor of the essence (maʿnā—literally "meaning") never missed their daily prayers. They transcended form from above not below and were therefore the first to recognize the necessity of exoteric forms for the preservation of the equilibrium of a human collectivity.

36. See S. H. Nasr, "Between the Rim and the Axis," in Islam and the Plight of Modern Man, London, 1976, chap. 1.

37. On the meaning of esoterism see F. Schuon, Esoterism as Principle and as Way, trans. by William Stoddart, London, 1981, Introduction; and L. Benoist, L'Esotérisme, Paris, 1963.

38. ". . . Orthodoxy is the principle of formal homogeneity proper to any authentically spiritual perspective; it is therefore an indispensible aspect of all genuine intellectuality." Schuon, Stations of Wisdom, trans. G. E. H. Palmer, London, 1961.

39. It is of much interest that the term orthodoxy is not found in Oriental languages and even in Arabic dominated by Islam which bears so many resemblances to Christianity. When one studies the Christian tradition, however, one realizes how essential this term is to describe various aspects of Islam itself and how misleading it is when orientalists call, let us say, Shīʿism and Sufism unorthodox whereas they both belong to the totality of Islamic orthodoxy, and also orthopraxy. See Nasr, Ideals and Realities of Islam, chaps. 5 and 6.

40. In Sunni Islam the ummah itself is the protector of the purity and continuity of the tradition; hence the principle of ijmāʿ or consensus which has been interpreted as the consensus of the religious scholars ('ulamāʾ) as well as the community as a whole. In Shīʿite Islam the function of preserving the tradition is performed by the Imam himself. See ʿAllāmah Ṭabāṭabāʾī, Shīʿite Islam, trans. S. H. Nasr, London and Albany (N.Y.), 1975, pp. 173ff.

41. In Judaism and Islam the law is an integral part of the religion and derives directly from the revelation. It is therefore traditional by definition. But even in Christianity which did not reveal a law, the law which was adopted by the Christian civilization of the Middle Ages from Roman and common law was still traditional, although because of the less direct relation of this law to the source of the Christian revelation, it became easier to reject the social aspects of Christian civilization at the time of the revolt against the Christian tradition than would have been possible in Islam or Judaism.

42. See R. Guénon, Autorité spirituelle et pouvoir temporel, Paris, 1929; A. K.

Coomaraswamy, *Spiritual Authority and Temporal Power in the Indian Theory of Government*, New Haven, 1942; S. H. Nasr, "Spiritual and Temporal Authority in Islam," in *Islamic Studies*, Beirut, 1967, pp. 6–13.

43. There are several notable works on tradition in its social aspect in European languages such as G. Eaton, *The King of the Castle: Choice and Responsibility in the Modern World*, London, 1977; M. Pallis, "The Active Life," in his *The Way and the Mountain*, London, 1960, pp. 36–61; A. K. Coomaraswamy, *The Religious Basis of the Forms of Indian Society*, New York, 1946; R. Guénon, *Introduction to the Study of the Hindu Doctrines*, Pt. 3, chaps. 5 and 6; and F. Schuon, *Castes and Race*, trans. Marco Pallis and Macleod Matheson, London, 1981.

44. For a discussion of these intellectual perspectives in Islam see Nasr, *Islamic Life and Thought*.

45. In later centuries "theosophy" associated with Boehme and his school in a sense replaced the earlier metaphysics of the Christian sages. The term "theosophy," although of Greek origin, did not become common in Christian intellectual life until the Renaissance.

46. "Il est impossible de nier que les plus illustres soufis, tout en étant 'gnostiques' par définition, furent en même temps un peu théologiens et un peu philosophes, ou que les grands théologiens furent à la fois un peu philosophes et un peu gnostiques, ce dernier mot devenant s'entendu dans son sense propre et non sectaire." Schuon, *Le Soufisme, voile et quintessence*, Paris, 1980, p. 105.

47. There is some difference in the way philosophy has been criticized by the traditional authors, the criticism of Schuon being more graded and shaded than that of Guénon who in order to clear the ground for the presentation of traditional doctrines opposed philosophy categorically (except for Hermeticism) identifying all philosophy with profane thought. See Guénon, *Introduction*, pt. 2, chap. 8. Schuon's more positive appreciation of philosophy in which he distinguishes between traditional philosophy and modern rationalism is found in many of his later writings esp. "Sur les traces de la notion de la philosophie," in his *Le Soufisme*, pp. 97–107.

48. See A. K. Coomaraswamy, "On the Pertinence of Philosophy," in *Contemporary Indian Philosophy*, ed. S. Radhakrishnan, London, 1936, pp. 113–34; as far as the Islamic tradition is concerned see S. H. Nasr, "The Meaning and Role of 'Philosophy' in Islam," *Studia Islamica* 36 (1973): 57–80.

49. On the meaning of theosophy see "Theosophie" by A. Faivre, in *Encyclopedia universalis*.

50. "When we sound the archetype, the ultimate origin of the form, then we find that it is anchored in the highest, not the lowest. . . . He who marvels that a formal symbol can remain alive not only for millennia, but that, as we shall yet learn, can spring to life again after an interval of thousands of years, should remind himself that the power from the spiritual world, which forms one part of the symbol, is everlasting." From W. Andrae, *Die Ionische Säule; Bauform oder Symbol?*, Berlin, 1933, pp. 65–66, quoted in A. K. Coomaraswamy, *The Vedas: Essays in Translation and Exegesis*, London, 1976, p. 146.

51. On this question see Guénon, *The Reign of Quantity and the Signs of Times*, trans. Lord Northbourne, Baltimore, 1973.

52. If half a century ago one had to read T. S. Eliot to become aware of the pathetic character of the spiritual condition of modern man, today there are numerous students of human society who have become aware that there is something deeply wrong with the premises upon which modernism is based and who have sought to study modern society from this point of view. See, for example, the well-known works of P. Berger such as *The Homeless Mind: Modernization and Consciousness*, New York, 1973; and those of I. Illich, *Celebration of Awareness*, New York, 1970; idem, *Energy and Equity*, London, 1974; idem, *Tools for Conviviality*, New York, 1973; and idem, *Tradition and Revolution*, New York, 1971.

There are numerous other criticisms of technology, science, the social order, etc., by other well-known figures such as L. Mumford, J. Ellul, and Th. Roszak. Roszak has in fact recorded many of these criticisms of various aspects of the modern world in his *Where the Wasteland Ends, The Unfinished Animal,* and *Person/Planet,* New York, 1980.

Despite the appearance of such works, however, it is amazing that those proponents of modernism who dominate a world which prides itself on being critical are so much lacking in a critical spirit when it comes to the examination of those premises and suppositions upon which the modernistic world view is based. "The *past,* out of which the tradition comes, is relativized [by the modernist relativizers] in terms of this or that socio-historical analysis. The *present,* however, remains strangely immune from relativization. In other words, the New Testament writers are seen as afflicted with a false consciousness rooted in their times, but the contemporary analyst takes the consciousness of *his* time as an unmixed intellectual blessing. The electricity- and radio-users are placed intellectually above the Apostle Paul." P. Berger, *A Rumor of Angels: Modern Society and the Rediscovery of the Supernatural,* New York, 1969, p. 51.

53. On traditional criticisms of the modern world see R. Guénon, *The Crisis of the Modern World,* trans. M. Pallis and R. Nicholson, London, 1975; and A. K. Coomaraswamy, "Am I My Brother's Keeper?" in his *The Bugbear of Literacy.*

54. Referring to his encounter with traditional authors, J. Needleman writes, "These were out for the kill. For them, the study of spiritual traditions was a sword with which to destroy the illusions of contemporary man." Needleman (ed.), *The Sword of Gnosis,* Baltimore, 1974, p. 9.

55. "When we look at human bodies, what we normally notice is their surface features, which of course differ markedly. Meanwhile on the inside the spines that support these motley physiognomies are structurally very much alike. It is the same with human outlooks. Outwardly they differ, but inwardly it is as if an 'invisible geometry' has everywhere been working to shape them to a single Truth.

"The sole notable exception is ourselves: our contemporary Western outlook differs in its very soul from what might otherwise be called 'the human unanimity' . . . If we succeed in correcting it [the misreading of modern science] we can rejoin the human race." H. Smith, *Forgotten Truth,* New York, 1976, pp. ix–x.

56. The well-known "Light Verse" is as follows: "Allah is the Light of the heavens and the earth. The similitude of His light is as a niche wherein is a lamp. The lamp is in a glass. The glass is as it were a shining star. (This lamp is) kindled from a blessed tree, an olive neither of the East nor of the West, whose oil would almost glow forth (of itself) though no fire touched it. Light upon light, Allah guideth unto His light whom He will. And Allah speaketh to mankind in allegories, for Allah is Knower of all things." Quran XXIV; 35—Pickthall translation.

Goethe who read the Quran when he was twenty-three years old wrote (in his *Aus dem Nachlass*):

> So der Westen wie der Osten
> Gehen Reines die zu kosten
> Lass die Grillen, lass die Schale
> Setze dich zum grossen Mahle.

58. As pointed out already the spread of modernism into the geographical Orient has destroyed to some extent the traditional civilizations of various parts of that world, but this does not mean that the sapiential dimension of the Oriental traditions in both their doctrinal and operative aspects which are of special concern to this study have been destroyed.

CHAPTER THREE

The Rediscovery of the Sacred: The Revival of Tradition

The words of wisdom are the lost objects of the faithful;
he must claim them wherever he finds them.
Ḥadīth of the Prophet of Islam

Remembering is for those who have forgotten.
Plotinus

The overall harmony and equilibrium of the cosmos required a movement within the heart and soul of at least a number of contemporary men to rediscover the sacred at the very moment when the process of secularization seemed to be reaching its logical conclusion in removing the presence of the sacred altogether from all aspects of human life and thought. The principle of cosmic compensation has brought to the fore the quest for the rediscovery of the sacred during the very period which the heralds of modernism had predicted to be the final phase of the depletion of human culture of its sacred content, the period whose dawn Nietzsche had declared a century ago when he spoke of the "death of God."[1] But many a contemporary man, having faced the terror of nihilism and the death of that which is human as a result of the effacing of the imprint of the Divinity upon the human face, has been confronted with the impelling attraction of the sacred which is both beyond and other than the secularized world that he calls "normal life." Such a person has felt the inner pull of the sacred at the center of his own being, the center which he carries with him wherever he may be. The quest for the rediscovery of the sacred, whether carried out consciously or in the form of groping in the dark, has become an element of the life of that humanity which has already experienced the loneliness of a world from which the Spirit has been banished. Needless to say, this quest has not always been successful but it has not always failed either, having reached its goal in a full and complete sense in those circles which have carried out the revival of tradition. The rediscovery of the sacred is ultimately and inextricably related to the revival of tradition, and the resuscitation of tradition and the possibility of living according to its tenets in the West during this century is the complete and final fulfillment of the quest of contemporary man for the rediscovery of the sacred.

The sapiential dimension which lies at the heart of tradition had become too weakened in the West to enable tradition to become revived during this century without authentic contact with the Oriental traditions which had preserved their inner teachings intact in both their doctrinal and operative aspects. Truncated and fragmented teachings of an originally esoteric nature issuing from the salons of Paris and other European cities were themselves too depleted of the presence of the sacred to enable modern Western man to rekindle the fire of the metaphysically penetrating intelligence and to enable the phoenix of sapience to arise from the ashes of a debilitating rationalism through recourse to what these circles offered. Already in the nineteenth century, what remained of knowledge of an originally sacred character had become more or less reduced to either occultism or a purely theoretical philosophy divorced from the possibility of realization, while even as theory it remained incomplete. That is why those who sought to rediscover sacred knowledge were attracted to the Orient despite the impossibility in most cases of gaining authentic knowledge of the Oriental traditions, especially as far as their inner dimensions were concerned.

The "lure" of the Orient is to be seen already in the eighteenth-century fascination in many European circles with China and also Egypt which, as far as the sources of traditional teachings are concerned, must be considered as an integral part of the Orient and the home of one of the most remarkable of traditional civilizations. Supposedly esoteric knowledge derived from Egypt, China, and other Eastern sources became a subject of discussion of occultist circles especially in France and such "restitutions" as the Egyptian Rite of

Cagliostro were carried out within Freemasonary.[2] Egyptology, as well as Orientalism in general, were closely associated at this time with the quest for a kind of knowledge which seemed to have been already lost in the mainstream of European thought. These disciplines, which in the nineteenth century became nearly completely "scientific" and rationalistic, were more in search of tradition and esoteric knowledge in the eighteenth century than is usually believed, although this search was rarely satisfied in a complete manner and certainly did not succeed in resuscitating the traditional point of view in such a way as to affect in any perceptible way the process of the desacralization of knowledge which was taking place at that time. Nor was this extensive transformation which was expected to happen in the West as a result of the dissemination of Oriental teachings and which was called a "second Renaissance" by Schopenhauer ever to take place during the nineteenth century when so many important works of Oriental wisdom were translated into European languages.[3]

Paradoxically enough, the nineteenth century, which from the metaphysical point of view marks the peak of the eclipse of tradition in the West, was also witness to the widespread interest in the study of the Orient and the translation of the sacred scriptures and works of a sapiential nature into various European languages by such master linguists as A. H. Anquetil Duperron, J. Hammer-Purgstall, and Sir William Jones. This was the period of intense activity in Orientalism which, despite its horrendous misdeeds, misinterpretations—both intentional and otherwise—condescending attitude toward natives, and servility to various political causes of European colonial powers, made available those hymns of gnosis and theophanies of pure metaphysics as the Upanishads,[4] the Tao-Te-Ching, and much of Sufi poetry. The history of Orientalism during this period is not our concern here for most of this activity was not related to either the rediscovery of the sacred or the revival of tradition but, in fact, served in many instances to destroy both the traditions it was studying and what remained of the Christian tradition which was often relativized by those who tried to make use of the presence of other religions to destroy the claim of Christians to the possession of truth in an absolute sense.[5] What concerns us here, therefore, is the case of the few philosophers and poets in the West who, being in quest of the sacred, sought to rediscover tradition in Oriental sources in an age which stood totally opposed to the traditional ideal.

Of all European countries, it was perhaps Germany where the influence of Oriental teachings was greatest partly because the Romantic movement possessed a greater intellectual content there than elsewhere and also because, as already mentioned, something of the Boehmian heritage still survived in his native land. To take one example, the translation into German of such masterpieces of Sufi poetry as the *Rose-Garden of Divine Mysteries* (*Gulshan-i rāz*) by Hammer-Purgstall had a profound effect upon notable German poets and created an avid interest in Oriental poetry and wisdom in a wide circle. Rückert was himself a translator of Persian and Arabic poetry as well as a poet of great quality who was influenced in his own works by Persian poetic symbols and images.[6]

The most notable figure of this period in Germany who was touched seriously on both the artistic and the intellectual planes by Oriental traditions, particularly Islam, was Goethe. He was intimately familiar with both the Quran and Islamic poetry, especially the works of Ḥāfiẓ, and even wrote a tragedy whose hero was the Prophet of Islam.[7] Goethe's grand response to that perfect wedding between metaphysical truth and poetic beauty which is the Divan of Ḥāfiẓ is the *West-östlicher Divan* which is unique in the annals of nineteenth-century European literature.[8] The opening verses,

> North and South and West are crumbling,
> Thrones are falling, kingdoms trembling:
> Come, flee away to purer East,
> There on patriarch's air to feast,
> There with love and drink and song
> Khiser's spring shall make thee young.

> There, pure and right where still they find,
> Will I drive all mortal kind
> To the great depths whence all things rise,
> There still to gain, in godly wise,
> Heaven's lore in earthly speech,
> Heads might break ere they could reach.[9]

have been often interpreted as Goethe's reaction to Napoleon's conquest of Europe. But his call is more fundamental than the response to a passing phenomenon of European history. It is a nostalgia for that immemorial tranquility of an Orient which is also the Origin and from which flows the fountain of eternal life guarded by Khiḍr,[10] an Orient still embedded in the peace and harmony of the traditional universe, before the shocking earthquakes of a world rebellious against Heaven and its imprint upon the human plane also reached the mountains and valleys of the East.

In England the quest for the Orient and the rediscovery of the sacred in various forms of archaic traditions included the revival of Platonism through the extensive translations of Floyer Sydenham and especially the remarkable scholar and Platonic philosopher Thomas Taylor. With the advent of Locke's *Essay Concerning Human Understanding*, the view of those who considered reason as a faculty which was developed in man "through the rationality displayed in the creation" triumphed over the older view that reason was "imparted from God directly to the mind of man" and therefore was wed to the Intellect and possessed a divine creative power.[11] The result was either the skepticism of a Hume concerning the power of reason or the religious activism of a John Wesley. The eighteenth century in England and Scotland was therefore one in which the Platonic concept of knowledge and of the process of knowing was nearly completely eclipsed. But a reaction soon set in against the prevalent philosophical tendencies, the reaction taking several different forms, of which the most important was the revival of Platonism.[12]

Thomas Taylor, who was the major factor in the revival of Platonism and in making the writings of Plato, the Neoplatonists, and Aristotle accessible in the English language, was not just a scholar of Greek. Rather, he belonged philosophically to the Platonic school and saw knowledge as the primary means of reaching the sacred. The premises of his world view stood opposed to the secularizing and rationalistic tendencies of his day. He still conceived of knowledge in a principial manner, as a way of attaining deliverance. The problem was that he stood outside the Christianity of his day and sought consciously to revive Greek paganism as if it were possible to resuscitate through a purely human agency a tradition whose animating spirit had already departed from the earthly plane.[13] Be that as it may, his edition of the complete works of Plato in 1804, along with so many other basic texts of Neoplatonism, played an important role in making accessible a traditional metaphysics, one of the most complete in the West, for those seeking an alternative to the secularizing philosophies and sciences of the time.[14] His work, in a sense, complemented the translation and introduction of Oriental doctrines into the English-speaking world, and many who were drawn to Taylor's works were likewise attracted to Oriental teachings. Taylor also influenced greatly such Romantic figures as Carlyle and Coleridge, but the most important personality whom he influenced was William Blake who was at the forefront of the movement seeking to reestablish the primacy of the sacred against all the prevalent tendencies of that day.

In recent years, Blake has appeared as a hero of those who seek to return to a more wholistic view of man and nature against the mechanistic and rationalistic conceptions of the world and of man represented by Bacon, Newton, and Locke, whom Blake opposed so strongly. The avid interest in Blake today is related closely to the intense search of those in the modern world who, tired and wary of the suffocating landscape of their secularized ambience, are seeking alternative philosophies and views of the cosmos. Moreover, rather than an eccentric poet of genius, as his contemporaries saw him, Blake appears today to many who are attracted to the traditional point of view as being more of a harbinger of certain aspects of tradition than just an individualistic rebel, and as a poet who was essentially traditional but who appeared as a rebel at a time when the established order and world view were themselves so antitraditional. The celebrated contemporary British poetess, Kathleen Raine, in fact believes that Blake possessed a secret and esoteric knowledge of an authentic traditional character.[15]

There is no doubt that he had knowledge of Western traditional sources and possibly some Oriental ones through translation. Also it is certain that he possessed visionary powers and combined a sense for the rediscovery of the sacred with poetic genius. Although his traditional knowledge was not complete and there are elements of an excessively individualistic nature in his artistic work which prevent his art from being characterized as traditional, there is no doubt that Blake represents one of the most powerful and effective attempts of the last century to convey the sense of the quest for the sacred and to criticize a world from which the gods and the angels seemed to have been banished. In his works, there is a strong sense, unique in its intensity in nineteenth-century English literature, of the struggle of the soul in its mortal combat against forces which would deprive it of the nourishment of the world of the Spirit and a revolt against limiting the scope of knowledge to that externalized reason which is the parody of the sanctifying intellect.[16] Blake is also the gate to the positive reappraisal of myth which was to be followed by his most important commentator, Yeats, and others during this century, and which is so closely allied to the quest for the rediscovery of the sacred.

In America also, amidst a strongly active and in many ways anti-traditional climate, the influence of the Orient was to be seen among those philosophers and poets most in quest of a sacred vision of life, such figures as Walt Whitman, Ralph Waldo Emerson, and the New England Transcendentalists in general. But it is especially in the works of Emerson that the attraction toward the Orient is to be seen most clearly, in the poet-philosopher for whom Asia was "a wonderland of literature and philosophy."[17] Emerson was especially inebriated by the message of the Upanishads, whose nondualistic doctrine contained so lucidly in the *Katha-Upanishad,* is reflected in his well-known poem "Brahma":

> *If the red slayer think he slays,*
> *Or if the slain think he is slain,*
> *They know not well the subtle ways*
> *I keep, and pass, and turn again.*

Emerson also concluded his essay on immortality with the story of Nachiketas drawn again from the *Katha-Upanishad.*[18]

In addition to Hindu sources, Emerson was greatly attracted to Persian poets, especially Saʿdī, and wrote an introduction for the first American edition of the translation of his *Gulistān* which appeared in 1865.[19] Moreover, he read other Oriental sources extensively and quotes Zoroaster often, although most of what he considered to be by Zoroaster were works of Oriental inspiration of the Hellenistic period attributed to the Persian prophet. The love of Emerson for these works of Oriental origin marks an important phase in America, paralleling what was occurring in Europe, a phase in which aid was sought from the surviving traditions of the East to resuscitate that *sapientia* which had become nearly completely lost in the West.

But neither such great poets as Goethe, Blake, or Emerson, nor for stronger reasons the prevalent occultism of nineteenth-century France associated with such names as Eliphas Lévi and Papus, could bring tradition back to the soil of the West in a total and complete way nor revive that *scientia sacra* which lies at the heart of all tradition. It remained for the Orient itself to bring about the revival of tradition in the West through the pen and words of those who lived in Europe or wrote in Western languages but who had been transformed intellectually and existentially by the traditional world view. The study of the quest of nineteenth-century figures, some of whom have been mentioned, for the rediscovery of the sacred in Oriental teachings and the attempt to regain knowledge of a traditional character in occultist and pseudoesoteric circles at that time, as well as the combination of these endeavours in such movements as the Theosophical Society and "spiritualism" with an Eastern coloring, provides a valuable background for the understanding of the significance of the appearance of authentic traditional teachings in the West during the early decades of this century. Such a study reveals in fact why a fresh restatement from the Orient was necessary at that time.

The dissemination of traditional teachings commenced in the West during the first two decades of this century when a small number of Europeans were given direct instruction and initiation into the esoteric schools of various Oriental traditions by authentic representatives of these traditions.[20] To be sure, such contacts had also existed occasionally during the nineteenth century, as for example in the case of H. Wilberforce Clarke who was received into Sufism and whose translations of Ḥāfiẓ and ʿUmar Suhrawardī are based on oral tradition as well as written sources. But what distinguished what occurred in the early part of this century from these already mentioned isolated cases was that, in contrast to the nineteenth century, the twentieth-century representatives of the traditional perspective possessed full knowledge of traditional teachings and were intellectually prepared to implant the tree of tradition upon the soil of the Western world with effects far beyond the rare contact with various Oriental traditions during the preceding decades.

The central figure who was most responsible for the presentation of the traditional doctrines of the Orient in their fullness in the modern West was René Guénon, a man who was chosen for this task by Tradition itself and who fulfilled an intellectual function of a supraindividual nature.[21] Guénon (1886–1951) was born and educated in France where he studied philosophy and mathematics before turning to various occult circles which were active in his youth when he was in quest of authentic knowledge which he could not discover in either the official university circles or in religious sources available to him at that time. But he could not discover what he was seeking in these occult groups any more than he could in the then accessible academic or religious organizations. In fact, he discovered within the so-called "esoteric" groups which he frequented all kinds of aberrations and outlandish pretensions which he was to study and to expose with such detail in later life. Sometime during the first few years of this century, when he was still a young man, he was initiated into Sufism and also received esoteric knowledge from authentic Hindu sources. Henceforth, he began to write on various traditional themes for the journal *Le Voile d'Isis* which under its later title *Études Traditionnelles* was to become the main vehicle for the exposition of the traditional perspective in Europe, containing articles not only by him and his students and associates but also by other outstanding masters of traditional doctrines such as Coomaraswamy and Schuon. The first book of Guénon, *Introduction générale à l'étude des doctrines hindoues*, published in Paris in 1921, was also the first full exposition of the main aspects of traditional doctrines. It was like a sudden burst of lightning, an abrupt intrusion into the modern world of a body of knowledge and a perspective utterly alien to the prevalent climate and world view and completely opposed to all that characterizes the modern mentality. During the next thirty years, Guénon was to produce a vast number of books, articles, and reviews which form an integral whole as if he had written them all at one sitting and then published them over the next few decades. This lack of a historical development, due also in part to the fact that his function was to express metaphysical and cosmological doctrines and not the operative and existential aspects of tradition nor scholarly research, appears all the more remarkable in that his personal life was transformed completely during this period. He openly embraced Islam, migrated to Cairo, married an Egyptian, lived in a traditional house near the Pyramids both physically and architecturally far away from his Paris residence, and was buried in a cemetery near Cairo which, even in the present semimodernized crowded climate of that city, is as far removed from the cultural ambience of his native France as one can imagine. Guénon, as he is reflected in his writings, seemed to be more of an intellectual function than a "man." His lucid mind and style and great metaphysical acumen seemed to have been chosen by traditional Sophia itself to formulate and express once again that truth from whose loss the modern world was suffering so grievously.

To accomplish such a task, Guénon had to be in a sense an extremist; he had to clear the ground completely in order to remove all possibility of error. He therefore adopted a polemical and uncompromising tone which has hindered many people from appreciating his exposition of traditional wisdom. To build the edifice of traditional knowledge he had to break down and remove the rubble of all that pretended to provide ultimate knowledge for modern man. He thereby began a systematic criticism of all that stood in the way of the understanding of tradition; playing a thankless iconoclastic role, Guénon devoted several studies to a detailed study and rejection of the various occultist, pseudoesoteric, and modernistic groups which pretended to possess sacred knowledge of either the Oriental or Western traditions. He was particularly critical of theosophy in the sense of the Theosophical Society of Mme. Blavatsky and Annie Besant, spiritualism of various kinds, and the modernistic movements in India affected by the West such as the Arya Samaj and Brahma Samaj, and discussed in detail the dangers of "initiation" into such pseudotraditional bodies from which he had suffered himself and which he knew well through personal experience.[22]

Guénon then set about to criticize the modern world itself, attacking not its accidental faults and shortcomings but the very premises upon which it stands. His *Crisis of the Modern World*, written in 1927, contains pages which seem "prophetic" today in retrospect, while his *The Reign of Quantity and the Signs of the Times* records in a masterly fashion the unfolding of the human cycle according to traditional principles relating much that has occurred and is occurring in the world today to perfectly intelligible principles.[23]

We are not concerned here with Guénon's criticism of the modern world as far as the social and political aspects of life are concerned. What is of particular interest for our study of the quest for the sacred in its sapiential aspect is his severe criticism of various modes of knowing prevalent in the modern world. As mentioned already, Guénon, who had studied European philosophy, was severely critical of all that is called modern philosophy, and in fact of "philosophy" as such, which he tried to refute completely as a legitimate manner of knowing principles. His criticism was extreme and uncompromising because he wanted to prevent any confusion between what modern man understands as philosophy and traditional metaphysics. His excess in this domain was due to the fact that he wanted at all costs to prevent metaphysics from being reduced to the category of profane thought. In his exaggeration, he overlooked the positive aspects of traditional philosophy, and even the term philosophy, to which Schuon was to point later.

Guénon was also thoroughly critical of modern science not because of what it has accomplished but because of the reductionism and also pretensions which have been associated with science in the modern world. His greatest criticism of modern science was its lack of metaphysical principles and its pretension, or rather the pretension of those who claim to speak from the "scientific point of view," to be *the* science or *the* way of knowing, whereas it is *a* science or *a* way of knowing concerned with a very limited domain of reality. This theme runs throughout Guénon's writings and he never tired of pointing out that the science of any domain would be legitimate provided it were not cut off from principles of a higher order and the traditional world view.[24] His criticism of modern science was a logical and intellectual one, based on neither sentiments nor even theological concerns derived from a particular form of revealed truth. Guénon in fact sought to demonstrate how it was possible to develop a science which was exact and "scientific" even in the contemporary sense but not divorced from metaphysical principles, choosing for this purpose the field of mathematics which he knew well.[25] Moreover, Guénon sought to expound the principles of some of the traditional sciences such as geometry and alchemy,[26] demonstrating that these sciences, far from being early stages of development of modern sciences which had now been outgrown, were sciences of another order providing a veritable knowledge of various aspects of cosmic reality, sciences which remained as valid today as in the days gone by if only one were to understand their symbolic language, sciences which were not in any way invalidated by other sciences developed later and dealing with the same subject matters.

Since Guénon was seeking to revive tradition through the presentation of Oriental doctrines, he also had to clear the ground of other misleading sources which also dealt with Oriental teachings, namely, works of orientalism. Here also, his criticism was massive and total and not based on discrimination between works of various degrees of value. To be sure, as already mentioned, most works of orientalism, although providing material for the study of the Orient, have been written from a point of view which is, to put it mildly, a hindrance to the understanding of the very subject the orientalists were, and in fact are still, trying in many cases to study. But there have also been works of both a scholarly and intellectual value produced by those who have been officially called orientalists.[27] Guénon rejected the whole enterprise of orientalism, neglecting worthwhile works, in order to avoid once again any error which might creep into the mind of the reader and prevent him from understanding traditional doctrines from their own point of view.

Parallel with this clearing of the ground, Guénon set about to expound metaphysics and cosmology from the traditional point of view and in relation to and as contained in the sapiential teachings of various traditions. His point of departure was Hinduism and his first purely metaphysical exposition was the *Man and His Becoming According to the Vedanta*. But he also dealt extensively with Islam and Taoism, the Kabbala, certain medieval esoteric currents in Christianity, and Hermeticism.[28] Moreover, Guénon wrote a number of works on general metaphysical and cosmological subjects such as *Oriental Metaphysics*, *Les États multiples de l'être*, *Symboles fondamentaux de la science sacré*, and *La Grande triade*. All in all, he was able to produce a vast corpus based on the primacy of knowledge and intelligence as their powers and possibilities are actualized by various objective modes of revelation which lie at the heart of the traditions that have governed the life of humanity over the ages. In his works is to be found one of the most important restatements of the doctrinal aspect of the knowledge of the sacred in modern times and they mark a major step in the rediscovery of sacred knowledge and the revival of tradition. Guénon did not establish another *ism* or one school of thought among others. There is no such thing as Guénonianism despite the misunderstanding of certain groups in Europe who call themselves Guénonians. What Guénon did emphasize is the necessity of following fully a living tradition and accepting the traditional perspective. But precisely because the modern world is what it is, one can refer to the reestablishment of the traditional perspective by him and others amidst a world alien to such a world view as the founding of a "school" or perspective, one which is both very much alive and pertinent to the contemporary world and distinct from different forms of modernism which, despite differences among themselves, stand opposed to it.

The work of Guénon in reviving the traditional point of view was complemented by another metaphysician of remarkable acumen and amplitude, Ananda K. Coomaraswamy (1877—1947), who was born of a Singalese father and an English mother. Like Guénon, Coomaraswamy began with the study of science but while the "abstract" bent of mind of Guénon had attracted him to mathematics, Coomaraswamy, who was always sensitive to the meaning of forms, was drawn to geology, a descriptive science in which he became an established authority. His temperament complemented that of Guénon in more than one way. While Guénon was a metaphysician not drawn greatly to artistic forms, Coomaraswamy was profoundly moved by forms of art and was in fact drawn to tradition when working as a geologist in the hills and mountains of Ceylon (Sri Lanka) and India he became witness to the rapid destruction of the traditional art and civilization of his homeland. Also Coomaraswamy was a meticulous scholar concerned with details while Guénon was essentially a metaphysician and mathematician concerned with principles.[29] Even in personal traits and styles of writing, the two men complemented each other, yet they were in perfect agreement about the validity of the traditional perspective and the metaphysical principles which lie at the heart of all traditional teachings.

Coomaraswamy was a man of immense energy who left a vast body of writings behind.[30] With the many works which introduced Oriental art, especially that of India, Sri Lanka, and Indonesia, to the West we are not concerned here. Suffice it to say that his years of maturity in England and especially the last thirty years of his life in America, where he was curator of Oriental art at the Boston Museum of Fine Arts, played a major role in bringing a vital aspect of Oriental civilizations, namely, their art, to the attention of the Western public. But Coomaraswamy was not a historian of art; his interest in the study of traditional art was in the truth which it conveyed. His studies were of an intellectual order, and in such works as the *Transformation of Nature in Art* and *The Christian and Oriental Philosophy of Art* he expounded a metaphysics of art which presents traditional art as a vehicle for the exposition of knowledge of a sacred order.

Like Guénon, Coomaraswamy also wrote in an unrelenting manner against modernism, emphasizing more than Guénon the devastations brought about by industrialization upon the traditional crafts and patterns of life in the West as well as in the Orient itself. But Coomaraswamy also addressed himself to the intellectual issues involved; in fact, he undertook a series of works called the "Bugbear Series" at the end of his life, of which only the *Bugbear of Literacy* was published before his death and which sought to destroy the various false gods of modernism through recourse to intellectual principles.

As for metaphysics and cosmology, Coomaraswamy produced numerous articles and books in which he drew freely from Hindu, Buddhist, and Islamic sources as well as from Plato, Plotinus, Dionysius, Dante, Erigena, Eckhart, Boehme, Blake, and other representatives of the Western sapiential tradition. Like Guénon, he emphasized the unity of the truth which lies at the heart of all traditions, the unity to which Coomaraswamy devoted his well-known essay "Paths That Lead to the Same Summit."[31] Besides his several works on the Hindu and Buddhist traditions of which *Hinduism and Buddhism* is an intellectual synthesis, Coomaraswamy also wrote such purely metaphysical works as *Recollection, Indian and Platonic, On the One and Only Transmigrant,* and *Time and Eternity.*

Coomaraswamy was deeply concerned with myth and symbol, with the so-called primitive mentality and traditional anthropology. His studies of religious symbolism and the traditional significance of myth played a major role in the resuscitation of interest in myth and symbol among many scholars of religion despite the so-called demythologizing tendency so evident in certain schools of Protestant and even Catholic theology. Coomaraswamy also devoted many studies to the traditional sciences ranging from his essay on the symbolism of zero in Indian mathematics to his treatise on the distinction between the traditional doctrine of graduation and modern evolution. Altogether, his works presented traditional teachings in the language of contemporary scholarship and with such immense learning and clarity of expression that, despite the nearly total opposition of modern milieus against his ideas when he first began to expound them, he wielded a great deal of influence among a vast spectrum of scholars and thinkers ranging from art historians to physicists, an influence which continues to this day. At the heart of this remarkable intellectual edifice lay the concept of knowledge of the sacred and sacred knowledge; in fact his works, as those of Guénon, were themselves the product of an intellect which breathed and functioned in a world of sacred character, a world which reflects the very substance of intelligence itself.

The task of the completion of the revival and exposition of traditional teachings in the contemporary world was to be carried out by Frithjof Schuon (b. 1907) whose works crown the body of contemporary traditional writings. If Guénon was the master expositor of metaphysical doctrines and Coomaraswamy the peerless scholar and connoisseur of Oriental art who began his exposition of metaphysics through recourse to the language of artistic forms, Schuon seems like the cosmic intellect itself impregnated by the energy of divine grace surveying the whole of the reality surrounding man and elucidating all the concerns of human existence in the light of sacred knowledge. He seems to be endowed with the intellectual power to penetrate into the heart and essence of all things, and especially religious universes of form and meaning, which he has clarified in an unparalleled fashion as if he were bestowed with that divine gift to which the Quranic revelation refers as the "language of the birds." No wonder that one of the leading American historians of religion, Huston Smith, says concerning him, "The man is a living wonder; intellectually *à propos* religion, equally in depth and breadth, the paragon of our time. I know of no living thinker who begins to rival him."[32]

Schuon has written of not only traditional doctrines but also the practical and operative aspects of the spiritual life. He has written of rites, prayer, love, faith, the spiritual virtues, and the moral life from the sapiential point of view. Moreover, he has expanded the horizon of traditional expositions to include certain aspects of the Christian tradition, especially Orthodoxy which was passed over by Guénon, as well as the American Indian tradition and Shintoism. He has expounded in all its grandeur the metaphysics of virgin nature and, being himself an outstanding poet and painter in addition to a metaphysician, has written some of the most remarkable pages on the metaphysics of traditional art and the spiritual significance of beauty.

Most of Schuon's numerous works have been translated into English although some are available still only in their original French and German.[33] These works include a series on comparative religion from the point of view of the *sophia perennis*, including his first work to be translated into English *The Transcendent Unity of Religions*,[34] and books devoted somewhat more particularly, although not exclusively, to specific traditions, such works as *Language of the Self*, concerned mostly with Hinduism; *In the Tracks of Buddhism,* which also includes a section on Shintoism; *Understanding Islam, Dimensions of Islam,* and *Islam and the Perennial Philosophy,* dealing with different facets of Islam including both Shī'ism and Sufism; *Le Soufisme, voile et quintessence,* devoted nearly completely to Sufism, as well as *Gnosis: Divine Wisdom* which contains sections on the Christian tradition. In *Spiritual Perspectives and Human Facts* and *Light on the Ancient World* he has dealt with the crisis of modern civilization and surveyed many facets of human history from the traditional point of view, while in such works as *L'Oeil du coeur* and *Stations of Wisdom* he has elucidated some of the most complex metaphysical and cosmological questions as well as elements of the practical aspect of the realization of knowledge. As for most of his recent works such as *Logic and Transcendence, Formes et substance dans les religions, Esoterism as Principle and as Way,* and *Du Divin à l'humain* (which is the synopsis of all his metaphysical teachings), they deal more than anything else with sacred knowledge and the ultimately sacred character of the faculty which knows. They are the final testament of pure gnosis reflecting both upon the object of knowledge and the subject or consciousness whose root is the Sacred as such.

The concern of Schuon in these works has been to elaborate the meaning of all that is human in the light of the Divine and with the aim of making possible the return to the Divine through a mode which is primarily sapiential but which is always wed to love and faith. Schuon speaks from the point of view of realized knowledge not theory, and his writings bear an "existential" impact that can only come from realization. No one can understand the message of these words and remain "existentially" the same. No wonder that upon the appearance of his first three books, an English Catholic could write,

> The Transcendent Unity of Religions, L'Oeil du coeur and Spiritual Perspectives and Human Facts not only show an understanding of Christian truth, precisely as truth, . . . but also exhibit an interior dimension in that understanding which no mere scholarship could produce. If in the Transcendent Unity he speaks of the way of Grace as one who understands that Divine economy in relation to the esoteric and exoteric paths of Islam, and in principle, in relation to exotericism and esotericism as such, in Spiritual Perspectives he speaks of Grace as one in whom it is operative and as it were in virtue of that operation. The book has a fulness of light which we have no right to find in the twentieth century, or perhaps in any other century.[35]

With Schuon's writings the full-fledged revival of tradition as related to the rediscovery of the sacred in the heart of all traditions and by virtue and through the aid of tradition in the heart of virgin nature, sacred art, and the very substance of the human being has taken place, making it possible amidst a world suffocating from the poisonous atmosphere of nihilism and doubt for those who "are called" to gain access to knowledge of the highest order rooted in the sacred and therefore inseparable from the joy and light of certitude.

The traditional point of view expanded with such rigor, depth, and grandeur by Guénon, Commaraswamy, and Schuon has been singularly neglected in academic circles and limited in diffusion as far as its "horizontal" and quantitative dissemination is concerned. But its appeal in depth and quality has been immeasurable. Being the total truth, it has penetrated into the hearts, minds, and souls of certain individuals in such a way as to transform their total existence. Moreover, ideas emanating from this quarter have had an appeal to an even larger circle than that of those who have adopted totally and completely the traditional point of view, and many scholars and thinkers of note have espoused certain basic traditional theses. As far as those who must be considered as belonging to the small circle of traditional authors are concerned, one should mention first of all Titus Burckhardt, residing in Switzerland, who has presented several basic works of Islamic esoterism in European languages with a lucidity and transparency of mind that is incredible and has also enriched the field of art with numerous studies of sacred art, accomplishing especially for Islamic art what Coomaraswamy had done for Hindu and Buddhist art.[36] In France Leo Schaya has applied traditional principles to produce one of the most penetrating studies on the Kabbala to appear in this century. In Italy G. Evola, who collaborated with Guénon, wrote several major studies on Hinduism, Hermeticism, and other traditions in a spirit akin to that of Guénon, while in recent years such figures as E. Zolla have continued to present a series of works of a traditional character especially on traditional literature and certain of the traditional sciences.

Outside of continental Europe it has been primarily England which has been the site of activity of traditional authors of significance. Here Marco Pallis, of Greek origin but living in Great Britain, who had traveled to the Himalayas in search of botanical specimens but returned with flowers of Buddhist wisdom, was the first person to present Tibetan Buddhism in an authentic manner to the West and is the author of the famous *Peaks and Lamas,* which was one of the very few serious works on the Oriental traditions available in European languages before the Second World War.[38] Also in this same land, for years Martin Lings has been making available treasures of Islamic esoterism from the traditional point of view and applying his intimate knowledge of spirituality combined with a gift for poetry to shed new light upon such figures of English literature as Shakespeare.[39] Here also such Catholic scholars and artists as Eric Gill and Bernard Kelly fell under the sway of the teachings of Guénon, Coomaraswamy, and Schuon, as have a number of orthodox figures. The activity of traditional authors has gradually gravitated around the journal *Studies in Comparative Religion,* which has now become perhaps the leading traditional journal in the Western world,[40] but the circle of those concerned with tradition has also widened steadily over the past few decades.[41]

As for America, the number of those who belonged fully to the traditional perspective had been very limited until recent years, despite the long presence in that land of Coomaraswamy whose writings influenced numerous scholars of whom few embraced the traditional point of view fully. But in America such scholars as J. E. Brown have sought to study the American Indian tradition from the traditional point of view,[42] while a number of scholars of religion such as H. Smith and V. Danner have produced important works of traditional character in recent years[43] and an ever greater number of figures covering a wide spectrum continue to be drawn to different elements of tradition, without their adopting the traditional point of view as such.[44]

The presence of the works and the emanation of ideas of those who revived tradition in the West have had an influence in one way or another upon many well-known figures in different fields of intellectual endeavor and scholarship, including the eminent historian of religion M. Eliade (at least in his earlier works), the foremost French authority of Islamic philosophy H. Corbin, the German scholar and critic L. Ziegler, the Indologist H. Zimmer, the mythologist J. Campbell, the art historian M. Schneider, the French philosopher G. Durand, the celebrated English poetess and scholar Kathleen Raine, and the remarkable economist turned traditional philosopher and theologian E. C. Schumacher.[45]

The revival of tradition in the West based upon the exposition of authentic Oriental doctrines and teachings has also had an echo in the

Orient, itself faced with the destruction of its own millennial traditions as a result of the onslaught of modernism.[46] Some of the works of traditional authors have been translated into Oriental languages ranging from Tibetan to Arabic and have provided intellectual arguments against certain tenets of modernism, arguments whose formulation had been for the most part impossible for most Orientals themselves, usually unaware of the deeper forces which have brought about modernism and often suffering from an inferiority complex vis-à-vis the modern West.[47] Needless to say, however, those among the modernized Orientals who have grasped the meaning of these traditional works have been limited in number, as can be seen by the intellectual quality of the response to the modern world which usually issues from those in the East who have become affected by modernism to any appreciable degree or from those still traditional but addressing the modern world of whose nature they are ignorant.

The quest for the sacred and the revival of tradition have also taken place in a more partial and limited but sometimes profound manner outside the major movement for the revival of tradition already outlined, although it was without doubt the sinking of the roots of authentic traditional teachings on the soil of Europe that transformed the cosmic ambience and created an opening in this cosmic sector which is the West to enable traditional teachings to spread to the West from other sources. The craving for the Orient has drawn many people in quest, not of wealth or worldly glory, but of the Land of Light to various countries of the East ranging from Japan to Morocco, which from the traditional point of view is part of the Orient. Not all these quests have resulted in serious contacts or the transmission of traditional knowledge, even when the possibility has arisen to encounter authentic representatives of the Oriental traditions.

There were, however, exceptions. Such Japanese masters as Roshi Tachibana and Hindus as Śri Ramana Maharshi and Anandamoyi Ma have emanated a presence, as well as spiritual instruction, which has crossed the ocean and the land to reach certain circles in the West. Likewise, the emanation of the teachings of certain Sufi masters from many different parts of the Islamic world has reached the West during the last few decades. Moreover, many representatives of these traditions, some authentic and others modernized, have traveled in ever greater numbers to Europe and America, ranging from a Vivekananda, who had a missionary zeal to present a modernized version of the Vedanta to the West but who nevertheless remained related to the teachings of the great Indian saint Ramakrishna,[48] to the prolific Japanese expositor of Zen, D. T. Suzuki, to the remarkable lamas forced out of Tibet after the Chinese invasion and the Sufi masters who have visited the West with increasing frequency during the past few years. This fresh, direct contact with the Orient has of course been of significance in the revival of tradition in the West, despite the role played by the army of pseudogurus and yogis in creating the confusion which characterizes the modern world. It also remains a fact that for many people it is difficult, without access to the traditional teachings connected with those who revived tradition in the West, to grasp the significance of what they do encounter in Oriental teachings, although there are exceptions and there is of course the question of different temperaments which require different types of instruction. The traditional circle, as described above, is like the Intellect or *Buddhi* of the domain of tradition in the modern world, casting its light and presence as the faculty which discriminates the true from the false, and elucidates, clarifies, and integrates the world in which different spiritual modes and ways, including those of work or service and love, function along with the way of knowledge which is the concern par excellence of the Intellect.

The revival of tradition has also involved to some degree, besides Oriental doctrines, the reappraisal of the classical Greek tradition, although the need still remains in the present day for the full reevaluation of the Greek intellectual heritage in the light of tradition. Already, however, there have been several studies of the Pythagorean-Platonic tradition based not upon the Renaissance and post-Renaissance humanism which has colored the study of Greek philosophy in the West ever since, but upon the perspective which sees the Pythagorean-Platonic school as being related to the universal Tradition. The discovery of the Pythagorean scale by von Thimus during the last century, followed by the studies on harmonics of H. Keyser and in recent years the appreciation of Plato as a Pythagorean philosopher[49] by E. McClain and others, represents the rediscovery of an important element of the Greek tradition. Also the extensive works of R. A. Schwaller de Lubicz on Egypt, as well as on Hermeticism, based on traditional principles and sources, seem astounding, especially when one speaks to those who knew him personally.[50]

These and other studies in different arts and sciences represent another facet of the rediscovery of the sacred and the revival of tradition with which we are concerned here. There have existed amidst this most antitraditional period of art attempts to practice once again the traditional art of both Eastern and Western origin, ranging from the revival of calligraphy to architecture, and to rediscover the intellectual principles of the arts in both East and West.[51] Important elements of traditional mathematics, especially geometry, have been reconstituted.[52] Much interest is to be seen in many circles in the meaning of traditional science itself and the significance of these sciences as at least alternative modes of knowledge of cosmic reality.

Another contemporary phenomenon related to the quest for the rediscovery of the sacred is the increase of interest in the study of myth and symbols. One can detect much change from the days when men like Frazer, whom Coomaraswamy called "hewers of wood," were collecting myths without the least interest in their inner significance to the contemporary interest shown by a significant number of scholars of religion and art, as well as philosophers and psychologists, in myths and symbols as keys for the understanding of both traditional man and the way he envisaged the cosmic environment. The identification of myth with the unreal is hardly as automatic in disciplined intellectual discourse today as a century ago. Yet, although some have now realized the significance of myth and symbol as distinct from facts, in the same way that a geologist would distinguish a crystal from opaque rock, in most cases there is still no light in which the crystal of myth could display its real qualities. That light can only come from a living tradition without which the study of myths and symbols, even if appreciated, usually dwindles to psychological interpretations or, at best, a science emptied of spiritual significance. The revival of the study of myths and symbols in modern times certainly signifies the quest of contemporary man for a universe of meaning and the sacred, but this quest cannot achieve its goal without the help of and through recourse to tradition itself. The study of myth and symbol cannot result in the knowledge of the sacred but is the means to this knowledge, provided the mind which studies myths and symbols is already transformed by the light and grace of tradition.

Strangely enough, the quest for the sacred is to be seen even in certain sectors of modern science which epitomizes secular knowledge and has been the primary force for the secularization of the world since the seventeenth century. Needless to say, that type of reason which has surrendered itself to the results of an empirical science refuses to see the metaphysical implications of modern science. In fact, scientistic philosophers are much more dogmatic than many scientists in denying any metaphysical significance to the discoveries of science. But the physicists themselves, or at least many of the outstanding figures among them, have often been the first to deny scientism and even the so-called scientific method. Much of the most serious theological discussions of the past decades have issued from the quarter of scientists rather than philosophers, and especially theologians, who seem, paradoxically enough, just about the last group to grasp the significance of the work of many scientists seeking to go beyond the scientific reductionism which has played such a role in the desacralization of nature and of knowledge itself.[53]

Let us take a look at contemporary physics with an independent mind and without becoming either mesmerized by the unscientific extrapolations of science into fantastic views of the cosmos, which seem to change with about the same rapidity as dress fashions, or hypnotized by the lure of the microscope.[54] Most of the major discoveries of physics since Einstein's 1905 theory of special relativity was announced have been the result not of induction or empirical observation but the consideration of aesthetic factors, search for unity, symmetry, and harmony. How often have well-known physicists proposed a theory which they have supported because it was mathematically speaking more "elegant"? Why is there this search for unity in the study of the laws of nature and, in fact, the attainment of ever greater or higher stages of unity? What about the appeal of Einstein in 1905 and Dirac in 1929 to symmetry, leading respectively to the special theory of relativity and antimatter, long before experimental evidence could be provided? Finally, how can one evaluate the so-called Pythagorean period of modern physics covering the era from Bohr to de Broglie, when very important contributions based on Pythagorean harmony and with full knowledge of musical harmony were made to modern physics? One could interpret these episodes as confirmations within the domain of modern physics of principles of a metaphysical and cosmological order not belonging to the physical sciences themselves. Such an interpretation would do no injustice to physics. It is, in fact, today of greater attraction to many physicists than the type of so-called philosophical interpretation which would claim that all is relative because of the theory of relativity or that free will is proven because of Heisenberg's indeterminacy principle. To be sure, traditional principles cannot be proven through modern physics but this physics, to the extent that it corresponds to an aspect of reality, can be a legitimate science whose ultimate significance can be grasped only through traditional metaphysics. In fact, this science could in principle be integrated into a higher form of knowledge if only this knowledge were available in such a manner as to transform the intellectual climate of the contemporary world and if modern science were to accept the limitations inherent in its premises and assumptions.[55]

Another aspect of modern physics brings us back to the meaning of intelligence and consciousness themselves. To study a particle like the electron means to relate, in a much more direct manner than in classical physics, the intelligence of the agent which knows to that which is known. In fact, by its behavior the electron seems to possess a kind of intelligence itself. No matter how deeply the heart of matter is pierced there is seen order and intelligibility which demonstrate the penetration of intelligence into the very heart of what is called material manifestation, until the stage bordering on chaos is reached where that which is called material simply ceases to exist.[56] Man's consciousness must be seen even in physics as an integral part of that reality which the physicist seeks to study, to the extent that Eugene Wigner, one of the founders of quantum mechanics, calls consciousness the first absolute reality and outward reality secondary reality.[57] The consciousness which is the direct reflection and ray of the Intellect and the substance of sacred knowledge is seen as an element with which the physicist has no choice but to be concerned, whether the mystery of human subjectivity and the divine origin of consciousness is understood and accepted by him or not.

Likewise, the idea of the world standing out there comprised of mutually exclusive objects whose motions and relations are studied by the physicist in an order which is ultimately mechanical has been questioned by such physicists as David Bohm, who now speaks of an "implicate order" resembling certain Oriental cosmological doctrines.[58] The birth and death of symmetrical particles from "nothing" and to "nothing" have also challenged the idea of the presence of the vacuum in modern science. What appears physically as emptiness is actually an ocean of virtual objects even from the physical point of view. What appears as empty in the cosmos is much more akin to the Far Eastern void and also the ether of traditional Western cosmologies than the vacuum of Newtonian physics. No wonder that during recent years there have appeared a score of works seeking to relate modern physics to Oriental esoteric doctrines, some comparing the no-thingness of modern physics to the Buddhist doctrine of the impermanence of things,[59] others the constant motion of particles to the cosmic dance of Śiva, and yet others the idea of emptiness and the vacuum of modern physics to the Taoist void and similar conceptions.[60] Not all of these studies have displayed a full grasp of the Oriental doctrines involved and many deal with traditional teachings from a profane point of view. But the fact that there is and has been much interest even among such leading physicists as Erwin Schrödinger, Carl Friedrich von Weizäcker, Wigner, and Bohm, as well as many others, in Oriental cosmological and metaphysical teachings points to a groping, even within physics, which is the heart of modern science, for the sacred and a world view not bound by the reductionism of a quantitative science imposed upon the nature of reality as such.[61] For there is no doubt that since nature is not man-made but comes from the source of the sacred or the Sacred as such, if limitations placed upon it by a desacralized mode of knowing were to be removed, the sacred would manifest itself of its own accord. The light has not ceased to exist in itself. The cosmos seems to have become dark, spiritually speaking, only because of the veil of opacity surrounding that particular humanity called modern. Actually, any attempt to go beyond reductionist science and to introduce a nonmaterialistic world view is a quest, albeit unconsciously, for the rediscovery of the sacred even if the quest does not succeed as a result of its being cut off from tradition, that veritable source of the sacred that resides at the heart of each religion by virtue of which the message of that other grand revelation that is the cosmos becomes comprehensible and meaningful in an operative manner.

The concern for the sacred is observed in an even more open manner in the contemporary interest in ecology and the conservation of nature. Although because of the neglect of the spiritual element, which is an essential factor in the economy of the cosmos, many ecological concerns have failed to bear fruit, still the recent awareness of the interrelation among all living beings now emphasized even by agnostic scientists carries within it once again the urge for the rediscovery of the sacred, even if the necessary metaphysics of nature is not usually available or is neglected.[62] For example, the Gaia hypothesis, which sees the earth not as a complex of dead, material components accidentally supporting life and somehow keeping the right temperature to make life possible for "hundreds of millions" of years but as a living being which itself controls the condition of various elements such as air, associated with life, is impregnated with metaphysical significance.[63] It is not only the name of the Greek goddess for earth which this theory resuscitates but the traditional doctrine that the earth is a great animal already stated by Plato in the *Timaeus* and repeated by numerous medieval philosophers and scientists in the Islamic world as well as among Jews and Christians. It is also an echo of the traditional doctrine of the sacrifice of the primordial man at the beginning of the cosmogonic process whether those who devised the Gaia hypothesis on purely scientific grounds were aware of it or not.

There are numerous serious scientists working with ecological questions who realize that the whole is greater than its parts and that the quest for wholeness is inseparable from the quest for holiness. The founder of the New Alchemy Institute at Cape Cod, one of the most important institutions of this kind in America, who is himself a reputable scientist once told us that somehow through the study of ecology the sacred has reentered into the world view of contemporary science.[64] There are many scientists engaged in various kinds of ecological studies who would confirm his point of view[65] while others accept the reality of this thesis even if they shun the usage of the word sacred.

In quite another realm of science, namely neurology and the study of the brain, there are again those among leading scientists who refuse to reduce man to a complicated machine or a behaviorally determined mechanism as do certain psychologists and who confirm the reality of the mind against the view of certain positivist philosophers like Ryle and Ayer who question even the meaning of the term mind.[66] The confirmation of the mind or consciousness independent of its material instrument which is the brain is yet another aspect of this search for the sacred and the evasion of that reductionism which closes the door to the perfume of the sacred within the breathing space of contemporary man. That is why all kinds of research carried out in the fields of parapsychology to show the independence of the mind from matter or even Kirlian photography developed particularly in Russia where direct study of spiritual questions is, to put it mildly, problematic, all indicate a religious urge toward the rediscovery of the sacred in a world dominated by the emphasis upon phenomena and despite the common error of failing to distinguish between the Spirit and the psyche.

The search for wholeness has manifested itself also in medicine and all the other sciences which are concerned with the human body including the rediscovery of the spiritual significance of the body.[67] Concern with wholistic medicine, natural foods, natural bodily rhythms, and the like, despite all the fads and commercial exploitations, represent a desire to return to that primordial harmony of man with the natural environment, which being created by God is the theater of His Wisdom and Power and contains a sacred presence. That is why for so many people this type of concern has become practically a "religion" engaging their whole being as if it could satisfy even their need for the Sacred as such.[68]

Although modern psychoanalysis is a veritable parody of traditional psychology and psychotherapy connected with the spiritual transformation of the soul, one observes increasingly in recent years attempts to break away from the mold Freud and also Jung have cast upon this discipline and to rediscover traditional techniques of curing the ills of the soul.[69] This is of course a very dangerous ground for ultimately only God has the right to treat the soul of man which belongs to Him alone. Without the protection of tradition the application of traditional techniques is a most dangerous one. Nevertheless, the attempt is now being made to break at least the tyranny of this agnostic and atheistic type of psychoanalysis that has been prevalent in the West during this century and to study those traditional sciences of the soul which are anchored in sacred knowledge and see the well-being of the soul in its wedding to the Spirit.[70] Again in these attempts one can detect the quest for the rediscovery of the Sacred even if here as in so many other domains the quest has not always been successful and has not been able to discover a science which could safely treat the deeper problems of the soul in such a way that the soul would be protected from the darkening influences of the lower psyche.

As far as philosophy is concerned, the mainstream of European and American thought has been completely dominated by that desacralization of knowledge discussed earlier and become reduced to either logic or an irrationalism based on anxiety, despair, and the like. Yet, besides the main schools of Anglo-Saxon and American positivism and continental existentialism and *Existenz* philosophy, there have appeared in recent years a number of Western philosophers whose concern has been essentially the revival of traditional philosophy and even metaphysics. Such figures as G. Durand in France and F. Brunner in Switzerland represent such a tendency as do many of the younger French philosophers now called "les nouveaux philosophes." After years of opposition to classical proofs for the existence of God as being meaningless, there have appeared once again, during the past decade or two, certain thinkers who are reexamining these classical proofs and seeking to revive what would amount to natural theology.[71] In as much as the destruction of natural theology was the final phase and end result of the destruction of the sacred character of knowledge and the divorce between Intellect and reason, such a resuscitation of the, properly speaking, intellectual faculties of the mind, even if it be in a partial manner, is in its own way another indication of the current movement in certain quarters towards the rediscovery of the sacred.

Parallel with these and many other contemporary movements in the arts, the sciences, and philosophy, which are too extensive to enumerate here, there has also taken place, in many parts of the Western world and particularly in America, the spread of Oriental religions and especially their mysticisms ranging from authentic transmission of a tradition to demonic counterfeits which only remind one of Christ's prophecy about many false prophets arising at the end of time. There have also appeared such phenomena as drug-induced mysticism, natural and even black magic, appropriation of techniques of meditation outside of their traditional context, and all kinds of bewildering experiments and experiences offered to a world hungering for anything which would enable it to break the confines of a stifling materialistic ambience and searching for an experience of the not-ordinary.[72]

Finally, a word must be said about the quest to revive certain lost or forgotten dimensions of the Christian tradition itself and to rediscover the presence of the sacred within the life and thought of those who, although nominally Christian, have relegated religion to a peripheral role in their lives. Christianity, being a living tradition, has certainly the possibility for such a restitution, although during the past few decades what in fact has taken place in the main body of the Church in the West is the intrusion of modernism into the heart of the religion itself. Nevertheless, despite all the antitraditional ideas which have gained acceptance even within religious circles that were orthodox until yesterday, there have been attempts to make use of techniques of meditation and metaphysical doctrines drawn from Oriental traditions and to resuscitate certain dimensions of the Christian tradition in conformity with universes of religious meaning discovered elsewhere. There are those who consider themselves "American Indian or Buddhist Christians" without at all meaning a crass eclecticism.[73] There are also those who have sought recourse to Orthodox spirituality whose sapiential doctrines and methods of realization have been kept more intact while, at the very moment when many Western theologians are introducing secularism into the citadel of religion itself, there is an amazing rise of interest in the sapiential and mystical dimension of the Christian tradition. In America, at least, the quest for the sacred in the Oriental traditions which marked the postwar decades, especially the 1960s, has now turned to a large extent to the attempt to rediscover the Christian tradition itself, especially those aspects of it which were lost or eclipsed after the Middle Ages.[74] To a certain extent also the same tendency can be observed among many secularized Jews. Of course, in these instances, as in the case of the new cults and sects, there have also been, from the traditional point of view, all kinds of exaggerations, false pretensions, and attempts at synthesis which are no more than amalgamations which cannot but harm the integrity of the tradition in question.

When one gazes over this complex pattern which constitutes the religious life of contemporary man in quest of the rediscovery of the sacred, the revival of tradition in the West becomes even more of paramount significance, for this resuscitated knowledge of a principial order provides the criterion for distinguishing the wheat from the chaff, the true from the false, and especially the counterfeit. Not everything that is nontraditional is antitraditional. There is the third category of the counterfeit of tradition or countertradition which begins to play an ever greater role in the modern world.[75] The revival of interest in the rediscovery of the sacred can become meaningful and operative only in the bosom of tradition which is "what attaches all things human to the Divine Truth."[76] Otherwise, this fragmented delving into the residues of traditional teachings, the search for the sacred and even the playing with symbols and doctrines of a sacred origin without full dedication to the sacred can become an aberration rather than a means of integration, leading even to chaos and dissolution. But, if carried out in the matrix of tradition, the quest for the sacred observable in so many domains of contemporary life and thought can lead to the reestablishment of the Truth and the rehabilitation of man in the light of that Truth which also resides at the center of his being. Such a rehabilitation which is a veritable resurrection can take place at least for that type of man whose inner being still resonates to the call of the sacred. And at the heart of this call is to be found that *scientia sacra* which is inseparable from the very substance and root of intelligence and which constitutes the foundation of tradition, the "sacred science" whose attainment is the raison d'être of human existence.

NOTES

1. It is remarkable how so many so-called radical theologians have sided with Nietzsche in talking about the "death of God" in order not to remain behind current fashions, whereas what one would expect from a theologian's interpretation of current nihilism is the reassertion of the saying of Meister Eckhart, "the more you blaspheme the more you praise God," and the Gospel saying, "Slander must needs come but woe unto him who bringeth it about." As could be expected, many sociologists have predicted the continuation of the secularizing movement in the modern world as a natural confirmation of their own secular point of view. This tendency is to be expected more in sociology than in theology seeing the nature of the origins of the discipline called sociology. But even among sociologists there are those, like P. Berger, who assert that from a sociological point of view there is reason to believe that faith in the supernatural and quest for the sacred will continue to survive even in modern society. Berger adds, however, that "those to whom the supernatural is still, or again, a meaningful reality find themselves in the status of a minority, more precisely, a *cognitive minority*—a very important consequence with far-reaching implications." P. Berger, *A Rumor of Angels*, p. 7.

2. See Faivre, *L'Ésotérisme au XVIIIᵉ siècle*, p. 171.

3. Eliade explains the reason why this so-called "second Renaissance" did not take place: "But the 'Renaissance' did not come about for the simple reason that the study of Sanskrit and other oriental languages did not succeed in passing beyond the circle of philologians and historians, while, during the Italian Renaissance, Greek and classical Latin were studied not only by the grammarians and humanists but also by the poets, artists, philosophers, theologians, and men of science." "Crisis and Renewal in History of Religions," *History of Religions* 5/1 (Summer 1965): 3.

We would add that, first of all, Oriental traditions could not possibly have brought about a renaissance if by renaissance is meant that antitraditional revolt against the Christian tradition which is the source of most of what characterizes the modern world and which marks the point of departure of Western civilization from the rest of the world; and second, the European Renaissance was a fall, a discovery of a new earth at the expense of the loss of a heaven and therefore in conformity with the downward flow of the cosmic cycle, while a traditional "renaissance" would imply a restoration from on high against the downward pull of the stream of historic time. In any case, a traditional restoration, which would in fact have been a veritable renaissance, could not possibly take place through the translation of texts alone and in the absence of that authentic knowledge which would make the appropriate understanding of these texts possible.

4. The translation of the Upanishads by Anquetil Duperron into Latin from the Persian *Sirr-i akbar* was particularly important in introducing nineteenth-century Europe to a sacred text of a purely metaphysical character. It is interesting to note that this basic work, presented by the translator to Napoleon in 1804, was from the Persian translation of the Mogul prince Dārā Shukūh, the translation having been carried out in Benares in the eleventh/seventeenth century and being itself the result of one of the most remarkable encounters between the esoteric dimensions of Islam and Hinduism. See D. Shayegan, *Hindouisme et Soufisme, les relations de l'Hindouisme et du Soufisme d'après le "Majma' al-bahrayn" de Dârâ Shokûh*, Paris, 1979.

5. The history of Orientalism and Western views toward various Oriental traditions has been dealt with in many works. See, as far as the Islamic world is concerned, for example, N. Daniel, *Islam, Europe and Empire*, London, 1968; Y. Moubarac, *Recherches sur la pensée chrétienne et l'Islam dans les temps modernes et à l'époque contemporaine*, Beirut, 1977; and J. Fück, *Die arabischen Studien in Europa bis in den Anfang des 20. Jahrhunderts*, Leipzig, 1955.

6. See A. M. Schimmel (ed.), *Orientalische Dichtung in den Übersetzung Friedrich Rückerts*, Bremen, 1963. In her introduction the editor discusses the influence of the Orient on Western and esp. German literature.

7. On Goethe and the East see Taha Hussein Bey, "Goethe and the East," in *Goethe: UNESCO's Hommage on the Occasion of the Two Hundredth Anniversary of His Birth*, Paris, 1949, pp. 167–79; F. Strich, *Goethe und die Weltliteratur*, Bern, 1957, esp. "Die Öffnende Macht des Orients," pp. 154–70; H. H. Schaeder, "Goethes Erlebnis des Ostens," in *Vierteljahrschrift des Goetheges.* 2 (1937): 125–39; and H. Krüger, *Weltend, Goethe und der Orient*, Weimar, 1903.

8. On the significance of this work see K. Viëtor, *Goethe the Poet*, "West-Eastern Divan," pp. 219–30.

9. *Goethe's Reineke Fox, West-Eastern Divan, and Achilleid*, trans. in the original meters by A. Rogers, London, 1890, pp. 199–200.

10. Khiḍr or the "Green prophet" represents an ever present initiatic function in the Islamic tradition similar to that of Elias in Judaism. Khiḍr (or Khaḍir) is considered as the guardian of the fountain of life which from the sapiential point of view symbolizes the water of sacred knowledge. On Khiḍr and his iconography in Islamic art see A. K. Coomaraswamy, "Khwāja Khadir and the Fountain of Life, in the Tradition of Persian and Mughal Art," *Ars Islamica* 1 (1934):173–82.

11. See G. M. Harper, *The Neoplatonism of William Blake*, Chapel Hill, N.C., 1961, p. 3.

12. On Platonism in England see E. Cassirer, *The Platonic Renaissance in England*, trans. J. P. Pettegrove, London, 1953, dealing with the earlier Cambridge Platonists up to the Age of Reason; and J. H. Muirhead, *The Platonic Tradition in Anglo-Saxon Philosophy*, London, 1931, which however neglects certain important figures including Taylor.

13. On Thomas Taylor and his writings see K. Raine and G. M. Harper (eds.), *Thomas Taylor the Platonist: Selected Writings*, Princeton, 1969.

14. On the bibliography of Taylor see W. E. Axon and J. J. Welsh, *A Bibliography of the Works of Thomas Taylor, the Platonist*, Westwood, N.J., 1975.

15. Kathleen Raine has composed several works on Blake but the most important as far as traditional teachings are concerned is *Blake and Tradition*, 2 vols., Princeton, 1968.

". . .for Blake himself, no less than Ellis and Yeats, seemed to have a knowledge whose sources were not divulged, as knowledge of the ancient Mysteries was kept secret among initiates. I began to understand that in those Mysteries was to be found the ordering principle—I know now that the key for which many have sought is traditional metaphysics with its accompanying language of symbolic discourse." Ibid., pp. xxv–xxvi.

16. It is interesting that Blake has attracted Oriental scholars, esp. Muslims who have devoted several scholarly works to him. See, for example, A. A. Ansari, *Arrows of Intellect; A Study in William Blake's Gospel of the Imagination*, Aligarh, 1965; and Gh. Sabri-Tabrizi, *The "Heaven" and "Hell" of William Blake*, London, 1973. A. K. Coomaraswamy also admired Blake whom he called "the most Indian of modern Western minds," and some of his early essays such as "The Religious Foundations of Life and Art," in Coomaraswamy and A. J. Penty (eds.), *Essays in Post-Industrialism: A Symposium in Prophecy*, London, 1914, pp. 33ff. are deeply "Blakean." Coomaraswamy also continued to quote Blake profusely throughout his later works. See R. Lipsey, *Coomaraswamy 3: His Life and Work*, Princeton, 1977, pp. 105ff.

On Blake and the traditional doctrine of art as expounded by Coomaraswamy, Schuon, and Burckhardt see B. Keeble, "Conversing with Paradise: William Blake and the Traditional Doctrine of Art," *Sophia Perennis* 1/1(Spring 1975):72–96.

17. F. I. Carpenter, *Emerson and Asia*, Cambridge, Mass., 1930, p. 27; see also A. Christy, *The Orient in American Transcendentalism; a Study of Emerson, Thoreau and Alcott*, New York, 1932; and W. Staebler, *Ralph Waldo Emerson*, New York, 1973. See also E. Zolla, "Naturphilosophie and Transcendentalism Revisited," *Sophia Perennis* 3/2(Autumn 1977):65–94.

18. See Swami Paramananda, *Emerson and Vedanta*, Boston, 1918; and Carpenter, op. cit.

19. On Emerson and Persian poetry see J. D. Yohannan, "Emerson's Translations of Persian Poetry from German Sources," *American Literature* 14 (Jan. 1943):407–20. See also M. A. Ekhtiar, *From Linguistics to Literature*, Tehran, 1962, pt. 2.

20. Some had received knowledge from Taoist and other Far Eastern sources, such as A. de Pourvourville, known as Matgioi, the author of the well-known *La Voie rationnelle*, Paris, 1941, and *La Voie métaphysique*, Paris, 1936; and others from Islamic esoteric circles, such as ʿAbd al-Hādī, who was to translate into French the celebrated *Risālat al-ahadiyyah* (*Treatise on Unity*) attributed to Ibn ʿArabī. See *Le Traité de l'Unité dit d'Ibn Arabî*, Paris, 1977, pp. 19–48.

21. Numerous works and studies have appeared on Guénon, mostly in his mother tongue, French. See, for example, J. Marcireau, *René Guénon et son oeuvre*, Paris, 1946; P. Chacornac, *La Vie simple de René Guénon*, Paris, 1958; P. Serant, *René Guénon*, Paris, 1953; L. Meroz, *René Guénon ou la sagesse initiatique*, Paris, 1962; and J. Tourniac, *Propos sur René Guénon*, Paris, 1973, and *Planète plus* (*L'homme et son message—René Guénon*), Paris, 1970. Some of these works, like that of P. Chacornac, for example, are reliable and of a traditional character, and others of a problematic nature.

As for authentic traditional studies and commentaries upon Guénon see A. K. Coomaraswamy, "Eastern Wisdom and Western Knowledge," in his *Bugbear of Literacy*; M. Pallis, "A Fateful Meeting of Minds: A. K. Coomaraswamy and R. Guénon," in *Studies in Comparative Religion*, Summer–Autumn 1978, pp. 176–88; F. Schuon, "Definitions," *France-Asie*, no. 80 (Jan. 1953):1161–64. There are several other articles, some by traditional authors, on Guénon in this issue which is dedicated to his memory; and G. Eaton, "Two Traditionalists," in his *The Richest Vein*, London, 1949.

22. His two major works in this domain are *Le Théosophisme—histoire d'une pseudo-religion*, Paris, 1921; and *L'Erreur spirite*, Paris, 1923. There are also studies devoted to these subjects in his *Aperçus sur l'initiation*, Paris, 1980; and *Initiation et réalisation spirituelle*, Paris, 1952.

23. Many of the works of Guénon were translated into English but a large number remain available only in the original French. Those translated into English include: *Introduction to the Study of the Hindu Doctrines*, *Man and His Becoming according to the Vedanta*, trans. R. Nicholson, London, 1945; *Crisis of the Modern World*, trans. M. Pallis and R. Nicholson, London, 1962; *Symbolism of the Cross*, trans. A. Macnab, London, 1958; *East and West*, trans. W. Massey, London, 1941; *The Reign of Quantity and the Signs*

of the Times, trans. Lord Northbourne, London, 1953; and *Oriental Metaphysics* in Needleman (ed.), *The Sword of Gnosis.* A number of his articles have also been translated and published mostly in *Studies in Comparative Religion.*

24. See, for example, "Sacred and Profane Science," in his *Crisis of the Modern World,* pp. 37–50 (also trans. A. K. Coomaraswamy, *Viśva-Bharati Quarterly* 1 [1935]:11–24).

25. He achieved this task in the field of infinitesimal calculus whose principles he related to more universal principles of a metaphysical order. See his *Les Principes du calcul infinitésimal,* Paris, 1946.

26. See, for example, *The Symbolism of the Cross,* dealing with the metaphysical symbolism of space and geometric patterns and *La Grande triade,* Paris, 1980, much of which deals with alchemical symbolism along with metaphysics.

27. An example of this type of orientalism is the works of L. Massignon, the great French Islamicist, whose works are not only important from a purely scholarly point of view but also expound in an authentic fashion certain important aspects of the Islamic tradition.

28. He paid much less attention to certain aspects of Christianity and also Buddhism and in fact corrected his earlier appraisal of Buddhism, which was from the exclusively Brahmanic point of view, as a result of his contacts with Coomaraswamy and Marco Pallis. This is one of the rare instances of change of view in the writings of Guénon where one can detect a revision concerning a particular subject.

29. Marco Pallis, himself a distinguished traditional author, writes concerning Coomaraswamy: "An intellectual genius well describes this man in whose person East and West came together, since his father belonged to an ancient Tamil family established in Sri Lanka while his mother came of an English aristocratic stock. An immensely retentive memory coupled with command of many languages both classical and current constituted the equipment of this prince among scholars. In the matter of checking his references Coomaraswamy was meticulously scrupulous where Guénon was the reverse." M. Pallis, "A Fateful Meeting of Minds: A. K. Coomaraswamy and R. Guénon," p. 179.

30. On his writings see R. Ettinghausen, "The Writings of Ananda K. Coomaraswamy," *Ars Islamica* 9 (1942):125–42; and R. Lipsey, *Coomaraswamy,* pp. 293–304. A working bibliography of Coomaraswamy is being prepared by R. P. Coomaraswamy, while J. Crouch has completed an exhaustive bibliography to be published soon.

As for works on Coomaraswamy himself there are the full-fledged biographies by R. Lipsey, *Coomaraswamy,* and P. S. Sastri, *Ananda K. Coomaraswamy,* New Delhi, 1974, and several works dedicated to him and containing sketches, testimonials, etc. Among these the several works of S. Durai Raja Singham contain a wealth of biographical information as well as testimonials. For example, his *A New Planet in Thy Ken: Introduction to Kala-Yogi Ananda K. Coomaraswamy,* Kuantan, Malaya, 1951; also *Hommage to Ananda K. Coomaraswamy: A Garland of Tributes,* Kuala Lumpur, 1948; *Hommage to Ananda K. Coomaraswamy (A Memorial Volume),* Kuala Lumpur, 1952; and *Remembering and Remembering Again and Again,* Kuala Lumpur, 1974. See also K. Bharata Iyer (ed.), *Life and Thought,* London, 1947; and R. Livingston, *The Traditional Theory of Literature,* Minneapolis, 1962. See also *Sophia Perennis* 3/2 (1977), dedicated to Coomaraswamy and devoted to "Tradition and the Arts" including the article of W. N. Perry on Coomaraswamy and Guénon and a section of poems by contemporary poets inspired by traditional doctrines, poets such as Kathleen Raine, Peter Wilson, Peter Russell, Cristina Campo, and Philip Sherard. Finally, see the more recent work of M. Bagchee, *Ananda Coomaraswamy, A Study,* Varanasi, 1977.

31. Originally published in *Motive,* May 1944, and which appeared later as chap. 3 of his *Bugbear of Literacy.*

32. H. Smith, statement made on the occasion of the publication of the English translation of Schuon's *Logic and Transcendence* and printed on the back of the 1975 paperback edition of the work.

33. The books of Schuon include *De l'unité transcendante des religions,* Paris, 1979;

L'Oeil du coeur, Paris, 1974; *Perspectives spirituelles et faits humains*, Paris, 1953; *Sentiers de gnose*, Paris, 1957; *Castes et races*, Paris, 1979; *Les Stations de la sagesse*, Paris, 1958; *Images de l'esprit*, Paris, 1961; *Comprendre l'Islam*, Paris, 1961; *Regards sur les mondes anciens*, Paris, 1965; *Logique et transcendance*, Paris, 1970; *Forme et substance dans les religions*, Paris, 1975; *L'Esotérisme comme principe et comme voie*, Paris, 1978; *Le Soufisme, voile et quintessence*; *Du Divin à l'humain*; *Christianisme/Islam—Visions d'oecuménisme ésotérique*; and *Sur les traces de la Religion pérenne*; *Leitgedanken zur Urbesinnung*, Zurich and Leipzig, 1935; and the two volumes of poetry, *Tage- und Nachtebuch*, Bern, 1947, and *Sulamith*, Bern, 1947.

Schuon's books translated into English are: *The Transcendent Unity of Religions; Spiritual Perspectives and Human Facts; Language of the Self*, trans. M. Pallis and D. M. Matheson, Madras, 1959; *Gnosis: Divine Wisdom*, trans. G. E. H. Palmer, London, 1977; *Stations of Wisdom*, trans. G. E. H. Palmer, London, 1978; *Understanding Islam; Light on the Ancient Worlds; In the Tracks of Buddhism*, trans. M. Pallis, London, 1968; *Dimensions of Islam*, trans. P. Townsend, London, 1970; *Logic and Transcendence; Islam and the Perennial Philosophy*, trans. P. Hobson, London, 1976; and *Esoterism as Principle and as Way*, trans. W. Stoddart, London, 1981.

For an evaluation of the writings of Schuon see L. Benoist, "L'Oeuvre de Frithjof Schuon," *Etudes Traditionelles* 79/459 (1978):97–101.

We are now preparing an anthology of his writings to appear soon care of the Crossroad Publishing Company in New York.

34. R. C. Zaehner, who changed his perspective several times during his writing career, at one point opposed the theses of Schuon completely and wrote, "Mr. Frithjof Schuon, in his *Transcendent Unity of Religions*, has tried to show that there is a fundamental unity underlying all the great religions. The attempt was worth making if only to show that no such unity can, in fact, be discovered." *The Comparison of Religions*, Boston, 1958, p. 169. To this assertion of Zaehner we would only add the phrase "by those who have no intellectual intuition of the supra-formal essence and who therefore should not be legitimately concerned with trying to understand or discern the supra-formal unity of which Schuon speaks." In his preface to the American edition of the *Transcendent Unity of Religions* another eminent scholar of religion, H. Smith, has presented extensive arguments to show why the method of Schuon and other traditional authors is in fact the only possible way of realizing the inner truth of religions and bringing about harmony among them without sacrificing a single form, doctrine, or rite of a divine origin.

35. B. Kelly, "Notes on the Light of the Eastern Religions with Special Reference to the Works of Ananda Coomaraswamy, René Guénon and Frithjof Schuon," *Dominican Studies* 7 (1954): 265.

36. Burckhardt has also written several basic works on the traditional sciences. His major writings include: *An Introduction to Sufi Doctrine*, trans. D. M. Matheson, London, 1976; *Sacred Art East and West*, trans. Lord Northbourne, London, 1967; *The Wisdom of the Prophets of Ibn 'Arabi*, trans. A. Culme-Seymour, Gloucestershire, 1975; *Alchemy: Science of the Cosmos, Science of the Soul*, trans. W. Stoddart, Baltimore, 1971; *The Art of Islam*, trans. J. P. Hobson, London, 1976; and *Moorish Culture in Spain*, trans. A. Jaffa, London, 1972.

37. See Schaya, *The Universal Meaning of the Kabbala*, trans. N. Pearson, London, 1971. He has also published many articles in the *Études Traditionnelles* of which he is now editor.

38. Pallis who is both an accomplished musician and mountain climber has also written on both nature and music from the traditional point of view and been instrumental, along with M. Lings, P. Townsend, R. C. Nicholson, W. Stoddart, G. Palmer, the late D. M. Matheson, P. Hobson, Lord Northbourne—himself the author of works on tradition—and several other selfless scholars, in making much of the work of Guénon and Schuon available in English. See Pallis, *The Way and the Mountain*, London, 1960; *Peaks and Lamas*, London, 1974; and *A Buddhist Spectrum*, London, 1980.

39. See his *Shakespeare in the Light of Sacred Art*, London, 1966; also his *A Sufi Saint of*

the Twentieth Century, London and Berkeley, 1971; *What is Sufism?*, London, 1981; and *Ancient Beliefs and Modern Superstitions*, London, 1979.

40. This journal in a sense complements the older *Études Traditionnelles* but has a larger audience and also a more extended field of concern. For a collection of some of the articles in the journal see Needleman (ed.), *The Sword of Gnosis*.

During recent years other journals with a traditional point of view have seen the light of day of which the most notable perhaps was the *Sophia Perennis* that was published by the Iranian Academy of Philosophy from 1975 through 1978.

Other journals such as *Conoscenza religiosa* (Italy), *Religious Studies* (Australia), and *Temenos* (England) also possess a traditional perspective with different kinds of emphasis. As for the *Studi tradizionali* published also in Italy, it is more than anything else of a "Guénonian" character.

41. There are many other notable traditional authors whose names cannot all be mentioned here. Some like Gai Eaton have gained fairly wide recognition as writers while others like Lord Northbourne have remained known to a more exclusive audience. W. Stoddart is preparing a full bibliography of traditional works written during this century.

42. See esp. his well-known work *The Sacred Pipe*, Baltimore, 1972.

43. There are a number of scholars mostly in the field of comparative religion and Islamic studies who have carried out important scholarly studies and translations from Oriental languages from the traditional point of view. This group includes H. Smith, W. N. Perry, V. Danner, R. W. J. Austin, J. L. Michon and W. Chittick whose works in Islamic studies and comparative religion are well known in scholarly circles.

44. Such figures include not only scholars like J. Needleman but also important religious thinkers like Thomas Merton.

45. His posthumous work *Guide for the Perplexed* is one of the most easily approachable introductions to traditional doctrines available today.

46. Such Oriental scholars and thinkers as the late Shaykh ʿAbd al-Ḥalīm Maḥmūd, the former rector of al-Azhar University, H. Askari, M. Ajmal, A. K. Brohi, and Y. Ibish in the Islamic world; A. K. Saran and Keshavram Iyengar in India; R. Fernando in Sri Lanka; and Sh. Bando in Japan may be mentioned among figures directly influenced in a major way by those who have revived tradition in the West.

47. This is a theme which cannot be dealt with here but which we have treated extensively in many of our Persian writings including our introduction to the Persian translation of Guénon's *Crisis of the Modern World* (*Buḥrān-i dunyā-yi mutajaddid*), trans. D. Dihshīrī, Tehran, 1971; see also our *Islam and the Plight of Modern Man*.

48. On the enigma of Vivekananda in relation to Ramakrishna see F. Schuon, *Spiritual Perspectives and Human Facts*, pp. 113–22.

49. The now extensive amount of literature on traditional harmonics and Pythagorean musical theory are based on the pioneering work of A. von Thimus, *Die harmonikale Symbolik des Altertums*, Berlin, 1868–76, as resuscitated and extended by H. Kayser in such works as *Der hörende Mensch*, Berlin, 1932; *Akróasis: The Theory of World Harmonics*, Boston, 1970; *Orphikon. Eine harmonikale Symbolik*, Basel-Stuttgart, 1973; and numerous other studies. On his life and works see R. Haase, *Ein Leben für die Harmonik der Welt*, Basel-Stuttgart, 1968.

These teachings were brought to America mostly by the Swiss pianist and musicologist E. Levy who also wrote about them and taught them to many students. See his "The Pythagorean Table," with S. Levarie, *Main Currents in Modern Thought*, March–April 1974, pp. 117–29; and their *Tone: A Study in Musical Acoustics*, Kent, Kans., 1968. In recent years a number of more accessible works have spread the knowledge of traditional musical theories as they apply to various disciplines further afield. See E. McClain, *The Pythagorean Plato: Prelude to the Song Itself*, Stony Brook, N.Y., 1978; idem, *The Myth of Invariance*, Boulder, Colo., and London, 1978; idem, "The Kaʿba as Archetypal Ark," *Sophia Perennis* 4/1 (Spring 1978):59–74; R. Brumbugh, *Plato's Mathematical Imagination*, New York, 1968; and A. T. de Nicolàs, *Meditation through the Ṛg Veda: Four Dimensional Man*, New York, 1976.

50. Once when we were in Cairo discussing Schwaller de Lubicz's study of things Egyptian with the celebrated Egyptian architect Hasan Fathy who knew him well, the aged architect, who is far from being a gullible person, told us that the French scholar seemed to have known the principles of Egyptian art and archaelogy a priori, before even arriving in Egypt, and terminated his studies, finished the cycle of his work, and left Egypt before the revolution with a clear premonition of what was to occur. Fathy is convinced that Schwaller de Lubicz's knowledge of the Egyptian tradition had come from an esoteric source which his archaeological studies only confirmed and that his knowledge was not the fruit of ordinary archaeological and art historical studies.

51. See, for example, S. Kramrish, *The Hindu Temple*, 2 vols., New York, 1980; B. Rowland, *Art in East and West*, Boston, 1966; idem, *The Art and Architecture of India: Buddhist, Hindu, Jain*, Baltimore, 1971; and H. Zimmer, *The Art of Indian Asia; Its Mythology and Transformations*, ed. J. Campbell, 2 vols., New York, 1955.

52. See, for example, K. Critchlow, *Islamic Patterns*, London, 1975; idem, *Time Stands Still*, London, 1980; R. Alleau, *Aspects de l'alchimie traditionnelle*, Paris, 1970; M. Ghyka, *Philosophie et mystique du nombre*, Paris, 1952; and E. Zolla, *Meraviglie della natura: l'alchimia*, Milan, 1975.

53. On different types of movement against reductionism such as consciousness research, frontier physics, morphic science, and the like see Roszak, *Person/Planet*, pp. 50–54 and pp. 327–28 for references to works in such fields.

54. We have in mind such completely unscientific extrapolations carried out in popularized descriptions of the scientific universe by men like C. Sagan and the evolutionist theology of Teilhard de Chardin with which we shall deal more extensively later.

55. We shall deal with this issue and the traditional criticism of modern science in chap. 6.

56. This would correspond to the *materia prima* of traditional cosmology. See his "Cosmology and Modern Science."

57. "Our inability to describe our consciousness adequately, to give a satisfactory picture of it, is the greatest obstacle to our acquiring a rounded picture of the world." E. Wigner, quoted by Sir J. Eccles, *The Brain and the Person*, Sydney, 1965, p. 3; see also E. Wigner, *Symmetries and Reflections*, Cambridge, Mass., 1970.

58. See D. Bohm, *Wholeness and the Implicate Order*, London, 1980, esp. chap. 7, "The Enfolding-Unfolding Universe and Consciousness," pp. 172ff., where he summarizes his views speaking of the life of the universe as an unfolding rather than evolution. Of course from the traditional point of view as far as consciousness is concerned the unfolded reality was already at the beginning and nothing can be added to its pure unconditional state by any process whatsoever of change and becoming.

59. One author calls the discovery of the fundamental impermanence of things, the discontinuity of matter and the absence of substance in modern physics as "une confirmation éclatante des principes essentiels du Bouddhisme." R. Linssen, "Le Bouddhisme et la science moderne," *France-Asie*, no. 46–47 (Jan.–Feb. 1950), p. 658.

60. See the well-known works of F. Capra, *The Tao of Physics*, New York, 1977; R. G. Siu, *The Tao of Science: An Essay on Western Knowledge and Eastern Wisdom*, Cambridge, Mass., 1958. Such types of writing have proliferated during the past few years. C. F. von Weizsäcker has even established a research foundation for the study of Eastern wisdom and Western science. See W. I. Thompson, *Passage About Earth*, New York, 1974, chap. 5, where the activities of this foundation are described.

61. It is amazing to note that even with the help of computers it is not possible to solve all the different aspects of a three body problem. How strange it is that people still think about reducing the whole of the visible universe to the activity of physical particles whose reality is exhausted by a mathematical treatment of their physical properties!

62. We have dealt with the question of the encounter of man and nature, its historical background in the Occident, and metaphysical principle pertaining to nature, in *Man and Nature*, London, 1976.

63. After carrying out scientific research on the interdependence of various elements and forces on the surface of the earth, Lovelock and Epton, who first proposed the Gaia hypothesis, write, "This led us to the formulation of the proposition that living matter, the air, the oceans, the land surface were parts of a giant system which was able to control temperature, the composition of the air and sea, the pH of the soil and so on so as to be optimum for survival of the biosphere. The system seemed to exhibit the behaviour of a single organism, even a living creature. One having such formidable powers deserved a name to match it; William Golding, the novelist, suggested Gaia, the name given by the ancient Greeks to their Earth goddess." J. Lovelock and S. Epton, "The Quest for Gaia," *New Scientist*, Feb. 6, 1975, p. 304.

64. This statement was made to us by John Todd during the ceremony of his receiving the Threshold Award at the New Alchemy Institute in 1980. On his ecological ideas see Nancy Todd (ed.), *Book of the New Alchemists*, New York, 1980; John Todd and Nancy Todd, *Tomorrow is Our Permanent Address*, New York, 1980.

65. For example, the Lindesfarne experiment conveys the same concern with the rediscovery of the sacred through the study of both ecological and traditional sciences. See W. J. Thompson, *Passages About Earth*, and his other later works which are all concerned in one way or another with the Lindesfarne experiment. See also the *Lindesfarne Letters* which appears periodically.

66. "I want to discredit such dogmatic statements [about man being simply a complicated machine] and bring you to realize how tremendous is the mystery of each one of us." Eccles, op. cit., p. 1.

Also, "Contrary to this physicalist creed, I believe that the prime reality of my experiencing self cannot with propriety be *identified* with some aspects of its experiences and its imaginings—such as brains and nervous and nerve impulses and even complex spatio-temporal patterns of impulses. The evidence presented in these talks show that these events, in the material world are necessary but not sufficient causes for conscious experiences and for my consciously-experiencing self." Ibid., p. 43.

67. This does not mean that this concern with the human body has succeeded in actually discovering the sacred significance of the body. On the contrary, it has often led to the worst kinds of perversions from both the moral and spiritual points of view.

68. In this as in other cases the lack of a traditional world view and the actual practice of a traditional way prevents such concerns from being anything more than partial and fragmentary, never able to transform the being of the person who has become attracted to the "natural" way of eating or natural methods of being treated medically usually for deeper spiritual reasons of which he is often not totally aware.

69. It might appear on the surface that Jung is dealing with traditional psychology whereas his treatment of traditional doctrines and symbols is a perversion of them so that he is, in a sense, more misleading than Freud who is openly against all that tradition stands for. See T. Burckhardt, "Cosmology in Modern Science," in Needleman (ed.), *The Sword of Gnosis*, pp. 153–78; idem, *Alchemy*, esp. chaps. 9–11; W. N. Perry, "The Revolt against Moses," *Studies in Comparative Religion*, Spring 1961, pp. 103–19; and F. Schuon, "The Psychological Imposture," *Studies in Comparative Religion*, Spring 1961, pp. 98–102. On traditional psychology see H. Jacobs, *Western Psychotherapy and Hindu Sadhana: A Contribution to Comparative Studies in Psychology and Metaphysics*, London, 1961; and A. K. Coomaraswamy, "On the Indian and Traditional Psychology, or Rather Pneumatology," in Lipsey (ed.), *Coomaraswamy 2: Selected Papers—Metaphysics*, Princeton, 1977, pp. 333–78. The two volumes of Coomaraswamy edited by R. Lipsey include both essays not published previously, such as the one on psychology, and some which had appeared in earlier collections, such as *Figures of Speech and Figures of Thought* and *Why Exhibit Works of Art?*, as well as articles from various learned journals.

J. Sinha in his classical work *Indian Psychology: Perception*, London, 1934, states, "There is no empirical psychology in India. Indian psychology is based on metaphysics" (p. 16). This statement holds true for all traditional psychology, which is a science of the soul in the light of the *scientia sacra*.

70. "There is no science of the soul without a metaphysical basis to it and without spiritual remedies at its disposal." Schuon, *Logic and Transcendence*, p. 14.

On the current search for the discovery of traditional science of the soul see J. Needleman (ed.), *On the Way to Self Knowledge*, New York, 1976; also E. Fromm, D. T. Suzuki, and R. DeMartino, *Zen Buddhism and Psychoanalysis*, New York, 1960, one of numerous works seeking to draw from Buddhist sources for the recreation of a viable science of the soul.

As for works of modern psychologists and psychoanalysts opposed to the prevalent materialistic influences upon these disciplines see A. Maslow, *The Psychology of Science*, New York, 1966.

71. The classical proofs such as the moral, experiential, teleological, cosmological, and ontological have been resuscitated of late in one form or another by such contemporary philosophers and theologians as R. Green, A. Plantinga, H. Malcolm, M. Adler, B. J. F. Lonergan, and R. Swinburne. This does not mean that the nexus between reason and the Intellect has been reestablished among such thinkers. But it does mean that a step has been taken in the other direction and away from the debasing of reason and its severance from the certitude of intellection, a step which was to lead with Hume and esp. the post-Hegelian critics of reason to an irrationalism which did not go beyond reason but fell below it.

Islamic theological and philosophical proofs for the existence of God which are in fact similar to those of St. Thomas and other Christian theologians have been discussed and analyzed in terms of modern philosophical ideas by W. L. Craig in his *The Kalām Cosmological Argument*, London, 1979; the author considers the *kalām* argument based on the impossibility of an infinite temporal regress as being defendable in contemporary philosophical terms. This is just one example of the renewal of interest in traditional philosophical proofs for the existence of God. Of course the proofs are not themselves affected by whether a particular generation of Western philosophers appreciates them or not.

72. The discernment of the true from the false in this bewildering world, and even a study of the present day scene, is beyond the confines of this study but certainly there is a need to survey the whole situation once again from the traditional point of view. For a description of the so-called "new religions" in America see J. Needleman, *The New Religions*, New York, 1977; and Needleman and G. Baker (eds.), *Understanding the New Religions*, New York, 1978.

73. Such authors as A. Graham, B. Griffiths, and T. Merton have written extensively on the positive role that living spirituality can play on the revival of the contemplative disciplines within Christianity and have even put certain Oriental forms of meditation into practice. There are, however, others whose approach is, to put it mildly, much less serious.

74. See J. Needleman, *Lost Christianity*, New York, 1980, which deals with the significance of this question in the religious life of many seekers today without exhausting the different facets of the problem.

75. On the countertradition see R. Guénon, *The Reign of Quantity*.

76. "La tradition est ce qui rattache toute chose humaine à la Verité Divine." F. Schuon, "L'esprit d'une oeuvre," *Planète plus* (*L'homme et son message—René Guénon*), April 1970, p. 36.

CHAPTER FOUR

Scientia Sacra

The Good Religion is Innate Wisdom: and the forms
and virtues of Innate Wisdom are of the same stock
as Innate Wisdom itself.

Dēnkard

A fund of omniscience exists eternally in our heart.

Tipiṭaka

S *ientia sacra* is none other than that sacred knowledge which lies at
the heart of every revelation and is the center of that circle which
encompasses and defines tradition. The first question which presents
itself is, how is the attainment of such a knowledge possible? The
answer of tradition is that the twin source of this knowledge is
revelation and intellection or intellectual intuition which involves the
illumination of the heart and the mind of man and the presence in
him of knowledge of an immediate and direct nature which is tasted
and experienced, the sapience which the Islamic tradition refers to as
"presential knowledge" (*al-ʿilm al-ḥuḍūrī*).[1] Man is able to know and
this knowledge corresponds to some aspect of reality. Ultimately in
fact, knowledge is knowledge of Absolute Reality and intelligence
possesses this miraculous gift of being able to know that which is and
all that partakes of being.[2]

Scientia sacra is not the fruit of human intelligence speculating upon
or reasoning about the content of an inspiration or a spiritual experience which itself is not of an intellectual character. Rather, what is
received through inspiration is itself of an intellectual nature; it is
sacred knowledge. The human intelligence which perceives this mes-

sage and receives this truth does not impose upon it the intellectual nature or content of a spiritual experience of a sapiential character. The knowledge contained in such an experience issues from the source of this experience which is the Intellect, the source of all sapience and the bestower of all principial knowledge, the Intellect which also modifies the human recipient that the Scholastics called the potential intellect. Here the medieval distinction between the active and passive or potential intellect[3] can serve to elucidate the nature of this process of the illumination of the mind and to remove the error of seeing the sapiential and intellectual content of spiritual experience as being the result of the human mind meditating upon or reasoning about the content of such an experience, whereas spiritual experience on the highest level is itself of an intellectual and sapiential nature.

From another point of view, that of the Self which resides at the center of every self, the source of the *scientia sacra* revealed to man is the center and root of human intelligence itself since ultimately "knowledge of the Substance is the substance of knowledge," or knowledge of the Origin and the Source is the Origin and Source of knowledge. The truth descends upon the mind like an eagle landing upon a mountain top or it gushes forth and inundates the mind like a deep well which has suddenly burst forth into a spring. In either case, the sapiential nature of what the human being receives through spiritual experience is not the result of man's mental faculty but issues from the nature of that experience itself. Man can know through intuition and revelation not because he is a thinking being who imposes the categories of his thought upon what he perceives but because knowledge is being. The nature of reality is none other than consciousness, which, needless to say, cannot be limited to only its individual human mode.

Of course not everyone is capable of intellection or of having intellectual intuition no more than everyone is capable of having faith in a particular religion. But the lack of possibility of intellection for everyone does not invalidate the reality of such a possibility any more than does the fact that many people are not able to have faith invalidate the reality of a religion. In any case for those who have the possibility of intellectual intuition there is the means to attain a knowledge of a sacred character that lies at the heart of that objective revelation which constitutes religion and also at the center of man's being. This microcosmic revelation makes possible access to that *scientia sacra* which contains the knowledge of the Real and the means of distinguishing between the Real and the illusory.

What we have designated as *scientia sacra* is none other than metaphysics if this term is understood correctly as the ultimate science of the Real. This term possesses certain unfortunate connotations because, first of all, the prefix *meta* does imply transcendence but not immanence and also it connotes a form of knowledge or science that comes after physics whereas metaphysics is the primary and fundamental science or wisdom which comes before and contains the principles of all the sciences.[4] Second, the habit of considering metaphysics in the West as a branch of philosophy, even in those philosophical schools which have a metaphysical dimension, has been instrumental in reducing the significance of metaphysics to just mental activity rather than seeing it as a sacred science concerned with the nature of Reality and wed to methods for the realization of this knowledge, a science which embraces the whole of man's being.[5] In Oriental languages such terms as *prajña*, *jñāna*, *maʿrifah*, or *ḥikmah* connote the ultimate science of the Real without their being reduced to a branch of another form of knowledge known as philosophy or its equivalent. And it is in this traditional sense of *jñāna* or *maʿrifah* that metaphysics, or the "science of the Real," can be considered as identical with *scientia sacra*.

If *scientia sacra* lies at the heart of each tradition and is not a purely human knowledge lying outside of the sacred precinct of the various traditions, then how can one speak of it without remaining bound within a single religious universe? The response to this question has led certain scholars and philosophers engaged in "comparative philosophy" in the context of East and West to speak of "meta-philosophy" and a meta-language which stands above and beyond the language of a particular tradition.[6] From the traditional point of view, however, the language of metaphysics is inseparable from the content and meaning it expresses and bears the imprint of the message, this language having been developed by the metaphysicians and sages of various traditions over the ages. Each tradition possesses one or several "languages of discourse" suitable for metaphysical doctrines and there is no need whatsoever to create a meta-language or invent a new vocabulary today to deal with such matters, since the English language is heir to the Western tradition and the several perfectly suitable metaphysical languages of the West such as those of Platonism, Thomism, and the school of Palamite theology. Moreover, contemporary traditional authors have already resuscitated the symbolic and intellectual aspects of modern languages which have decayed in their symbolic and hierarchic aspects but which nevertheless contain metaphysical possibilities because of the very nature of human language.[7] These authors have created a perfectly suitable language for the expression of *scientia sacra* drawing occasionally from such sacred languages as Sanskrit and Arabic for certain key concepts. In any case a meta-language to express a meta-philosophy in order to expound traditional metaphysics is totally unnecessary. The language needed has been already forged from existing European languages which, although reflecting the gradual degradation of thought from an intellectual point of view, have also preserved the possibility of revival precisely because of their inalienable link with the classical languages of the West and the traditional metaphysics expressed in them, and even in the earlier phases of the life of modern European languages.

If one were to ask what is metaphysics, the primary answer would be the science of the Real or, more specifically, the knowledge by means of which man is able to distinguish between the Real and the illusory and to know things in their essence or as they are, which means ultimately to know them *in divinis*.[8] The knowledge of the Principle which is at once the absolute and infinite Reality is the heart of metaphysics while the distinction between levels of universal and cosmic existence, including both the macrocosm and the microcosm, are like its limbs. Metaphysics concerns not only the Principle in Itself and in its manifestations but also the principles of the various sciences of a cosmological order. At the heart of the traditional sciences of the cosmos, as well as traditional anthropology, psychology, and aesthetics stands the *scientia sacra* which contains the principles of these sciences while being primarily concerned with the knowledge of the Principle which is both sacred knowledge and knowledge of the sacred par excellence, since the Sacred as such is none other than the Principle.

The Principle is Reality in contrast to all that appears as real but which is not reality in the ultimate sense. The Principle is the Absolute compared to which all is relative. It is Infinite while all else is finite. The Principle is One and Unique while manifestation is multiplicity. It is the Supreme Substance compared to which all else is accident. It is the Essence to which all things are juxtaposed as form. It is at once Beyond Being and Being while the order of multiplicity is comprised of existents. It alone *is* while all else becomes, for It alone is eternal in the ultimate sense while all that is externalized partakes of change. It is the Origin but also the End, the alpha and the omega. It is Emptiness if the world is envisaged as fullness and Fullness if the relative is perceived in the light of its ontological poverty and essential nothingness.[9] These are all manners of speaking of the Ultimate Reality which can be known but not by man as such. It can only be known through the sun of the Divine Self residing at the center of the human soul. But all these ways of describing or referring to the Principle possess meaning and are efficacious as points of reference and support for that knowledge of the Real that in its realized aspect always terminates in the Ineffable and in that silence which is the "reflection" or "shadow" of the nonmanifested aspect of the Principle upon the plane of manifestation. From that unitary point of view, the Principle or the Source is seen as not only the Inward but also the Outward[10], not only the One but also the essential reality of the many which is but the reflection of the One. At the top of that mountain of unitive knowledge there resides but the One; discrimination between the Real and the unreal terminates in the awareness of the nondual nature of the Real, the awareness which is the heart of gnosis and which represents not human knowledge but God's knowledge of Himself, the consciousness which is the goal of the path of knowledge and the essence of *scientia sacra*.[11]

The Ultimate Reality is at once Absolute and Infinite since no finite reality can be absolute due to its exclusion of some domain of reality. This reality is also the Supreme Good or the Perfection which is inseparable from the Absolute. Reality, being at once Absolute, Infinite, and Supreme Goodness or Perfection, cannot but give rise to the world or multiplicity which must be realized for otherwise that Reality would exclude certain possibilities and not be infinite. The world flows from the infinitude and goodness of the Real for to speak of goodness is to speak of manifestation, effusion, or creation and to speak of infinity is to speak of all possibilities including that of the negation of the Principle in whose direction the cosmogonic process moves without ever realizing that negation completely, for that total negation would be nothingness pure and simple.

Goodness is also from another point of view the image of the Absolute in the direction of that effusion and manifestation which marks the descent from the Principle and constitutes the world. Herein lies the root of relativity but it is still on the plane of Divinity. It is relatively *in divinis* or what could be called, using the well-known Hindu concept, the Divine *māyā*.[12] Relativity is a possibility of that Reality which is at once Absolute and Infinite; hence that reality or the Absolute gives rise to that manifestation of the good which in descending hierarchy leads to the world. The world is ultimately good, as asserted by various orthodox traditions,[13] because it descends from the Divine Goodness. The instrument of this descent is the reflection of the Absolute upon the plane of that Divine Relativity, the reflection which is none other than the Supreme Logos, the source of all cosmic perfections, the "place" of the archetypes, the "Word" by which all things were made.[14]

Since the world or manifestation or creation issues from that Reality which is at once Absolute, Infinite, and Perfection or Goodness, these Hypostases of the Real or the Divine must be also reflected in the manifested order. The quality of absoluteness is reflected in the very existence of things, that mysterious presence of each thing which distinguishes it from all other things and from nothingness. Infinitude is reflected in the world in diverse modes in space which is indefinite extension, in time which is potentially endless duration, in form which displays unending diversity, in number which is marked by endless multiplicity, and in matter, a substance which partakes potentially of endless forms and divisions. As for Goodness, it is reflected in the cosmos through quality itself which is indispensable to existence however eclipsed it might become in certain forms in the world of multiplicity which are removed as far as possible from the luminous and essential pole of manifestation. Space which preserves, time which changes and transforms, form which reflects quality, number which signifies indefinite quantity and matter which is characterized by limitless substantiality are the conditions of existence of not only the physical world but the worlds above reaching ultimately the Divine Empyrean and the Divine Hypostases of Absoluteness, Infinity, and Perfection themselves.

Moreover, each of the Divine Hypostases is reflected in a particular manner in the five conditions of existence. Absoluteness is reflected in space as center, in time as the present moment, in matter as the ether which is the principle of both matter and energy, in form as the sphere which is the most perfect of forms and generator of all other regular geometric forms that are potentially contained in it, and in number as unity which is the source and principle of all numbers. Infinitude is reflected in space as extension which theoretically knows no bound, in time as duration which has logically no end, in matter as the indefiniteness of material substantiality, in form as the unlimited possibility of diversity, and in number as the limitlessness of quantity. As for Perfection, it is reflected in space as the contents or objects in space reflecting Divine Qualities and also as pure existence which as the Sufis say is the "Breath of the Compassionate" (*nafas al-raḥmān*), in space and time likewise as shapes and events possessing quality, in form as beauty and in number as that qualitative aspect of number always related to geometric forms which is usually associated with the idea of Pythagorean number. *Scientia sacra* sees these aspects of cosmic existence as reflections upon the plane or the multiple planes of manifestation of the Supreme Hypostases of Absoluteness, Infinitude, and Goodness which characterize the Real as such. It also sees each of these conditions of existence as reflecting directly an aspect of the Divinity: matter and energy the Divine Substance, form the Logos, number the Divine Unity which is inexhaustible, space the infinite extension of Divine Manifestation, and time the rhythms of the universal cycles of existence which the Abrahamic traditions allude to in passing as far as their official, formal theologies are concerned and which Hinduism highlights, referring to them as days and nights in the life of Brahma.

Since metaphysics as developed in the Occident has almost always been related to ontology, it is important to pause a moment and discuss the relation of Being to the Principle or Ultimate Reality. If Being is envisaged as the principle of existence or of all that exists, then It cannot be identified with the Principle as such because the Principle is not exhausted by its creating aspect. Being is the first determination of the Supreme Principle in the direction of manifestation, and ontology remains only a part of metaphysics and is incomplete as long as it envisages the Principle only as Being in the sense defined. But if Being is used to embrace and include the sense of Absoluteness and Infinity, then it can mean both the Supra-Being or Reality beyond Being and Being as its first determination, even if only the term *Being* is used. Such seems to be the case with *esse* as employed by certain of the Scholastics and also *wujūd* in some of the schools of Islamic philosophy and theosophy.[15]

The distinction between Being and being, Being and existence, existence and essence or quiddity and the relation between quiddity or essence and existence in existents lies at heart of medieval Islamic, Jewish, and Christian philosophy and has been discussed in numerous works of medieval thought. From the point of view of *scientia sacra* what caused this profound way of envisaging reality to become unintelligible and finally rejected in the West was the loss of that intellectual intuition which destroyed the sense of the mystery of existence and reduced the subject of philosophy from the study of the act of existence (*esto*) to the existent (*ens*), thereby gradually reducing reality to pure "it" divorced from the world of the Spirit and the majesty of Being whose constant effusions uphold the world which appears to the senses as possessing a continuous "horizontal" existence divorced from the "vertical" Cause or Being per se. That Islamic philosophy did not end with that impasse which marks the study of ontology in Western philosophy is due to its insistence upon the study of Being and its act rather than existents and to the wedding of this philosophy, by Suhrawardī and those who were to follow him, to spiritual experience which made the experience of Being not only a possibility but the source for all philosophical speculation concerning the concept and reality of being.[16]

The Ultimate Reality which is both Supra-Being and Being is at once transcendent and immanent. It is beyond everything and at the very heart and center of man's soul. *Scientia sacra* can be expounded in the language of one as well as the other perspective. It can speak of God or the Godhead, Allah, the Tao, or even *nirvāna* as being beyond the world, or forms or *samsāra*, while asserting ultimately that *nirvāna* is *samsāra*, and *samsāra*, *nirvāna*. But it can also speak of the Supreme Self, of *Ātman*, compared to which all objectivization is *māyā*. The Ultimate Reality can be seen as both the Supreme Object and the Innermost Subject, for God is both transcendent and immanent, but He can be experienced as immanent only after He has been experienced as transcendent. Only God as Being can allow man to experience the Godhead as Supra-Being. The unitive knowledge which sees the world not as separative creation but as manifestation that is united through symbols and the very ray of existence to the Source does not at all negate the majesty of transcendence. Without that majesty, the beauty of Divine Proximity cannot be beheld and integral metaphysics is fully aware of the necessity, on its own level, of the theological formulations which insist upon the hiatus between God and man or the Creator and the world. The metaphysical knowledge of unity comprehends the theological one in both a figurative and literal sense, while the reverse is not true. That is why the attainment of that unitive knowledge is impregnated with the perfume of sanctity which always strengthens the very foundations of the religion with which the formal theology in question is concerned, while the study of formal theology can never result in that *scientia sacra* which simply belongs to another dimension and which relies upon another aspect of the functioning of the Intellect upon the human plane.

Metaphysics does not only distinguish between the Real and the apparent and Being and becoming but also between grades of existence. The hierarchic nature of reality is a universal assertion of all traditions and is part and parcel of their religious practices as well as their doctrines, whether conceived in terms of various hosts and orders of angels as described in the famous *Celestial Hierarchies* of Dionysius, or levels of light and darkness as in certain schools of Islamic esoterism, or as various orders of gods and titans as in religions with a mythological structure such as Hinduism. Even in Buddhism for which the Supreme Principle is seen as the Void or Emptiness rather than Fullness, the vast intermediate worlds are depicted with remarkable power and beauty in both Buddhist cosmological texts and Buddhist art. The emphasis upon the hierarchic structure of reality in traditional doctrines is so great that a famous Persian poem states that he who does not accept the hierarchy of existence is an infidel (*zindīq*). Here again *scientia sacra* which is concerned with the nature of reality is distinguished from theology as usually understood, which can remain satisfied with what concerns man directly and a simpler view of reality based on God and man without emphasis upon the hierarchy of existence, although even in theology many schools have not failed to take into consideration the existence if not always the full significance of the intermediate planes of reality.[17]

The relation between the various levels of reality or hierarchy of existence cannot be fully understood without taking into consideration another important notion found in one way or another in all the complete expressions of the *scientia sacra*, this notion being that of necessity to which is contrasted the notion of possibility. The distinction between necessity and possibility is the cornerstone of the philosophy of Ibn Sīnā (Avicenna) who has been called the "philosopher of being" and father of medieval ontology.[18] But the significance of both of these terms is of a purely metaphysical order and cannot be limited to the philosophical realm, even if this be traditional philosophy. It is the fruit of intellection rather than ratiocination as are in fact many of the tenets of traditional philosophy which veil in a syllogistic garb intuitions of a purely metaphysical nature. The presence of the notions of necessity and possibility in both Hindu and Far Eastern doctrines point in fact to realities of a universal order not at all limited to one particular mode of exposition or school of metaphysics.

Necessity is opposed to possibility conceptually but, if the meaning of possibility is understood fully, it will be seen that in one sense it complements necessity and is opposed to necessity only in one of its meanings. The root of possibility is related to potentiality and also "puissance," all three words being derived from *posse*, which means "to be able to." Possibility has in fact two meanings: one, the quality or character of something that can exist or not exist; and two, the quality or character of something which has the power and capability to perform or carry out an act. In the first sense the quiddities of things are possible, or contingent; an object can exist or not exist and there is no logical or metaphysical contradiction whether, let us say, a horse exists or not. In this sense but on a higher level, the archetypes or what Islamic metaphysics call *al-aʿyān al-thābitah* or "immutable essences"[19] are also possible beings, only God being necessary. Taken in this meaning of the term, possibility is opposed to necessity while things which do exist and therefore must exist have become necessary not through their own essence but through the Necessary Being which alone is necessary in Itself. That is why, to use the language of Islamic philosophy again, they are called *al-wājib biʾl-ghayr*, literally "that which is made necessary by other than itself," the "other" being ultimately the Necessary Being.

In the second sense of the meaning of possibility as power, it is not opposed to necessity but complements it as far as the Principle is concerned. God is Absolute Necessity and Infinite Possibility, the omnipotence of God reflected in the Divine Attribute *al-Qādir* in the Quran, meaning exactly possibility in this second sense. Whatever happens in this world is according to the Will of God but also in conformity with a Divine Possibility. God could not will what is not possibility in this sense for He would then negate His own Nature. Whatever claims a blind type of religious voluntarism might make, God's omnipotence cannot contradict His Nature and when the Gospel claims, "With God all things are possible," it is referring precisely to this Infinite Possibility of God.

Each world brought into being corresponds to a Divine Possibility and gains existence through the Divine Will which operates on different levels, sometimes appearing as contradictory to the eyes of the earthly creature. But there is never anything arbitrary about what God wills; His wisdom complements His Will and His Nature remains inviolable.

As far as necessity is concerned, it can be said that although the medieval philosophers called pure Being the Necessary Being, strictly speaking only the Beyond Being or Ultimate Reality is necessity in Itself and necessary with respect to Itself. Being is necessary vis-à-vis the world so that from the point of view of the world or of multiplicity, it can be legitimately considered as the Necessary Being. But Being can also be considered as Possibility as such which must be distinguished from the possibilities which are qualities of Being. These qualities possess two aspects: they are contingent or possible in relation to the Principle or Essence, that is, they can exist or not exist, and they are necessary in their content and so participate in the necessity of the Essence. From the consideration of these two aspects one can see that there are two kinds of possibilities: those which reflect necessity and those which reflect contingency. The first kind engenders objects which definitely exist and the second those which can possibly not exist.

God gives existence to possibilities which are so many reflections and reverberations of Being and from this breathing of existence upon the quiddities of possibilities the world and, in fact, the myriad of worlds are born. That Divine Relativity or *māyā*, as it is projected toward nothingness and away from the Source, produces privative modalities and inversions of these possibilities whose origin is positive reflection and inversion, polarization of light and casting of shadows, luminous Logos and dark Demiurge. Being as Possibility is Itself the supreme veil of the Reality which in Itself is not only Infinite but also Absolute, that Essence which is beyond all determination.[20]

To speak of the veil is to be concerned with one of the key concepts with which *scientia sacra* is concerned, one which, however, has not been as much emphasized in Western metaphysical doctrines as it has in the East, although it is certainly mentioned by such figures as Eckhart and Silesius who allude to the Divine Relativity and are aware of its significance for the understanding of how the roots and principles of manifestation are to be found in the Principle Itself. The veil is none other than what the Hindus call *māyā* and the Sufis *ḥijāb*. The fact that *māyā* has now become practically an English word points to the necessity of dealing with such a concept in the exposition of traditional doctrines and the lack of an appropriate term in the English language to convey all that *māyā* signifies.

Māyā is usually translated as illusion and from the nondualistic or Advaitist point of view *māyā is* illusion, only *Ātman*, the Supreme Self, being real. But *māyā* is also creativity and "Divine Play" (*līlā*). On the principial level she is relativity which is the source of separateness, exteriorization, and objectivization. She is that tendency toward nothingness which brings manifestation into being, the nothingness which is never reached but which is implied by the cosmogonic movement away from the Principle. Infinitude could not but include the possibility of separation, division, and externalization which characterize all that is other than the Principle.[21] *Māyā* is the supreme veil and also the supreme theophany which at once veils and reveals.[22] God being good cannot but radiate His goodness and this tendency toward radiation or manifestation implies that movement away from the Source which characterizes cosmic and even metacosmic levels of reality away from the Origin which alone is absolutely real. *Māyā* is almost the same as the Islamic *raḥmah*, the Divine Mercy, whose "breath" existentiates the world, the very substance of the world being *nafas al-raḥmān*, the Breath of the Compassionate[23] in the same way that one can call *māyā* the breath of *Ātman*. For Hinduism, however, the creation of the world or the casting of the veil of *māyā* upon the Absolute Self or *Ātman* is expressed as "Divine Play," while for Islam this externalization which is none other than the activity of *māyā* is envisaged as the love of God to be "known," the origin of the world being the revelation of God to Himself according to the famous tradition of the Prophet (*ḥadīth*), "I was a hidden treasure, I desired to be known, hence I created the world in order to be known."[24]

Formal theology envisages God and the world or the Creator and the created in a completely distinct and "absolute" manner and is therefore unable to provide answers for certain fundamental questions intellectually, questions which can be dealt with only from the perspective of the *scientia sacra* and the doctrine of *māyā* or veil which, on the highest level, implies introduction of relativity into the principial plane without, however, reaching the level of the Absolute which remains beyond all duality and relativity. Since there is a world which is relative, the roots of this world must exist in the principial order itself and this root is none other than the Divine *māyā* which veils and manifests the One upon all planes of reality. She is the Feminine, at once Mary and Eve. Evil issues from the exteriorizing activity of *māyā* but Existence which remains pure and good finally prevails over evil as Eve was forgiven for her sins by the spiritual inviolability and victory of Mary.

Māyā acts through both radiation and reverberation or reflection, first preparing the ground or plane of manifestation and then manifesting both the radiation and reverberation which take place on this plane. To use an image of Schuon,[25] if we envisage a point which symbolizes the Absolute or the Supreme Substance, the radii symbolize the radiation, the circumference the reflection or reverberation of the center and the area of the whole circle, Existence itself,[26] or a particular level of existence in which *māyā* repeats her act. *Māyā* is the source of all duality even on the principial level causing the distinction between the Essence and the Qualities. It is also the source of the dualism between subject and object even on the highest level beyond which there is but the One, in which knower and known, or subject and object are one. But *māyā* does not remain bound to the principial level alone. She is self-projected through various levels of cosmic existence which a *ḥadīth* calls the seventy thousand veils of light and darkness and which can be summarized as the three fundamental levels of angelic, animic, and physical existence.

On each level there is a manifestation or reflection of the Supreme Substance and the action of *māyā*. For example, on the physical or material plane, the reflection of Substance is the ether which is the invisible support and origin of the physical elements. The reverberation of *māyā* is matter and its radiation energy. Moreover, the two main tendencies of *māyā*, which are conservation and transformation, translate themselves into space and time in this world and the many worlds and cycles which transform these worlds on the cosmic level. There is, to be sure, an immense gulf which separates various worlds and an almost complete incommensurability between the animic and the material worlds and also between the angelic or spiritual world and the animic. But through all these levels *māyā* remains *māyā*, being at once the revealer of the Real and Its veil, in herself the intermediary and isthmus between the Infinite and the finite.

Māyā in its aspect of illusion is also the cause for this impossibility of encompassing Reality in a closed system of thought so characteristic of profane philosophy. The Absolute is blinding evidence or something incomprehensible to those who do not possess the eye or intuition to grasp it conceptually. In any case, ratiocination, belonging to the realm of relativity, cannot be used to prove or perceive the Absolute which remains beyond the reach of all attempts of the relative to comprehend It. But intelligence can know the Absolute and in fact only the Absolute is completely intelligible. Below that level, the activity of *māyā* enters into play and brings about an element of ambiguity and uncertainty. If there were to be such a thing as pure relativity, it would be completely unintelligible. But even in the relative world which still bears the imprint of the Absolute, the element of ambiguity and unintelligibility of *māyā* enters into all mental activity which would seek to transgress beyond its legitimate function and try to enmesh the Absolute in a finite system of thought based upon ratiocination.[27] Human thought as mental activity cannot become absolutely conformable to the Real as a result of *māyā*, whereas direct knowledge or intellection has such a power. The plight of innumerable schools of modern philosophy and their failure to achieve the task of encompassing the Real through the process of purely human thought is caused by the power of *māyā* which exercises its illusory spell most upon those who would deny her reality.

Closely related to the doctrine of *māyā* is the question of evil and its meaning in the light of the absolute goodness of the Origin and Source, a question which lies at the heart of the problems of theodicy, especially as they have been discussed in the Abrahamic world over the ages. This problem, namely, how can a God who is both omnipotent and good create a world which contains evil, is insoluble on the level of both formal theology and rationalistic philosophy. Its answer can be found only in metaphysics or *scientia sacra*, the eclipse of which has caused many men to lose their faith in religion and the religious world view precisely because of their inability to gain access to a doctrine which would solve this apparent contradiction. From the metaphysical point of view there is not just the question of the omnipotence of God, there is also the Divine Nature which the Divine Will cannot contradict. God cannot will to cease to be God. Now, this Divine Nature is not limited to Being; as already mentioned, it is the Absolute and Infinite Reality which is the Beyond Being or Supra-Being of which Being is the first determination in the direction of manifestation or creation. The Divine Nature or Ultimate Reality is both infinite and good and therefore wills to radiate and manifest Itself. From this radiation issue the states of existence, the multiple worlds, hence separation, elongation from the Source from which results what manifests itself as evil on a particular plane of reality. To speak of Infinity is to speak of the possibility of the negation of the Source in the direction of nothingness, hence of evil which one might call the "crystallization or existentiation of nothingness." Since only God—who is both the Beyond Being and Being—is Good, as the Gospels assert, all that is other than God partakes of that element of privation which is the source of evil. The will of God as the Godhead or the Beyond Being is the realization of the possibilities inherent in Its Infinitude and hence that separation from the Source which implies evil. But precisely because manifestation is a possibility of Infinite Reality, the existence of the world in itself is not evil nor does the element of evil appear in any of the worlds still close to the Divine Proximity.[28] Now, the Will of God as Being operates within the radiation and reverberation caused by *māyā* and the very Nature of that Infinite Reality which is the Supra-Being. The Will of God on this level opposes concrete forms of evil according to the criteria established by various revelations and always in the light of the total good and in accordance with the economy of a particular traditional mode of life. On this level the Will of God is opposed to various types of evil without being able to eradicate existence as such, which would amount to negating the Divine Nature Itself. There are in reality two levels of operation of the Divine Will or even two Divine Wills, one related to the Absolute and Infinite Reality which cannot but manifest and create, hence, separation, elongation, and privation which appear as evil; and the second related to the Will of Being which opposes the presence of evil in accordance with the divine laws and norms which constitute the ethical structures of various traditional worlds.

To relate evil to the infinity of that Reality which is also the All-Possibility, does not mean to deny the reality of evil on a particular level of reality. The existence of evil is inseparable from the relative level in which it manifests itself. One cannot simply say that evil does not exist as do even certain traditional masters of gnosis who, gazing with constancy upon the overwhelming goodness of the Divine Principle, in a sense circumvent evil and pass it by.[29] But this is of course not the case of all the traditional sages, many of whom have provided the metaphysical key for the understanding of evil. From the point of view of *scientia sacra*, although real on the relative plane of reality, evil has no reality as a substance and in itself as a thing or object. Evil is always partial and fragmented. It must exist because of the ontological hiatus between the Principle and manifestation but it remains always limited and bound while goodness is unlimited and opens unto the Infinite. Also as far as the Will of God is concerned, God wills evil not as evil but as part of a greater good to which this segmented reality called evil contributes. That is why evil is never evil in its existential substance but through that privation of a good which plays a role in the total economy of the cosmos and contributes to a greater good. Every disequilibrium and disorder is of a partial and transient nature contributing to that total equilibrium, harmony, and order which is the cosmos.[30]

The doctrine of *māyā* or *ḥijāb* enables us to understand the metaphysical roots of that which appears as evil. This doctrine explains evil as privation and separation from the Good and also as an element contributing to a greater good, although within a particular ambience or plane of existence, evil remains evil as a result of either privation or excess. If this doctrine is fully understood then it is possible to comprehend the meaning of evil as such. But even in this case it is not possible for man to understand such or such an evil, only God being totally and completely intelligible. In any case, although the Divine Will wills everything that exists including what appears as evil, as far as man, who is both intelligent and has a free will, is concerned, God wills for him only the good. The best way of solving the question of evil and theodicy is in fact to live a life which would make possible the actualization of the *scienta sacra* in one's being. This realization or actualization is the best possible way of understanding the nature of the Good and the why of terrestrial human existence which, being removed from God, cannot but be marred by the fragmentation, dissipation, and privation that appears as evil and that is as real as that plane of reality upon which it manifests itself. Evil ceases to exist, however, on a higher plane, where transient and partial disorders contribute to a greater order and privation to a greater good.

Closely allied to the question of good and evil is that of free will and determinism which has also occupied philosophers and theologians in the Abrahamic world over the ages but which also is of central concern in other traditional climates such as that of India as evidenced by the discussion of correct action in the *Bhagavad-Gītā*. In this question also there is no possibility of going beyond the either-or dichotomy as long as one remains on the level of formal theology or rationalistic philosophy as witnessed by centuries of debates among theologians and philosophers in Judaism, Christianity, and Islam. From the metaphysical point of view, however, the whole debate appears as sterile and fragmented through the fact that both sides attribute a quality of absoluteness to that which is relative, namely the human plane. Metaphysically speaking, only the Ultimate Reality is absolute and at once pure necessity and pure freedom. Only God is completely necessary and free, being both Absoluteness and Infinitude. Now, on the human plane, we are already on the level of relativity, therefore there cannot be either absolute determination or absolute free will. Something of both must manifest itself on the level of human relativity. If only one of these two conditions were to be present, the plane of relativity would no longer be relative but absolute. Man's freedom is as real as himself. He ceases to be free in the sense of independent of the Divine Will to the extent that he ceases to be separated ontologically from God. At the same time, man is determined and not free to the extent that an ontological hiatus separates him from his Source and Origin, for only God is freedom. Journeying from the relative toward the Absolute means at once losing the freedom of living in error and gaining freedom from the tyranny of all the psycho-material determinations which imprison and stifle the soul. In God there is pure freedom and pure necessity and only in Him is man completely free and also completely determined but with a determination which, being nothing but man's own most profound nature and the root of his being, is none other than the other face of freedom, total and unconditional.

Intelligence is a divine gift which pierces through the veil of *māyā* and is able to know reality as such. It is a ray of light which pierces through the veils of cosmic existence to the Origin and connects the periphery of existence, upon which fallen man lives, to the Center wherein resides the Self. The Intellect is itself divine and only human to the extent that man participates in it. It is a substance as well as a function; it is light as well as vision. The Intellect is not the mind nor is it reason which is the reflection of the Intellect upon the human plane, but it is the root and center of consciousness and what has been traditionally called the soul. In the technical sense, however, the soul must be considered as the equivalent of the *anima* or *psyche* in which case the Intellect is *spiritus* or *nous* from whose marriage with the passive and feminine psyche is born that gold which symbolizes the perfection of the sanctified soul.

The metacosmic principle which is the Intellect is the source of both knowledge and being, of the subjective conscience which knows and the objective order which is known. It is also the source of revelation which creates a nexus between man and the cosmos and of course the metacosmic Reality. The Logos or *Buddhi* or *ʿaql*, as the Intellect is called in various traditions, is the luminous center which is the generating agent of the world—for "it was by the Word that all things were made"—of man, and of religion. It is God's knowledge of Himself and the first in His creation. Moreover, as there is a hierarchy of cosmic existence, so are there levels of consciousness and degrees of descent of the Intellect through various levels of existence until man is reached, in whose heart the ray of Intellect still shines, although it is usually dimmed by the passions and the series of "falls" that have separated man from what he really is.

Yet, even the consciousness of fallen man and the intelligence which shines within him, although a distant reflection of the Intellect, nevertheless display something of the miracle of the Intellect which is at once supernatural and natural. Perhaps the most immediate experience of man is his subjectivity, the mystery of inwardness and a consciousness which can reflect upon itself, opening inwardly unto the Infinite which is also bliss. No less of a miracle is the power of objectivity, the power of human intelligence to know the world in an objective manner and with a categorical certitude which no amount of sophism can destroy. Finally, there is the mystery of the adequation of knowledge, of the fact that our intelligence corresponds to the nature of reality and that what man knows corresponds to aspects of the Real.[31] But these are all mysteries as long as man is cut off from the light of intellectual intuition or intellection. Otherwise, in the light of the Intellect itself both the subjective and objective powers of intelligence are perfectly intelligible.

As already stated, *scientia sacra* cannot be attained without intellection and the correct functioning of intelligence within man. That is why those who are cut off from this inner sacrament[32] not only repudiate the teachings of this sacred knowledge but also offer rationalistic arguments against them based usually on incomplete or false premises, expecting the heavens to collapse as a result of this sound and fury which metaphysically signifies nothing. Intellection does not reach the truth as a result of profane thought or reasoning but through an a priori direct intuition of the truth. Reasoning may act as an occasion for intellection but it cannot be the cause of intellection. For that very reason the fruit of intellection cannot be nullified or negated by any form of reasoning which, based on the limitations of the person who uses reasoning, often results in error pure and simple. This assertion does not mean of course that intellection is against logic or that it is irrational. On the contrary, there is no truth which can be considered illogical, logic itself being an ontological reality of the human state. But the role and function of reasoning and the use of logic in metaphysics and profane philosophy are completely different, as different as the use of mathematics in the rosette of the Chartres Cathedral or a cupola of one of the mosques of Isfahan and in a modern skyscraper.

Although the Intellect shines within the being of man, man is too far removed from his primordial nature to be able to make full use of this divine gift by himself. He needs revelation which alone can actualize the intellect in man and allow it to function properly. The day when each man was also a prophet and when the intellect functioned in man "naturally" so that he saw all things *in divinis* and possessed a direct knowledge of a sacred character is long past. The traditional doctrines themselves emphasize that in the later unfolding of the cosmic cycle it is only revelation or *avatāric* descent that enables man to see once again with the "eye of the heart" which is the "eye of the intellect." If there are exceptions, these are exceptions which only prove the rule and in any case "the wind bloweth where it listeth."

Revelation in its esoteric dimension makes possible, through initiation, access to higher levels of man's being as well as consciousness. The appropriate rites, the traditional cadre, forms and symbols, and the grace issuing from revelation provide keys with which man is able to open the doors of the inner chambers of his being and with the help of the spiritual master to journey through the cosmic labyrinth with the result of finally attaining that treasure which is none other than the pearl of gnosis. Revelation actualizes the possibilities of the intellect, removes impediments of the carnal soul which prevent the intellect from functioning, and makes possible the transmission of an initiatic knowledge which at the same time resides within the very substance of the intellect. There is an unbridgeable hiatus between intelligence sanctified by revelation and the intelligence which, cut off from this source and also from its own root, is reduced to its reflection upon the human mind and atrophied into that truncated and fragmented faculty which is considered scientifically as intelligence.[33]

As far as the relation between the intellect and revelation is concerned, it is fundamental to say a few words on the rapport between intellectuality and sacred scripture which has been so forgotten in the modern world. Without reviving spiritual exegesis, it is not possible to rediscover *scientia sacra* in the bosom of a tradition dominated by the presence of sacred scripture. Scripture possesses an inner dimension which is attainable only through intellection operating within a traditional framework and which alone is able to solve certain apparent contradictions and riddles in sacred texts. Once intellectual intuition becomes inoperative and the mind a frozen lake over which ideas glide but into which nothing penetrates, then the revealed text also veils its inner dimension and spiritual exegesis becomes reduced to archaeology and philology, not to speak of the extrapolation of the subjective errors of the present era back into the age of the revelation in question. Clement and Origen become thus transformed into modern exegetes for whom the New Testament is little more than an ethical commentary upon the social conditions of first-century Palestine.

In the Oriental world, including the Judeo-Christian tradition, the spiritual science of exegesis has never died out completely. The sacred text serves as the source for the formal world of the tradition in question, including its ritual and liturgical practices and its sacred art, as well as the intellectual aspect of the tradition extending from formal theology, philosophy, and the science of symbols to *scientia sacra* itself which crowns the inner message conveyed by the sacred text and which is attained through the intelligence that is sanctified by that very sacred scripture.[34] In Islam, dominated by the blinding presence of the Quran, every aspect of the tradition has been related to the Holy Book and the category of exegetes[35] has ranged from those concerned with the Divine Law to the gnostics who have penetrated through that spiritual hermeneutics or *taʾwīl*[36] to the pearl of wisdom residing behind the veil of the external forms of the Holy Book. Such masterpieces of Sufism as the *Mathnawī* of Jalāl al-Dīn Rūmī are in reality commentaries upon the Quran, not to speak of the numerous esoteric commentaries of such masters as Ibn ʿArabī,[37] Ṣadr al-Dīn al-Qūnyawī,[38] ʿAbd al-Razzāq al-Kāshānī, Rashīd al-Dīn Aḥmad Mībudī, and others. Both *scientia sacra* and all the ancillary traditional sciences in Islam may be said to issue forth from the fountainhead of the inner wisdom contained in the Quran in the same way that Hinduism considers the traditional sciences to be the limbs of the Vedas. Spiritual hermeneutics is the means whereby the intelligence, sanctified by revelation, is able to penetrate into the heart of revelation to discover that principial truth which is the very root and substance of intelligence itself. In this process the microcosmic manifestation of the Intellect, which is the source of inner illumination and intellection, unveils the inner meaning of that macrocosmic manifestation of the Intellect which is revelation or more specifically, sacred scripture. Moreover, the same truth pertains *mutatis mutandis* to the interpretation of the inner meaning of that other revealed book which is the cosmos itself.

Scientia sacra envisages intelligence in its rapport not only with revelation in an external sense but also with the source of inner revelation which is the center of man, namely the heart. The seat of intelligence is the heart and not the head, as affirmed by all traditional teachings. The word *heart, hṛdaya* in Sanskrit, *Herz* in German, *kardia* in Greek, and *cor/cordis* in Latin, have the root hrd or krd which, like the Egyptian Horus, imply the center of the world or a world.[39] The heart is also the center of the human microcosm and therefore the "locus" of the Intellect by which all things were made. The heart is also the seat of sentiments and the will, the other elements of which the human being is constituted. Profound emotions as well as will have their origin in the heart as does intelligence which constitutes the apex of the microcosmic ternary of powers or faculties. It is also in the heart that intelligence and faith meet and where faith itself becomes saturated with the light of sapience. In the Quran both faith (*īmān*) and intelligence (*ʿaql*) are explicitly identified with the heart (*al-qalb*),[40] while in Hinduism the Sanskrit term *śraddhā*, which is usually translated as faith, means literally knowledge of the heart.[41] In Latin also the fact that *credo* and *cor/cordis* are derived from the same root points to the same metaphysical truth. This traditional exegesis of language reveals not only the relation of principial knowledge to the heart but also the important metaphysical principle that integral intelligence is never divorced from faith but that, on the contrary, faith is necessary in the actualization of the possibilities of intellection within the cadre of a revelation. That intelligence which is able to attain to the knowledge of the sacred is already sanctified and rooted in the center of the human state where it is never divorced from either faith or love. In the heart, knowledge in fact always coincides with love. Only when externalized does knowledge become related to the mind and the activity of the brain, and love to that substance which is usually called the soul.

This externalization of the intelligence and its projection upon the plane of the mind is, however, a necessary condition of human existence without which man would not be man, the creature who is created as a thinking being. Dialectical intelligence identified with the mind is not in itself negative; in fact, human intelligence in its fullness implies the correct functioning of both the intelligence of the heart and that of the mind, the first being intuitive and the second analytical and discursive. The two functions together make possible the reception, crystallization, formulation, and finally communication of the truth. Mental formulation of the intuition received by the intelligence in the heart becomes completely assimilated by man and actualized through the activity of the mind. This in fact is one of the main roles of meditation in spiritual exercises, meditation being related to the activity of the mind. Through this process also the light received by the heart is communicated and transmitted, such an activity being necessary because of the very nature of the content of the intuition received by the intelligence residing in the heart, the content which, being good, has to give of itself and, like all goodness, shine forth.[42] The human being needs to exteriorize certain inner truths in order to be able to interiorize, to analyze in order to synthesize, synthesis needing a phase of analysis. Hence, the need of man for language which proceeds from holy silence and returns again to it, but which plays a vital role in the formulation of the truth issuing from the first silence and in preparing man for return to the second silence which is synthesis after analysis, return to unity after separation.[43]

Symbolically, the mind can be considered as the moon which reflects the light of the sun which is the heart. The intelligence in the heart shines upon the plane of the mind which then reflects this light upon the dark night of the terrestrial existence of fallen man. *Scientia sacra* which issues from the total intelligence of the heart,[44] therefore, also includes the dialectic of the mind. In fact, some of the greatest dialecticians in both East and West have been metaphysicians who have realized the supreme station of knowledge. What tradition opposes is not the activity of the mind but its divorce from the heart, the seat of intelligence and the location of the "eye of knowledge," which the Sufis call the eye of the heart (*'ayn al-qalb* or *chishm-i dil*) and which is none other than the "third eye" of the Hindu tradition. It is this eye which transcends duality and the rational functioning of the mind based upon analysis and which perceives the unity that is at once the origin and end of the multiplicity perceived by the mind and the mind's own power to analyze and know discursively. That is why the Sufis chant:

> *Open the eye of thy heart so that thou wilst see the Spirit*
> *So that thou wilst see that which cannot be seen.*[45]

The attempt of the rational mind to discover the Intellect through its own light is seen by tradition to be futile because the object which the rational faculty is trying to perceive is actually the subject which makes the very act of perception by the rational faculty possible. A mind which is cut off from the light of the intelligence of the heart and which seeks to find God is unaware that the light with which it is seeking to discover God is itself a ray of the Light of God. Such a mind cannot but be like a person wandering in the desert in the brightness of day with a lamp in his hand looking for the sun.[46] Blindness does not issue from reason but from reason being cut off from the intellect and then trying to play the role of the intellect in the attainment of knowledge. Such an attempt cannot but result in that desacralization of knowledge and of life that one already observes in members of that segment of humanity which has chosen to take its destiny into its own hands and live on the earth as if it were only of this earth.

Since *scientia sacra* is expressed outwardly and does not remain only on the level of the inner illumination of the heart, it is necessary to understand something of the kind of language it employs. The formal language used for the expression of *scientia sacra*, and in fact nearly the whole spectrum of traditional teachings, is that of symbolism. *Scientia sacra* can be expressed in human words as well as in landscape paintings, beating of drums, or other formal means which convey meaning. But in all cases symbolism remains the key for the understanding of its language. Fortunately, during this century much has been written on the veritable significance of symbols, and it has been shown, especially in works identified with the circle of traditional writers, that symbols are not man-made signs, but reflections on a lower level of the existence of a reality belonging to the higher order.[47] Symbols are ontological aspects of a thing, to say the least as real as the thing itself, and in fact that which bestows significance upon a thing within the universal order of existence. In the hierarchic universe of traditional metaphysics, it can be said that every level of reality and everything on every level of reality is ultimately a symbol, only the Real being Itself as such. But on a more limited scale, one can say that symbols reflect in the formal order archetypes belonging to the principial realm and that through symbols the symbolized is unified with its archetypal reality.[48]

There are, moreover, symbols which are "natural" in the sense of being inherent in the nature of certain objects and forms through the very cosmogonic process which has brought forth these forms upon the terrestrial plane. There are other symbols which are sanctified by a particular revelation that is like a second creation. The sun is "naturally" the symbol of the Divine Intellect for anyone who still possesses the faculty of symbolic perception and in whom the "symbolist spirit" is operative. But the same sun is sanctified in a special manner in solar cults such as Mithraism and gains a special significance in a particular traditional universe as has wine in Christianity or water in Islam. The Sufi poets may use the symbolism of wine in the first sense of symbol but it is the Christic descent which has given that special significance to wine in the Eucharist as a sanctified symbol that remains bound to the particular world which is Christian.[49]

Scientia sacra makes use of both types of symbolism in the exposition of its teachings but is always rooted in its formal aspect in the tradition in which it flowers and functions and by virtue of which the very attainment of this sacred knowledge is possible in an operative manner. Sufism may draw occasionally from Hindu or Neoplatonic formulations and symbols, but its formal world is that of the Quran and it is the grace issuing from the Quranic revelation which has made the attainment of gnosis in Sufism possible. It is in fact the living tradition that molds the language of discourse of metaphysics and that chooses among the symbols available to it those which best serve its purpose of communicating a doctrine of a sapiential and sacred nature. On the one hand, symbolism can be fully understood only in the light of a living spirituality without which it can become a maze of riddles; on the other hand, symbols serve as the means whereby man is able to understand the language of *scientia sacra*.

Finally, it must be emphasized that traditional metaphysics or *scientia sacra* is not only a theoretical exposition of the knowledge of reality. Its aim is to guide man, to illuminate him, and allow him to attain the sacred. Therefore, its expositions are also points of reference, keys with which to open certain doors and means of opening the mind to certain realities. In their theoretical aspect they have a provisional aspect in the sense of the Buddhist *upāya*, of accommodating means of teaching the truth. In a sense, *scientia sacra* contains both the seed and the fruit of the tree of knowledge. As theory it is planted as a seed in the heart and mind of man, a seed that if nurtured through spiritual practice and virtue becomes a plant which finally blossoms forth and bears fruit in which, once again, that seed is contained. But if the first seed is theoretical knowledge, in the sense of *theoria* or vision, the second seed is realized gnosis, the realization of a knowledge which being itself sacred, consumes the whole being of the knower and, as the sacred, demands of man all that he is. That is why it is not possible to attain this knowledge in any way except by being consumed by it.

> The result of my life can be summarized in three words;
> I was immature, I matured and I was consumed.[50]
>
> RŪMĪ

NOTES

1. On the meaning of this term see Nasr, *Islamic Science—An Illustrated Study*, London, 1976, p. 14.

2. "Toute connaissance est, par définition, celle de la Réalité absolue; c'est à dire que la Réalité est l'objet nécessaire, unique, essentiel de toute connaissance possible." Schuon, *L'Oeil du coeur*, p. 20.

3. Islamic as well as Jewish and Christian philosophers of the medieval period distinguished between the Active Intellect (*al-ʿaql al-faʿʿāl*, *intellectus agens*, *ha-sekhel*

hapoᵓel) which is the origin of knowledge and the potential or "material" intellect (*al-ᶜaql al-hayūlānī, intellectus materialis, ha-sekhel ha-hyulaᵓni*) which receives knowledge, and emphasized the intellectual nature of what is received by the human mind from the Divine Intellect. On the doctrine of the intellect in Islam see Ibn Sīnā, *Le Livre des directives et remarques,* trans. A. M. Goichon, Paris-Beirut, 1951, pp. 324ff; al-Fārābī, *Epistola sull'intelletto,* trans. F. Lucchetta, Padua, 1974; F. Rahman, *Prophecy in Islam, Philosophy and Orthodoxy,* Chicago, 1979; and J. Jolivet, *L'Intellect selon Kindī,* Leiden, 1971. As for the medieval Western world in general see E. Gilson, *History of Christian Philosophy in the Middle Ages,* New York, 1955; also M. Shallo, *Lessons in Scholastic Philosophy,* Philadelphia, 1916, pp. 264ff; and R. P. de Angelis, *Conoscenza dell'individuale e conoscenza dell'universale nel XIII e XIV secolo,* Rome, 1922. H. A. Wolfson has also dealt with this issue in many of his writings including *The Problem of the Soul of the Spheres,* Washington, 1962; *Essays in the History of Philosophy and Religion,* ed. I. Twersky and G. H. Williams, Cambridge, Mass., 1979; *Philo: Foundations of Religious Philosophy in Judaism,* Cambridge, Mass., 1968; *Christianity and Islam,* Cambridge, 1948; and "Extradeical and Intradeical Interpretations of Platonic Ideas," *Journal of the History of Ideas* 22/1 (Jan.–March 1961):3–32.

4. The Platonic view which sees knowledge descending from the realm of the "ideas" to the world, or from the Principle to manifestation, is more akin to the sapiential perspective than the Aristotelian one which moves from manifestation to the Principle or from physics to metaphysics.

5. On the distinction between metaphysics and profane philosophy see Guénon, *Introduction to the Study of Hindu Doctrines,* pp. 108ff; and idem, "Oriental Metaphysics," in Needleman (ed.), *Sword of Gnosis,* pp. 40–56.

6. This issue has been discussed by T. Izutsu, among others, in his *The Concept and Reality of Existence,* Tokyo, 1971; also his *Unicité de l'existence et création perpétuelle en mystique islamique,* Paris, 1980.

7. The service rendered by traditional authors to French, English, and German, the primary languages employed by them, in reviving them as languages for metaphysical discourse and in resuscitating their symbolic quality is the very reverse of the process being carried out by many modern analytical philosophers and positivists to cleanse European languages of their metaphysical content, reducing them to unidimensional languages reflecting the unidimensional minds which use such forms of language.

The concern of certain traditional authors with etymology and the revival of the significance of the root meaning of words is closely linked with this need to bring to the fore once again the symbolic possibilities hidden in the very structure of words which were once used by human beings who lived in the world of the sacred and who possessed the "symbolist spirit" which was directly reflected in their language. The still extant sacred and archaic languages are a witness to the remarkable treasury of metaphysics embedded in the very structure of language itself. In fact, in certain societies to this day metaphysics is taught as a commentary upon a sacred or archaic language, for example, in certain schools of Sufism. As far as Sufism is concerned see J. L. Michon, *Le Soufi marocain Aḥmad ibn ᶜAjība et son miᶜrāj. Glossaire de la mystique musulman,* Paris, 1973, especially pp. 177ff.

See also E. Zolla, *Language and Cosmogony,* Ipswich, U.K., 1976; and J. Canteins, *Phonèmes et archetypes,* Paris, 1972.

8. This element comprises the heart of all traditional doctrine while the method concerns means of attaching oneself to the Real. On the relation between doctrine and method see M. Pallis, "The Marriage of Wisdom and Method," *Studies in Comparative Religion* 6/2 (1972):78–104.

9. Some contemporary scholars such as R. Panikkar (in his *Inter-religious Dialogue,* New York, 1978) have contrasted the Buddhist *Shunyata* and the Christian Pleroma but, metaphysically speaking, the concept of Ultimate Reality as emptiness and as fullness complement each other like the *yin-yang* symbol and both manifest themselves in every integral tradition. Even in Christianity where the symbolism of Divine Fullness is emphasized and developed with remarkable elaboration in Franciscan theology, esp.

that of St. Bonaventure, the complementary vision of emptiness appears in the teachings of the Dominican Meister Eckhart who speaks of the "desert of the Godhead."

10. In one of the most difficult verses to comprehend from the exoteric point of view the Quran states, "He is the First and the Last; the Outward and the Inward" (LVII; 3).

11. This is the view of the Advaita Vedanta in Hinduism and of the transcendent Unity of Being (*waḥdat al-wujūd*) in Sufism which, because of the myopia of a reason divorced from the sanctifying rays of the Intellect, have been often mistaken for pantheism. See Nasr, *Three Muslim Sages*, Cambridge, Mass., 1964, pp. 104–8; also T. Burckhardt, *Introduction to Sufi Doctrine*, pp. 28–30.

12. See Schuon, *Du Divin à l'humain*, pt. 2, "Ordre divin et universel."

13. The point of view of Manichaeism which sees the world as evil rather than good is primarily initiatic and not metaphysical, that is, it begins not with the aim of understanding the nature of things but of providing a way for escaping from the prison of material existence. Buddhism possesses a similar practical perspective but, of course, with a different metaphysical background since it belongs to a different spiritual universe.

14. Islam and Hinduism join the Judeo-Christian tradition in confirming that it was by the Word that all things were made. The Quran asserts, "Verily, when He [Allah] intends a thing, His Command is, "Be" [*kun*], and it is!" (XXXVI; 82—Yusuf Ali translation). Here the imperative form of the verb "to be," namely *kun*, being identified with the Word or Logos.

15. One can interpret Thomistic metaphysics which begins and ends with *esse* as including the notion of the Real in its completely unconditioned and undetermined sense although this term could be complemented by the term *posse* to denote the All-Possibility of the Divine Principle. From this point of view one can assert that despite the sensualist epistemology of St. Thomas, criticized earlier because of its denial of the possibility of intellectual intuition, Thomism contains in its dogmatic content truths of a truly metaphysical nature which reflect knowledge of a principial order and which can serve as support for metaphysical contemplation.

In Islamic philosophy such a figure as Ṣadr al-Dīn Shīrāzī speaks about *wujūd* (which means literally "being") in such a manner that it is definitely to be identified with the Supreme Principle rather than its first self-determination. The Supreme Name of God in Islam, namely, Allah, implies also both Being and Beyond Being, both the personal Deity and the Absolute and Infinite Reality, both God and the Godhead of Meister Eckhart.

16. See the introduction of Corbin to Ṣadr al-Dīn Shīrāzī, *Le Livre des pénétrations métaphysiques*, Tehran-Paris, 1964, where he contrasts the destiny of ontology in the Islamic world ending with Sabziwārī and his like and in the West terminating with Heidegger, showing the chasm which distinguishes the Islamic theosophical and philosophical schools from *Existenz* philosophy. See also Izutsu, *The Concept and Reality of Existence;* and Nasr, "Mullā Ṣadrā and the Doctrine of the Unity of Being," *Philosophical Forum*, December 1973, pp. 153–61.

17. In Islam such a widespread theological school as Ashʿarism is characterized by its rejection of the hierarchy of existence in conformity with its atomistic and voluntaristic point of view.

18. On this question see Nasr, *An Introduction to Islamic Cosmological Doctrines*, chap. 12, "The Anatomy of Being." In Arabic "necessity" is *wujūb* and "possibility" *imkān*, which in the context of Avicennan ontology we translate as "contingency."

19. On the immutable essences see T. Burckhardt, *Introduction to Sufi Doctrine*, pp. 62–64.

20. "Nous pouvons discerner [dans l'absolument Réel] une tridimensionalité, elle aussi intrinsèquement indifférenciée mais annonciatrice d'un déploiement possible: ces dimensions sont l'"Être', la 'Conscience', la 'Félicité'. C'est en vertu du troisième élément—immuable en soi—que la Possibilité divine déborde et donne bien, 'par amour', à ce mystère d'extériorisation qu'est le Voile universel, dont la chaine est faite des mondes, et la traine, des êtres." Schuon, "Le problème de la possibilité," in *Du Divin à l'humain*.

21. To which Islamic metaphysics refer as *mā siwa'Llāh*, literally, "all that is other than Allah."

22. "*Māyā* is likened to a magic fabric woven from a warp that veils and a weft that unveils." Schuon, "*Atmā-Māyā*," p. 89. On the metaphysical significance of *māyā* as both veil and principle of relativization and manifestation of the Absolute see, besides this article, the chap. "*Māyā*" in Schuon's *Light on the Ancient Worlds*, pp. 89–98.

23. On the Breath of the Compassionate see Ibn al-ʿArabī, *The Bezels of Wisdom*, trans. R. W. J. Austin, New York, 1980, "The Wisdom of Leadership in the Word of Aaron," pp. 241ff. Also Nasr, *Science and Civilization in Islam*, chap. 13.

24. Called the *ḥadīth* of *kanz al-makhfī* (The Hidden Treasure).

25. See his "*Atmā-Māyā*."

26. As far as the highest level is concerned, Islamic metaphysics calls the reverberation "the most sacred effusion" (*al-fayḍ al-aqdas*) and the radii "the sacred effusion" (*al-fayḍ al-muqaddas*), the first being the archetype of all things (*al-aʿyān al-thābitah*) and the second the Breath of the Compassionate which externalizes and existentiates them on various planes of reality.

27. "The desire to enclose universal Reality in an exclusive and exhaustive 'explanation' brings with it a permanent disequilibrium due to the interference of *Māyā*." Schuon, *Light on the Ancient Worlds*, p. 91.

28. The Quranic doctrine that Iblīs was a *jinn* and made of fire signifies that the presence of evil does not make itself felt on the cosmic plane until the descent reaches into the animic realm.

29. The Intellect as it operates in man does not begin with a knowledge of the world but with an a priori knowledge of the Divine Good which it perceives before it even comes to understand evil. That is why some metaphysicians, led through intellection to a direct understanding of the Good in itself, do not even have a desire to understand evil and pass it by as if it did not exist. There is, of course, also the experiential aspect to consider. A saint who has destroyed evil not in the whole world but around himself might be said to breathe already in the atmosphere of paradise and therefore be oblivious to the evils of terrestrial existence which do not exist as such for him. This attitude is to be found among certain of the great Sufis who assert that evil simply does not exist without bothering to provide the metaphysical evidence as to what one means by such a statement and from what point of view can one say that evil does not exist.

30. *Cosmos* literally means "order" in Greek. The opposite of cosmos is nothing but chaos.

31. The principle of adequation does not negate our earlier assertion that *māyā* prevents containing and comprehending reality in a system derived from ratiocination, for we are speaking here of intellection and intelligence not ratiocination and thought of a purely human character.

32. Not only in the Islamic tradition whose spirituality is essentially sapiential is intelligence considered as God's greatest gift to man (according to the well-known saying attributed to ʿAlī ibn Abī Ṭālib, "God did not bestow upon His servants anything more precious than intelligence"), but even in Christianity which is primarily a way of love the Hesychasts consider the essence of the prayer of Jesus itself to be the actualization and descent of intelligence into the human heart.

33. See Schuon, *In the Tracks of Buddhism*, p. 83.

34. "A point de vue doctrinal, ce qui importerait le plus, ce serait de retrouver la science spirituelle de l'exégèse, c'est-à-dire de l'interpretation métaphysique et mystique des Écritures; les principes de cette science, dont le maniement présuppose de toute evidence une haute intelligence intuitive et non une simple acuité mentale, ont été exposés par Origène et d'autres, et mis en pratique par les Pères et par les plus grands saints. En d'autres termes, ce qui manque en Occident, c'est une intellectualité fondé, non sur l'érudition et le scepticisme philosophique, mais sur l'intuition intellectuelle actualisée par le Saint-Esprit sur la base d'une exégèse tenant compte de tous les plans et de tous les niveaux de l'entendement; cette exégèse implique aussi la science du symbolisme, et celle-ci s'étend à tous les domaines de l'expression formelle, notamment à l'art sacré, qui, lui englobe la liturgie, au sens le plus large, aussi bien que l'art

158 · *Knowledge and the Sacred*

proprement dit. L'Orient traditionel ne s'étant jamais éloigné de cette manière d'envisager des choses, la compréhension de ses métaphysiques, ses exégèses, ses symbolismes, et ses arts seraient pour l'Occident, d'un intérêt vital." Schuon, "Que peut donner l'Orient à l'Occident?" *France-Asie*, no. 103 (Dec. 1954):151.

35. There are in fact numerous works in Islamic languages on the "categories" of commentators usually called *Ṭabaqāt al-mufassirīn*, while a clear distinction is made between exoteric commentary (*tafsīr*) and inner or esoteric commentary (*ta'wīl*).

36. *Ta'wīl*, which in Islamic esoterism means to reach the inner meaning of the sacred text and which should not be confused with the pejorative sense in which it is occasionally used as meaning individualistic interpretation of the sacred text, contains a profound metaphysical significance in its very etymology for it means, literally, "to take back to the beginning," implying that to reach the inner meaning (*bāṭin*) from the outward sense (*zāhir*) is also to return to the origin or beginning of that truth whose very descent implies also externalization. On the question of *ta'wīl* see Corbin, *En Islam iranien*, vol. 3, pp. 222ff. and pp. 256ff., where it is discussed with reference to the Quran; and Nasr, *Ideals and Realities of Islam*, chap. 2.

37. The well-known *Ta'wīl al-qur'ān* (*The Spiritual or Hermeneutic Commentary upon the Quran*) attributed to Ibn 'Arabī is actually by a later member of his school, 'Abd al-Razzāq al-Kāshānī, while Ibn 'Arabī himself wrote a monumental commentary, discovered by O. Yahya, which, however, has not as yet been printed.

38. The major commentary of Qunyawī on the *Sūrat al-fātiḥah*, the opening chapter of the Quran, is being edited and translated by W. Chittick and is to appear soon.

39. See R. Guénon, "The Heart and the Cave," in *Studies in Comparative Religion* 4 (Spring 1971):69–72.

40. Hence *īmān* is often identified with knowledge and when God is referred to as *al-mu'min*, traditional commentators do not translate that Name as "He who has faith" as one would expect from the literal meaning but as "He who has knowledge which illuminates the creature and transforms him."

41. See H. Köhler, *Śraddhā—In der Vedischen und Altbuddistischen Literatur*, Wiesbaden, 1973. This issue has been dealt with in detail by W. C. Smith in his *Faith and Belief*. Smith draws attention quite rightly to the fact that, before modern times, belief as opinion was not a religious category and faith was related to knowledge not to belief in the tentative sense in which this term is used today. This does not mean that the more traditional sense of the term belief which is still alive cannot be fully resuscitated.

42. In traditional Islamic educational circles the ability to teach metaphysics is considered as the sign of the teacher's complete assimilation of the subject in such a manner that his intellect has reached the level of *al-'aql bi'l-malakah* (*intellectus habitus*) and the knowledge in question has become for him *bi'l-malakah*, that is, completely digested and assimilated.

43. What Islamic metaphysics calls *al-jam' ba'd al-farq*.

44. Some of the most profound metaphysical doctrines expounded in works of Islamic philosophy and theosophy are described under the title of *al-wāridāt al-qalbiyyah*, literally, "that which has entered the heart." In fact, one of the books of Sadr al-Dīn Shīrāzī, one of the greatest of Islamic metaphysicians, bears such a title. See Nasr, *The Transcendent Theosophy of Sadr al-Dīn Shīrāzī*, London, 1978, p. 49.

45.

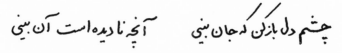

46. This is the imagery of the famous poem of Shabistarī from the *Gulshan-i rāz*:

There is many a fool who seeks the luminous sun
In the desert with a lamp in his hand.

47. On the meaning and science of symbols see L. Benoist, *Signes, symboles et mythes*, Paris, 1977; H. Sedlmayr, *Verlust der Mitte*, Salzburg, 1976; R. A. Schwaller de Lubicz, *Symbol and the Symbolic*, trans. R. and D. Lawlor, Brookline, Mass., 1978; G. Dumézil, *Mythe et épopée*, 2 vols., Paris 1968–71 (dealing mostly with myths but of course also symbolism); H. Zimmer, *Myths and Symbols in Indian Art and Civilization*, ed. J. Campbell, New York, 1963; M. Eliade, *Images and Symbols*, trans. Ph. Mairet, New York, 1961; R. Alleau, *La Science des symboles*, Paris, 1976; and J. C. Cooper, *An Illustrated Encyclopaedia of Traditional Symbols*, London, 1978.

48. For primordial man the symbolized *was* in fact the symbol since he still lived in the unfragmented reality of the paradisal state. Something of this primordial point of view has survived among some of the so-called primitive peoples among whom the "symbolist spirit" is still alive and who identify in their perception of things the object symbolized and the symbol. This is the reverse of idolatry which reduces the symbol to the physical object which is supposed to symbolize it, while in the perspective in question the object symbolizing an archetypal reality is "elevated" to the level of that reality and becomes a transparent form through which that reality is reflected and manifested.

49. "Natural symbolism, which assimilates, for example, the sun to the divine Principle, derives from a 'horizontal' correspondence; revealed symbolism, which makes this assimilation spiritually effective—in ancient solar cults and before their 'petrifaction'—derives from a 'vertical' correspondence; the same holds good for gnosis, which reduces phenomena to 'ideas' or archetypes. Much might be said here on the natural symbolism of bread and body—or of body and blood—and their 'sacramentalisation' by Christ; likewise the sign of the Cross, which expresses with its two dimensions the respective mysteries of the Body and Bread and the Blood and Wine, has, of course, always had its metaphysical sense but received its quasi-sacramental virtue—at least in its specifically Christian form—through the incarnated Word, in other terms, it is necessary for the *Avatara* to 'live' a form in order to make it 'effective', and that is why sacred formulae or divine Names must come from Revelation in order to be capable of being 'realised'." Schuon, *Stations of Wisdom*, p. 97.

50.

حاصل عمرم سه سخن بیش نیست   خام بدم پخته شدم سوختم

CHAPTER FIVE

Man, Pontifical and Promethean

لحظه ای درخود نگر تا کیستی   ازکجائی وزچه جائی چیستی

Look within yourself a moment and ask who art thou?
From where doest thou comest, from which place,
What art thou?
Rūmī

Was ist der Menschen Leben, ein Bild der Gottheit.
What is the life of man, an image of the Godhead.
Hölderlin

The concept of man as the pontiff, *pontifex*, or bridge between Heaven and earth, which is the traditional view of the *anthrōpos*, lies at the antipode of the modern conception of man[1] which envisages him as the Promethean earthly creature who has rebelled against Heaven and tried to misappropriate the role of the Divinity for himself. Pontifical man, who, in the sense used here, is none other than traditional man, lives in a world which has both an Origin and a Center. He lives in full awareness of the Origin which contains his own perfection and whose primordial purity and wholeness he seeks to emulate, recapture, and transmit. He also lives on a circle of whose Center he is always aware and which he seeks to reach in his life, thought, and actions. Pontifical man is the reflection of the Center on the periphery and the echo of the Origin in later cycles of time and generations of history. He is the vicegerent of God (*khalīfatallāh*) on earth, to use the Islamic term,[2] responsible to God for his actions, and the custodian and protector of the earth of which he is given dominion on the condition that he remain faithful to himself as the central terrestrial figure created in the "form of God," a theomorphic being living in this world but created for eternity. Pontifical man[3] is aware of his role as intermediary between Heaven and earth and his entelechy as lying beyond the terrestrial domain over which he is allowed to rule provided he remains aware of the transient nature of his own journey on earth. Such a man lives in awareness of a spiritual reality which transcends him and which yet is none other than his own inner nature and against which he cannot rebel, save by paying the price of separation from all that he is and all that he should wish to be. For such a man, life is impregnated with meaning and the universe peopled with creatures whom he can address as thou. He is aware that precisely becasue he is human there is both grandeur and danger connected with all that he does and thinks. His actions have an effect upon his own being beyond the limited spatio-temporal conditions in which such actions take place. He knows that somehow the bark which is to take him to the shore beyond after that fleeting journey which comprises his earthly life is constructed by what he does and how he lives while he is in the human state.

To be sure, the image of man as depicted in various traditions has not been identical. Some have emphasized the human state more than others and they have envisaged eschatological realities differently. But there is no doubt that all traditions are based on the central and dominant images of the Origin and the Center and see the final end of man in the state or reality which is other than this terrestrial life with which forgetful or fallen man identifies himself once he is cut off from revelation or religion that constantly hearken man back to the Origin and the Center.

Promethean man, on the contrary, is a creature of this world. He feels at home on earth, earth not considered as the virgin nature which is itself an echo of paradise, but as the artificial world created by Promethean man himself in order to make it possible for him to forget God and his own inner reality. Such a man envisages life as a big marketplace in which he is free to roam around and choose objects at will. Having lost the sense of the sacred, he is drowned in transience and impermanence and becomes a slave of his own lower nature, surrender to which he considers to be freedom. He follows passively the downward flow of the cycle of human history in which he takes pride by claiming that in doing so he has created his own destiny. But still being man, he has a nostalgia for the Sacred and the Eternal and thus turns to a thousand and one ways to satisfy this need, ways ranging from psychological novels to drug-induced mysticism.

He also becomes stifled by the prison of his own creation, wary of the destruction he has wrought upon the natural environment and the vilification of the urban setting in which he is forced to live. He seeks for solutions everywhere, even in teachings by which pontifical man, or traditional man, has lived over the ages. But these sources are not able to help him for he approaches even these truths as Promethean man. This recently born creature, who has succeeded in wreaking havoc upon the earth and practically upsetting the ecological balance of the natural order itself in only some five centuries,[4] is little aware that to overcome the impasse into which modern man has thrown himself as a result of attempting to forget what it really means to be man he must rediscover himself. He must come to understand the nature of man as that pontifical and central creature on this earth who stands as witness to an origin from which he descends and a center to which he ultimately returns. The traditional doctrine of man and not the measurement of skulls and footprints is the key for the understanding of that *anthrōpos* who, despite the rebellion of Promethean man against Heaven from the period of the Renaissance and its aftermath, is still the inner man of every man, the reality which no human being can deny wherever and whenever he lives, the imprint of a theomorphic nature which no historical change and transformation can erase completely from the face of that creature called man.

In recent decades many attempts have been made to trace the stages of the "disfiguration of the image of man in the West"[5] beginning with the first stages of the Promethean revolt in the Renaissance, some of whose causes are to be seen already in the late Middle Ages, and terminating with the infrahuman condition into which modern man is being forced through a supposedly humanistic civilization. The tracing of this disfiguration could not in fact be anything other than the tracing of one facet of that process of the desacralization of knowledge and of life already outlined in the first part of this book. The decomposition and disfiguration, in the history of the West, of the image of man as being himself *imago Dei*, came into the open with that worldly humanism which characterizes the Renaissance and which is most directly reflected in its worldly art.[6] But there are certain elements of earlier origin which also contributed to this sudden fall, usually interpreted as the age of the discovery of man at the moment when the hold of the Christian tradition upon Western man was beginning to weaken. One of the elements is the excessive separation between man as the seat of consciousness or the I and the cosmos as the "not-I" or a domain of reality from which man is alienated. This attitude was not unrelated to the excessive separation of the spirit from the flesh in official Christian theology even if this chasm was filled by the Hermetic tradition, especially its alchemical aspect, and affected even the daily life of the medieval community through the craft guilds. The "angelism" of medieval theology, although containing a profound truth, considered only one aspect of the traditional *anthrōpos*, allowing the rebellion against such a view by those who thought that in order to discover the spiritual significance of nature and the positive significance of the body, they had to deny the medieval concept of man. The Renaissance cult of the body, even if by some freak of history it had manifested itself in India, could not have been opposed to Hinduism in the same way that it was opposed to Christianity in the West.

The other elements which brought about the destruction of the image of pontifical man and helped the birth of that Promethean rebel with whom modern man usually identifies himself were mostly associated with the phenomena of the Renaissance itself and its aftermath or had their root in the late medieval period. These factors include the destruction of the unity and hierarchy of knowledge which resulted from the eclipse of the sapiential dimension of tradition in the West. From this event there resulted in turn the emptying of the sciences of nature of their esoteric content and their quantification, the rise of skepticism and agnosticism combined with a hatred of wisdom in its Christian form, and the loss of knowledge based upon certitude,[7] which was itself the result of reducing Being to a mental concept and a denial of its unifying and sanctifying rays.

From an intellectual point of view the main stages in the process of the disfiguration of pontifical man into the Promethean can be traced to the late Middle Ages because they include the excessively rigid Aristotelianization of Western thought in the thirteenth century identified by some with Averroes. This "exteriorization" of Christian thought was followed by the secularization of the science of the cosmos in the seventeenth century, itself a result of the "naturalization" of Christian man as a well-contented citizen of this world. This period was in turn succeeded by the divinization of time and historical process associated in the nineteenth century with the name of Hegel and others who made of change and becoming the foundation of reality and the criterion of the truth itself. The development of Aristotelian philosophy and theology in a Christian mold was itself of course not antitraditional. It even provided a metaphysical language of great power and dogmatic assertions of remarkable depth. But, as already mentioned, it did exteriorize the process of knowledge. Furthermore, Averroism in the Western world, and in contrast to the Islamic world itself from which Averroes (Ibn Rushd) himself hailed, depleted the cosmos of its "soul," helping the secularization of the cosmos which was also to affect deeply the destiny of Western man himself.[8]

The seventeenth-century scientific revolution not only mechanized the conception of the world but also of man, creating a world in which man found himself as an alien. Furthermore, the scientism which issued from this century and the apparent success of Newtonian physics led to the establishment of a whole series of so-called sciences of man which to this day emulate an already outmoded physics. The modern sciences of man were born in an atmosphere of positivism associated with a figure like Auguste Comte who simply reversed the traditional rapport between the study of *Deus, homo,* and *natura* in creating his famous three stage theory of human progress, which is based on the total misunderstanding of the nature of man and is a parody of traditional doctrines concerning human existence on earth.[9] The Comptean science of man and his society can be only characterized as ignorance, or *avidyā,* characteristic of the Dark Age, parading as science. Despite the refutation of the mechanistic physics upon which most sciences of man are based today and strong criticism of the type of anthropology which sees in man no more than a mammal walking upright, most of those disciplines usually identified as the social sciences and even humanities still suffer from an inferiority complex vis-à-vis the natural sciences and mathematics which forces them to adopt a world view alien to the very nature of man.

As for the Hegelian turning of permanence into change and dialectical process, it not only deprived man of the image of immutability which constitutes a basic feature of the traditional concept of man but it also played a major role in the humanization of the Divinity which was to lead to the final phase of the secularization of the life of modern man. Hegel "equated" man's finite consciousness with the Divine Infinite Consciousness. From his position there was but one step to Feurbach's assertion that man's awareness of Infinite Consciousness is nothing more than the consciousness of the Infinite within human consciousness itself. Instead of man being seen as the image of God, the relation was now reversed and God came to be regarded as the image of man and the projection of his own consciousness. Promethean man not only sought to steal fire from Heaven but even to kill the gods, little aware that man cannot destroy the image of the Divinity without destroying himself.

As far as the traditional doctrine of man is concerned, it is based in one way or another on the concept of primordial man as the source of perfection, the total and complete reflection of the Divinity and the archetypal reality containing the possibilities of cosmic existence itself. Man is the model of the universe because he is himself the reflection of those possibilities in the principial domain which manifest themselves as the world. Man is more than merely man so that this way of envisaging his rapport with respect to the cosmos is far from being anthropomorphic in the usual sense of this term. The world is not seen as the reflection of man qua man but of man as being himself the total and plenary reflection of all those Divine Qualities whose reflections, in scattered and segmented fashion, comprise the manifested order.

In traditions with a strongly mythical character this inward relationship between man and the cosmos is depicted in the myth of the sacrifice of the primordial man. For example, in the Iranian religions the sacrifice of the primordial man is associated with the creation of the world and its various orders and realms, different parts of the "body" of the primordial man being associated with different orders of creatures such as animals, plants, and minerals. Sometimes, however, a more particular relationship is emphasized as in those Zoroastrian sources where Gāyomart, who is the first man, is associated with the generation of the minerals, for as the *Greater Bundahišn* says, "When Gayōmart was assailed with sickness, he fell on his left side. From his head lead came forth, from his blood zinc, from his marrow silver, from his feet iron, from his bones brass, from his fat crystal, from his arms steel, and from his soul as it departed, gold."[11]   In Hinduism there is the famous passage in the *Ṛg-Veda* (X,90) according to which, from the sacrifice of Puruṣa or primordial man, the world and the human race consisting of the four castes are brought into being, the *brahmins* from his mouth, the *rājanyas* or *kṣatriyas* from his arms, the *vaiśyas* from his belly, and the *śūdras* from his feet, his sacrifice, or *yājñas*, being the model of all sacrifice.[12] Primordial man is the archetype of creation as he is its purpose and entelechy. That is why according to a *hadīth*, God addresses the Prophet of Islam, whose inner reality is the primordial man par excellence in the Islamic tradition, in these terms, "If thou wert not, I would not have created the world."[13] This perspective envisages the human reality in its divine and cosmic dimensions in exact opposition to philosophical anthropomorphism. Man does not see God and the world in his image but realizes that he is himself in his inner reality that image which reflects the Divine Qualities and by which cosmic reality is created, the possibilities being contained in the Logos "by which all things were made."

The metaphysical doctrine of man in the fullness of his being, in what he is, but not necessarily what he appears to be, is expounded in various languages in the different traditions with diverse degrees of emphasis which are far from being negligible. Some traditions are based more upon the divinized human receptacle while others reject this perspective in favor of the Divinity in Itself. Some depict man in his state of fall from his primordial perfection and address their message to this fallen creature, whereas others, while being fully aware that the humanity they are addressing is not the society of perfect men living in paradise, address that primordial nature which still survives in man despite the layers of "forgetfulness"[14] and imperfection which separate man from himself.

That primordial and plenary nature of man which Islam calls the "Universal or Perfect Man" (*al-insān al-kāmil*)[15] and to which the sapiential doctrines of Graeco-Alexandrian antiquity also allude in nearly the same terms, except for the Abrahamic and specifically Islamic aspects of the doctrines absent from the Neoplatonic and Hermetic sources, reveals human reality to possess three fundamental aspects. The Universal Man, whose reality is realized only by the prophets and great seers since only they are human in the full sense of the word, is first of all the archetypal reality of the universe; second, the instrument or means whereby revelation descends into the world; and third, the perfect model for the spiritual life and the ultimate dispenser of esoteric knowledge. By virtue of the reality of the Universal Man, terrestrial man is able to gain access to revelation and tradition, hence to the sacred. Finally, through this reality which is none other than man's own reality actualized, man is able to follow that path of perfection which will finally allow him to gain knowledge of the sacred and to become fully himself. The saying of the Delphic oracle, "Know thyself," or that of the Prophet of Islam, "He who knoweth himself knoweth his lord," is true not because man as an earthly creature is the measure of all things but because man is himself the reflection of that archetypal reality which *is* the measure of all things. That is why in traditional sciences of man the knowledge of the cosmos and the metacosmic reality are usually not expounded in terms of the reality of terrestrial man. Rather, the knowledge of man is expounded through and in reference to the macrocosm and metacosm, since they reflect in a blinding fashion and in an objective mode what man is if only he were to become what he really is. The traditional doctrine of Primordial or Universal Man with all its variations—Adam Kadmon, Jen, Puruṣa, *al-insān al-kāmil,* and the like—embraces at once the metaphysical, cosmogonic, revelatory, and initiatic functions of that reality which constitutes the totality of the human state and which places before man both the grandeur of what he can be and the pettiness and wretchedness of what he is in most cases, in comparison with the ideal which he carries always within himself. Terrestrial man is nothing more than the externalization, coagulation, and often inversion and perversion of this idea and ideal of the Universal Man cast in the direction of the periphery. He is a being caught in the field of the centrifugal forces which characterize terrestrial existence as such, but is also constantly attracted by the Center where the inner man is always present.

It is also by virtue of carrying this reality within himself and bearing the characteristics of a theomorphic being, because he is such a being in his essential reality, that man remains an axial creature in this world. Even his denial of the sacred has a cosmic significance, his purely empirical and earthly science going to the extent of imposing the danger of destroying the harmony of the terrestrial environment itself.[17] Man cannot live as a purely earthly creature totally at home in this world without destroying the natural environment precisely because he is not such a creature. The pontifical function of man remains inseparable from his reality, from what he is. That is why traditional teachings envisage the happiness of man in his remaining aware and living according to his pontifical nature as the bridge between Heaven and earth. His religious laws and rites have a cosmic function[18] and he is made aware that it is impossible for him to evade his responsibility as a creature who lives on the earth but is not only earthly, as a being strung between Heaven and earth, of both a spiritual and material mold, created to reflect the light of the Divine Empyrean within the world and to preserve harmony in the world through the dispensation of that light and the practice of that form of life which is in accordance with his inner reality as revealed by tradition.[19] Man's responsibility to society, the cosmos, and God issues ultimately from himself, not his self as ego but the inner man who is the mirror and reflection of the Supreme Self, the Ultimate Reality which can be envisaged as either pure Subject or pure Object since It transcends in Itself all dualities, being neither subject nor object.

The situation of man as bridge between Heaven and earth is reflected in all of his being and his faculties. Man is himself a supernaturally natural being. When he walks on the earth, on the one hand he appears as a creature of the earth; on the other, it is as if he were a celestial being who has descended upon the earthly realm.[20] Likewise, his memory, speech, and imagination partake at once of several orders of reality. Most of all his intelligence is a supernaturally natural faculty, a sacrament partaking of all that the term supernatural signifies in Christianity, yet functioning quasi-naturally within him with the help of revelation and its unifying grace. That is why, while even in this world, man is able to move to the other shore of existence, to take his stance in the world of the sacred and to see nature herself as impregnated with grace. He is able to remove that sharp boundary which has been drawn between the natural and the supernatural in most schools of official Christian theology but which is not emphasized in the same manner in other traditions and is also overcome in the sapiential aspects of the Christian tradition itself.

Metaphysically speaking then, man has his archetype in that primordial, perfect, and universal being or man who is the mirror of the Divine Qualities and Names and the prototype of creation. But each human being also possesses his own archetype and has a reality *in divinis* as a possibility unto himself, one which is unique since that person reflects the archetype of the human species as such in the same way that every point on the circumference of a circle reflects the center and is yet distinct from other points. The reality of man as a species as well as of each human being has its root in the principial domain. Therefore man as such, as well as each human being, comes into the world through an "elaboration" and process which separates him from the Divine and departs from the world through paths, which in joy or sorrow depending on his life on earth, finally lead him back to the Divine.

This "elaboration" concerning the genesis of man is expounded in one form or another in all sapiential teachings but not in exoteric religious formulations whose point of view is the immediate concern of man for his salvation, so that they leave aside certain doctrines or only allude to them in passing, while esoterism, being concerned with the truth as such, takes such questions into consideration as we see in the case of exoteric Judaism on the one hand and the Kabbala on the other. In the Christian West, especially in modern times when the esoteric and sapiential teachings had become much less accessible than before, the religious point of view seemed to assert only the doctrine of creation *ex nihilo* without further explanation of what *ex nihilo* might mean metaphysically as Ibn ʿArabī, for example, had done for the term *al-ʿadam* which is the Quranic term used for creation "from nothing."[21]

As a result, many nineteenth-century thinkers felt that they had to choose between either the creationist view or the Darwinian theory of evolution and naturally chose the latter as appearing more "plausible" in a world which had forfeited the view of permanence and immutability to that of constant change, process, and becoming and where the higher states of existence had lost their reality for those affected by the leveling process of modern thought. Even today, certain scientists who realize the logical and even biological absurdity of the theory of evolution and some of its implications and presuppositions believe that the only other alternative is the *ex nihilo* doctrine, unaware that the traditional metaphysical doctrine interprets the *ex nihilo* statement as implying an elaboration of man's being *in divinis* and through stages of being preceding his appearance on earth. This doctrine of man, based on his descent through various levels of existence above the corporeal, in fact presents a view of the appearance of man which is neither illogical nor at all in disagreement with any scientific facts—and of course not necessarily hypotheses and extrapolations—provided one accepts the hierarchy of existence, or the multiple levels of reality which surround the corporeal state. As we shall see in our later discussion of the theory of evolution, the whole modern evolutionary theory is a desperate attempt to substitute a set of horizontal, material causes in a unidimensional world to explain effects whose causes belong to other levels of reality, to the vertical dimensions of existence.

The genesis of man, according to all traditions, occurred in many stages: first, in the Divinity Itself so that there is an uncreated "aspect" to man. That is why man can experience annihilation in God and subsistence in Him (the *al-fanā'* and *al-baqā'* of Sufism) and achieve supreme union. Then man is born in the Logos which *is* in fact the prototype of man and another face of that same reality which the Muslims call the Universal Man and which each tradition identifies with its founder. Next, man is created on the cosmic level and what the Bible refers to as the celestial paradise, where he is dressed with a luminous body in conformity with the paradisal state. He then descends to the level of the terrestrial paradise and is given yet another body of an ethereal and incorruptible nature. Finally, he is born into the physical world with a body which perishes but which has its principle in the subtle and luminous bodies belonging to the earlier stages of the elaboration of man and his genesis before his appearance on earth.[22]

Likewise, the Quran speaks of man's pre-eternal (*azalī*) covenant with God when he answered God's call, "Am I not your Lord?" with the affirmative, "Yea,"[23] the "Am I not your Lord?" (*alastu birabbikum*) symbolizing the relation between God and man before creation and so becoming a constantly repeated refrain for all those sages in Islam who have hearkened man to his eternal reality *in divinis* by reminding him of the *asrār-i alast* or the mysteries of this preeternal covenant. This reminding or unveiling, moreover, has always involved the doctrine of the elaboration of man through various states of being. When Ḥāfiẓ, in his famous poem,

> *Last night* [dūsh] *I saw that the angels beat at the door*
> *of the Tavern*
> *The clay of Adam, they shaped and with the mold of love*
> *they cast*[24]

speaks of *dūsh* or "dark night" preceding the morning light, he is alluding symbolically to that unmanifested state where the primordial substance of man was being molded in the Divine Presence preceding the day of manifestation and his descent on earth; but even this substance molded by the angels was itself an elaboration and descent of man from his uncreated reality *in divinis.*

It is remarkable that, while traditional teachings are aware that other creatures preceded man on earth, they believe that man precedes them in the principial order and that his appearance on earth is the result of a descent not an ascent. Man precipitates on earth from the subtle state appearing out of the cloud or on a chariot as described in various traditional accounts, this "cloud" symbolizing the intermediary condition between the subtle and the physical. He appears on earth already as a central and total being, reflecting the Absolute not only in his spiritual and mental faculties but even in his body. If Promethean man finally lost sight completely of the higher levels of existence and was forced to take recourse in some kind of mysterious temporal process called evolution which would bring him out of the primordial soup of molecules envisaged by modern science, pontifical man has always seen himself as the descent of a reality which has been elaborated through many worlds to arrive on earth in a completed form as the central and theomorphic being that he is. From his point of view as a being conscious of not only earthly, horizontal causes but also Heaven and the vertical dimension of existence and chains of causes, the monkey is not what man had once been and is no longer, but what he could never be precisely because of what he always is and has been. Pontifical man has always been man, and the traditional perspective which is his views the presence of the monkey as a cosmic sign, a creature whose significance is to display what the central human state excludes by its very centrality. To study the state of the monkey metaphysically and not just biologically is to grasp what man is not and could have never been.

Traditional sciences of man have spoken at length about the inner structure and faculties of man as well as the significance of his body and its powers. One discovers in such sources the repeated assertion that man has access to multiple levels of existence and consciousness within himself and a hierarchy of faculties and even "substances" which in any case cannot be reduced to the two entities of body and soul or mind and body, reflecting the dualism so prevalent in post-Cartesian Western thought. This dualism neglects the essential unity of the human microcosm precisely because duality implies opposition and, in contrast to trinity, is not a reflection of Unity. On the first level of understanding the human microcosm, therefore, one must take into consideration the tripartite nature of the human being consisting of spirit, soul, and body—the classical *pneuma, psychē,* and *hylē* or *spiritus, anima,* and *corpus* of Western traditions both Graeco-Alexandrian and Christian—at least as far as Christian Hermeticism is concerned. The soul is the principle of the body, but in the "normal" human being is itself subservient to the spirit and reaches its salvation and beatitude through its wedding to the spirit of which so many alchemical texts speak.[25]

This tripartite division, however, is a simplification of a more complex situation. Actually man contains within himself many levels of existence and layers. Such traditions as Tantrism and certain schools of Sufism as well as Western Hermeticism speak not of body as opposed to soul and spirit but of several bodies of man of which the physical body is only the most outward and externalized envelope. Man possesses subtle as well as spiritual bodies in conformity with the different worlds through which he journeys. There is, moreover, an inversion between various levels of existence so that man's soul (used here in the general sense of all that is immaterial in his being), molded in this world by his actions, becomes externalized in the intermediate world as his "body." It is in reference to this principle that the Imams of Shī'ism, referring to the posthumous states of man and especially the "perfect man" represented by the Imams, have declared," *Arwāḥunā ajsādunā wa ajsādunā arwāḥunā*" (Our spirits are our bodies and our bodies are our spirits).[26] The sojourn of man through the levels of existence and forms, which the popular interpretation of Indian religions identifies with a return to the same level of reality and the esoteric dimension of the Abrahamic traditions with multiple levels of reality,[27] corresponds to his journey within himself and through all the layers of his own being.

Man possesses an incorruptible ethereal body as well as a radiant spiritual body corresponding to the other "earths" of the higher states of being. In the same way that to speak of body and soul corresponds to the perspective of heaven or several heavens and earth, to envisage the several bodies of man corresponds to seeing the higher levels of reality as each possessing its own heaven and earth. After all, through the grace of the Amidha Buddha man is born in the "Pure Land" and not "pure heaven," but here the symbolism of land includes the paradisal and heavenly.[28] It is the celestial earth to which also Islamic esoterism refers often, and which played such an important role in Zoroastrianism, where the earth itself was conceived as having been originally an angel.[29]

The various "bodies" of the inner man have been envisaged in very different terms in different traditions but everywhere they are related to the realization of sacred knowledge and the attainment of virtue. The beauty of man's physical body is God-given and not for him to determine. But the type of "body" attained either in the posthumous state or through initiatic practices and ways of realization depends upon how man spends that precious gift which is human life, for once this life comes to an end the door, which is open toward the Infinite, closes. Only man can pass through the door while enjoying possibilities of the human state. It makes literally all the difference in the world whether man *does* pass through that door while he has the possibility or not.[30]

In any case, as far as the positive and not negative and infernal possibilities are concerned, the various bodies of the Buddhas and Bodhisattvas mentioned in northern schools of Buddhism and so central to Buddhist eschatology and techniques of meditation, the Hindu *chakras* as centers of the subtle bodies and energies, the *ōkhēma symphyēs* ("psychic vehicle") of Proclus or the *laṭāʾif* or subtle bodies of Sufism, all refer to the immense reality unto which the human microcosm opens if only man were to cease to live on the surface of his being. Certain schools also speak of the man of light and the whole anatomy and physiology of the inner man, which is not the subject of study of modern biology but which, nevertheless, affects the human body, the physical body itself reflecting the Absolute on its own level and possessing a positive nature of great import for the understanding of the total nature of man.[31]

The human body is not the seat of concupiscence but only its instrument. Although asceticism is a necessary element of every authentic spiritual path, for there is something in the soul that must die before it can reach perfection, the body itself is the temple of God. It is the sacred precinct in which the Divine Presence or the Divine Light[32] manifests itself as asserted not only in the Oriental religions but also in Hesychasm within Orthodox Christianity where the keeping of the mind within the body and the Divine Name within the center of the body, which is the heart, plays a crucial role. This perspective is also to be found in Christian Hermeticism but has not been greatly emphasized in Western Christian theology.[33]

The human body consists of three basic elements: the head, the body, and the heart. The heart, which is the invisible center of both the subtle and the physical body, is the seat of intelligence and the point which relates the terrestrial human state to the higher states of being. In the heart, knowledge and being meet and are one. The head and the body are like projections of the heart: the head, whose activity is associated with the mind, is the projection of the intelligence of the heart and the body the projection of being. This separation already marks the segmentation and externalization of man. But the compartmentalization is not complete. There is an element of being in the mind and of intelligence in the body which become forgotten to the extent that man becomes engrossed in the illusion of the Promethean mode of existence and forgets his theomorphic nature. That is why modern man, who *is* Promethean man to the extent that such a perversion of his own reality is possible, is the type of man most forgetful of the tranquility and peace of mind which reflects being and of the intelligence of the body. That is also why those contemporary men, in quest of the sacred and the rediscovery of pontifical man, seek, on the one hand, techniques of meditation which would allow the agitated mind to simply be and to overcome that excessive cerebral activity which characterizes modern man and, on the other hand, to rediscover the wisdom and intelligence of the body through yoga, Oriental forms of medicine, natural foods, and the like. Both attempts are in reality the quest for the heart which in the spiritual person, aware of his vocation as man, "penetrates" into both the head and the body, integrating them into the center, bestowing a contemplative perfume to mental activity and an intellectual and spiritual presence to the body which is reflected in its gestures and motions.[34]

In the prophet, the *avatār*, and the great saint both the face and the body directly manifest and display the presence of the heart through an inwardness which attracts toward the center and a radiance and emanation of grace which inebriates and unifies. For those not blessed by the vision of such beings, the sacred art of those traditions based on the iconography of the human form of the founder or outstanding spiritual figures of the tradition is at least a substitute and reminder of what a work of art man himself is. To behold a Japanese or Tibetan Buddha image, with eyes drawn inward toward the heart and the body radiating the presence of the Spirit which resides in the heart, is to grasp in a concrete fashion what the principial and ideal relation of the heart is to both the head and the body which preserve their own intelligible symbolism and even their own wisdom, whether a particular "mind" cut off from its own roots is aware of it or not.

The central and "absolute" nature of the human body is also to be seen in man's vertical position which directly reflects his role as the axis connecting heaven and earth. The clear distinction of his head protruding toward heaven reflects his quest for transcendence. The chest reflects glory and nobility, of a more rigorous nature in the male and generous in the female, and the sexual parts hierogenesis, divine activity whose terrestrial result is the procreation of another man or woman who miraculously enough is again not merely a biological being although outwardly brought into the world through biological means.[35] From the perspective of *scientia sacra* the human body itself is proof that man has sprung from a celestial origin and that he was born for a goal beyond the confines of his animality. The definition of man as a central being is reflected not only in his mind, speech, and other internal faculties but also in his body which stands at the center of the circle of terrestrial existence and possesses a beauty and significance which is of a purely spiritual nature. The very body of man and woman reveals the destiny of the human being as a creature born for immortality, as a being whose perfection resides in ascending the vertical dimension of existence, having already reached the center of the horizontal dimension. Having reached the point of intersection of the cross,[36] it is for man to ascend its vertical axis which is the only way for him to transcend himself and to remain fully human, for to be human is to go beyond oneself. As Saint Augustine has said, to remain human, man must become superhuman.

Man also possesses numerous internal faculties, a memory much more prestigious than those who are the product of modern education can envisage[37] and one which plays a very positive role in both intellectual and artistic activity of traditional man. He possesses an imagination which, far from being mere fantasy, has the power to create forms corresponding to cosmic realities and to play a central role in religious and even intellectual life, far more than can be conceived by the modern world whose impoverished view of reality excludes the whole domain of what might be called the imaginal, to distinguish it from the imaginary.[38] Man also possesses that miraculous gift of speech through which he is able to exteriorize the knowledge of both the heart and the mind. His speech is the direct reflection and consequence of his theomorphic nature and the Logos which shines at the center of his being. It is through his speech that he is able to formulate the Word of God and it is also through his speech in the form of prayer and finally the quintessential prayer of the heart which is inner speech and silent invocation that he himself becomes prayer. Man realizes his full pontifical nature in that theophanic prayer of Universal Man in which the whole creation, both Heaven and earth, participate.

From the point of view of his powers and faculty man can be said to possess essentially three powers or poles which determine his life, these being intelligence, sentiment, and will. As a theomorphic being he possesses or can possess that absolute and unconditioned intelligence which can know the truth as such; sentiments which are capable of going beyond the limited conditions of man and of reaching out for the ultimate through love, suffering, sacrifice, and also fear;[39] and a will which is free to choose and which reflects the Divine Freedom.

Because of man's separation from his original perfection and all the ambivalence that the human condition involves as a result of what Christianity calls the fall, none of these powers function necessarily and automatically according to man's theomorphic nature. The fall of man upon the earth, like the descent of a symbol from a higher plane of reality, means both reflection and inversion which in the case of man leads to perversion. Intelligence can become reduced to mental play; sentiments can deteriorate to little more than gravitation around that illusory coagulation which we usually call ourselves but which is only the ego in its negative sense as comprising the knots of the soul; and the will can be debased to nothing other than the urge to do that which removes man from the source of his own being, from his own real self. But these powers, when governed by tradition and imbued with the power of the light and grace which emanates from revelation, begin to reveal, like man's body, dimensions of his theomorphic nature. The body, however, remains more innocent and true to the form in which God created it, whereas the perversion of man and his deviation from his Divine Prototype is manifested directly in this intermediate realm with which man identifies himself, namely, the realm of the will and the sentiments and even the mental reflection of the intelligence, if not the intelligence itself. In the normal situation which is that of pontifical man, the goal of all three human powers or faculties, that is, intelligence, the sentiments, and will, is God. Moreover, in the sapiential perspective both the sentiments and the will are related to intelligence and impregnated by it, for how can one love without knowing what one loves and how can one will something without some knowledge at least of what one wills?

The understanding of the reality of man as *anthrōpos* can be achieved more fully by also casting an eye upon the segmentations and divisions of various kinds which characterize mankind as such. The original *anthrōpos* was, according to traditional teachings, an androgynic figure although some traditions speak of both a male and a female being whose union is then seen as the perfection identified with the androgynic state.[40] In either case, the wholeness and perfection inherent in the human state and the bliss which is associated with sexual union belong in reality to the androgynic state before the sexes were separated. But the dualities which characterize the created order and which manifest themselves on all levels of existence below the principial, such as *yin-yang*, *puruṣa-prakṛti*, activity and passivity, form and matter, could not but appear upon the plane of that androgynic reality and give birth to the male and the female which do not, however, correspond to pure *yin* and pure *yang*. Since they are creatures they must contain both principles within themselves with one of the elements of the duality predominating in each case. The male and the female in their complementarity recreate the unity of the androgynic being and in fact sexual union is an earthly reflection of that paradisal ecstasy which belonged to the androgynic *anthrōpos*. But that androgynic reality is also reflected in both man and woman in themselves, hence both the sense of complementarity and rivalry which characterizes the relation between the sexes. In any case the distinction between the male and female is not only biological. It is not even only psychological or spiritual. It has its roots in the Divine Nature Itself, man reflecting more the Absoluteness of the Divine and the woman Its Infinitude. If the face of God towards the world is envisaged in masculine terms, His inner Infinitude is symbolized by the feminine as are His Mercy and Wisdom.[41] Human sexuality, far from being a terrestrial accident, reflects principles which are ultimately of a metacosmic significance. It is not without reason that sexuality is the only means open for human beings, not endowed with the gift of spiritual vision, to experience "the Infinite" through the senses, albeit for a few fleeting moments, and that sexuality leaves such a profound mark upon the soul of men and women and affects them in a manner far more enduring than other physical acts. To understand the nature of the male-female distinction in the human race and to appreciate the positive qualities which each sex displays is to gain greater insight into the nature of that androgynic being whose reality both the male and female carry at the center of their being.[42]

Man is not only divided according to sex but also temperament of which both sexes partake. The four temperaments of traditional Galenic medicine which have their counterparts in other schools of traditional medicine concern not only the physical body but also the psychic substance and in fact all the faculties which comprise what we call the soul. They affect not only the sentiments but also the will and even the modes of operation of intelligence which in themselves remain above the temperamental modifications. The same could be said of the three *guṇas* of Hindu cosmology, those fundamental tendencies in the primary substance of the universe, or *prakṛti*, which concern not only the physical realm but also human types.[43] One can say that human beings are differentiated through the dual principles of *yin-yang*; the three *guṇas*, which are *sattva*, the ascending, *raja*, the expansive, and *tamas*, the descending tendencies; and the temperaments which have a close correlation with the four natures, elements, and humors as expounded in various cosmological schemes.[44]

Human types can also be divided astrologically, here astrology being understood in its cosmological and symbolic rather than its predictive sense.[45] Astrological classifications, which are in fact related to traditional medical and physical typologies, concern the cosmic correspondences of the various aspects of the human soul and unveil the refraction of the archetype of man in the cosmic mirror in such a way as to bring out the diversity of this refraction with reference to the qualities associated with the zodiacal signs and the planets. Traditional astrology, in a sense, concerns man on the angelic level of his being but also unveils, if understood in its symbolic significance, a typology of man which reveals yet another facet of the differentiation of the human species. The correspondence between various parts of the body as well as man's mental powers to astrological signs and the intricate rapport created between the motion of the heavens, various "aspects" and relations between planets and human activity are also a means of portraying the inward link that binds man as the microcosm to the cosmos.

Mankind is also divided into castes and races, both of which must be understood in their essential reality and without the pejorative connotations which have become associated with them in the modern world. The division of humanity into castes does not necessarily mean immutable social stratification for there have been strictly traditional societies, such as the Islamic, where caste has not existed as a social institution in the same way it was found in ancient Persia or in India. The traditional science of man sees the concept of caste as a key for the understanding of human types. There are those who are contemplative by nature and drawn to the quest of knowledge, who have a sacerdotal nature and in normal times usually fulfill the priestly and intellectual functions in their society. There are those who are warriors and leaders of men, who possess the courage to fight for the truth and to protect the world in which they live, who are ready to sacrifice themselves in battle as the person with a sacerdotal nature sacrifices himself in prayer to the Divinity. Members of this second caste have a knightly function and in normal times would be the political leaders and warriors. Then there are those given to trade, to making an honest living and working hard to sustain and support themselves and those around them. They have a mercantile nature and in traditional societies comprise those who carry out the business and economic functions of normal society. Finally, there are those whose virtue is to follow and to be led, to work according to the dictates of those who lead them. These castes which Hinduism identifies as the *brahman, kṣatriya, vaiśya,* and *śūdra* are not necessarily identified with birth in all societies.[46] In any case, as far as the study of human types is concerned, they are to be found everywhere in all times and climes wherever men and women live and die. They represent fundamental human types complementing the tripartite Neoplatonic division of human beings into the pneumatics, psychics, and "hylics" (the *hylikoi* of the Neoplatonists). To understand the deeper significance of caste is to gain an insight into a profound aspect of human nature in whatever environment man might function and live.[47]

Finally, it is obvious that human beings are divided into racial and ethnic types. There are four races, the yellow, the red, the black, and the white, which like the four castes act as the pillars of the human collectivity, four symbolizing stability and being associated with the earth itself with its four cardinal directions and the four elements of which the physical world is composed. Each race is an aspect of that androgynic reality and possesses its own positive features. In fact, no one race can exhaust the reality of the human state, including human beauty which each race, both its male and female members, reflect in a different fashion. The very plenitude of the Divine Principle and richness of the reality of the Universal Man, who is the theater for the theophany of all the Divine Names and Qualities, requires this multiplicity of races and ethnic groups which in their unbelievable variety manifest the different aspects of their prototype and which together give some idea of the grandeur and beauty of that first creation of God which was the human reality as such, that primordial reflection of the face of the Beloved in the mirror of nothingness.

The division of mankind into male and female, the various temperamental types, astrological divisions of human beings, different natures according to caste, various racial types, and many other factors along with the interpenetration of these modes of perceiving the human state, reveal something of the immense complexity of that creature called man. But as analysis leads in turn to synthesis, this bewildering array of types all return to that primordial reality of the *anthrōpos* which each human being reflects in himself or herself. To be human is to be human wherever and whenever one may live. There is therefore a profound unity of traditional mankind which only the traditional science of man can comprehend without reducing this unity to a uniformity and a gross quantitative equality that characterizes so much of the modern concern for man and the study of the human state.

Through all these differences of types, tradition detects the presence of that pontifical man born to know the Absolute and to live according to the will of Heaven. But tradition is also fully aware of the ambivalence of the human state, of the fact that men do not live on the level of what they are in principle, but below themselves, and of the imperfection of all that participates in what is characteristically human. This trait includes even those direct manifestations of the Absolute in the relative which comprise religion with revelation at its heart. Man is such a being that he can become prophet and spokesman for the Word of God, not to speak of the possibility of the divinized man which certain traditions like Islam, based on the Absolute itself, reject. But even in these cases there is a human margin and within each religion there exists an element of pure, unqualified Truth and a margin which already belongs to the region where the Truth penetrates into the human substance.[48] Moreover, revelation is always given in the language of the people to whom God addresses Himself. As the Quran says, "And We never sent a messenger save with the language of his folk that he might make [the message] clear for them."[49] Hence the multiplicity of religions in a world with multiple "humanities." The human state therefore gives a certain particularity to various revelations of the Truth while the heart of these revelations remains above all form. In fact, man himself is able to penetrate into that formless Essence through his intelligence sanctified by that revelation and even come to know that the formless Truth is modified by the form of the recipient according to the Divine Wisdom and Will, God having Himself created that recipient which receives His revelation in different climes and settings.[50]

How strange it appears that agnostic humanism, which remains content with the vessel without realizing the origin of the divine elixir that the human vessel contains, should be only a half-way house to that which is inhuman! Pontifical man has lived on the earth for millennia and continues to survive here and there despite the onslaught of modernism. But the life of Promethean man has been indeed short-lived. The kind of humanism associated with the Promethean revolt of the Renaissance has led in only a few centuries to the veritably infrahuman which threatens not only the human quality of life but the very existence of man on earth. The reason for such a phenomenon, which seems so unexpected from the perspective of Promethean man, is quite obvious from the traditional point of view. It lies in the fact that to speak of the human is to speak, at the same time, of the Divine. Although scholars occasionally discuss what they call Chinese or Islamic humanism, there has in fact never been a humanism in any traditional civilization similar to the one associated with the European Renaissance and what followed upon its wake. Traditional civilizations have spoken of man and of course created cultures and disciplines called the humanities of the highest order but the man they have spoken of has never ceased to be that pontifical man who stands on the axis joining Heaven and earth and who bears the imprint of the Divine upon his very being.

It is this basic nature of man which makes a secular and agnostic humanism impossible. It is not metaphysically possible to kill the gods and seek to efface the imprint of the Divinity upon man without destroying man himself; the bitter experience of the modern world stands as overwhelming evidence to this truth. The face which God has turned toward the cosmos and man (the *wajhallāh* of the Quran)[51] is none other than the face of man toward the Divinity and in fact the human face itself. One cannot "efface" the "face of God" without "effacing" man himself and reducing him to a faceless entity lost in an anthill. The cry of Nietzsche that "God is dead" could not but mean that "man is dead" as the history of the twentieth century has succeeded in demonstrating in so many ways. But in reality the response to Nietzsche was not the death of man as such but of the Promethean man who had thought he could live on a circle without a center. The other man, the pontifical man, although forgotten in the modern world, continues to live even within those human beings who pride themselves in having outgrown the models and modes of thought of their ancestors; he continues to live and will never die.

That man who remains man and continues to survive here and there even during this period of eclipse of spirituality and the desacralization of life is the being who remains aware of his destiny which is transcendence and the function of his intelligence which is knowledge of the Absolute. He is fully aware of the preciousness of human life, which alone permits a creature living in this world to journey beyond the cosmos, and is always conscious of the great responsibility which such an opportunity entails. He knows that the grandeur of man does not lie in his cunning cleverness or titanic creations but resides most of all in the incredible power to empty himself of himself, to cease to exist in the initiatic sense, to participate in that state of spiritual poverty and emptiness which permits him to experience Ultimate Reality. As the Persian poet Saʿdī says,

> *Man reaches a stage where he sees nothing but God;*
> *See how exalted is the station of manhood.*[52]

Pontifical man stands at the perigee of an arc half of which represents the trajectory through which he has descended from the Source and his own archetype *in divinis* and the other half the arc of ascent which he must follow to return to that Source. The whole constitution of man reveals this role of the traveler who becomes what he "is" and is what he becomes. Man is fully man only when he realizes who he is and in doing so fulfills not only his own destiny and reaches his entelechy but also illuminates the world about him. Journeying from the earth to his celestial abode, which he has left inwardly, man becomes the channel of grace for the earth, and the bridge which joins it to Heaven. Realization of the truth by pontifical man is not only the goal and end of the human state but also the means whereby Heaven and earth are reunited in marriage, and the Unity, which is the Source of the cosmos and the harmony which pervades it, is reestablished. To be fully man is to rediscover that primordial Unity from which all the heavens and earths originate and yet from which nothing ever *really* departs.

NOTES

1. By man is meant not the male alone but the human state whose archetypal reality is the androgyne reflected in both the male and female. Man in English signifies at once the male and the human being as such like the Greek *anthrōpos*, the German *mensch* or the Arabic *insān*. There is no need to torture the natural structure of the English language to satisfy current movements which consider the use of the term "man" as a sexist bias, forgetting the second meaning of the term as *anthrōpos*.

2. On the Islamic conception of man and the meaning of this term see G. Eaton, *King of the Castle*, chap. 5; G. Durand, *Science de l'homme et tradition*, Paris, 1979, esp. chap. 3, entitled "*Homo proximi orientis*: science de l'homme et Islam spirituel"; and Nasr, "Who is Man? The Perennial Answer of Islam," in Needleman (ed.), *The Sword of Gnosis*, pp. 203–17.

See also "Man as Microcosm," in T. Izutsu, *A Comparative Study of the Key Philosophical Concepts in Sufism and Taoism—Ibn ʿArabî and Lao-Tzû, Chuang-Tzû*, Pt. 1, Tokyo, 1966, pp. 208ff., where the whole doctrine of the universal man (or *khalīfah*) as expounded in Ibn ʿArabī's *Fuṣūs al-ḥikam* is elaborated with great clarity. In pts. 2 and 3 of this work the Taoist concept of man is likewise elucidated and finally compared in a masterly fashion with the Islamic.

3. Needless to say, the title of pontiff given to the Catholic pope symbolizes directly the central function of this office as the "bridge" between God and His church as well as between the church and the community of the faithful, but this more particular usage of the term does not invalidate the universal significance of the "pontifical" function of man as such.

4. Certain modern observers of the environmental crisis, who want at the same time to defend the misdeeds of modern man, seek to extrapolate the devastation of the planet to earlier periods of human history in order to decrease the burden of responsibility of modern man by including even goats to explain why the ecological balance is being destroyed. While one cannot deny the deforestation of certain areas or erosion of the soil during the Middle Ages or even earlier, there is no doubt that there is no comparison between the intensity, rapidity, or extent of destruction of the natural environment during the past few centuries and what occurred during the previous long periods of history when traditional man lived on the surface of the earth.

5. This is the title of a well-known essay of G. Durand. See his *On the Disfiguration of the Image of Man in the West*, Ipswich, U.K., 1976.

6. There is no doubt that there were many attempts to rediscover traditional teachings in the Renaissance esp. in the field of the traditional sciences. See J. F. Maillard, "Science sacrée et science profane dans la tradition ésotérique de la renaissance," *Cahiers de l'Université Saint Jean de Jérusalem*, vol. I, Paris, 1974, pp. 111–26. But this fact cannot at all obliterate the truth that secularizing humanism and the rationalism connected with the notion of *virtù*, according to which man was able to command any situation rationally, characterize and dominate the Renaissance world view, especially as it concerns man. This conception of man based on an aggressive rationalism combined with skepticism was to enter the mainstream of European thought, both literary and scientific, through such figures as Montaigne and Galileo. On *virtù* and the concept of Renaissance man as "the rational artist in all things," see A. C. Crombie, "Science and the Arts in the Renaissance: The Search for Truth and Certainty, Old and New," *History of Science*, 18/42 (Dec. 1980): 233.

7. This hatred of wisdom has been combined, in what is characteristically modern philosophy, with a fear that God may somehow threaten the petty mental constructions which modern man has substituted for wisdom. "God, for the philosophic spirit, is an external menace to the human wisdom that man, deprived of Divine Intellect, contrives for himself." Durand, op. cit., pp. 20–21.

8. On this process see S. H. Nasr, *Man and Nature*, chap. 2.

9. On the traditional criticism of Comte see R. Guénon, *La Grande triade*, Paris, 1980, chap. 20.

10. For a criticism of the positivism inherent in modern anthropology see Durand, "Hermetica ratio et science de l'homme," in his *Science de l'homme et tradition*, pp. 174ff. See also the capital work of J. Servier, *L'Homme et l'invisible*, which, using scientific data, refutes nearly all the presumptions of modern anthropology.

11. Quoted in R. C. Zaehner, *The Teachings of the Magi*, London, 1956, p. 75; see also M. Molé, *Le Problème zoroastrien et la tradition mazdéenne*, Paris, 1963. The alchemical significance of this passage which relates the alchemical symbolism of metals to the inner or physiological aspect of the microcosm is evident. It is also of great significance to note that according to the *Bundahišn*, the form of Gāyomart was spherical as also asserted in Plato's *Symposium* concerning the form of the primordial man. This geometric symbolism indicated that just as all geometric figures and solids are generated by and contained in the circle and the sphere which are the primordial form in two and three dimensions, primordial man is the origin of all humanity and, in fact, cosmic existence and "comprehends," in a metaphysical sense, all cosmic existence.

See also the various works of M. Eliade dealing with sacrifice and religious rites including *Patterns in Comparative Religion*, trans. R. Sheed, New York, 1958; *Traité d'histoire des religion*, Paris, 1964; and *Gods, Goddesses, and the Myths of Creation*, New York, 1967.

12. The Person (Puruṣa) has a thousand eyes, a thousand heads, a thousand feet:
Encompassing Earth on every side, he rules firmly-established in the heart.
The Person, too, is all This, both what has been and what is to come . . .
With three parts the Person is above, but one part came-into-existence here:
Thence, he proceeded everywhere, regarding Earth and Heaven.
Of him was Nature born, from Nature Person born:
When born, he ranges Earth from East to West.
Whereas the Angels laid-out the sacrifice with the Person of their offering, . . .
From that sacrifice, when the offering was all accomplished, the Verses and Liturgies were born,
The Metres, and the Formulary born of it.
Therefrom were born horses, and whatso *beasts* have *cutting* teeth in both jaws.
Therefrom were born cows, and therefrom goats and sheep.
When they divided the Person, how-many-fold did they arrange him?
What was his mouth? What were his arms? How were his thighs and feet named?
The Priest was his mouth; of his arms was made the Ruler;
His thighs were the Merchant-folk; from his feet was born the Servant.
The Moon was born from his Intellect; the Sun from his eye.

Rg Veda, X, 90, trans. A. K. Coomaraswamy on the basis of the translation of N. Brown. See Coomaraswamy, *The Vedas, Essays in Translation and Exegesis*, London, 1976, pp. 69–71.

13.

$$\text{لَوْلَاكَ وَلَاخَلَقْتُ الأَفْلَاكَ}$$

14. This is a specifically Islamic image, since Islam sees the cardinal sin of man in his forgetfulness (*ghaflah*) of who he is although he still carries his primordial nature (*al-fitrah*) within himself, the man as such to which in fact the Islamic message addresses itself. See Schuon, *Understanding Islam*, pp. 13–15.

15. The term *al-insān al-kāmil* was first used as a technical term by Ibn 'Arabī although its reality constitutes the second *Shahādah, Muhammad^un rasūlallāh*, and of course was present from the beginning of the Quranic revelation. After Ibn 'Arabī the doctrine was presented in a more systematic fashion by 'Abd al-Karīm al-Jīlī in his *al-Insān al-kāmil* and also by 'Azīz al-Dīn Nasafī in the work bearing the same name. See. T. Burckhardt, *De l'homme universel*; and M. Molé (ed.), *'Azizoddin Nasafi, Le Livre de l'homme parfait (Kitāb al-insān al-kāmil)*, Tehran-Paris, 1962. A complete translation of the Jīlī work is being prepared in English by V. Danner for the Classics of Western Spirituality Series being published by the Paulist Press.

16. All traditions teach of the presence of more than one self within us, and we still speak of self-discipline which means that there must be a self which disciplines and another which is disciplined. Coomaraswamy has dealt with this theme in many of his writings, for example, "On the Indian Traditional Psychology, or Rather Pneumatology," in Lipsey (ed.), *Coomaraswamy 2: Selected Papers, Metaphysics*, pp. 333ff.

On the traditional doctrine of the inner man see also V. Danner, "The Inner and Outer Man," in Y. Ibish and P. Wilson (eds.), *Traditional Modes of Contemplation and Action*, Tehran, 1977, pp. 407–12.

17. The very fact that one of the species living on earth called man can destroy the natural environment is itself an indication that he is not simply an earthly creature and that his actions possess a cosmic dimension. This only proves, for those whose vision has not become atrophied by the limitations of modern thought, that man is more than a purely biological specimen with a somewhat larger brain than the other primates.

18. Both Jews and Muslims within the Abrahamic family of traditions and Hindus in quite another world believe that the practice of their rites and various aspects of their sacred law uphold the cosmos. In Hinduism the gradual decline of man and his natural environment through a cosmic cycle are explicitly associated with degrees of practice of the Law of Manu. The same correspondence between the practice of rites and the sustenance of the cosmic order is also emphasized in nearly every other tradition ranging from the Egyptian to the American Indian.

19. "Man is either Viceroy or else he is an animal that claims special rights by virtue of its cunning and the devouring efficiency of teeth sharpened by technological instruments, an animal whose time is up. If he is such an animal, then he has no rights—he is no more nor less than meat—and elephants and lions, rabbits and mice must in some dim recess of their being rejoice to see the usurper develop the means of his own total destruction. But if he is Viceroy, then all decay and all trouble in the created world that surrounds him is in some measure to be laid to his count." Eaton, *King of the Castle*, p. 123.

20. By this assertion we do not mean that traditional man is only that half-angelic creature of a certain type of Christian piety who is alienated from nature. Traditional man who saw himself as custodian of nature nevertheless buried his dead and did not consider himself a purely natural being, although he lived in complete harmony with nature.

21. See Ibn 'Arabī, *The Wisdom of the Prophets (Fuṣūṣ al-Ḥikam)*, trans. from Arabic to French with notes by T. Burckhardt and trans. from French to English by A. Culme-Seymour, pp. 23 and 35; also Ibn al-'Arabī, *Bezels of Wisdom*, chap. 2.

22. The genesis of man and his prenatal existence in various higher states of existence is expounded in great detail in Jewish esoterism. See L. Schaya, "La genèse de l'homme," *Études Traditionnelles*, no. 456–57 (Avril–Septembre 1977):94–131, where he discusses the birth, descent, loss of original purity, and the regaining of man's original state according to Jewish sources concluding that, "Né de Dieu, l'être humain est destiné, après ses multiples naissances et morts, à renaître en Lui, en tant que Lui" (p. 131); and idem, *The Universal Meaning of the Kabbalah*, pp. 116ff. See also F. Warrain, *La Théodicée de la Kabbale*, Paris, 1949, pp. 73ff.; and G. Scholem, *Major Trends in Jewish Mysticism*, Jerusalem, 1941, lectures 6 and 7.

23. Quran VII; 172. On the significance of this verse see Nasr, *Ideals and Realitites of Islam*, pp. 41ff.

24. *The Divan*, trans. H. Wilberforce Clarke, vol. 1, Calcutta, 1891, p. 406.

25. Hermeticism as reflected in alchemical texts contains a most profound anthropology which is now attracting the attention of those Western anthropologists who have realized the inadequacies of the modern science bearing this name and are in search of a science which would deal with the *anthrōpos*, not the two-legged animal that modern, secularized man envisages him to be. On the wedding between the soul and the Spirit in alchemy see T. Burckhardt, *Alchemy*, chap. 17.

26. Ṣadr al-Dīn Shīrāzī and later Islamic metaphysicians have dealt extensively with eschatological questions centered around the doctrine of the subtle body and its relation with the soul as it is molded by human action to which this *hadīth* refers. See especially the commentary of Ṣadr al-Dīn Shīrāzī upon the *Uṣūl al-kāfī* of Kulaynī containing the sayings of the Imams and also his commentary upon Suhrawardī's *Hikmat al-ishrāq*. See Corbin, "Le Thème de la résurrection chez Mollâ Sadrâ Shîrâzî (1050/1640) commentateur de Sohrawardî (587/1191)," in *Studies in Mysticism and Religion presented to Gershom G. Scholem*, Jerusalem, 1968, pp. 71–115.

27. On the metaphysical interpretation of the popular Indian notion of transmigration see Coomaraswamy, "On the One and Only Transmigrant," *Journal of the American Oriental Society* 44, supplement no. 3, and in Lipsey, *Coomaraswamy*, vol. 2.

28. One must also remember the meaning of "land" in the ancient Icelandic *Land-Náma-Bók*, which has been compared by Coomaraswamy in certain respects to the *Ṛg-Veda*. See his *The Ṛg Veda as Land-Náma-Bók*, in his *The Vedas—Essays in Translation and Exegesis*, pp. 117–59.

The *Ṛg Veda* itself (I, 108, 9 and X, 59, 4) refers to the three worlds as "earths." Likewise, the Kabbalah speaks of not only the earthly paradise or "upper earth" (*Tebel*) but also of six other earths of a more fragmentary nature so that there are altogether seven earths as stated by the *Zohar* and the *Sefer Yetsirah*. See Schaya, *The Universal Meaning of the Kabbalah*, pp. 108–9.

29. See Corbin, *Spiritual Body and Celestial Earth*, trans. N. Pearson, Princeton, 1977, where these doctrines are fully expounded. Corbin even speaks of "geosophy" as a wisdom about the earth and a sacred knowledge of the earth, including the celestial earth totally distinct from what geography or geology is concerned with.

30. Traditional eschatologies, whose complex doctrines cannot be treated here, all assert that only in this life as a human being can one take advantage of the central state into which one is born and pass to the spiritual abode and that there is no guarantee that one will be born into a central state after death unless one has lived according to tradition and in conformity with the Divine Will.

31. The physiology of the "man of light" is developed within Islamic esoterism particularly in the Central Asiatic school associated with the name of Najmal-Dīn Kubrā. See Corbin, *The Man of Light in Iranian Sufism*, trans. N. Pearson, Boulder, Colo., and

London, 1978; and idem, *En Islam iranien*, vol. 3. It is also developed fully in the Kabbala (for example, in the *Zohar*) as well as in the ancient Iranian religions which speak often of the cosmic dimensions of man in terms of light symbolism. See B. T. Anklesaria, *Zand-Ākāsīh, Iranian or Greater Bundahišn*, Bombay, 1956; and J. C. Coyajee, *Cults and Legends of Ancient Iran and China*, Bombay, 1963.

32. The title of one of Suhrawardī's most famous works is *Hayākil al-nūr* (*The Temples of Light*). The Arabic work *haykal* (pl. *hayākil*) here rendered as temple means also body; the title refers to the symbolism of the body as the temple in which is present the light of God.

33. There are of course exceptions not only in the medieval period in such figures as Dante but also in the later period in the writings of Paracelsus and even during the last century in the poetry of William Blake.

On the doctrine of the spiritual significance of the body in connection with the "subtle body" see G. R. S. Mead, *The Doctrine of the Subtle Body in Western Tradition*, London, 1919; and of more recent origin, C. W. Leadbeater, *Man Visible and Invisible*, Wheaton, Ill., 1969; and on a more popular level D. Tanseley, *Subtle Body, Essence and Shadow*, London, 1977.

34. One hardly need mention how important gesture is in traditional societies and how it is related to sacred symbols which manifest themselves in all facets of traditional civilizations including their art. The *mudras* in both Hinduism and Buddhism are a perfect example of the central role played by gesture.

On the heart, head, and body of man and their spiritual significance see Schuon, "The Ternary Aspect of the Human Microcosm," *Gnosis, Divine Wisdom*, pp. 93–99.

35. See Schuon, *Du Divin à l'humain*, pt. 3.

36. The horizontal and vertical dimensions of the cross symbolize the Universal Man who contains all the possibilities of existence, both horizontal and vertical, within himself. See R. Guénon, *Symbolism of the Cross*.

37. Some interest has been taken in recent years on reviving the traditional doctrines concerning memory. See F. Yates, *The Art of Memory*, Chicago, 1966.

38. This is a term used first by Corbin in French to distinguish the positive role of the imagination from all the pejorative connotations connected with the word "imaginary."

In recent years after three centuries of neglect, certain European philosophers and scholars have turned their attention to a serious reappraisal of the traditional teaching concerning the imagination. Among this group one must mention especially G. Durand who has established a center in Chambéry, France, named "Centre de recherche sur l'Imaginaire" for the study of the world of imagination. See his *Les Structures anthropologiques de l'Imaginaire*, Paris, 1979; also Corbin, *Creative Imagination in the Sufism of Ibn ʿArabī*, trans. R. Manheim, Princeton, 1969. See also R. L. Hart, *Unfinished Man and the Imagination*, New York, 1968.

39. For modern man the sentiment of fear has come to have only a negative significance as result of the loss of the sense of majesty and grandeur associated with the Divinity. In the traditional context, however, the Biblical saying, repeated by St. Paul and the Prophet of Islam, "the beginning of wisdom is the fear of God" (*raʾs al-hikmah makhāfatallāh*), remains of permanent significance since it corresponds to the nature of things and the most urgent and real needs of man as a being created for immortality.

40. For example, in India while in Tantrism there is reference to the androgynic figure *Ardhanārī*; in the Śivite school the androgynic state is usually represented iconographically by the union of Śiva and Parvatī who are sometimes fused as one figure half male and half female, in which case Śiva is known as *Ardhanārīśvara*.

On the significance of the androgyne and some of the contemporary applications of the meaning of its symbol see E. Zolla, *The Androgyne, Fusion of the Sexes*, London, 1981; also K. Critchlow, *The Soul as Sphere and Androgyne*, Ipswich, U.K., 1980.

41. It is not accidental that in so many sacred languages these qualities possess a feminine form such as the Arabic *rahmah* ("mercy") and *hikmah* ("wisdom").

42. The attempt by modern man to destroy the qualitative differences between the

sexes in the name of some kind of egalitarianism is only a consequence of the further elongation of Promethean man from the archetypal reality of the human state and therefore an insensitivity to this precious qualitative difference between the sexes.

43. On the *gunas* see Guénon, *Man and His Becoming According to the Vedanta*, chap. 4.

44. On their relation see Nasr, *Islamic Science—An Illustrated Study*, pp. 159ff.

45. For the traditional treatment of astrological human types see al-Bīrūnī, *Elements of Astrology*, trans. W. Ramsey Wright, London, 1934; Burckhardt, *The Mystical Astrology of Ibn ʿArabī*, London, 1977; R. Z. Zoller, *The Lost Key to Prediction*, New York, 1980; M. Gauguelin, *The Cosmic Clocks*, London, 1969; and J. A. West and J. G. Toonder, *The Case for Astrology*, London, 1970.

46. On the metaphysical significance of caste see Schuon, "Principle of Distinction in the Social Order," in his *Language of the Self*, pp. 136ff.

47. It is possible for a human being to possess more than one caste characteristic, the most eminent example being of course the prophet-kings of the Abrahamic traditions who possessed both the sacerdotal and knightly natures in the most eminent degree, Melchizedik being the primal example of the union of these natures as well as spiritual and temporal authority.

48. See Schuon, "Understanding and Believing" and "The Human Margin," in Needleman (ed.), *The Sword of Gnosis*, pp. 401ff.

49. Quran (XIV; 4—Pickthall translation).

50. We shall deal more extensively with this question in chap. 9.

51. In all traditions the significance of the "face" is emphasized since it bears the direct imprint of the Divine upon the human. In the Quran there are several references to the "face of God" which have become sources of meditation for many Muslim sages. See, for example, H. Corbin, "Face de Dieu et face de l'homme," *Eranos-Jahrbuch* 36 (1968): 165–228, which deals mostly with the teachings of Qāḍī Saʿīd Qummī, on the significance of the face of God in relation to the human face and all that determines the humanity of man.

52.

رداد می بجانی که بجرخدا بنید   نبکر که تا چه حد است مقام آدمیت

CHAPTER SIX

The Cosmos as Theophany

Nel suo profondo vidi che s'interna,
legato con amore in un volume,
ciò che per l'universo si squaderna:
sustanze e accidenti e lor costume
quasi conflati insieme, par tal modo
che ciò ch'i' dico è un semplice lume.

In the depth I saw ingathered, bound by love in one
single volume, that which is dispersed in leaves
throughout the universe: substances and accidents and
their relations, as though fused together in such a way
that what I tell is but a simple light.[1]

Dante

Although the goal of sacred knowledge is the knowledge of the
Sacred as such, that is, of that Reality which lies beyond all
cosmic manifestation, there is always that stage of the gathering of
the scattered leaves of the book of the universe, to paraphrase Dante,
before journeying beyond it. The cosmos plays a positive role in
certain types of spirituality that any integral tradition must account
for and include in its total perspective, which is not to say that the
adept of every kind of spiritual path need study the pages of the
cosmic book. But precisely because the cosmos *is* a book containing a
primordial revelation of utmost significance and man a being whose
essential, constitutive elements are reflected upon the cosmic mirror
and who possesses a profound inner nexus with the cosmic ambience
around him, sacred knowledge must also include a knowledge of the

cosmos which is not simply an empirical knowledge of nature nor even just a sensibility toward the beauties of nature, no matter how noble this sensibility of the kind expressed by so many English Romantic poets might be.

In the traditional world there is a science of the cosmos—in fact many sciences of the cosmos or cosmological sciences which study various natural and cosmic domains ranging from the stars to minerals, but from the point of view of metaphysical principles. All traditional cosmology is in fact the fruit of the applications of metaphysical principles to different domains of cosmic reality by an intelligence which is itself still wed to the Intellect and has not completely surrendered to sensorial impressions. Such sciences also do deal with the natural world and have produced knowledge of that world which is "scientific" according to the current understanding of this term, but not only scientific.[2] Even in these instances, however, the aim of such traditional sciences has been not to produce knowledge of a particular order of reality in a closed system, and cut off from other orders of reality and domains of knowledge, but a knowledge which relates the domain in question to higher orders of reality as that knowledge itself is related to higher orders of knowledge.[3] There is such a thing as traditional science distinct from modern science dealing with the same realms and domains of nature which are treated in the sciences today. Yet these traditional sciences, although of much importance in understanding the rise of modern science, which in many cases employed their outward content without comprehending or accepting their world view, have a significance wholly other than the modern sciences of nature.[4]

The traditional sciences of the cosmos make use of the language of symbolism. They claim to expound a *science* and not a sentiment or poetic image of the domain which is their concern, but a science which is expounded in the language of symbolism based on the analogy between various levels of existence. In fact, although there are numerous cosmological sciences, sometimes even several dealing with the same realm and within a single tradition, one can speak of a *cosmologia perennis* which they reflect in various languages of form and symbol, a *cosmologia perennis* which, in one sense, is the application and, in another, the complement of the *sophia perennis* which is concerned essentially with metaphysics.

There is also another type of the "study" of the cosmos in the traditional context which complements the first. That is the contemplation of certain natural forms as reflecting Divine Qualities and the vision of the cosmos *in divinis*. This perspective is based on the power of forms to be occasions for recollection in the Platonic sense and the *essential* and of course not *substantial* identity of natural forms with their paradisal origin. Spiritual realization based on the sapiential perspective implies also this "metaphysical transparency of natural forms and objects" as a necessary dimension and aspect of "seeing God everywhere."[5] In reality the traditional cosmological sciences lend themselves to being such a support for contemplation besides making available a veritable science of various realms of the cosmos. What is in fact traditional cosmology but a way of allowing man to contemplate the cosmos itself as an icon! Therefore, both types of knowledge of the cosmos, as viewed from the perspective of sacred knowledge and through eyes which are not cut off from the sanctifying rays of the "eye of the heart," reveal the cosmos as theophany.[6] To behold the cosmos with the eye of the intellect is to see it not as a pattern of externalized and brute facts, but as a theater wherein are reflected aspects of the Divine Qualities, as a myriad of mirrors reflecting the face of the Beloved, as the theophany of that Reality which resides at the Center of the being of man himself. To see the cosmos as theophany is to see the reflection of one-Self in the cosmos and its forms.

In traditions based upon a sacred scripture the cosmos also reveals its meaning as a vast book whose pages are replete with the words of the Author and possess multiple levels of meaning like the revealed book of the religion in question. This perspective is to be found in Judaism and Islam where the eternal Torah and the Quran as the *Umm al-kitāb* are seen as prototypes of both the revealed book and that other grand book or virgin nature which reflects God's primordial revelation. In Christianity also, where there is greater emphasis upon the Son as Logos than on the book, the vision of the universe as the book of God is not only present but has been repeated through the ages especially in the utterance of those who have belonged to the sapiential perspective. In fact, this view, so majestically depicted by Dante, did not disappear until the inner meaning of revelation itself became inaccessible. Exegesis turned to the interpretation of the outward, literal meaning of the sacred text while cosmic symbols were becoming facts and, instead of revealing the cosmos as theophany, were limiting the reality of the world to the categories of mass and motion. The veiling of pontifical man and his transformation to the Promethean could not but result in the cosmic book becoming illegible and sacred Scripture reduced to only its outward meaning.

In Islam the correspondence between man, the cosmos, and the sacred book is central to the whole religion. The sacred book of Islam is the written or composed Quran (*al-Qurʾān al-tadwīnī*) as well as the cosmic Quran (*al-Qurʾān al-takwīnī*). Its verses are called *āyāt* which means also signs or symbols to which the Quran itself refers in the verse, "We shall show them our portents upon the horizon [*āfāq*] and within themselves [*anfus*], until it be manifest unto them that it is the truth" (XLI; 53).[7] The *āyāt* are the Divine Words and Letters which comprise at once the elements of the Divine Book, the macrocosmic world and the inner being of man. The *āyāt* manifest themselves in the Holy Book, the horizons (*āfāq*) or the heavens and earth and the soul of man (*anfus*). To the extent that the *āyāt* of the sacred book reveal their inner meaning and man's outer faculty and intelligence become wed once again to the inner faculties and the heart, and man realizes his own being as a sign of God, the cosmos manifests itself as theophany and the phenomena of nature become transformed into the *āyāt* mentioned by the Quran, the *āyāt* which are none other than the *vestigia Dei* which an Albertus Magnus or John Ray sought to discover in their study of natural forms.[8] Likewise, the theophanic aspect of virgin nature aids in man's discovery of his own inner being. Nature is herself a divine revelation with its own metaphysics and mode of prayer, but only a contemplative already endowed with sacred knowledge can read the gnostic message written in the most subtle manner upon the cliffs of high mountains, the leaves of the trees,[9] the faces of animals and the stars of the sky.

In certain other traditions of a primordial character where the revelation itself is directly related to natural forms as in the tradition of the American Indians, especially those of the Plains, and in Shinto-ism, the animals and plants are not only symbols of various Divine Qualities but direct manifestations of the Divine Principle in such a way that they play a direct role in the cultic aspect of the religion in question. Moreover, in such traditions there exists a knowledge of nature which is direct and intimate yet inward. The Indian not only sees the bear or the eagle as divine presences but has a knowledge of what one might call the eagle-ness of the eagle and the bear-ness of the bear as if he saw in these beings their Platonic archetypes. The revelation of God in such cases embraces both men and nature in such a way that would be inconceivable for that exteriorized reason of postmedieval man who externalized his alienation from his own inner reality by increasing his sense of aggression and hatred against nature, an aggression made somewhat easier by the excessively rigid distinction made in Western Christianity between the supernatural and the natural. In any case, the animal masks of certain archaic traditions or the waterfalls of Taoist paintings depicting the descent of the One into the plane of multiplicity are neither animism in its pejorative sense nor a naive projection of the human psyche upon creatures of the external world. They are epiphanies of the Sacred based on the most profound knowledge of the very essence of the natural forms involved. They represent a knowledge of the cosmos which is not by any means negated or abrogated by what physics may discover about the dynamics of a waterfall or anatomy about the animal in question. One wonders who knows more about the coyote, the zoologist who is able to study its external habit and dissect its cadaver or the Indian medicine man who identifies himself with the "spirit" of the coyote?[10]

Not only do the traditional sciences of the cosmos study the forms of nature with respect to their essential archetypes and do contemplatives within these traditions view the phenomena of virgin nature as theophanies, but also the astounding harmony of the natural world is seen as a direct result and consequence of that sacrifice of the primordial man described in different metaphysical or mythical languages in various traditions. The unbelievable harmony which pervades the world, linking the life cycles of fishes on the bottom of tropical oceans to land creatures roaming northern tundras in an incredible pattern, has been all but neglected by Western science until very recent times. But it forms an important element of that traditional science of nature which, whether in terms of the Pythagorean theory of harmony related to the World Soul or in other terms, remains always aware of that harmony between animals, plants, and minerals, between the creatures of various climes and also between the physical, subtle, and spiritual realms of beings which make the life of the cosmos possible. This harmony, whose grand contour has been only partly revealed by some recent ecological studies, is like the harmony of the parts of the human body as well as of the body, soul, and spirit of pontifical or traditional man and, in fact, is profoundly related to this concretely experienced harmony of man because this latter type of harmony, like that of the cosmos, is derived from the perfect harmony of the being of the Universal Man who is the prototype of both man and the cosmos. If the cosmos is a crystallization of the sounds of music and musical harmony a key for the understanding of the structure of the cosmos from planetary motion to quantum energy levels, it is because harmony dwelt in the very being of that archetypal reality through which all things were made. If God is a geometer who provides the measure by which all things are made, He is also the musician who has provided the harmony by which all things live and function and which is exhibited in a blinding and miraculous fashion in the cosmos.

The cosmos has of course its own laws and rhythms. Modern science speaks of laws of nature and even in modern physics, although this concept has been modified, the idea of statistical laws dominating over aggregates remains while the laws of macrophysics continue to be studied as the proper subject of science. Through a long history related to the rise of the idea of natural law as opposed to revealed law in the Christian tradition, whose own laws were in fact general spiritual and moral injunctions rather than a detailed codified law as in Judaism and Islam, a cleavage was created in the mind of Western man between laws of nature and spiritual principles. While the integral Christian tradition was alive in the Middle Ages, the cleavage was overcome by sapiential and even theological teachings such as those of Erigena and Saint Thomas which related natural laws themselves to God's Wisdom and Power. Nevertheless there was no Divine Law in the sense of the Islamic *Sharīʿah* within Christianity itself which could be seen in its cosmic aspect to include the laws according to which other beings in the cosmos function. The cleavage was never totally overcome so that with the advent of the revolt against the medieval synthesis during the Renaissance, the "laws of nature" and the "laws of God" as found in religion began to part ways to the extent that viewing the laws whose functioning is to be observed everywhere in the cosmos as Divine Law became soon outmoded and relegated to the pejorative category of "anthropomorphism." Moreover, since Christianity emphasizes the importance of the unparalleled event of the birth of Christ and his miraculous life, the evidence of religion seemed to many a European mind to rely upon the miracle which breaks the regularity of the laws observed in nature, whereas that regularity itself is no less evidence of the primacy of the Logos and the Wisdom of God reflected in His creation.[11] The fact that the sun does rise every morning is, from the sapiential point of view, as much a cause for wonder as if it were to rise in the West tomorrow.

It is of interest to note how Islam views this same subject of law. The Quranic revelation brought not only as set of ethical practices and a spiritual path for its followers but also a Divine Law, the *Sharīʿah*, by which all Muslims must live as the means of surrendering their will to God's will.[12] By extension the *Sharīʿah* is seen by Muslims as embracing all orders of creation and corresponding to what is understood in Western intellectual history as "laws of nature." Many an Islamic source has spoken of the Divine Law of this or that animal.[13] Interestingly enough, the Greek word for cosmic law, *nomos*, which reached Muslims through translations of Greek texts, especially of the *Laws* of Plato, became Arabized as *nāmūs*—the *Laws* of Plato itself being called *Kitāb al-nawāmīs*. Through such figures as al-Fārābī in his *Ārāʾ ahl al-madīnat al-fāḍilah* (*The Views of the Inhabitants of the Virtuous State*),[14] it entered into the mainstream of Islamic thought and its meaning became practically synonymous with the *Sharīʿah*. To this day Muslim philosophers and theologians, as well as simple preachers in the pulpit, speak of the *nawāmīs al-anbiyāʾ*, the Divine Laws brought by the prophets and *nāmūs al-khilqah*, the Divine Law which governs creation. There is no difference of nature between them. God has promulgated a law for each species of being and order of creatures which for man becomes religious law or the *Sharīʿah* as understood in its ordinary sense. The only difference is that other creatures have not been given the gift of free will and therefore cannot rebel against the laws which God has meant for them, against their "nature"[15] while man, being the theomorphic creature that he is, participates also in the Divine Freedom and can revolt against God's laws and himself. From a metaphysical point of view the rebellion of man against Heaven is itself proof of man's being made "in the image of God," to use the traditional formulation.

In this crucial question as in so many others, the Islamic perspective joins that of other Oriental traditions where no sharp distinction is made between the laws governing man and those governing the cosmos. The Tao is the origin of all things, the law governing each order of existence and every individual being within that order. Each being has its own Tao. Likewise *dharma* is not limited to man; all creatures have their own *dharma*. From the point of view of *scientia sacra* all laws are reflections of the Divine Principle. For man to discover any "law of nature" is to gain some knowledge of the ontological reality of the domain with which he is concerned. Moreover, the discovery of such laws is always through man's own intelligence and the use of logic which reflects an aspect of his own ontological reality. Therefore, in an ultimate sense, the study of the "laws of nature" is inseparable from the study of the reality of that Universal Man or macrocosmic reality whose reflection comprises the cosmos. It is a study of man himself. To study the laws of the cosmos, like studying its harmony or the beauty of its forms, is a way of self-discovery provided the subject carrying out such a study does not live in a truncated order of reality in which the study of the external world serves only to fragment further man's soul and alienate him from himself, creating, paradoxically enough, a world in which man himself no longer has a place.

What pertains to cosmic laws also holds true for causes which are reduced to the purely material in modern science as if the material order of reality could be totally divorced from other cosmic and metacosmic orders. The traditional sciences take into consideration not only the material or immediate causes of things but also the nonmaterial and ultimate ones. Even the four Aristotelian causes, the formal, material, efficient, and final, are systematized approximations of all the causes involved in bringing about any effect, for these causes include not only what is outwardly understood by the formal, efficient, and final causes but all that such causes mean metaphysically. The formal cause includes the origin of a particular form in the archetypal world, the efficient cause the grades of being which finally result in the existentiation of a particular existent, and the final cause a hierarchy of beings belonging to higher orders of reality that terminates with the Ultimate Cause which is the Real as such. It is in fact in this perspective that many later metaphysical rather than only rationalistic commentators of Aristotle viewed the significance of the Aristotelian four causes.

In any case, the causes which are responsible for various effects in the natural world are not limited to the natural world but embrace all orders of being. Moreover, these causes operate within man himself and between man and his cosmic environment. Each being in fact is related by a set of causes to the milieu in which it exists, the two being inseparable.[16] Man is bound to his world not only by the set of physical causes which bind him to that world but also by metaphysical ones. The net of causality is much vaster than that cast by those sciences which would limit the cosmos to only its material aspect and man to a complex combination of the same material factors caught in the mesh of that external environment which penetrates within him and determines his behavior and manner of being. Modern behaviorism is in many ways a parody of the Hindu doctrine of *karma* which expresses the central importance of causality in the domain of manifestation without either limiting it to only the psycho-physical realm or denying the possibility of deliverance, or *mokṣa*, from all chains of cause and effect, even those belonging to higher levels of existence. To behold the cosmos as theophany is not to deny either the laws or the chain of cause and effect which pervade the cosmos but to view the cosmos and the forms it displays with such diversity and regularity as reflections of Divine Qualities and ontological categories rather than a veil which would hide the splendor of the face of the Beloved.

To achieve such a goal and see the cosmos as theophany and not veil, it is necessary to return again and again to the truth that reality is hierarchic, that the cosmos is not exhausted by its physical aspect alone. All traditional cosmologies are based in one way or another on this axial truth. Their goal is to present in an intelligible fashion the hierarchy of existence as reflected in the cosmos. The "great chain of being" of the Western tradition, which survived in the West until it became horizontalized and converted from a ladder to Heaven to an evolutionary stream moving toward God knows where,[17] was a synthesis of this idea which has its equivalence in Islam,[18] India, and elsewhere, even if not as thoroughly elaborated in all traditions. The cosmologies which appeal to the immediate experience of the cosmos by terrestrial man have no other aim but to convey this metaphysical and central truth concerning the multiple states of existence in a vivid and concrete fashion. Cosmologies based on Ptolemaic astronomy or other astronomical schemes based on the way the cosmos presents itself to man are not in any way invalidated by the rejection of this geocentric scheme for the heliocentric one, because they make use of the immediate experience of the natural world as symbol rather than fact, a symbol whose meaning like that of any other symbol cannot be grasped through logical or mathematical analysis.

If one understands what symbols mean, one cannot claim that medieval cosmologies are false as a result of the fact that if we were standing on the sun we would observe the earth moving around it. The fact remains that we are not standing on the sun and if the cosmos, from the vantage point of the earth where we were born, does possess a symbolic significance, surely it would be based on how it *appears* to us as we stand on earth. To think otherwise would be to destroy the symbolic significance of the cosmos. It would be like wanting to understand the meaning of a *maṇḍala* by looking at it under a microscope. In doing so one would discover a great deal about the texture of the material upon which the *maṇḍala* has been drawn but nothing about the symbolic significance of the *maṇḍala* which was drawn with the assumption that it would be looked upon with the normal human eye. Of course, in the case of the cosmos the other ways of envisaging and studying it, as long as they conform to some aspect of cosmic reality, also possess their own profound symbolism—such as, for example, the heliocentric system, which was in fact known long before Copernicus, or the vast dark intergalactic spaces—but the destruction of the immediate symbolism of the cosmos as it presents itself to man living on earth cannot but be catastrophic.

To look upon the vast vault of the heavens as if one lived on the sun creates a disequilibrium which cannot but result in the destruction of that very earth that modern man abstracted himself from in order to look upon the solar system from the vantage point of the sun in the absolute space of classical physics. This disequilibrium would not necessarily have resulted had the type of man who rejected the earth-centered view of the cosmos been the solar figure, the image of the supernal Apollo, the Pythagorean sage, who in fact knew of the heliocentric astronomy without this knowledge causing a disruption in his world view. But paradoxically enough, this being who abstracted himself from the earth to look upon the cosmos from the sun, through that most direct symbol of the Divine Intellect, was the Promethean man who had rebelled against Heaven. The consequences could, therefore, not be anything but tragic.

The destruction of the outward symbol of traditional cosmologies destroyed for Western man the reality of the hierarchic structure of the universe which these cosmologies symbolized and which remains independent of any particular type of symbolism used to depict it. This structure could be and in fact has been expressed by other means, ranging from traditional music which reflects the structure of the cosmos to mathematical patterns of various kinds to metaphysical expositions not directly bound to a particular astronomical symbolism. The exposition of the hierarchic levels of reality as the "five Divine Presences" (*al-haḍarāt al-ilāhiyyat al-khams*) by the Sufis, such as Ibn ʿArabī, is a perfect example of this latter kind.[19] Ibn ʿArabī speaks of each principal order of reality as a *haḍrah* or "Divine Presence" because, metaphysically speaking, being or reality is none other than presence (*haḍrah*) or consciousness (*shuhūd*). These presences include the Divine Ipseity Itself (*hāhūt*), the Divine Names and Qualities (*lāhūt*), the archangelic world (*jabarūt*), the subtle and psychic world (*malakūt*), and the physical world (*mulk*).[20] Each higher world contains the principles of that which lies below it and lacks nothing of the lower level of reality. That is why in God one is separate from nothing. Although these presences possess further inner divisions within themselves, they represent in a simple fashion the major level of cosmic existence and metacosmic reality without there being the need to have recourse to a particular astronomical symbolism. This does not mean, however, that certain other later cosmologists did not point to correlations between these presences and various levels of the hierarchic cosmological schemes that still possessed meaning for those who beheld them.

In Islam we encounter numerous cosmological schemes associated with the Peripatetics, Illuminationists, the Ismāʿīlīs, alchemical authors like Jābir ibn Hayyān, Pythagoreans, various schools of Sufism, and of course the cosmologies based upon the language and text of the Quran and related to its inner meaning, which served as source of inspiration and principle for the other cosmologies drawn from diverse sources.[21] But throughout all of these cosmological schemes, there remains the constant theme of the hierarchic universe manifested by the Divine Principle and related intimately to the inner being of man. The same theme is found at the center of those sometimes bewildering cosmologies found in India, in Kabbalistic and Hermetic texts, in the oral traditions of the American Indians, in what survives of ancient Sumerian and Babylonian religions, among the

Egyptians, and practically everywhere else.[22] The diversity of symbolism is great but the presence of the vision of the cosmos as a hierarchic reality bound to the Origin and related to man not only outwardly but also inwardly persists as elements of what we referred to earlier as *cosmologia perennis*. This vision is that of pontifical man and therefore has had to be present wherever and whenever pontifical man, who is none other than traditional man, has lived and functioned.

Likewise, these traditional cosmologies as perceived within the sapiential perspective have been concerned with providing a map of the cosmos as well as depicting it as an icon to be contemplated and as symbol of metaphysical truth. The cosmos is not only the theater wherein are reflected the Divine Names and Qualities. It is also a crypt through which man must journey to reach the Reality beyond cosmic manifestation. In fact man cannot contemplate the cosmos as theophany until he has journeyed through and beyond it.[23] That is why the traditional cosmologies are also concerned with providing man with a map which would orient him within the cosmos and finally enable him to escape beyond the cosmos through that miraculous act of deliverance with which so many myths have been concerned.[24] From this point of view the cosmos appears as a labyrinth through which man must journey in a perilous adventure where literally all that he is and all that he has is at stake, a journey for which all traditions require both the map of traditional knowledge and the spiritual guide who has himself journeyed before through this labyrinth.[25] It is only by actually experiencing the perilous journey through the cosmic labyrinth that man is able to gain a vision of that cathedral of celestial beauty which is the Divine Presence in its meta-cosmic splendor.[26]

Having journeyed through and beyond the cosmos, man, who is then "twice born" and a "dead man walking" in the sense of being spiritually resurrected here and now, is able finally to contemplate the cosmos and its forms as theophany.[27] He is able to see the forms of nature *in divinis* and to experience the Ultimate Reality not as transcendent and beyond but as here and now.[28] It is here that the cosmos unveils its inner beauty ceasing to be only externalized fact or phenomenon but becoming immediate symbol, the reflection of the noumenon, the reflection which is not separated but essentially none other than the reality reflected. The cosmos becomes, to use the language of Sufism, so many mirrors in which the various aspects of the Divine Names and Qualities and ultimately the One are reflected. The Arabic word *tajallī* means nothing but this reflection of the Divine in the mirror of the cosmos which, metaphysically speaking, is the mirror of nothingness.[29] Objects appear not only as abstract symbols but as concrete presence. For the sage a particular tree is not only a symbol of the grade of being which he has come to know through his intelligence and the science of symbolism that his intelligence has enabled him to grasp. It *is* also a tree of paradise conveying a presence and grace of a paradisal nature.

This immediate experience, however, is not only not separate from the science of symbols, of sacred geometry, and of the significance of certain sacred forms, but it provides that immediate intuition which only increases the grasp of such sciences and makes possible their application to concrete situations. Zen gardens are based on the science of sacred geometry and the metaphysical significance of certain forms but cannot be created by just anyone who might have a manual on the symbolism of space or rock formations. The great gardens are expressions of realized knowledge leading to the awareness of natural forms as "presence of the Void," which in turn has made possible the application of this knowledge to specific situations resulting in some of the greatest creations of sacred art. The same rapport can be found *mutatis mutandis* elsewhere in traditions which do not emphasize as much as Zen knowledge of natural forms as immediate experience but where complete teachings in the cosmological sciences are available. Everywhere the knowledge of cosmic symbols goes hand in hand with that direct experience of a spiritual presence which results from spiritual realization, although there are always individual cases where a person may be given the gift of experiencing some aspect of the cosmos or a particular natural form as theophany without a knowledge of the science of symbolism or, as is more common in the modern world, a person may have the aptitude to understand the meaning of symbols, which is itself a precious gift from Heaven, but lack spiritual realization and therefore lack the possibility of ever experiencing the cosmos as theophany. In the sapiential perspective, in any case, the two types of appreciation of cosmic realities usually go hand in hand, and certainly in the case of the masters of gnosis, complement each other.

Of special significance among cosmological symbols which are related to the contemplation of the cosmos as theophany and the experience of the presence of the sacred in the natural order are those connected with space. Space and time along with form, matter or substance, and number determine the condition of human existence and in fact of all existence in this world. Tradition therefore deals with all of them and transforms all of them in order to create that sacred world in which traditional man breathes. The symbolism of number is revealed through its qualitative aspect as viewed in the Pythagorean tradition, and certain theosophers in the West have even spoken of an "arithmosophy" to be contrasted with arithmetic. Form and matter are sacralized through their symbolic rapport and their relation to the archetypal realities reflected by forms on the one hand and the descent or congelation of existence, which on the physical plane appears as matter or substance,[30] on the other. The nature of time is understood in its relation to eternity and the rhythms and cycles which reflect higher orders of reality, as we shall see in the next chapter. Finally space, which is central as the "container" of all that comprises terrestrial existence, is viewed not as the abstract, purely quantitative extension of classical physics but as a qualitative reality which is studied through sacred geometry.

Qualitative space is modified by the presence of the sacred itself. Its directions are not the same; its properties are not uniform. While in its empty vastness it symbolizes the Divine All-Possibility and also the Divine Immutability, it is the progenitor of all the geometric forms which are so many projections of the geometric point and so many reflections of the One, each regular geometric form symbolizing a Divine Quality.[31] If Plato specified that only geometers could enter into the temple of Divine Knowledge, it was because, as Proclus was to assert in his commentary upon the *Elements* of Euclid, geometry is an ancillary to metaphysics.[32] The orientation of cultic acts, the construction of traditional architecture, and many of the traditional sciences cannot be understood without grasping the significance of the traditional conception of qualified space. What is the experience of space for the Muslim who turns to a particular point on earth, wherever he might be, and then is blessed one day to enter into the Ka'bah itself beyond the polarization created upon the whole earth by this primordial temple built to celebrate the presence of the One? Why are the remarkable Neolithic structures of Great Britain round and why do the Indians believe that the circle brings strength? Most remarkable of all is the immediate experience of a wholly other kind of space within a sacred precinct. How did the architects of the medieval cathedrals create a sacred space which is the source of profound experience even for those Christians who no longer follow their religion fully? In all these and numerous other instances what is involved is the application of a traditional science of space which makes possible the actualization of a sacred presence and also the contemplation of an element of the cosmic reality as theophany. It is through this science of qualified space that traditional science and art meet and that cosmological science and experience of the sacred become wed in those places of worship, rites, cites of pilgrimage, and many other elements which are related to the very heart of tradition.

This science is closely associated with what has been called "sacred geography" or even "geosophy," that symbolic science of location and space concerned with the qualitative aspects of points on earth and the association of different terrestrial sites with traditional functions, ranging from the location of sanctuaries, burial sites, and places of worship to places for the erection of gardens, planting of trees, and the like in that special form of sacred art associated with the Japanese garden and the traditional art of the Persian garden with all its variations, ranging from Spanish gardens to the Mogul ones of India. The science of sacred geography ranges from, on the one hand, popular and often folkloric practices of geomancy in China to the most profound sensitivity to the grace of the Divine Presence which manifests itself in certain natural forms and locations on the other.

This science is thus closely allied to that particular kind of sapience which is wed to the metaphysics of nature and that spiritual type among human beings who is sensitive to the *barakah* or grace that flows in the arteries of the universe. Such a person is drawn by this *barakah* into the empyrean of spiritual ecstasy like an eagle that flies without moving its wings upon an air current which carries it upward toward the illimitable expanses of the heavenly vault. For such a person nature is the supreme work of sacred art; in traditions based upon such a perspective, like Islam or the American Indian tradition, virgin nature as created by God *is* the sanctuary par excellence. The mosque of the Muslim is the earth itself as long as it has not been defiled by man, and the building called the mosque only extends the ambience of this primordial mosque which is virgin nature into the artificial urban environment created by man. Likewise, for the American Indian, that wilderness of enchanting beauty which was the American continent before the advent of the white man was the cathedral in which he worshiped and wherein he observed the greatest works of art of the Supreme Artisan, of *Wakan-Tanka*. This perspective, moreover, is not limited to only certain traditions but is to be found in one way or another within all integral traditions. This sensitivity to the *barakah* of nature and the contemplation of the cosmos as theophany cannot but be present wherever pontifical man lives and breathes, for nature is a reflection of that paradisal state that man still carries within the depth of his own being.

Such a vision has, needless to say, become blurred and is denied in the world of Promethean man whose eminently successful science of nature has blinded human beings to possibilities of other sciences and other means of beholding and understanding nature. Moreover, this negation and denial has occurred despite the fact that the cosmos has not completely followed man in his rapid fall. It might be said that, although both nature and man have fallen from that state of perfection characterized as the paradisal state, what still remains of virgin nature is closer to that prototype than the type of Promethean man who increases his domination upon the earth every day. That is why what does remain of virgin nature is so precious not only ecologically but also spiritually. It is the only reminder left on earth of the normal condition of existence and a permanent testament to the absurdity of all those modern pretensions which reveal their true nature only when seen in the light of the truth. Excluding revealed truth, nothing in the orbit of human experience unveils the real nature of the modern world and the premises upon which it is based more than the cosmos, ranging from the starry heavens to the plants at the bottom of the seas. That is why Promethean man has such an aggressive hatred for virgin nature; why also the love of nature is the first sign among many contemporaries of their loss of infatuation with that model of man who began his plunder of the earth some five centuries ago.

During the last few years so many critiques have been written of modern science and its recent handmaid, technology,[33] that one hardly needs to go once again into all the arguments ranging from the ecological and demographic to the epistemological and theological. In any case that would require a major separate study of its own. But to bring out fully the meaning of the traditional sciences of nature and the significance of the cosmos as theophany, it is necessary to recapitulate the main points of criticism made of modern science by the traditional authorities and from the traditional point of view. The first point to assert in order to remove all possible misunderstanding is that the traditional criticisms against modern science are not based on sentiments, fanaticism, illogicality, or any of the other terms with which anyone who criticizes modern science is usually associated. The traditional critique is based on intellectual criteria in the light of the metaphysical truth which alone can claim to be knowledge of a complete and total nature.[34] That is why traditional authors never deny the validity of what modern science has actually discovered provided it is taken for what it is. The knowledge of any order of reality is legitimate provided it remains bound to that order and within the limits set upon it by both its method and its subject matter. But this would in turn imply accepting another science or manner of knowing which, being of a more universal nature, would set the boundary within which that science could function legitimately.

Herein lies the first and foremost criticism of modern science. In declaring its independence of metaphysics or any other science, modern science has refused to accept the authority which would establish the boundary for its legitimate activity. That is why despite all the pious platitudes and even well-intentioned and earnest pleading of honest scientists, modern science does transgress beyond the realm which is properly its own and serves as background for monstrous philosophical generalizations which, although not at all scientific but scientistic, feed upon the tenets and findings of the sciences and the fact that modern science has signed its declaration of independence from metaphysics. Moreover, by token of the same fact, the metaphysical significance of scientific discoveries remains totally neglected by the supposedly scientifically minded public which usually knows very little about science but is mesmerized by it. And here again, despite the loud protests of some reputable scientists, instead of the metascientific significance of what science has actually discovered becoming revealed, the reverse process takes place whereby, through wild interpolations and usually well-hidden assumptions, metaphysical truths become rejected in the name of scientific knowledge. What tradition opposes in modern science is not that it knows so much about the social habits of ants or the spin of the electron but that it knows nothing of God while functioning in a world in which it alone is considered as science or objective knowledge.

This divorce of science from metaphysics is closely related to the reduction of the knowing subject to the *cogito* of Descartes. It is usually forgotten that despite all the changes in the field of modern physics, the subject which knows, whether the content of that knowledge be the pendulum studied by Galileo or wave functions of electrons described mathematically by de Broglie, is still that reason which was identified by Descartes with the individual human ego who utters *cogito*. The other modes of consciousness and manners of operation of the mind are never considered in modern science. The findings of that reason which is wed once again to the Intellect and that mind which is illuminated by the light of the "eye of the heart" is not considered as science at all, especially as this term is used in the English language.[35] Hence, the irrevocable limitation of a science caught within the mesh of the functioning of only a part of the human mind but dealing with a subject of vast import which it then seeks to solve in manners that are characteristically "unscientific," namely, intuition, artistic beauty, harmony, and the like. Many first-rate scientists, in contrast to most philosophers of science, would in fact accept our contention that, if one considers all that which is called science has achieved even in modern times, one cannot speak of *the* "scientific method" but has to accept the assertion that science is what scientists do, which might include playing with possibilities of musical harmony to solve certain physical problems.

Despite the reality of this assertion, however, the rationalism inherent in what the modern world considers to be science continues and has had its lethal effect upon the humanities, the social sciences, and even philosophy and theology. Strangely enough, precisely because of the inherent limitation of the original epistemological premises of modern science, more and more modern science has come to see in the objective world not what is there but what it has wanted to see, selecting what conforms to its methods and approaches and then presenting it as the knowledge of reality as such. Modern men, influenced by science, think that according to the scientific point of view one should only believe what one can see, whereas what has actually happened is that science has come to see what it believes according to its a priori assumptions concerning what there is to be seen.[36] This epistemological limitation combined with the lack of general accessibility in the West since the rise of modern science to that *scientia sacra* of which we have spoken, has prevented this science from being integrated into higher orders of knowledge with tragic results for the human race. In fact, only a high degree of contemplative intelligence can enable man to look upon the sun and see at once the visible symbol of the Divine Intellect and an incandescent mass diffusing energy in all directions.[37]

These limitations of modern science are to be seen also in its neglect of the higher states of being and its treatment of the physical world as if it were an independent order of reality. This neglect of the unmanifested and in fact nonphysical aspects of reality has not only impoverished the vision of cosmic reality in a world dominated by scientism, but it has caused confusion between vertical and horizontal causes and brought about incredible caricatures of the cosmic reality as a result of relegating to the physical domain forces and causes which belong to higher orders of existence. It is not accidental that the more physics advances in its own domain, the more does it become aware of its need for another complete paradigm which would take into consideration domains of reality that many physicists feel almost intuitively to exist, but which have been cast aside from the world view of classical and modern physics.[38]

One of the consequences of this systematic neglect of higher orders of existence has been the denial of life as an animating principle or energy which has penetrated into the physical realm. Rather, life is seen as an accidental consequence of molecular motion according to that well-known reductionist point of view that does not realize that if life or consciousness "result" from certain activities of molecules and their combinations, they must either have already been present there in some way or come from elsewhere.

This difficulty in solving the question of the origin and meaning of life, despite its being discussed over the centuries by vitalists and mechanists, is related to the desacralization of the world which became the subject matter of seventeenth-century science and the gradual deformation and finally destruction of the concept of the World Soul. In all traditional cosmologies there is an *Anima mundi* or its equivalent like the *Janna Caeli* of antiquity, *Spenta Armaiti* of Mazdaean cosmology, or the Universal Soul (*al-nafs al-kulliyyah*) of Islamic sources. This soul must not of course be confused with the immanent

Deity, and belief in the World Soul does not imply a kind of pantheism. But the World Soul played a major cosmological function as the soul of the natural order and its link with the Intellect. It also had a central epistemological role as the Divine Sophia identified often with the Virgin Mary as the Theotokos, the Soul in which the Son of the Intellect is born, or as Fāṭimah who is the mother of the Imams who embody and symbolize the Divine Light.

In the West the World Soul was typified by the Virgin. Its expulsion from the world of modern man, which was also a direct consequence of Cartesian dualism, was almost synchronous with the loss of the significance of Mary in the rites and doctrines of the Christian churches of those countries where the scientific world view was developing most rapidly.[39] Gradually, the very idea of *animated* meaning "possessing a soul" or "ensouled" (*enpsychos*) was replaced by "moved" (*kinētos*) which soon came to mean moved by history. The *Anima mundi* or *Weltgeist* became the *Zeitgeist* of Hegel and the other dialectical philosophers. Instead of the cosmos being animated by a soul which was its intermediary link with the Intellect as we find in many traditional schools of cosmology and philosophy especially in Islam,[40] it became the passive instrument of an ambiguous *Zeitgeist* which could not but mean the apparent tyranny of becoming over Being Itself, if one is permitted such an elliptical formulation. The consequence of this change for religion as such was immense. It was not long before men began to change the very rites and doctrines of religion not according to the inspiration received from the Holy Ghost or *Heilige Geist* but from the *Zeitgeist*, or "the times" with which everyone tries to keep up.

Moreover, this impoverishment of the reality with which modern science deals removed from the consciousness of modern man, influenced by this science and the philosophies derived from it, the reality of that intermediate world which has been traditionally referred to as the imaginal world to which we had occasion to refer before. Without this world which stands between the purely intelligible and the physical world and which possesses its own nonmaterial forms, there is no possibility of a total and complete cosmology nor of the explanation of certain traditional teachings concerning eschatology. Nor is it possible to comprehend those mysterious cities and palaces, those mountains and streams which appear in both traditional myths and cosmological schemes. Where is the Holy Mountain wherein is to be found the Grail? Where are those cities of the imaginal world which in Islam are called Jābulqā and Jābulsā[41] and which Suhrawardī considered to exist in the eighth clime, in that land of "no-where" which he called *nā kujā ābād*, literally *u-topia*? When the eighth clime was destroyed, the gnostic and visionary *u-topia* could not but become the utopia of those European secularists and atheists who, often aided by certain messianic ideas, sought to establish the kingdom of God on earth without God, as if the good without the Good had any meaning. When the *Weltgeist* became *Zeitgeist*, history replaced the Divinity, and *nā kujā ābād*, instead of being the abode of the gnostic in which he contemplated paradisal forms, became the utopia in whose name so much of what has remained of tradition has been destroyed throughout the world.

This neglect of the multiple levels of existence by the modern scientific perspective has forced the exponents of this science to take recourse to belief in the uniformity of "laws of nature" over long periods of time and expanses of space. This theory which is called "uniformitarianism" and which underlies all those geological and paleontological speculations which speak of millions of years past was rapidly promoted from the status of hypothesis to that of "scientific law"; and when most honest scientists are asked on what basis do they believe that the laws of nature, the so-called constants of the law of gravitation, the law of electromagnetic theory or quantum jumps have always been the same, they answer that since there is no other choice they have adopted the uniformitarian thesis. Actually from the modern scientific point of view itself there is of course no other way of speaking about what was going on in the planetary systems eons ago except by considering the laws of physics to be uniform and simply admitting that this science cannot provide an answer to such questions without extrapolating cosmic and natural laws back into earlier periods of time or into the future. Of course it is not the physical conditions which modern science assumes to have been the same but the laws and forces which bring about different physical conditions at different times while supposedly remaining uniform themselves. As far as these laws and forces are concerned, whatever means are employed by modern science to check whether or not there were changes in such laws and forces in the past are themselves based on the condition of the uniformity of the laws and forces used to carry out the process of checking. A science aware of its limits would at least distinguish between what it means to say that the specific weight of aluminum is such and such or how many protons are found in the nucleus of a helium atom and to claim that such and such an astronomical event occurred 500 million years ago or a particular geological formation was formed so many millions or even billions of years ago. One wonders what exactly the word *year* means in such a statement and what assumptions are made upon the nature of reality to give the kind of definition of years which is usually given when a question such as this is posed to a scientist.

What is most unfortunate from the traditional point of view in this presumptuous extrapolation of physical laws to include long stretches of time, and in fact all time as such, is that it results in the total neglect and even negation of cosmic rhythms, the qualitatively different conditions which prevail in the cosmos in different moments of the cosmic cycle and that absorption of the whole physical world into its subtle principle at the end of a cosmic cycle. The denial of the traditional doctrine of cycles or even one cycle which ends with the majestic and tremendous events described in all sacred scriptures and associated with eschatology is one of the greatest shortcomings of modern science because it has made eschatology to appear as unreal. It has helped destroy in the name of scientific logic, but in reality as a result of a presumptuous extrapolation based on metaphysical ignorance, the reality of that vision of ultimate ends which gives significance to human life and which over the ages has had the most profound effect upon the behavior of man as an ethical being. It has also destroyed in the minds of those affected by scientism the grandeur of creation and the meaning of the sacrifice of primordial man. That is why this science has been so impervious to the amazing harmony that pervades the heavens and the earth. Where does this harmony come from? This question, which is metaphysical but which has profound scientific consequences, has been left unanswered as a result of the hypothesis of uniformitarianism which is metaphysically absurd but which passes as scientific law as a result of the loss of vision of the hierarchic universe and understanding of cosmic rhythms.

Also, closely related to this loss of the awareness of the vertical dimension of existence, is the reductionism so characteristic of modern science which we have had occasion to mention already in conjunction with the process of the desacralization of knowledge. From the point of view of *scientia sacra*, this reductionism is the inversion of the traditional doctrine according to which each higher state of existence "contains" the lower, the Principle containing the root of all that is real in all realms of metacosmic and cosmic existence. In this reversal of the normal rapport between grades of being, the Spirit is reduced to the psyche, the psyche to biological form, living forms to aggregates of material components, etc. Of course one cannot lay the responsibility for all the levels of this reductionism at the feet of physics; but even on the nonmaterial levels, the effect of a purely phenomenal science wed to the sensually verifiable is to be observed, as, for example, the reduction of the Spirit to the psyche so characteristic of the modern world and concern with proofs of the existence of not only the psychic but also the spiritual through various experiments which indirectly emulate the physical sciences.[42]

To be sure, a group of biologists and others concerned with the life sciences have at least tried to resist this reductionism on the level of life forms, for those who are concerned with such sciences know fully well how the whole is a totally other entity than its parts, that form signifies a reality which is irreducible to its physical or chemical components and that the energy associated with life functions differently from material energy. This "morphic" science, to quote the terminology used by L. L. Whyte,[43] is closely akin to the *Naturphilosophie* tradition and is fully supported by such important biologists as A. Portmann,[44] who has opposed scientific reductionism as far as "forms" are concerned. In fact there is a whole critique of modern science based on this perspective and the quest for the study of forms of nature from a wholistic point of view;[45] but the fact that such a critique has been made does not hide the fact that reductionism continues to be associated with modern science, and especially with the world view of its popularizers, and that this reductionism is one of the main obstacles which prevents modern man from seeing the reflection of the hierarchy of existence in the mirror of cosmic manifestation.

This reductionism has its opposite but complementary pole in the completely unjustifiable generalization of science and its findings in such a way that it passes itself off as a science of things as such or metaphysics and, despite the denial of many of its practitioners, plays the role of a theology while hiding the presence of God and drawing a veil over the vestiges of God upon the face of His creation. Being a science of the world wed to a particular manner of envisaging and studying the external, modern science nevertheless claims absoluteness as *the* science of the world as it is, which could not but be the function of a "divine science." Hence it cannot but usurp the place of metaphysics and theology for those who see in it the only possible way of gaining certitude while everything else appears to them as conjecture.[46]

A science which thus reduces the scope of both knowledge and reality to its particular manner of envisaging the world, and that aspect of the world which can be envisaged by its way of seeing things, cannot but aid in the secularization of the world and the spread of agnosticism. This is especially true since this science functions in a world in which its tenets become almost automatically generalized far beyond the confines acceptable to many scientists themselves because this "world" is already one molded to a great extent by the generalization of scientific thought, especially in its earlier seventeenth-century form. By refusing to consider the several facets of a particular reality and by reducing symbols to facts, this science cannot but contribute to that agnosticism and desacralization of knowing and being which characterizes the modern world,[47] although such would not necessarily have had to be the case had this type of science been integrated into knowledge of a higher order.

The traditional perspective sees as the reason behind these limitations of modern science a concept of nature which goes back even before the seventeenth century to the traditional schools of Christian thought where, despite a Hildegard of Bingen, Saint Francis, or Saint Bonaventure,[48] a kind of polemical attitude was entertained toward nature at least in the official theology.[49] It was in Christian Hermeticism and alchemy that one had to seek an integral vision of nature and its spiritual significance.[50] The quantification of nature by the seventeenth-century physics was carried out upon a natural order which was already depleted of its sacred presence. But this science rapidly accentuated this alienation of man from nature and the mutilation of nature whose catastrophic results now face contemporary man. The mainstream of Western thought saw in nature an obstacle to the love of God. Furthermore, Promethean man and the humanism associated with him had an innate hatred for nature as a reality possessing its own harmony, equilibrium, and beauty not invented or created by man and opposed in principle to the tenets of humanism.

These elements, added to the more active than contemplative mentality of Western man, especially in the modern period, complemented each other to make possible that disrupting and finally destructive relationship which Western man has entertained vis-à-vis nature at the expense of veiling its sacramental qualities and its revelatory function as theophany.

That is why there is and there must be another science of nature which is not metaphysics or *scientia sacra* itself but its application to the realm of nature. Such a science would not exclude what is positive in modern science but would not be bound by its limitations.[51] It would not veil but reveal the theophanic character of the cosmos and relate the knowledge of the sensible domain to higher levels of reality and finally to Reality as such.[52] It would be a science whose matrix would be the Intellect and not the dissected *ratio* associated with the Cartesian *cogito*. Such a science existed already in traditional civilizations and embraced *their* sciences of the sensible order which in many cases were of considerable breadth and depth. Its principles are still to be found in *scientia sacra* from which could be created a science to embrace and integrate the sciences of nature of today once they are shorn of the rationalistic and reductionist propositions, which do not have to be their background, but which have accompanied them since their birth during the Scientific Revolution. Only such an embrace can nullify the disruptive and, in fact, dissolving effect of a partial knowledge which parades as total knowledge or is paraded by others as such. Those "others" include not only scientistic philosophers but many philosophers and historians of science infected by a dogmatic positivism[53] and a number of modern mystifiers and pseudognostics who, instead of integrating science into the gnostic vision, have mutilated the verities of gnosis into a pseudoscientific science fiction which is no more than another way of generalizing the partial knowledge represented by modern science into total knowledge, but with esoteric pretensions.[54] This other science which is traditional in the most profound sense of implying a transmission in conformity with the destiny of the person who is able to possess such a knowledge[55] cannot but manifest itself when *scientia sacra* becomes a reality once again, because it is none other than the application of this supreme form of knowledge to the cosmic realm.

It is not possible to say whether such a science which is intermediary between pure metaphysics and modern science can be created and expounded to integrate modern science in time to prevent the applications of this science in the form of modern technology from bringing further devastation upon nature and destruction upon man himself. What is certain, however, is that however omnipotent Promethean man may feel himself to be, it is nature that shall have the final say.[56] It is her rhythms and norms which shall finally predominate. Since truth always triumphs according to the old Latin adage *vincit omnia veritas*, and nature is closer to the truth than the artificial world created by Promethean man, she cannot but be the final victor.

The spiritual man, whose mind is sanctified by the Intellect and whose outward eyes have gained a new light issuing from the eye of the heart, does not even see himself in such a dichotomy. He is always on nature's side for he sees in her the grand theophany which externalizes all that he is inwardly. He sees in the forms of nature the signatures of the celestial archetypes and in her movements and rhythms the exposition of a metaphysics of the highest order. To such a person nature is at once an aid to spiritual union, for man needs the world in order to transcend it, and a support for the presence of that very reality which lies at once beyond and within her forms created by the hands of the Supreme Artisan. To contemplate the cosmos as theophany is to realize that all manifestation from the One is return to the One, that all separation is union, that all otherness is sameness, that all plenitude is the Void. It is to see God everywhere.

NOTES

1. See Dante Alighieri, *The Divine Comedy, Paradiso*, trans. with a commentary by C. S. Singleton, Princeton, 1975, p. 377. Singleton explains (pp. 576–77) some of the symbolism of this remarkable passage including the reference of *squaderna* to the number four and the verb *s'interna* to the triune God.

2. In contrast to those who have spoken of Eastern wisdom and Western science and have tried to pay tribute to the East by exalting its wisdom and belittling its "science" which is then considered to be the crowning achievement of the West, we believe that besides Eastern wisdom, which of course possesses an exalted nature and is of inestimable value, the sciences of the Oriental civilizations are also of much significance in making available alternative sciences and philosophies of nature to those prevalent in the West. It is of much interest to note that in contrast to this juxtaposing of Eastern wisdom and Western science of the early part of this century, many seekers of authentic knowledge today are practically as much interested in Eastern sciences as in Eastern wisdom. We do not of course want to depreciate in any way Eastern wisdom without whose knowledge the traditional sciences would become meaningless. But we wish to defend the significance of the traditional sciences against those who would

claim that the Oriental civilizations may have contributed something to philosophy or religion but little of consequence to the study of nature. Despite the presence of practitioners of acupuncture and Hatha Yoga in practically every European and American city and the appearance of a whole library of popular works on the Oriental sciences, one still encounters such a point of view rather extensively.

3. On the traditional meaning and significance of cosmology see T. Burckhardt, "Nature de la perspective cosmologique," *Études Traditionnelles* 49 (1948): 216–19; also his "Cosmology and Modern Science," in J. Needleman (ed.), *The Sword of Gnosis*, esp. pp. 122–32. As far as Islamic cosmology is concerned see Nasr, *An Introduction to Islamic Cosmological Doctrines*.

4. The modern discipline of the history of science, with a few notable exceptions, is able to trace the historical link between the traditional sciences and the modern ones but is not capable of unraveling their symbolic and metaphysical significance precisely because of its own philosophical limitations and its totally secularized conception of knowledge. On the difference between traditional and modern science see R. Guénon, "Sacred and Profane Science," in his *Crisis of the Modern World*, pp. 37–50; and Nasr, "Traditional Science," in R. Fernando (ed.), vol. dedicated to A. K. Coomaraswamy (in press).

5. On the theme of seeing the Divine Presence in all things see Schuon, "Seeing God Everywhere," in his *Gnosis, Divine Wisdom*, pp. 106–21.

6. Theophany, literally, "to show God," does not mean the incarnation of God in things but the reflection of the Divinity in the mirror of created forms.

7.

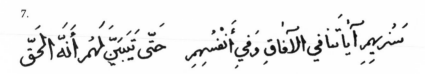

8. We have developed this idea extensively in our various works on the Islamic sciences esp. *An Introduction to Islamic Cosmological Doctrines*, prologue; *Science and Civilization in Islam*, p. 24; and *Ideals and Realities of Islam*, pp. 54ff.

9. According to a famous Persian Sufi poem,

> Upon the face of every green leaf is inscribed
> For the people of perspicacity, the wisdom of the Creator.

10. On the spiritual significance of the identification of the American Indian with the spirit of a particular animal see J. Brown, *The Sacred Pipe*, Brown, Okla., 1967, esp. pp. 44ff., "Crying for a Vision"; C. Martin, *Keepers of the Game*, Los Angeles, 1980; A. I. Hallowell, "Bear Ceremonialism in the Northern Hemisphere," *American Anthropologist* 28/1 (1926):1–175; and *Artscanada* nos. 184–87 (Dec. 1973–Jan. 1974), which contains much documentation of interest concerning the relation between American Indians and the animal world.

11. This does not mean that the significance of miracles is to be denied or belittled in any way. Even Islam, which emphasizes the order in the universe as the most evident proof of the power and wisdom of the One, asserts that there cannot be prophecy without miracles (*iʿjāz*), which in fact occupies an important position in Islamic theological discussions.

12. For the meaning of the *Sharīʿah* and its significance for Muslims see Nasr, *Ideals and Realities of Islam*, chap. 4.

13. Works on Islamic natural history take this practically for granted; in Arabic various species are often referred to as *ummah* which means a religious community bound by a particular Divine Law such as the *ummah* of Islam or Judaism. On the spiritual meaning of the animal kingdom having its own laws and religious significance

see Ikhwān al-Safāʾ, *Der Streit zwischen Mensch und Tier*, trans. F. Dieterici, Olms, 1969; and into English by J. Platts as *Dispute between Man and the Animals*, London, 1869.

14. See al-Fārābī, *Idées des habitants de la cité vertueuse*, trans. R. P. Janssen, Cairo, 1949. An English translation with commentary and annotations was completed by R. Walzer before his death and is to be published soon by the Oxford University Press.

15. The Ashʿarites reject the idea of the "nature" of things and laws relating to these "natures." But they do so in the name of an all-embracing voluntarism which transforms these "laws" into the direct expressions of the Will of God. Although this kind of totalitarian voluntarism is opposed to the sapiential perspective which is based on the integral nature of the Godhead including both His Wisdom and Power and not just His Power or Will, as far as the present argument is concerned, even the Ashʿarite position would be included by the thesis here presented. They, too, like other schools of Islamic thought, see all laws governing both the human and the nonhuman world as expressions of the Divine Will even if they do not distinguish between what God wills and what reflects His Nature which cannot not be.

16. On the metaphysical relation between a particular being and the milieu in which it exists see Guénon, *Les États multiples de l'être.*

17. On the chain of being see the still valuable work of A. Lovejoy, *The Great Chain of Being*, Cambridge, Mass., 1961.

18. For Islamic sources on the chain of being (*marātib al-mawjūdāt*) see Nasr, *Introduction to Islamic Cosmological Doctrines*, pp. 202ff.

19. On the "Five Divine Presences" see F. Schuon, *Dimensions of Islam*, pp. 142–58.

20. The last three worlds have their own subdivisions, the *malakūt* including also the lower angels, and being identified with the soul which has the possibility of journeying to and through the other realms or presences.

21. There is as yet no exhaustive work which would embrace all the different kinds of cosmology developed in Islamic thought. We have dealt with some of the most important ones in our *Introduction to Islamic Cosmological Doctrines.*

It should be remembered that in Islam as in other traditions the whole of cosmology has also been expounded in terms of music since traditional music has a cosmic dimension and corresponds to the structure, rhythms, and modalities of the cosmos. That is why traditional sciences of music emphasize so much the cosmic and metacosmic correspondences of musical modes, melodies, and rhythms.

On the correspondence between music and the cosmos in Islam see R. D'Erlanger, *La Musique arabe*, 5 vols., Paris, 1930–1939; N. Caron and D. Safvat, *Les Traditions musicales*, vol. 2, Iran, Paris, 1966; Ibn ʿAlī al-Kātib, *La Perfection des connaissances musicales*, trans. A. Shiloah, Paris, 1972; A. Shiloah, "L'Epître sur la musique des Ikhwān al-Safāʾ," *Revue des Études Islamiques*, 1965, pp. 125–62, and 1967, pp. 159–93; and J. During, "Elements spirituels dans la musique traditionnelle iranienne contemporaine," *Sophia Perennis* 1/2 (1975): 129–54 (which deals with the spiritual and initiatic rather than cosmological aspect of traditional music).

See also the classical work of A. Daniélou, *Introduction to the Study of Musical Scales*, London, 1943, which deals with the metaphysical and cosmological foundations of Indian music. This correspondence between cosmology and music is to be found wherever traditional music has survived along with the intellectual and spiritual tradition which has given birth to it.

22. On various cosmologies in the ancient world see C. Blacker and M. Loewe (eds.), *Ancient Cosmologies*, London, 1975. The essays in this volume having been written by different authors, although all informative, do not all possess the same point of view as far as their evaluation of the meaning of the traditional cosmological schemes is concerned.

23. On the gnostic journey through the cosmos in the Islamic tradition see Nasr, *Introduction to Islamic Cosmological Doctrines*, chap. 15.

24. Many traditional myths deal with the precarious and dangerous act of escaping from the prison of cosmic existence considered in its aspect of limitation. See, for example, Coomaraswamy, "Symplygades," in Lipsey (ed.), *Coomaraswamy*, vol. 1, pp. 521–44.

25. Some traditions envisage this labyrinth as so many dangerous mountains and valleys, dark forests and the like. The journey of Dante up the mountain of purgatory is a symbol of the journey through the cosmos seen as a mountain, a symbolism also found in ʿAṭṭār's *Conference of the Birds* (*Manṭiq al-ṭayr*) and in many other traditions. The symbolism of the cosmic mountain (the Mount Meru of Hinduism, Alborz of the Zoroastrians, the Qāf of Islam, etc.) is one of the most universal symbols to be found in various traditions. On the symbolism of mountain climbing as related to journeying through the cosmos see M. Pallis, "The Way and the Mountain," in his *The Way and the Mountain*, pp. 13–35.

26. The maze of such cathedrals as Chartres relate to this same principle and is based on exact knowledge of the traditional cosmological sciences. See K., C., and V. Critchlow, *Chartre Maze, A Model of the Universe*, London, 1976.

27. The Prophet of Islam has said, "Die before you die." It is the person who has followed this injunction who is able to contemplate cosmic forms as reflections of Divine Qualities rather than opaque veils which hide the splendor of their Source.

28. This is essentially the perspective of Zen which does not mean that one can experience the Divine in things by some form of naturalism which for many Western adepts of Zen is almost a carry over from a kind of sentimental nature mysticism into the world of Zen. Such people, in a sense, wish to experience Heaven without either faith in God or virtue which would qualify a being for the paradisal state, for what is the contemplation of natural forms *in divinis* except an experience of the paradisal state? In any case, there is no such thing as natural mysticism from the traditional point of view; in practice man cannot experience God as the immanent before experiencing Him as the transcendent, however these concepts are translated in different traditional languages. One could also say that man can realize the identity of *nirvāna* with *samsāra* provided he has already gone beyond *samsāra* and reached *nirvāna*.

29. That is why *tajallī* is translated as theophany. In his incomparable *Gulshan-i rāz*, Shabistarī says,

> Non-being is a mirror, the world the image [of the Universal Man], and man
> Is the eye of the image, in which the person is hidden.

See Nasr, *Science and Civilization in Islam*, p. 345.

30. We are not using matter here in its Aristotelian but in its everyday sense as the "stuff" or "substance" of which things are made.

31. During the last few years much interest has been shown in the West in the rediscovery of the meaning of sacred geometry. See, for example, K. Critchlow, *Time Stands Still*; idem, *Islamic Patterns*; and the various publications of the Lindesfarne Association including the *Lindesfarne Letters*, esp. no. 10 (1980), dealing with geometry and architecture.

32. See Proclus Lycius, *The Philosophical and Mathematical Commentaries of Proclus, on the First Book of Euclid's Elements*, trans. with commentary by Th. Taylor, London, 1792. This fundamental work elucidated by Taylor's important commentaries, contains the basis for the understanding of the relation of geometry to first principles. Of course although geometry is an ancillary to metaphysics, it is not only an ancillary. Rather, it is one of the most important of the traditional sciences in its own right and as these sciences are related to art.

33. It is really only since the early decades of the nineteenth century that technology in the West has become wed closely to modern science and has constituted its direct application. Before this relatively recent past, science and technology followed two very different courses with few significant reactions between them.

34. For traditional critiques of modern science see Guénon, "Sacred and Profane Science"; Schuon, *Language of the Self*, chap. 10; idem, *In the Tracks of Buddhism*, chap. 5; Lord Northbourne, *Religion in the Modern World*, London, 1963, esp. chap. 5; and F. Brunner, *Science et réalité*, Paris, 1954.

36. "Modern man was not—and is not—"intelligent" enough to offer intellectual resistance to such specious suggestions as are liable to follow from contact with facts

which, though natural, normally lie beyond the range of common experience; in order to combine, in one and the same consciousness, both the religious symbolism of the sky and the astronomical fact of the Milky Way, an intelligence is required that is more than just rational, and this brings us back to the crucial problem of intellection and, as a further consequence, to the problem of gnosis and esoterism. . . . Howbeit, the tragic dilemma of the modern mind results from the fact that the majority of men are not capable of grasping *a priori* the compatibility of the symbolic expressions of tradition with the material observations of science; these observations incite modern man to want to understand the 'why and where' of all things, but he wishes this 'wherefore' to remain as external and easy as scientific phenomena themselves, or in other words, he wants all the answers to be on the level of his own experiences: and as these are purely material ones, his consciousness closes itself in advance against all that might transcend them." Schuon, *Language of the Self*, pp. 226–27.

38. The attraction toward Oriental teachings about nature alluded to above is related to this same phenomenon. On the interest of contemporary physics in the traditional esoteric and mystical views of the universe see M. Talbot, *Mysticism and the New Physics*, New York, 1981.

39. "L'Ame du Monde est donc bien typifiée par la Vièrge Marie du Christianisme." J. Brun, "Qu'est devenu L'Ame due Monde?" *Cahiers de l'Université Saint Jean de Jérusalem*, no. 6, *Le Combat pour l'Ame du Monde*, Paris, 1980, pp. 164–65. This essay traces the steps by which the world as seen by modern man lost its soul.

On the relation of the Virgin Mary to the World Soul see the article of G. Durand, "La Vièrge Marie et l'Ame du Monde," in the same volume, pp. 135–67.

40. For example, among all the later Islamic philosophers who followed the Avicennan and Suhrawardian cosmologies such as Qāḍī Saʿīd Qummī, whose *Glosses upon the "Theology of Aristotle"*, containing an elaborate discussion of this subject, has been analyzed by C. Jambet in his "L'Ame du Monde et l'amour sophianique," in *Cahiers de l'Université Saint Jean de Jérusalem*, no. 6, *Le Combat pour l'Ame du Monde*, pp. 52ff.

41. On the meaning of these cities which appear in folk tales, poetry such as that of Niẓāmī as well as texts of philosopy and metaphysics see Corbin, *En Islam iranien*, vol. 2, p. 59.

42. It is the allure of empiricism which draws so many people to various kinds of spiritualism, magnetism, occultism, etc., where the supernatural is "proven" through phenomenal evidence. Although certain experiments in parapsychology have certainly demonstrated that there is more to reality than meets the eye and that the so-called scientific world view of a limited material-energy complex as the ultimate ground of all that constitutes reality cannot be sustained, no phenomenal evidence can prove the reality of the Spirit which lies beyond all phenomena and belongs to the realm of the noumena.

43. See his *Universe of Experience*, New York, 1974.

44. His numerous articles and essays in the *Eranos-Jahrbuch* over the years comprise a major statement of a nonreductionist "philosophy of nature" by a contemporary biologist. On Portmann see also M. Grene, *Approaches to a Philosophical Biology*, New York, 1965.

For a philosophy of science opposed to reductionism see also the works of M. Polanyi, *The Tacit Dimension*, New York, 1966; *Science, Faith and Society*, London, 1946; and *Knowing and Being*, London, 1969. His works have attracted during the past few years the attention of many students of science opposed to the reductionism inherent in the current scientific world view.

45. During the past few years much activity has taken place in Germany to criticize the segmented approach of modern science in the name of a more wholistic way of studying nature. There is even a review devoted to this subject with numerous articles by both scientists and philosophers who deal with this theme and its ramifications. See the *Zeitschrift für Ganzheitsforschung* (1957–).

On the criticism of modern science from this perspective see also W. Heitler, *Naturphilosophische Streifzüge*, Braunschweig, 1970; and his *Der Mensch und die naturwissenschaftliche Erkenntnis*, Braunschweig, 1970.

46. "Fondée non pas sur la considération de Dieu, mais sur une technique particulière, la science moderne cache Dieu et l'enveloppe au bien de s'ouvrir à la connaissance universelle et transcendante . . . ; elle n'est proprement ni divine ni révélatrice de Dieu et ne peut definir la réalité véritable du monde." F. Brunner, *Science et réalité*, p. 205. This work contains one of the most thorough intellectual criticisms of modern science by a contemporary European philosopher.

47. "Symbolic thought is gnostic, while scientific thought is agnostic; it believes that 'two and two make four' or it believes only what it sees, which amounts to the same thing." G. Durand, *On the Disfiguration of the Image of Man in the West*, Ipswich, U.K., 1977, p. 15.

48. St. Bonaventure could write concerning the beauties of nature as the reflection of God's beauty and wisdom:

> Whoever, therefore, is not enlightened
>   by such splendor of created things
>   is blind;
> whoever is not awakened by such outcries
>   is deaf;
> whoever does not praise God because of all these effects
>   is dumb;
> whoever does not discover the First Principle
>   from such clear signs
>   is a fool.

From E. Cousins (trans.), *Bonaventure: The Soul's Journey unto God*, p. 67. But it seems that many of those who followed him after the Middle Ages, even among theologians dominated to a great extent by nominalism, would have been classified by him according to the above definitions as blind, deaf, dumb, or fools.

49. "Il nous semble que la pensée occidentale, traditionnelle ou moderne, religieuse ou athée, propose de la Nature une notion 'mutilée' ou limitée, corrélative d'une attitude passionnelle ou polémique." G. Vallin, "Nature intégrale et Nature mutilée," *Revue philosophique*, no. 1 (Jan.–Mars 1974): 77.

50. "La pensée occidentale nous offre, notamment dans le Néoplatonisme, dans l'Hermétisme ou l'alchimie, ou chez un Scot Erigène, une approache ou un équivalent de ces que nous proposons d'appeler la 'Nature intégral'; mais c'est dans le cadre de la pensée orientale, et notamment de la métaphysique hindouiste du *Védanta* que cette 'structure' à la fois cosmologique et théologique nous paraît présenter toute son ampleur et sa richesse." Ibid., p. 84. We have also dealt with this question in our *Man and Nature*.

51. "C'est pourquoi il faut qu'il existe une autre science que la science moderne. Cet autre type de connaissance du monde n'exclut pas la science sous sa forme actuelle, si l'on envisage la perfection pour qui sous-tend et justifie dans une certaine mesure la pensée technique elle-même: la science véritable laisse subsister la science moderne comme une manifestation possible de l'esprit en nous." Brunner, op. cit., p. 208–9.

52. Through such a science "l'ordre sensible, après celui de l'âme, exprime finalement l'ordre de l'intelligence auquel appartiennent les lois suprêmes de la production du monde, de la vie spirituelle et du retour des êtres à Dieu." Brunner, op. cit., p. 215.

53. It is important to note that the founders of the discipline of the history of science, who were all either outstanding historians of thought or philosophers of science, were, with the exception of the much neglected P. Duhem, positivists. As a result, an invisible positivist air still dominates the minds of the scholars of this discipline despite several important exceptions such as A. Koyré, G. Di Santillana and, among the younger generation, N. Sivan and A. Debus. What is of special interest is that this positivism becomes rather aggressive when the question of the Oriental sciences and their metaphysical significance comes to the fore. That is why so few studies of the Oriental sciences which would reveal their significance as being anything more than quaint errors on the path of human progress have come out of those dominated by the

tacit positivism of this discipline, no matter how learned they might be. S. Jaki in his *The Road of Science and the Ways to God*, Chicago, 1978, has referred to this positivism in connection with its neglect of the role of Christian elements such as a Creator whose will rules over an orderly universe. Although we do not agree with his appreciation of Western science as a positive result of the particular characteristics of Christianity, we certainly share his concern for the limitations imposed upon the discipline of the history of science by the positivism of its founders.

54. The recent work, R. Ruyer, *La Gnose de Princeton: des savants à la recherche d'une religion*, Paris, 1974, supposedly by the group of scientists at Princeton interested in gnosis but most likely the thoughts of one person using a fictitious group, is an example of this kind of phenomenon. The thirst for sacred knowledge in the contemporary world is such that this work became popular in France where, during recent years, many pseudognostic and pseudoesoteric works by scientists have seen the light of day.

55. Traditions emphasize that this knowledge, although attainable, is not attainable by everyone because not only does it need preparation but can be taught only to the person who possesses the capability and nature to "inherit" such a knowledge. That is why some of the Muslim authorities like Sayyid Haydar Āmulī refer to it as inherited knowledge (*al-ʿilm al-mawrūthī*) which they contrast with acquired knowledge (*al-ʿilm al-iktisābī*). See Corbin, "Science traditionnelle et renaissance spirituelle," *Cahiers de l'Université Saint Jean de Jérusalem* 1 (1974):39ff.

56. "Nature . . . which is at the same time their sanctuary [of the American Indians], will end by conquering this artificial and sacreligious world, for it is the Garment, the Breath, the very Hand of the Great Spirit." Schuon, *Language of the Self*, p. 224.

CHAPTER SEVEN

Eternity and the Temporal Order

Zeit ist wie Ewigkeit und Ewigkeit wie Zeit,
So du nur selber nicht machst einen Unterscheid.

Eternity is as time, time as eternity,
If they are otherwise, the difference is in thee.[1]
Angelus Silesius

To-day, to-morrow, yesterday
With Thee are one, an instant aye.
Joshua Sylvester

Not only does man stand at the point of intersection of the vertical and horizontal axes of existence considered in their spatial symbolism, but he also lives at the moment when the eternal and the temporal meet. He is at once a being located in time and the process of change and one who is made for the Eternal and the Immutable and who is able to gain access to the Eternal even when living outwardly in the domain of becoming. He can, moreover, live in time and experience it not only as change and transience but also as the "moving image of eternity." In the same way that the periphery of the circle of existence reflects the Center which is everywhere and nowhere, the experience of that change which is called time reflects eternity in that whenever which is the ever-recurring now. As long as man is man, the vertical axis is open before him not only in the "spatial" sense of enabling him to climb to the higher levels of reality and ultimately to the Real as such, but also "temporally" in transcending the experience of profane time to reach the portal of eternity itself. Likewise, in the same way that the intermediate worlds possess their own space and form until one reaches the level of formless manifestation, so also do they possess their own "time" or what would correspond to time in the terrestrial realm of existence.

No better proof is needed of the meeting of the dimensions of time and eternity within man than the fact that man is aware of his own death, of his own mortality, which means that he is also given the possibility to envisage that which lies beyond the terminus a quo of terrestrial existence. Man's awareness of his mortality is in a sense proof of his immortality, of the fact that he was created for the Eternal. Moreover, there exists within normal man a natural attraction for the Eternal which is none other than the Absolute and the Sacred as such. The Eternal is like the original abode of the soul which, being lost, is sought by the soul everywhere in its earthly exile. The tranquility of a placid lake or the vibrating rays of the morning sun shining upon the mountain peaks evoke in man a sense of peace and the joy of a beauty which melts the hardness of the human soul and quells the agitations of a being caught in the tumultuous tides of the sea of becoming, of what Buddhism characterizes so powerfully as *samsāra*. This joy and sense of peace are none other than the mark of eternity as it touches the human soul. Pontifical man lives in time but as a witness to eternity.

Traditional teachings throughout the world are replete with references to the mysterious relationship between time and eternity both within man and in the objective order. Since all religion is concerned with the sacred, it is also concerned with the Eternal, for the Eternal *is* the Sacred as such and also all that is sacred bears the stamp of eternity. Moreover, man lives in time; his actions are determined by time; and he is finally devoured by time, for to be born in time is to die. Hence even archaic religions which, as we shall shortly see, have a very different conception of history and the march of time than do the Judeo-Christian ones, are as much concerned with saving man from the withering effect of the temporal process and enabling him to be saved from all-becoming as the Judeo-Christian traditions. To be seriously concerned with the human state, as all the traditions are despite the many differences between them, is to have to deal with a being living amidst temporality but who is marked by the signature of eternity, a being who is mortal yet made for immortality.

In the same way that intelligence is made to know the Absolute and can know only the Absolute absolutely, the knowledge of all other orders of reality partaking of an element of *māyā* which characterizes those states, it is easier for intelligence as previously defined to grasp the meaning of eternity than of time. Eternity is associated with immutability and permanence. It is an attribute of that reality which *is* but does not *become* and in fact transcends even Being. But this first veil upon the face of Absolute Reality shares with that Reality the attribute of eternity, for Being like Non-Being, in the metaphysical sense already defined, does not become. To gain an intellectual comprehension of the meaning of the Absolute is also to understand the Eternal. That same intellectual intuition which makes available through *scientia sacra* a principial knowledge of Ultimate Reality also provides a direct intuitive knowledge of the Eternal.

It is from this principial, metaphysical point of view that the definition of time seems more problematic than that of eternity to the extent that Saint Augustine could assert that he knew what time was but had difficulty defining it when asked. Modern analytical philosophers have tried to "solve" the problem of time by simply reducing it to a problem of language and of memory, as if one could explain the immediate experience of time by anything less immediate in such a way that the immediate experience would cease to exist. The analytical philosophers now speak of *before* an utterance, *with* an utterance, and *later than* an utterance instead of past, present, and future, hoping thereby to deny once and for all the human experience of past, present, and future. They lay the blame for the impossibility of solving the problem of time in classical philosophy on the "myth of passage"[2] which views time as a running river. Some philosophers of science try to associate the very reality of temporality with asymmetrical boundary conditions of physics,[3] while others as "idealists" have denied the reality of time altogether.[4] There is such a bewildering range of views and opinions concerning time in modern European philosophy that one could conclude that once man loses sight of the Eternal he no longer has any sense of the profound significance of time which has become the alpha and omega of his existence. He may talk about four-dimensional "world-lines" including and embracing time and space in a unity in the manner of modern physics but can hardly answer why, if he is located on only a limited segment of this four-dimensional complex, he can even speculate about what lies beyond this complex and "where" he as a conscious being will be when the world-line about which he is speculating now will reach a point corresponding to the end of his terrestrial life. It is questions such as these that have caused many modern continental philosophers in the West to look with skepticism upon the vacuum-cleaning activity of the positivists and analysts who would like to remove any metaphysical significance that time might still possess, since it ends with a supernatural event, namely, death, that only the philosopher in the Platonic sense has practiced facing.[5]

From the metaphysical point of view, in the same way that eternity is an attribute of that Reality which is at once Absolute and infinite, time is the characteristic of the dynamic potential of matter and energy which, as discussed already, result from the irradiation and effusion of the All-Possibility in the direction of nothingness. Once cosmic manifestation reaches the level of the physical world, the matter-energy of this world which corresponds to the principle of substance on this level of reality contains within its very nature a dynamism which entails change and becoming. Time is a consequence of this change. In this sense, the concept of time in modern physics as being a condition of material existence rather than an abstract absolute quantity as found in Newtonian physics is closer to traditional cosmologies. These cosmologies see both time and space as conditions of corporeality, and "abstracted" from it, rather than quantitative coordinates extending to infinity within which objects move and interact. It must be remembered that Aristotle considered time as the measurement of change.[6]

Moreover, since cosmic reality is characterized by the polarization between subject and object, there are two modes of time, one subjective and the other objective.[7] Objective time is cyclic by nature, one cycle moving within another with a quaternary structure which manifests itself on various levels ranging from the four parts of the day (morning, midday, evening, and night), the four seasons and the four ages of man (childhood, adolescence, maturity, and old age) to the four *yugas* of the Hindu cosmic cycle. As for subjective time, it is always related to the consciousness of past, present, and future which flow into one another, each possessing its own positive as well as negative aspects. The past is a reflection of the Origin, the memory of paradise lost and the reminder of faithfulness to tradition and what has been already given by God. But it is also related to imperfection, to all that man has left behind in his spiritual journey, the world that man leaves for the sake of God. The future is related to the ideal which is to be attained, the paradise that is to be gained. But it is also a sign of the loss of childhood and innocence and elongation and separation from the Origin which means also tradition. As for the present which is man's most precious gift, it is the point where time and eternity meet; it symbolizes hope and joy. It is the moment of faith and the door toward the nontemporal. Contemplation is entry into the eternal present which is now. But the present is also the moment associated with immediate pleasure, with instantaneous satisfaction which only accentuates the fleeting effect of time rather than the pacifying reflection of eternity.[8]

Hence both subjective and objective time have a relative reality which is no less than the reality of the being who is located in the spatio-temporal matrix. To deny their reality is valid only from the perspective of the Immutable which always is but does not become. *Scientia sacra*, therefore, while affirming this view on its own level, seeks to provide meaning for that experience which we call time and which is also real from the point of view of change and becoming like *māyā* itself, which does not exist from the "perspective" of *Ātman* but whose reality cannot be denied for those living in the embrace of *māyā*. From the total metaphysical point of view then, eternity is an attribute of the Absolute and Infinite Reality which, because of its Infinitude and Goodness, emanates outwardly and manifests the many levels of existence. Of these levels the physical possesses a matter combined with energy whose very dynamism necessitates that process of becoming and change of which time is a condition. But time itself is impregnated by the Eternal in such a way that every moment of time is a gate to the Eternal—the moment, the present, the now belong to the Eternal itself.

As far as spiritual experience is concerned, the present moment as the gateway to the Eternal is so significant that practically all the traditions of the world speak with nearly the same tongue concerning the present moment, the instant (*nû alzemâle*), the present now (*gegenwürtig nû*), and the eternal now (*ewigen nû*) of Meister Eckhart in which God makes the world,[9] the *waqt* or *ān* of Sufism whose "son" the Sufi considers himself to be (according to the well-known saying "the Sufi is the son of the moment"—*al-ṣūfī ibn al-waqt*),[10] the moment or point at which, according to Dante, all times are present.[11] This "now" is the gateway to eternity; it is to time what the point is to space. To be at the central point here and now is to live in the Eternal which is always the present. Hence the preciousness of the "moment" which man must not let pass him by for as the Buddhists say, "Get ye across this sticky-mire, let not the Moment pass, for they shall mourn whose Moment's past."[12] Forgetful man daydreams in either the past or the future evading the present moment which alone is real in the spiritual sense. Only he who lives in the eternal present is in fact awake. This moment is that "twinkling of the eye" in which all things were made[13] and which in the Upanishads appears as a name of God.[14] To live in this moment is to experience all that was, is, and will ever be.

The subjective experience of the eternal present, moreover, conditions and colors man's experience of time itself as does in fact the experience of anything which bears the fragrance of the immutable and the sacred. There is not just a single subjective experience of time but one subjective experience within another. Hence joy and happiness, issuing from that Supreme Substance which is pure bliss, shorten time since this experience brings man closer to the eternal now, while pain, agitation, and dispersion lengthen the subjective experience of time. That is why it is said that in the Golden Age time was longer than in the later ages. That is also why in such myths as that of the seven sleepers in the cave, the aṣḥāb al-kahf mentioned in the Quran, falling asleep in the cave for a short moment corresponded to the passage of several generations in the outside world.[15] In a sense, eternity penetrates into time in such a way that the closer man's experience approaches the realm of the eternal and the joy which is inseparable from it, the less is the subjective experience of time a burden on him so that duration passes by more rapidly.[16] If in the embrace of the earthly beloved hours pass as if they were but a moment, in union with the Divine Beloved all the eons of time past and future pass not only as if they were a moment but as they *are* actually a moment, in fact *the* supreme moment in which the spiritual man lives constantly. It is the now which all human beings experience at that moment which is their last earthly moment, namely, the moment of death. The now is at once an anticipation of that moment and a going beyond it in the sense of experiencing an inner resurrection even before bodily death.[17]

Eternity then is reflected in the present now, and the now is the solar gate through which the hero must pass to reach beyond the sea of becoming and the withering effect of time whose function it is to devour all that exists in its bosom. But from another point of view it is possible to refer to eternity as both being "before" and "after" the moment in which we stand and in fact before and after the world in which we have our present existence. Eternity is then before all that was and after all that will be, before and after meaning not in time but in principle. It is in this sense that the Islamic tradition speaks of *al-azal*, that is, preeternity and *al-abad* or posteternity, the two being in their own reality none other than *al-sarmad* or eternity as such.[18] The morning of *azal* referred to so often in Sufi poetry refers to eternity in its aspect of coming before all creation. It refers to that "early dawn" when man made his eternal covenant with God.[19]

Likewise, eternity is sometimes referred to as boundless time or timelessness as in late Zoroastrianism where boundless time or Zurvan is considered as the principle of both Ahura-Mazda and Ahriman, Zurvan meaning metaphysically the Eternal and etymologically boundless time.[20] Also, in later Greek thought Kronos as the father of Zeus was often identified with *chronos*, despite the fact that such an assimilation is etymologically inconceivable. In the context of the *Maitri Upanishad*, "time" is equivalent with eternity, here again "time" meaning boundless time, not time as it is usually understood. Since ontologically existence cannot be completely other than Being which is its principle, time also cannot be totally divorced from eternity in the sense that what man experiences in time comes from God and is related to Him. It is in this sense that the *Maitri Upanishad* distinguishes "two forms" of Brahman, as time and timelessness, but possessing one essence. It states: "From one who worships, thinking that 'Time [*kālas*] is Brahma', time [*kāla*, also death] reflows afar."

> *From Time flow forth all beings,*
> *From Time advance to full growth,*
> *And in Time again, win home,—*
> *"Time" is the formed and the formless, both.*[21]

This Time which contains all time is in reality none other than that moment which always is, the "in the beginning" which is always present. The "once upon a time" of folk tales is not a particular time but Time which is also the timeless, the Hebrew ʿ*olam* and the Greek *aiōn*. In certain languages such as Sanskrit fairy tales simply begin with "there is" (*asti*), implying directly the eternal present, while Persian stories begin with a statement known to every Persian-speaking child but which contains the whole metaphysical significance of that eternal moment which is beyond time and yet the point from which the story begins. The statement is: "There was one; there was no one; other than God there was no one."[22] The origin of time and all those events which we experience as taking place "in time" belong to that "once upon a time" which is no time and yet all times wherein belong both metaphysics and myths and symbols which, therefore, do not wither with time. They share in the immutability of that eternal moment from which all things are born.

Although the doctrine of the eternal now in its relation to time is universal and is to be found in the sacred scriptures and sapiential teachings of different traditions throughout the world, the attitude toward the experience of man in the stream of change and process which is called history is hardly the same among all religions. Nor is the question of the genesis of the world as it is related to the temporal process the same. Of course, all traditions are based on the doctrine of grades of existence issuing from the Supreme Principle but they envisage the unfolding of time differently, some basing themselves on a single act of creation and one period of the cosmic drama and others on many cycles which are repeated according to the rhythms that reflect the "days and nights of the life of Brahma," to put it in Hindu terms. There are also those traditions which live in space and for whom time and history are of little consequence, and those which live in time and which take history into account as being of religious and ultimate significance.

The difference between these perspectives which also is directly related to the cyclic and linear conceptions of the "march of time" or history can itself be explained by taking recourse to the traditional doctrine of cycles.[23] According to this doctrine in its Hindu form, each grand cosmic cycle (*kalpa*) consists of a thousand *yugas* which comprise "a day of Brahma."[24] Moreover, each smaller cosmic cycle concerning a particular humanity is comprised of four *yugas*, beginning with what the Greeks called the Golden Age (the *Kṛta Yuga* of Hindu sources) and ending with the Iron Age (*Kali Yuga*) whose termination also marks the end of the present terrestrial cycle of history. In one single cycle in which time is divided according to the *Tetractys*, that is, 4, 3, 2, 1, the Golden Age being the longest and the Iron Age the shortest, the process of change or what we interpret as the flow of time is very slow at the beginning, increasing its tempo as the cycle advances so that time, far from being linear and uniform, is itself qualitatively modified during different *yugas*. For men of the Golden Age, time as an element of "secular" change was not of any significance. Time was identified with cosmic rhythms like that of the seasons. Although the cycle never returns to the same point but follows a helical rather than circular motion,[25] the changes in nonrepeated patterns were too imperceptible to be of any consequence. It was only during later phases of the cycle that gradually the experience of time in its noncyclic aspect became consequential and that history began to gain significance.

This difference can perhaps be better understood by meditating a moment upon the symbolism of the hourglass which itself is an instrument for the measurement of time.[26] One unit of time during which the sand flows from the upper compartment into the lower could be considered as symbolizing one cosmic cycle. Now, as the cycle begins, although the sand is pouring through, there seems to be no perceptible change in the condition of the upper compartment which appears as being immutable. The reality of such a condition appears as one of permanence in which the particles of sand are "seen" as being in space and not in a time which would alter their condition in an ultimately significant way—in the same way that in the Golden Age, although individuals did grow old and die, the world in which they lived seemed to be located in a paradisal permanence in which the cosmos was rejuvenated by temporal cycles but not affected in a nonrenewable manner by time. For so-called primitive man, the cosmos and history were the same, in fact identical, as were time and transcendence and reality and the symbol. But as the sand continues its flow, the very situation of the upper compartment begins to change. It is not only the individual particles of sand that fall through the channel but the whole configuration of sand in the upper compartments begins to change and time gains a new significance.

The religions in which time is seen in a cyclic manner and where history is of little consequence as far as man's "salvation" is concerned are essentially those archaic religions based on the reality of human experience in earlier phases of the cosmic cycle and corresponding to the beginning of the flow of sand in the hourglass. It is the later religions, corresponding to the last phase of the unit of time measured by the hourglass, which had to take into account the temporal experience in a religious manner. Judaism, although in one respect a "primoridal" religion, was destined to play a major role in itself and also to serve as background for Christianity in the religious life of the humanity of the last phase of the human cycle, hence its concern with history and the metahistorical and metacosmic significance of the historical experience of the chosen people of Israel. Hinduism, on the other hand, remains based on the primordial perspective of cyclic time while having been able to rejuvenate itself and survive to this day. Zoroastrianism, in a sense, occupies an intermediate position between the religions of India and the Abrahamic ones as far as history is concerned,[27] while Islam being the last of the Abrahamic religions and yet a return to the primordial religion confirms the significance of man's actions in history while refusing to identify the truth itself with history in any way. It is of some significance that even the events of sacred history mentioned in both the Bible and the Quran have a more historical color in the former and a more symbolic one in the latter.[28]

In any case since it is the function of all religions to save men from the imperfections implied by their terrestrial state, they have had to deal with the significance of temporality in different ways depending on their point of departure and the "archetypal" reality which they represent on earth. There has developed as a result of these factors a cyclic as well as a linear conception of time and of history, the first associated with the non-Abrahamic and the second with Abrahamic religions. But even within the Abrahamic traditions the situation has not been the same in the three religions which comprise the members of this religious family. In Judaism, because of the presence of a long line of prophets, while the importance of history is confirmed, the flow of history is not strictly speaking linear nor has history been identified with the Deity through the doctrine of incarnation which marks the entrance of the truth into history. In Islam also the significance of what man accomplishes in this world either individually or collectively is fully emphasized, the world of time being called the "cultivating field" for eternity,[29] but it is categorically denied that anything that occurs in history affects the divine as such since Islam rejects strongly all incarnationism. Moreover, the Islamic conception of prophecy according to which truth was present from the beginning and is brought to the world over and over again by different prophets, ending with the Prophet of Islam after whom there will be no other prophet but the second coming of Christ, is based on a cyclic conception of time and not a linear one.[30]

It is most of all in Christianity that one can say that only one part of a complete cycle or one small cycle was taken and treated in a linear manner. As a result, Christianity in its exoteric formulations—not of course in its sapiential teachings which saw Christ as the Logos who said, "before Abraham was I am"—came to perceive history as marked by three fundamental points: the fall of Adam on earth, the incarnation of the Son of God as the second Adam in history, and the end of the world with the second coming of Christ. This view of the march of time, combined with the idea of the birth of Christ as a unique historical event and the incarnation of the Son in the matrix of time and of history, created a special religious situation which, once Christianity was weakened, gave way easily to that idolatry of the worship of history that characterizes much of the modern world. Although the concern of Marx with every detail of human life is a parody of the concerns of Talmudic Law, his putting history in the place of the Divinity is a Christian heresy and not an Islamic or Hindu one. While Christianity was strong, despite its emphasis upon history, the passage of days and years was sanctified by the continuous repetition of the events of the life of the founder and the saints. Christians, like followers of other religions, lived in the world whose very temporality was transformed by the ever-repeated themes of the life of Christ and the rites which flowed from the origins of the tradition along with the grace of the saints who perpetuated the spirit of the tradition over the ages. The worship of mammon as history or historical process came only in the wake of the desacralization of the Christian world, but it was precisely the secularization of the linear concept of time and historical process that gave rise to that historicism and denial of the truth as transcendent that characterizes much of modern thought. Otherwise, traditional Christian thought, like all traditional thought, had seen the solution to the problem of space and time through recourse to that Reality which is beyond space and time yet pervades and transforms both of them.[31]

The concern of Christianity with the linear time covering the period from the first coming of Christ to his second coming is also related to the point of view of the Abrahamic religions which, in their exoteric aspect, are concerned primarily with the practical goal of saving man rather than with the nature of things per se which is the concern of the esoteric. That is why in the exoteric formulations of these religions eschatology is simplified into the two opposite states of heaven and hell and the question of creation is reduced to the theological formulation of *creatio ex nihilo*. The question of intermediate states, the final consummation of all things in God, other cosmic cycles and humanities, the meaning of the "waters" upon which the light of God shone, the existence of beings *in divinis* before that event called creation, and so many other questions are left for the esoteric dimension of these traditions.

As far as the question of time is concerned, perhaps no issue demonstrates the inadequacy of the theological formulations in themselves and without the aid of sapiential doctrines than creation *ex nihilo*. In all the three Abrahamic religions there have been theologians who have claimed that God created the world from nothing and that the world has an origin in time, while there have been traditional philosophers who have insisted that there was no time when the world was not, since time is a condition of the world. Thousands of treatises have been written by Muslims, Jews, and Christians since John the Grammarian wrote his *De aeternitate mundi* against Proclus.[32] To this day in traditional Islamic circles of learning the problem of ḥudūth and qidam or "newness" and "eternity" of the world is debated,[33] since it represents a question which cannot be resolved logically on the level in which the theologies of the Abrahamic religions place themselves. It must either be accepted on faith or recourse must be had to that *scientia sacra* for which *ex nihilo* does not mean literally from nothing but rather from "possibilities" in the principial order which, to quote Ibn ʿArabī, have not as yet "smelled the perfume of existence" and which are existentiated and externalized upon the terrestrial plane from a preexistent state or even states. Creation in this sense is always a descent. A figure like Jalāl al-Dīn Rūmī has already provided the answer for the incessant debate between followers of ḥudūth and those of qidam, while those who have not been able to reach an understanding of the issue even in the traditional Islamic context have been those who simply have not comprehended the message of a work such as the *Mathnawī*.[34]

An element of these teachings concerning creation that does need to be mentioned is the doctrine of the renewal of creation at every instant (*tajdīd al-khalq fī kulli ānāt*), which characterizes much of the Sufi teachings concerning creation. The Sufis, like all those who speak of the moment or the now, take recourse to an "atomization of temporality," if such a term can be used, and believe that, although time as flow is indivisible, from another point of view it is no more than the repetition of the instant like the line which is formed by the repetition of spatial point.[35] During this instant or now the whole world returns to the Origin through the movement of contraction (*al-qabḍ*) and is recreated through expansion (*al-bast*) like the two phases of breathing. At every moment there is a fresh creation (*tajdīd al-khalq*) and the link between the Creator and His creation is incessantly renewed. As Jāmī says, "The universe is changed and renewed unceasingly at every moment and every breath. Every instant one universe is annihilated and another resembling it takes its place. . . . In consequence of this rapid succession, the spectator is deceived into the belief that the universe is a permanent existence."[36] This doctrine, which has the greatest import as far as the practical and operative aspects of Sufism are concerned, is a manner of viewing the problem of creation from the perspective of the eternal present itself from which nothing ever really departs. Furthermore, it complements the metaphysical doctrine which sees creation *ex nihilo* as the existentiation of the archetypes or essences which possess a precosmic reality *in divinis*.[37]

The deification of the historical process in secular terms has taken place in the modern world not only because the metaphysical teachings concerning time and eternity have been forgotten as a result of the desacralization of both knowledge and the world but also, as already mentioned, as a result of the particular emphasis of Christianity upon history which is not to be found in other traditions.[38] Christian thought, at least in its main line of development in the West, took history seriously, in the sense of believing in the irreversible directionality of history, the power which history possesses to introduce novelty of even a radical order, awareness of the uniqueness of each historic event which was to give rise in modern times to existentialism, the possibility of certain historical events to be decisive in a final way,[39] the religious significance of human involvement in historical movements and institutions, and the importance of human freedom in not only determining the individual man's future but also the whole of history. From these premises to those of Promethean man, who secularized all of them and decided to mold his own destiny and history, was but a single step. And from this secularization of the Christian conception of history combined with messianism, those materialistic and secular philosophies have been born which are based on the view that the historical process is the ultimately real itself, and that through material progress man is able to attain that perfection which was traditionally identified with the paradisal state, with the terrestrial and celestial Jerusalem located at the alpha and omega points of history which are also the present now. Through historicism, secular utopianism, and the idea of progress and evolution in a sense time has, for modern man, tried to devour eternity and usurp its place, replacing the eternal now in which the eternal and the temporal meet with the present moment as the fleeting instant of transient pleasures and sensations. Paradoxically enough, the end result of this process is that this divinized time has not only destroyed the possibility of the experience of eternity for those who have fallen under its hypnotic spell, but it has also eclipsed the meaning of perpetuity and historical continuity and hence the sense of history itself.[40]

The deification of historical process has become so powerful and such a compelling force that, in the souls of many human beings, it has taken the place of religion. Nowhere is this more evident than in the role that the theory of evolution plays in the mental and psychological life of those scientists who claim to look upon all things from a detached scientific point of view but who react with violent passion when the theory of evolution is discussed critically from any quarter—whether it be logical, theological, or scientific.[41] In many ways and for profound reasons, evolution has become the substitute for religion for many people who defend it with complete intolerance while claiming to be very reasonable and tolerant beings without any strong religious beliefs.[42] Others speak in categorical terms of the scientific method, then defend evolution on scientific grounds without being at all aware that their manner of accepting evolution as scientific has nothing to do with their own definition of what science is.[43] There lies in these attitudes a factor of the most profound nature which concerns the depth of the soul of man, for it involves the substitution of historical process for the Divinity and therefore brings out a response which is reserved for the sacred to which pontifical man always responds with the whole of his being. Moreover, this defense of evolution involves a battle for "faith," not scientific truth, for it provides the only way possible to veil over the penetration of the archetypal realities, of which the species are earthly reflections, upon the physical plane, and the sole means of providing some kind of a seemingly acceptable scheme to enable man to live in this world amidst the bewildering variety of the forms of nature but in forgetfulness of the transcendent One who is the source of this variety.

The criticisms which can be brought and have in fact been brought against the theory of evolution as currently understood, and of course not as man's vertical ascent toward his own eternal archetype, are at once metaphysical and cosmological, religious, logical, mathematical, physical and biological, including the domain of paleontology. Metaphysically, life comes before matter, the subtle world before life, the Spirit before the subtle world, and the Ultimate Reality before everything else, this "before" meaning in principle whatever may have been the chronological appearance of matter, life, and consciousness upon the theater of cosmic existence. Intellectual intuition which enables man to know *scientia sacra* provides this absolute certitude of the primacy of consciousness over both life and matter. It provides a knowledge of that hierarchy which issues from the Source in which all things are eternally present and to which all things return. It sees existents in gradation and their appearance on the temporal plane as elaborations of possibilities belonging to that vertical dimension or gradation.[44] Objects in this world "emerge" from what Islamic esoterism calls the 'treasury of the Unseen" (*khazānay-i ghayb*); nothing whatsoever can appear on the plane of physical reality without having its transcendent cause and the root of its being *in divinis*. There is, metaphysically speaking, no possibility of any temporal process adding something to the Divinity or to Reality as such. Whatever grows and develops is the actualization of a possibility which had preexisted in the Divine Order, this development or growth being always of an essence while total reality resides in the immutable world of the archetypes. Finally, metaphysically speaking, that which belongs to a lower scale of being can never give rise to what belongs by nature to a higher level. From the point of view of the *scientia sacra* the only meaning that the evolution of anything can have would be the actualization of the possibilities latent in that thing. Otherwise not all the eons of time can produce something out of nothing. The power of creation belongs to the creating Principle alone which is pure actuality itself. What evolution does is to deify the historical process not only by considering it as the ultimately real but also by transferring the power of *creatio ex nihilo* from the transcendent Divinity to it.

Also, from the metaphysical and cosmological points of view, form is the imprint of an archetype and a divine possibility and not an accident of a material congregate. Moreover, form is quality and qualities do not add up as do quantities. Even in the inanimate world green is not the sum of red and blue in the same way that four is the sum of two and two. Green possesses a qualitative reality which is simply not reducible to the qualities of the colors which, materially or quantitatively speaking, add up to constitute green. This principle is even more evident in life forms where the reality of any form is irreducible to its quantitative components. Would half a human body be qualitatively half of the complete human body? Forms of living beings have a qualitative reality which cannot evolve from any other form unless that form were also present "somewhere." And that "somewhere" cannot metaphysically have any locus but the archetypal world which is the origin of all forms.

From the purely religious point of view also, the evidence against evolution is universal even in traditions such as Hinduism, Jainism, and Buddhism where cosmic history is envisaged on grand scales and where there has been perfect awareness among those who read their sacred Scriptures that the world has been around much longer than six thousand years, that other creatures have preceded man on earth, and that the geological configuration of the world has changed. The same can be said of Islam where, over a thousand years ago, Muslim scientists were perfectly aware that sea shells on top of mountains meant that mountains had turned into seas and seas into mountains and that land animals had preceded man on earth and that sea animals had come before land animals.[45] In all sacred Scriptures and traditional sources whether they speak of creation in six days or of cosmic cycles lasting over vast expanses of time, there is not one indication that higher life forms evolved from lower ones. In all sacred books man descends from a celestial archetype but does not ascend from the ape or some other creature. Whatever concoctions of scriptural evidence have been made up to support modern evolutionary theory since the last century, they are based upon the forgetting of the traditional and sapiential commentaries and on interpreting the vertical scale of existence in a temporal and horizontal fashion as was done philosophically as a background for the rise of nineteenth-century evolutionary theory itself. The remarkable unanimity of sacred texts belonging to all kinds of peoples and climes surely says something about the nature of man. In any case, it is one more proof against those who would seek to make use of a particular text from one tradition or a few lines judiciously chosen from a certain scripture which would lend themselves more easily to misinterpretation in order to demonstrate religious support for the validity of the theory of evolution.

From a purely logical point of view it is difficult to explain how one can get, let us say, five pounds of barley out of a box in which there were originally only four. When one studies historical geology and paleontology one runs across many cases where the evolution of one form into another seems just as absurd. But this absurdity is brushed aside by positing long periods of time, with the illusion that somehow if you have enough time you can explain any problem. Whether one has a thousand years or a hundred million years, it is logically absurd that inert matter should become conscious or that a lower order of organization would by itself become a higher order of organization—apparently against not only logic but all that we know of the laws of physics. In logic no A can become B unless B is already in some way contained in A, and surely B can never come out of A if it possesses something more or is greater than A. No amount of evolutionary patience can change this primary human demand for logic. That is in fact why those who defend the theory of evolution usually make their definition so ambiguous as to be able to evade critical logical examination of the definition they provide.

There is even a mathematical criticism of the theory of evolution.[46] According to modern information theory, one cannot receive from any unit more information than has been put into it. Now, the cell can be considered as a unit containing a certain amount of information which in fact governs the activities of the life form in question. How can this information within the cell be increased without having new information put into it through some agent whatever it might be? One cannot study the cell as it is done today, accept information theory and at the same time accept the current interpretations of the theory of evolution according to which, through temporal processes and without an external cause, which itself must be of a higher order in the sense of being able to increase the information contained within a gene, the amount of information contained within the genes does increase and they "evolve" into higher forms.

As for arguments drawn from physics, it is well-known that life forms preserve their order and structure and use the energy connected with life to that end in a manner which is totally different and opposed to the second law of thermodynamics. The very appearance on earth of more complicated life forms during later stages in the life of the earth is opposed to the law of entropy and indicates the presence of another kind of energy at play. There are in fact many biologists who claim that there is not one but two different types of energy functioning in our terrestrial environment: one physical or connected with nonliving matter and the other with living things; and that the laws pertaining to the two are very different even if vital energy enters into play only when a particular set of material conditions are present and not before or after. Such scientists oppose strongly the possibility of inert matter evolving into life forms because of the fundamental differences between the two types of energy involved in the laws which govern each realm.[47]

As far as biological and paleontological evidence is concerned, there are numerous arguments outlined by experts in these fields many of whom hardly dare express their views until old age for fear of being ostracized by their professional colleagues. Nevertheless, the number of works by scientists in these fields, which point to the impossibility of the theory of evolution, the theory that E. F. Schumacher calls science fiction rather than science,[48] grows substantially every day and includes not only biologists but also geneticists, physiologists, and men from many other disciplines in the life sciences.[49] As for paleontological evidence, the first fact which confronts any student of the field is the appearance of new species in new geological periods in a sudden manner and over very extended areas. Unrelated major groups such as the vertebrates appear all of a sudden in the form of four orders and everywhere one detects the sudden rather than gradual appearance of complex organisms. Moreover, the stratigraphic record hardly ever reveals fossils which should exist as intermediates between the great groups, something which should be present if the theory of evolution as usually understood were to be accepted.[50] Furthermore, all the reasons given by defenders of evolution as to why the paleontological record does not in fact provide any such evidence have been refuted by numerous scientists.[51] As for plants, the situation is even more difficult to explain than is the case for animals. The paleontological record hardly supports the evolutionary hypothesis no matter how far it is stretched and how far-fetched is its interpretation.[52] The most damaging evidence comes of course from the lack of the trace of life in the pre-Cambrian and its sudden profusion afterwards. Anyone who studies this record with an open mind cannot but be impressed by the sudden appearance of a new force or energy upon the surface of the earth, manifesting itself and leaving its mark upon the geological record in a manner that can hardly be called evolutionary. The whole paleontological evidence of the Cambrian as distinct from the pre-Cambrian points to anything but the gradual evolution of life forms.[53] As for the post-Cambrian, the record reveals that nearly all the phyla of animals known were already present in the Cambrian—such as Porifera, Coelenterata, and Annelida—and that as far as phyla are concerned, no new classes have arisen since the Paleozoic with the exception of the Chordata.

The mutations of which many biologists speak and through which they seek to explain what they call evolution by leaps in fact never exceed a very limited boundary and represent either an anomaly or a decadence of the species in question. The hiatus remains unexplained by any of the mutations observed in biology unless one posits at other periods different forces acting on earth from those now observable. None of the variations which are presented by advocates of evolution as "buds" of a new species have in fact been anything more than variants within the framework of a specific species. There are animals which in a sense "imitate" animals of other orders such as whales which are mammals although they act as fishes; and yet fishes, reptiles, birds, and mammals remain distinct types and such creatures as whales and dolphins, far from proving evolutionary theories, only point to the immense creative power of nature. As for adaptations, there are some so complex that any evolutionary theory would be hard put to explain it, the action of a wise Creator being a much more logical solution.[54] That is why the more objective among biologists, even when they do accept the theory of evolution for what they feel is the lack of any other "scientific" alternative, remain fully aware of the fantastic and even "surrealistic" character of evolutionary theory as usually understood.[55] Certainly biology has not provided any proofs for this theory in the scientific sense of proof, but it has provided numerous obstacles which can only be overcome by a "leap of faith," which is only a parody of the faith that God has placed in the human soul for Himself and His messages. The criticisms against the evolutionary theory and problems associated with it are so numerous that certain modern scientists have even suggested that Darwinism and Lamarckism are burdens upon the science of biology itself and that this science should be allowed to develop without having to bear the burden of a philosophical assumption which does not correspond to its findings but in fact puts an immense constraint upon this science in order to enable modern man to continue to use this crutch for his unending worship of the historical and temporal process as reality.[56]

The few arguments outlined here in such a brief fashion are themselves the subject of another discourse and cannot be developed in detail in a study devoted to knowledge and the sacred. But because the theory of evolution, both in itself and in its wedding to various philosophies and even theologies, has played such a major role in the desacralization of what remained in the West of sacred knowledge and even of man's general sense of the sacred, it has been necessary to refer to these criticisms. It has also been important to mention the scientific objections to evolution because it is on the basis of a supposedly scientific foundation that evolution has been generalized to embrace the whole cosmos up to the Pleiades and the whole of knowledge including theology itself.

If in the nineteenth and early twentieth centuries evolutionary theory affected European philosophy in various ways, ranging from Nietzsche's superman to the emergent evolution of Samuel Alexander and the creative evolution of Henri Bergson, it nevertheless remained for the latter half of the twentieth century for this type of thought to enter into the realm of Catholic theology itself and to produce that Darwinization of theology, and the surrender of this queen of the sciences to the microscope,[57] which is represented by Teilhard de Chardin. Strangely enough, in this domain the French Jesuit was preceded by an Oriental, namely Śrī Aurobindo, who in his *Life Divine* had tried to provide an evolutionary interpretation of the Vedanta but who did not have the same influence or effect in India as Teilhard has had in the West.[58] It is in fact noteworthy to mention that, in the Orient, it is only in the Indian subcontinent that, as a result of Anglo-Saxon education with its heavy emphasis upon such evolutionary philosophers as Herbert Spencer, there has appeared not only a figure such as Aurobindo but a whole army of "evolutionary thinkers" of lesser eminence. Also it is from this world that that peculiar wedding between pseudospirituality and evolutionism, with talk of cosmic consciousness and the birth of a new humanity with evolved consciousness and the like, has spread to the rest of the world. Neither Buddhist Japan and China nor the Islamic world, despite the talk of Iqbal about the superman, produced the same blend of religion and evolution that we find in Aurobindo. It is therefore somewhat strange that the Western counterpart of Aurobindo should hail not from the land of Darwin but that of Claude Bernard and Cuvier.

From the traditional point of view Teilhard represents an idolatry which marks the final phase of the desacralization of knowledge and being, the devouring of the Eternal by the temporal process, if such were to be possible. It is therefore all the more strange that some should consider his work as "the resacralization of the profane world."[59] The fact that there has been such a flood of popularized writings about him, even journals being devoted to the study of his works[60] and that he has caught the attention of such a wide audience, including many not at all attracted to authentic religion, can only mean, in a world such as ours, that he caters to certain of the antitraditional and even countertraditional[61] tendencies of this world—most of all to that psychological formation which is the result of the domination of the evolutionary way of thinking upon the mind and psyche of most modern men.[62]

For Teilhard, evolution embraces not only living creatures but even nonliving matter. All cosmic matter which he addresses as "O Holy Matter!"[63] follows the law of "complexification" which leads the cosmic "stuff" to rise from stage to stage until it reaches man. All beings for him have a conscious inner face (not to be confused with the traditional Hindu doctrine that equates existence itself with consciousness) like man himself, and evolution also implies the evolution of consciousness from life and matter. This evolution has not only brought forth the biosphere to cover the earth but through human culture has led to the noosphere which has become imposed upon the biosphere. At a later stage of this supposed evolution human cultures will become one. Through the psychic concentration thus created a "hyperpersonal" consciousness will come into being at the "Omega point" where evolution will end in convergent integration, this point being God in as much as He determines the direction of history. It is through this fantastic mental sublimation of a crass materialism that Teilhard seeks to synthesize science and religion and give Christian significance to the evolutionary hypothesis *cum* science.

First of all, from the metaphysical and religious points of view this amalgamation rather than synthesis cannot be considered as anything but the inversion of the traditional doctrine of emanation and the generation of the hierarchy of existence. Theologically it is sheer idolatry as demonstrated by such assertions of Teilhard as, "There exists only matter becoming spirit. . . . Thus much matter [is needed] for thus much spirit,"[64] and the like. What is lacking completely in this perspective is awareness of the two kinds of rapport between the Principle and Its manifestation, that is, the relation of continuity and discontinuity. While the Principle is the source of the cosmos and nothing can exist without receiving existence from the source of Being which is to existence as the sun is to its rays, the Principle remains transcendent vis-à-vis all manifestation through a discontinuity which cannot be disregarded or overlooked by any authentic exposition of metaphysics. There is a world of difference between the traditional doctrine of the transcendent unity of being (*waḥdat al-wujūd* in its Islamic form) and a rationalistic pantheism that neglects the absolute transcendence of the One which is yet the source of all multiplicity.[65] For Teilhardism, it is not only the question of neglecting the aspect of discontinuity between the Principle and Its manifestation,[66] which would result in a kind of philosophical pantheism encountered often in the history of Western thought, but of even considering the Principle as the end product of the evolution of manifestation itself.

Teilhard tries to explain the transition of inert matter to life as the "coiling up of the molecule upon itself," forgetting the penetration of a new cosmic principle into the domain of inert matter as the cause for the sudden appearance of life on earth. This "coiling up," moreover, is nothing but a parody of spiritual concentration as his description of the transition of life to consciousness as "the threshold of reflection" is a parody of the divine creative act itself. He speaks about this process reaching, through evolution, the state of totality as if totality could have ever not been or could have ever lacked something which it gained later without ceasing to be totality! When one reads Teilhard carefully, one realizes that his faith lies in matter and in this world above all else without an awareness of how matter itself is generated by higher levels of existence.[67] When Teilhard says, "If, in consequence of some inner subversion, I should lose successively my faith in Christ, my faith in a personal God, my faith in the Spirit, it seems to me that I would continue to believe in the world. The *world*—the value, the infallibility and the goodness of the world—this *is*, in the last analysis, *the first and the only thing in which I believe*,"[68] he is expressing openly that worship of mammon which theologically could not but be called idolatry. And even when he asserts his faith in the Omega point evolving from evolutionary processes, he is denying the totality of all traditional teachings and clinging to only a truncated and subverted version of them, for Christ did say that he is the alpha *and* the omega; in the Quran God is called not only the last or omega (*al-ākhir*) but also the first (*al-awwal*), not only the outward (*al-ẓāhir*) but also the inward (*al-bāṭin*).

The criticism against Teilhard's amalgamation of religion and science cannot be limited to the religious pole but includes the scientific one as well. All the criticism brought against evolutionary and transformist theories in general apply to Teilhard as well who defended them not with scientific reasoning but with a "religious" passion. Moreover, Teilhard has been criticized for his views on biology and physiology with which he was not very familiar but from which he sought to draw philosophical and religious conclusions.[69] He sought to create a cosmic unity through the reduction of vital energy to physical energy and to equate the laws of living beings which possess finality in the biological sense[70] with those of inert matter which is of a very different nature, and in which the same kind of finality cannot be observed, although from the traditional metaphysical point of view, very far from that of Teilhard, everything in the universe possesses a purpose and an entelechy within the total harmony of the cosmos. His "unity" is more a uniformity, reducing all levels of cosmic reality to the material one rather than true unity which integrates instead of leveling and reducing things to their least common denominator.[71] Teilhard saw the world of nature as, in a sense, "Marxist," that is, solely determined by temporal and historical processes. As one of his scientific critics has asserted, however, "Nature is much more Platonist than Father Teilhard believes and not at all Marxist."[72]

If we have paused to criticize Teilhardism in the midst of this discussion of time and eternity, it is because the unveiling of the nature of this type of phenomenon is one of the most important tasks if one is to resuscitate traditional doctrines in an authentic manner, for it is not only the antitraditional but even more the countertraditional that veils the nature of tradition of which it is a veritable caricature. In fact, "Teilhardism is comparable to one of those cracks that are due to the very solidification of the mental carapace, and that do not open upward, toward the heaven of true and transcendent unity, but downwards toward the realm of psychism. Weary of its own discontinuous vision of the world, the materialist mind lets itself slide toward a false continuity or unity, toward a pseudo-spiritual intoxication, of which this falsified and materialized faith—or this sublimated materialism [of Teilhardism]—marks a phase of particular significance."[73] The slightest intuition of the immutable archetypes and the sense of the Eternal would have evaporated this fog of illusion which seeks to sublimate the temporal into the order of the Eternal of which it cannot be but a shadow.

The traditional response to either the Hegelian or Marxist reification and even deification of the historical process or, what is even more insidious from the traditional point of view, that mixture of evolutionism and theology found in Teilhard can be discovered not only in the metaphysical doctrines concerning eternity and the temporal order but also in those traditional philosophies of becoming which treat in a more directly philosophical way those currently popular philosophical theories which would make of the evolutionary process the progenitor of either the perfect society, or the Spirit or Omega point itself. One of these philosophies is that of Ṣadr al-Dīn Shīrāzī whose transubstantial motion (*al-ḥarakat al-jawhariyyah*) treats fully the significance of movement and becoming while remaining aware of the archetypal realities which manifest themselves through this "substantial becoming."[74] Likewise, Jalāl al-Dīn Rūmī deals extensively with dialectic and the opposition between what Hegel and Marx called thesis and antithesis without ever elevating the historic process to the level of the Truth which is by nature immutable and eternal.[75] It is such sources, whether Islamic or otherwise, that alone can explain the meaning of becoming, the scales of cosmic beings including living forms, the vertical hierarchy stretching from the lowest material form through man to the Divine Presence, and even the mutilation and inversion of these teachings in modern times. And for that very reason it is through the subversion of such traditional teachings that tradition itself is betrayed by forces which parade under a religious guise while helping to accomplish the final short-lived victory of the temporal over the Eternal, of the profane over the sacred.[76]

Ultimately the temporal can no more be made to replace the eternal and to consume it than can the sun be hidden in a well. The traditional doctrine of eternity and the temporal order cannot itself change or evolve because it belongs to the eternal order. This doctrine not only distinguishes between time and eternity but also "modes of time" in accordance with modes of consciousness.[77] Its concern is not only with profane time and God as the Eternal but also with those intermediate modes of becoming associated with eschatology whose final end *is* the abode of eternity in its absolute sense.[78] Finally, this doctrine is concerned with that present now which is eternity as it touches the plane of time, the moment which is both alpha and omega in which man encounters the Eternal that is the Sacred as such, the moment that is the sun-gate through which he passes to the Beyond, becoming finally what he always *is*, a star immortalized in the empyrean of eternity.

> *O soul, seek the Beloved, O friend, seek the Friend,*
> *O watchman, be wakeful: it behooves not a watchman to sleep.*
> *On every side is clamour and tumult, in every street are*
>   *candles and torches,*
> *For tonight the teeming world gives birth to the world*
>   *everlasting.*
> *Thou wert dust and art heart, thou wert ignorant and*
>   *art wise;*
> *He who has dragged thee this far shall drag thee to the*
>   *Beyond through His pull.*
>
>   RŪMĪ[79]

NOTES

1. F. Palmer, "Angelus Silesius: A Seventeenth Century Mystic," *Harvard Theological Review* 11 (1918): 171–202.
2. Associated with the name of the British philosopher D. C. Williams.
3. This view is of importance for modern physics but cannot explain either the reason for our experience of time or its nature. This view has been discussed by such well-known philosophers of science as K. R. Popper, H. Reichenbach, and A. Grünbaum.
4. Such a point of view has always had supporters ranging from McTaggart to those Greek metaphysicians like Parmenides who, looking at things from the point of view of permanence or Being, denied to becoming any reality at all.
5. On works of modern philosophy, esp. the analytical school dealing with time, see the article of J. J. C. Smart on time in the *Encyclopedia of Philosophy*, vol. 8, pp. 126–34.
6. On the Aristotelian notion of time and its medieval modifications and criticisms see H. A. Wolfson, *Crescas' Critique of Aristotle*, Cambridge, Mass., 1929. As far as the concept of time among Islamic philosophers is concerned see Nasr, *Introduction to Islamic Cosmological Doctrines*, chap. 13.
7. Certain modern philosophers such as H. Bergson and following him the modernized Muslim poet and philosopher, Muhammad Iqbal, have made a clear distinction between external time always measured by comparing spatial positions and inward or subjective time which Bergson calls duration. But from the traditional point of view this distinction is hardly new.
8. See F. Schuon, *Du Divin à l'humain*.
9. "Everything God made six thousand years ago and more when He made the world, God makes now instantly (*alzemâle*) . . . He makes the world and all things in this present Now (*gegen würtig nû*)." Eckhart, quoted from the Pfeiffer edition by A. K. Coomaraswamy, *Time and Eternity*, p. 117. This work is an amazing study replete with numerous quotations from the Hindu, Buddhist, Christian, and Islamic traditions on the metaphysics of time and eternity with special emphasis upon the present now in its relation to eternity.
10. This well-known dictum means that the Sufi lives in the eternal present which is the only access to the Eternal. It is also an allusion to the Sufi practice of *dhikr* or invocation which is related to the eternal present and which transforms, sanctifies, and delivers man by saving him from both daydreaming about the future or the past and by facing Reality which resides in the present, the present that experimentally is alone real.
11. "Il punto a cui tutti li tempi son presenti" (*Paradiso*, 17.17–18).
12. Quoted by Coomaraswamy in *Time and Eternity*, pp. 43–44.
13. The *Gulshan-i rāz* says

تراناکی که درک طرة العین   کاف و نون پیدآورد کردنیس

The Powerful One who in a blinking of an eye
Brought the two worlds into being through the k and n of kun

(the imperative of the verb "to be" in reference to Quran XXXVI; 82; see discussion in chap. 4, n. 14 above).

14. *Nimisa*, hence *naimisiyah* or "people of the moment" mentioned in the *Chāndogya Upanishad* which corresponds almost exactly to the Sufi *ibn al-waqt*.
15. Variations of the myth of the "sleepers of the cave" abound among nearly all peoples. For the spiritual significance of this myth and the Quranic account as they

affect the relation between Islam and Christianity see L. Massignon, "Recherche sur la valeur eschatologique de la Légende des VII Dormants chez les musulmans," *Actes 20ᵉ Congrès International des Orientalists*, 1938, pp. 302–3; and *Les Sept dormants d'Éphèse* (*Ahl al-kahf*) *en Islam et en Chrétienté*, 3 vols., avec le concours d'Emile Dermenghem, Paris, 1955–57.

16. We do not of course want to deny other psychological factors which facilitate the rapid passage of time including dispersions of all kinds. But it is noteworthy to remember that even in such cases the person in question experiences a rapid passage of time only if he is enjoying the activity in question, even if that act be spiritually worthless or even harmful. No one sitting on a needle experiences the rapid passage of time unless he is an ascetic who no longer feels the pain and whose consciousness is not associated with the negative character of that sensation, even if physiologically one would expect him to experience the pain.

17. The Catholic prayer asking for the blessings and mercy of the Virgin Mary now and at the moment of death indicates clearly the rapport between these two moments.

18. The three terms *sarmad*, *azal*, and *abad* refer to the same reality, namely, the Eternal, but under three different rapports: *sarmad* being eternity in itself, *abad* eternity with respect to what stands "in front of" the present moment of experience, and *azal* what stands behind and before this moment. *Azal* is related to the Eternal from which man has come and *abad* to the Eternal to which he shall journey after death, while from the point of view of eternity itself there is no before or after, all being *sarmad*.

19. Ḥāfiẓ says,

دوردکلطف ازل رهنمون شود حافظ   ورنه تا به ابد شرمسار خود باشم

May the pre-eternal [azal] *grace be the guide of Ḥāfiẓ,*
Otherwise I shall remain in shame until post-eternity [abad].

20. See R. C. Zaehner, *Zurvan, a Zoroastrian Dilemma*, Oxford, 1955.

21. Quoted in Coomaraswamy, *Time and Eternity*, p. 15, where he has dealt fully with the distinction between time and Time, the second being none other than eternity.

22. *Yikī būd yikī nabūd; ghayr az khudā hīchkī nabūd.*

23. This doctrine has been expounded and explained in numerous works of both a traditional and nontraditional character during the past half century. See, for example, Guénon, *Formes traditionnelles et cycles cosmiques*, Paris, 1970; and M. Eliade, *The Myth of the Eternal Return* (also published as *Cosmos and History*), trans. W. Trask, New York, 1974.

24. Considered by some to be 4,320,000,000 years.

25. This point is emphasized by Guénon in many of his works but overlooked by M. Eliade in his otherwise masterly study *Cosmos and History* or *The Myth of Eternal Return*.

26. On the symbolism of the hourglass see F. Schuon, "Some Observations on the Symbolism of the Hourglass," in his *Logic and Transcendence*, pp. 165–72.

27. On the Zoroastrian concept of history and the 12,000 year period which ends with the victory of light over darkness see A. V. Jackson, *Zoroastrian Studies*, New York, 1938, pp. 110–15; and H. S. Nyberg, "Questions de cosmogonie et de cosmologie mazdéene," *Journal Asiatique* 219 (1929): 2ff.

28. Many episodes of sacred history are found in both the Bible and the Quran although not always in the same versions. But the Quran seems to be much more interested in the transhistorical significance of these events for the soul of man and his entelechy rather than the understanding of God's will in history or historical events themselves. There is in fact a singular lack of concern with time as a dimension of reality as it is found even in traditional Western thought of the type associated with St. Augustine.

29. According to a ḥadīth, "This world is the cultivating field for the other world,"

الدنيا مزرعة الآخرة

that is, the fruit of man's actions in this world affect the state of his soul in the hereafter. It is perfectly possible to take the life of this world very seriously as it concerns man's final end without taking history as seriously as most Western thinkers have taken it. The case of Islam is a perfect case in point that there are not just two possibilities as many modern scholars claim, either the West taking history and this world seriously or the Oriental, and esp. Hindu, view for which history is of no consequence. Such a reductionist view fails to distinguish between this world as the cultivating ground for eternity and history as determining the nature of Reality or affecting it in some final and fundamental way.

30. See Abū Bakr Sirāj al-Dīn, "The Islamic and Christian Conceptions of the March of Time," *The Islamic Quarterly* 1 (1954): 179–93.

31. "The characteristic of the traditional solution of the space-time problem is that reality is both *in and out of* space, both *in and out of* time." W. Urban, *The Intelligible World, Metaphysics and Value*, New York, 1929, p. 270.

32. This famous work opposed the Biblical doctrine of the creation of the world *ex nihilo* to the Greek doctrine of the "eternity" of the world and became the source and beginning for numerous discussions and treatises on the subject which in Islamic philosophy is called *al-ḥudūth waʾl-qidam*. But the truth of this matter was not to be exhausted by its reduction to one of these categories, hence the incessant debate about the meaning of *ex nihilo* itself among Muslim, Jewish, and Christian authors to which Wolfson has devoted many studies, some of the most important of which have been assembled in his *Essays in the History of Philosophy and Religion*.

33. One of the most thorough philosophical discussions of this issue in Islamic philosophy during the past few decades is that of ʿAllāmah Ṭabāṭabāʾī in his *Uṣūl-i falsafah wa rawish-i riʾālizm*, 5 vols., Qum, 1332–50 (A. H., solar).

34. Jalāl al-Dīn Rūmī discusses the theme of *ḥudūth* and *qidam* in both his poetical and prose works of which one of the most astonishing is in the *Fīhi mā fīhi*. See *Discourses of Rumi*, trans. A. J. Arberry, London, 1961, pp. 149–50.

35. That is why Coomaraswamy in his *Time and Eternity* deals so extensively with atomism, Hindu, Buddhist, and Islamic. He also discusses in detail why the now is ever-present and yet not "part" of time.

36. *Lawāʾih*, trans. E. H. Whinfield and M. M. Kazvīnī, London, 1978, pp. 42–45.

37. On the renewal of creation in Sufism see T. Izutsu, "The Concept of Perpetual Creation in Islamic Mysticism and Zen Buddhism," in Nasr (ed.), *Mélanges offerts à Henry Corbin*, pp. 115–48; idem, "Creation and the Timeless Order of Things: A Study in the Mystical Philosophy of ʿAyn al-Quḍāt," *Philosophical Forum*, no. 4 (1972):124–40. We have also dealt with this issue in *Science and Civilization in Islam*, esp. chap. 13; and Burckhardt, *Introduction to Sufi Doctrine*, chap. 10.

38. If all of the ways in which Christianity has emphasized the significance of history be considered, even Judaism would have to be excluded leaving Christianity as the only religion with such a particular attitude toward history.

39. The Christian idea of *kairos*, a welcome time, the right and proper time, or the fullness of time, mentioned in the Gospel of Luke, contains the seed of that further theological elaboration of the meaning of history which is of concern here.

40. It is amazing how so many young people of the present day lack an awareness of or interest in history, seeking to live as if they had no history.

41. We use the term evolution here to mean the belief that through natural agencies and processes one species is transformed into another and not adaptations, modifications, and changes which do occur within a particular species in adapting itself to a changed set of natural conditions. Some scientists in fact distinguish between trans-

formism implying change of one species into another and evolution as the biological transformations within a species. See M. Vernet, *Vernet contre Teilhard de Chardin*, Paris, 1965 p. 30. If we use evolution in the sense of transformism in biology it is because it contains a more general philosophical meaning outside the domain of biology not to be found in the more restricted term transformism.

42. "For in its turn Evolution has become the intolerant religion of nearly all educated Western men. It dominates their thinking, their speech and the hopes of their civilization." E. Shute, *Flaws in the Theory of Evolution*, Nutley, N.J., 1976, p. 228.

43. In the late nineteenth century the president of the American Association and an avowed defender of "the scientific method," Professor Marsh, said, "I need offer no argument for evolution, since to doubt evolution is to doubt science, and science is only another name for truth." Quoted in D. Dewar, *Difficulties of the Evolution Theory*, London, 1931, p. 3. One wonders by what definition of science such a statement, which is so typical when the question of evolution is discussed, can be called scientific.

44. On this theme see Coomaraswamy, "Gradation, Evolution and Reincarnation," in his *Bugbear of Literacy*, chap. 7. See also his *Time and Eternity*, pp. 19–20, where he discusses traditional doctrine of gradation and the "seminal reason" of St. Augustine.

45. See, for example, al-Bīrūnī, *Kitāb al-jamāhir fī maʿrifat al-jawāhir*, Hyderabad, 1935, p. 80. This has led certain Western scholars to claim that such Muslim scientists were exponents of Darwinism before Darwin. See J. Z. Wilczynski, "On the Presumed Darwinism of Alberuni Eight Hundred Years before Darwin," *Isis* 50 (Dec. 1959):459–66, which follows the earlier studies of Fr. Dieterici and others. But as we have sought to show in our *Introduction to Islamic Cosmological Doctrines*, pp. 147–48, and elsewhere, the Muslim sources are referring to the traditional theory of gradation rather than the Darwinian theory of evolution.

46. This type of criticism has been developed extensively by A. E. Wilder Smith, who is a biochemist, pharmacologist, and mathematician. See his *Man's Origin, Man's Destiny*, Wheaton, Ill., 1968; *A Basis for a New Biology*, Stuttgart, 1976; and *Herkunft und Zukunft des Menschen*, Basel, 1966.

47. An extensive argument concerning the difference between physical energy associated with inert matter and vital energy associated with living forms is given by M. Vernet in his *La Grande illusion de Teilhard de Chardin*, Paris, 1964.

48. See his *Guide for the Perplexed*, p. 133, where Schumacher writes, "Evolutionism is not science; it is science fiction, even a kind of hoax."

49. Among the growing number of scientific works critical of the theory of evolution one can mention D. Dewar, *The Transformist Illusion*, Murfreesboro, 1955; his already cited *Difficulties of the Evolution Theory*; Shute, op. cit.; L. Bounoure, *Déterminisme et finalité*, Paris, 1957; E. L. Grant-Watson, *Nature Abounding*, London, 1941; and G. Sermonti and R. Fondi, *Dopo Darwin*, Milan, 1980.

During the past few years a number of works against the Darwinian theory of evolution have appeared from specifically Christian circles but from the scientific and not just theological or religious point of view. See, for example, D. Gish, *Evolution, the Fossils Say No*, San Diego, Calif., 1980; B. Davidheiser, *Evolution and Christian Faith*, Phillipsburg, N.J., 1978; H. Hiebert, *Evolution: Its Collapse in View?*, Beaverledge, Alberta, Canada, 1979; and H. M. Morris, *The Twilight of Evolution*, Grand Rapids, Mich., 1978. Most of these works base the religious aspect of their criticism solely upon Christian sources without reference to other traditions, but they also all rely upon scientific criticism of the theory of evolution and not just "Biblical evidence".

50. "Some biologists appreciate the fact that the lack of fossils intermediate between the great groups requires explanation unless the doctrine of evolution in any of its present forms is to be abandoned." Dewar, *Difficulties of Evolution Theory*, p. 141.

51. Ibid., pp. 142ff.

52. In the case of plants, "geological problems raised by paleo-botany are so great that a botanist must question the evolutionary sequence of plant forms." Shute, op. cit., p. 14.

53. Referring to the lack of a trace of life in the pre-Cambrian, Shute writes, "These

despairing suggestions point up the remarkable dilemma of the evolutionist who leans on Palaeontology for its customary support. What greater degree of disproof could Palaeontology provide? Millions of years of 'NO' is indeed a resounding 'NO'!" Shute, op. cit., p. 6.

54. "Every text on Evolution or on Biology is replete with illustrations of adaptation. I do not wish to repeat too many of these, but to adduce a few of the little-known and more extraordinary adaptations—adaptations so complex and refined that evolutionary theory must be very hard pressed to explain them. The notion of a designing, all-wise Creator fits them much better." Shute, *Flaws in the Theory of Evolution*, pp. 122–23.

55. One of the leading biologists of France, J. Rostand, writes, "The world postulated by transformism is a fairy world, phantasmagoric, surrealistic. The chief point, to which one always returns, is that we have never been present even in a small way at *one* authentic phenomenon of evolution." Yet he adds, "I firmly believe—because I see no means of doing otherwise—that mammals have come from lizards, and lizards from fish; but when I declare and when I think such a thing, I try not to avoid seeing its indigestible enormity and I prefer to leave vague the origin of these scandalous metamorphoses rather than add to their improbability that of a ludicrous interpretation." Quoted in Burckhardt, op. cit., p. 143.

56. It is amazing that two of the leading biologists of Italy should write at the end of a major criticism of Darwinism, "Il risultato a cui crediamo di dover condurre non pùo essere, pertanto, che il sequente: la biologia non ricaverà alcun vantaggio nel sequire gli orientamenti di Lamarck, di Darwin e degli iperdarwinisti moderni; al contrario, essa dere allontanarsi quanto prima della strettoie e dai vicoli ciechi del mito evoluzionistico, per riprendere il suo cammino sicuro lungo le strade aperte e luminose della Tradizione." G. Sermonti and R. Fondi, *Dopo Darwin*, pp. 334–35. This work contains a wealth of scientific arguments drawn all the way from biochemistry through paleontology against the evolutionary theory of Darwin.

57. "The speculations of Teilhard de Chardin provide a striking example of a theology that has succumbed to microscopes and telescopes, to machines and to their philosophical and social consequences, a 'fall' that would have been unthinkable had there been here the slightest direct intellective knowledge of the immaterial realities. The 'inhuman' side of the doctrine in question is highly significant." Schuon, *Understanding Islam*, p. 32.

58. On Śrī Aurobindo and Teilhard de Chardin and their "evolutionary religion" see R. C. Zaehner, *Evolution in Religion: A Study in Śrī Aurobindo and Pierre Teilhard de Chardin*, Oxford, 1971; also his *Matter and Spirit, Their Convergence in Eastern Religions, Marx, and Teilhard de Chardin*, New York, 1963, which is a study of religion from the Teilhardian perspective. As Zaehner points out, in the case of both Śrī Aurobindo and Teilhard de Chardin, there is a passionate belief in evolution and the salvation of the whole of humanity in the Marxist sense along with the "mystical" vision of the spiritual world which Zaehner interprets as a new synthesis but which from the traditional point of view cannot but be the eclipse of *Ātman* by *māyā* to such a degree that it can only occur in the deep twilight of a human cycle before the blinding Sun of the Self lifts once again all veils of illusion, evaporates all clouds of doubt, and melts all those idols of perversion and inversion of the truth.

59. See P. Chanchard, *Man and Cosmos—Scientific Phenomenology in Teilhard de Chardin*, New York, 1965, whose chap. 8 is entitled "The Resacralization of the Profane World." He writes, "Here is the real meaning of Teilhard's work. . . . It is a matter of *resacralizing a profane world by giving even the profane its own sacred character*" (p. 170).

60. On Teilhard de Chardin see P. Smulders, *Theologie und Evolution, Versuch über Teilhard de Chardin*, Essen, 1963; E. Rideau, *Teilhard de Chardin: a Guide to His Thought*, trans. R. Hague, London, 1967; H. de Lubac, *The Eternal Feminine*, trans. R. Hague, London, 1971; H. de Lubac, *The Faith of Teilhard de Chardin*, trans. R. Hague, London, 1965; C. Cuénot, *Teilhard de Chardin et la pensée catholique*, Paris, 1965; and M. Barthélemy-Madaule, *Bergson et Teilhard de Chardin*, Paris, 1963. There is a veritable flood of writings on him mostly by admirers or apologists while the most acute criticisms of a scientific nature have come from such French scientists as M. Vernet.

61. "The modern psyche is dominated by time, matter, change and is relatively blind to space, Substance and Eternity. To oppose one's thoughts to the Theory of Evolution is to think in a way which is contrary to the common tendency of the modern psyche." M. Negus, "Reactions to the Theory of Evolution," in *Studies in Comparative Religion*, Summer–Autumn 1978, p. 191.

62. Teilhard's type of pseudospiritual evolutionism could not in fact have gained wide support without that psychological attitude that has been already molded by the influence of the ideas of progress and evolution.

63. This being metaphysically a caricature and parody of "O Holy Mother," for the Virgin represents esoterically the maternal and expansive element of the Divine, the feminine *materia in divinis* which generates the Logos.

64. From his *L'Énergie humaine*, Paris, 1962, p. 74 and p. 125. On Teilhardian idolatry see K. Almquist, "Aspects of Teilhardian Idolatry," *Studies in Comparative Religion*, Summer–Autumn, 1978, pp. 195–203.

65. The prevalent error of orientalists in identifying such doctrines as *waḥdat al-wujūd* in Sufism with pantheism originates from the same error that lies at the origin of Teilhardian pantheism, except that the orientalists at least do not pretend to speak for Catholic theology.

66. "All errors concerning the world and God consist either in a 'naturalistic' denial of the discontinuity and so also of transcendence—whereas it is on the basis of this transcendence that the whole edifice of science should have been raised—or else in a failure to understand the metaphysical and 'descending' continuity which in no way abolishes the discontinuity starting from the relative." Schuon, *Understanding Islam*, pp. 108–9.

67. See Almquist, op. cit., p. 201, where the spiritual substance which through coagulation finally produces matter is discussed in the light of the primacy of consciousness and subjectivity with which all knowing of necessity begins.

68. Quoted in Almquist, op. cit., pp. 202–3.

69. "Teilhard n'était pas un biologiste; la physiologie générale en particulier lui était étrangère. Il en résulte que les déductions qu'il tire des perspectives qu'il prend sur le plan philosophique et religieux se trouvent faussées, dès lors que les bases elles-mêmes sur lesquelles il entendait se fonder, s'effondrent." Vernet, *La Grande illusion de Teilhard de Chardin*, p. 107.

70. On finality in this sense see L. Bounoure, *Déterminisme et finalité*.

71. "Certains font honneur à Teilhard d'avoir conçu une unité cosmique; or, cette unité est fausse. Tout réduire à une seule et même énergie physique d'où découleraient tous les phénomènes, selon des processus purement matériels, ne répond pas, nous venons de le voir, à la realité du monde et de la vie. Telle a été l'immense illusion de Teilhard." Vernet, op. cit., p. 123.

72. "La nature est plus platonicienne que ne le croit le P. Teilhard et pas du tout marxiste." R. Johannet, introd. to *Vernet contre Teilhard de Chardin*, p. 22, n. 2.

73. T. Burckhardt, "Cosmology and Modern Science," in J. Needleman (ed.), *The Sword of Gnosis*, p. 153.

74. The doctrine of transubstantial motion presents, within the cadre of traditional teachings, one of the most systematically exposed and logically appealing formulations of the meaning of change in the light of permanence. It is associated with the school of Ṣadr al-Dīn Shīrāzī, who instead of limiting motion to the four accidents of quality, quantity, position, and place as did the Peripatetics, also accepts motion in the category of substance without in any way denying the reality of the immutable archetypes or essences. For an explanation of this difficult doctrine see the articles of Sayyid Abu'l-Hasan Qazwīnī and ʿAllāmah Ṭabāṭabāʾī in S. H. Nasr (ed.), *Mullā Ṣadrā Commemoration Volume*, Tehran, 1380 (A. H., solar); also, S. H. Nasr, *Islamic Life and Thought*, pt. 3, pp. 158ff.; and idem, *Ṣadr al-Dīn Shīrāzī*, pp. 932–61.

75. It is this fact that has caused certain modern Marxists in the Islamic world to claim Mawlānā Jalāl al-Dīn Rūmī as their ancestor, misinterpreting completely the dialectic of Rūmī with its vertical and transcendent dimension to make it conform to the Hegelian-Marxist one.

76. It is interesting to note that if such movements in Hinduism and Christianity have resulted in figures like Śri Aurobindo and Teilhard de Chardin, in Buddhism and Islam they have given rise to that unholy wedding of ideas taken from these religions and Marxism by those who have called themselves Buddhist Marxists and Islamic Marxists. The political consequences of the thought of the first group should at least cause a moment of pause for those who hoist the banner of Islamic Marxism.

77. For example, in Sufism certain authorities distinguish between external time (*zamān-i āfāqī*, literally "time of the horizons") and inward time (*zamān-i anfusī*, literally "time of the souls") in reference to the Quranic verse already cited concerning the manifestation of the portents (*āyāt*) of God "upon the horizons (*āfāq*) and within themselves (*anfus*)." They also state that each world through which the spiritual adept journeys has its own "time." On *zamān-i āfāqī* and *zamān-i anfusī* see H. Corbin, *En Islam iranien*, vol. 1, pp. 177ff.

78. No exposition of traditional doctrines would be complete without a discussion of eschatology which constitutes an essential teaching of every religion and whose full significance can only be grasped through the esoteric dimension of tradition and the *scientia sacra* which provides the necessary metaphysical knowledge for the treatment of the subject. The bewildering complexity of eschatological realities which lie beyond the ken of man's earthly imagination can only be grasped through the revealed truths as they are elucidated and elaborated by an intelligence imbued with the sense of the sacred, but even in this case it is not possible to say the last word about them.

79.

Trans. R. A. Nicholson, in *Selected Poems from the Dīvāni Shamsi Tabrīz*, Cambridge, 1898, pp. 141–43 (revised).

It is so significant that Zaehner in his already cited work on Teilhard de Chardin and Śri Aurobindo quotes from this poem as an affirmation of the evolution of spirit from matter, whereas this whole poem is about the death of the saint himself, that is Rūmī, and the miracle of the return of the purified and sanctified soul which has itself descended from the realm of the Eternal into the stream of becoming back to the abode of the Beloved.

CHAPTER EIGHT

Traditional Art as Fountain of Knowledge and Grace

Law and art are the children of the Intellect.
Plato, LAWS

Beauty absolutely is the cause of all things being in
harmony (*consonantia*) and of illumination (*claritas*);
because, moreover, in the likeness of light it sends forth
to everything the beautifying distributives of its over
fontal raying; and for that it summons all things to itself.
Dionysius the Areopagite, DE DIVINIS NOMINIBUS

Tradition speaks to man not only through human words but also
through other forms of art. Its message is written not only upon
pages of books and within the grand phenomena of nature but also
upon the face of those works of traditional and especially sacred art
which, like the words of sacred scripture and the forms of nature, are
ultimately a revelation from that Reality which is the source of both
tradition and the cosmos. Traditional art is inseparable from sacred
knowledge because it is based upon a science of the cosmic which is
of a sacred and inward character and in turn is the vehicle for the
transmission of a knowledge which is of a sacred nature. Traditional
art is at once based upon and is a channel for both knowledge and
grace or that *scientia sacra* which *is* both knowledge and of a sacred
character. Sacred art which lies at the heart of traditional art has a
sacramental function and is, like religion itself, at once truth and
presence, and this quality is transmitted even to those aspects of

traditional art which are not strictly speaking sacred art, that is, are not directly concerned with the liturgical, ritual, cultic, and esoteric elements of the tradition in question but which nevertheless are created according to traditional norms and principles.[1]

To understand how traditional art is related to knowledge of the sacred and sacred knowledge, it is necessary first of all to clarify what is meant by traditional art. Since we have already identified religion with that which binds man to God and which lies at the heart of tradition, it might be thought that traditional art is simply religious art. This is not at all the case, however, especially since in the West from the Renaissance onward, traditional art has ceased to exist while religious art continues. Religious art is considered religious because of the subject or function with which it is concerned and not because of its style, manner of execution, symbolism, and nonindividual origin. Traditional art, however, is traditional not because of its subject matter but because of its conformity to cosmic laws of forms, to the laws of symbolism, to the formal genius of the particular spiritual universe in which it has been created, its hieratic style, its conformity to the nature of the material used, and, finally, its conformity to the truth within the particular domain of reality with which it is concerned.[2] A naturalistic painting of Christ is religious art but not at all traditional art whereas a medieval sword, book cover, or even stable is traditional art but not directly religious art although, because of the nature of tradition, indirectly even pots and pans produced in a traditional civilization are related to the religion which lies at the heart of that tradition.[3]

Traditional art is concerned with the truths contained in the tradition of which it is the artistic and formal expression. Its origin therefore is not purely human. Moreover, this art must conform to the symbolism inherent in the object with which it is concerned as well as the symbolism directly related to the revelation whose inner dimension this art manifests. Such an art is aware of the essential nature of things rather than their accidental aspects. It is in conformity with the harmony which pervades the cosmos and the hierarchy of existence which lies above the material plane with which art deals, and yet penetrates into this plane. Such an art is based on the real and not the illusory so that it remains conformable to the nature of the object with which it is concerned rather than imposing a subjective and illusory veil upon it.

Traditional art, moreover, is functional in the most profound sense of this term, namely, that it is made for a particular use whether it be the worshiping of God in a liturgical act or the eating of a meal. It is, therefore, utilitarian but not with the limited meaning of utility identified with purely earthly man in mind. Its utility concerns pontifical man for whom beauty is as essential a dimension of life and a need as the house that shelters man during the winter cold. There is no place here for such an idea as "art for art's sake," and traditional civilizations have never had museums nor ever produced a work of art just for itself.[4] Traditional art might be said to be based on the idea of art for man's sake, which, in the traditional context where man is God's vicegerent on earth, the axial being on this plane of reality, means ultimately art for God's sake, for to make something for man as a theomorphic being is to make it for God. In traditional art there is a blending of beauty and utility which makes of every object of traditional art, provided it belongs to a thriving traditional civilization not in the stage of decay, something at once useful and beautiful.

It is through its art that tradition forges and forms an ambience in which its truths are reflected everywhere, in which men breathe and live in a universe of meaning in conformity with the reality of the tradition in question. That is why, in nearly every case of which we have a historical record, the tradition has created and formalized its sacred art before elaborating its theologies and philosophies. Saint Augustine appears long after the sarcophagus art of the catacombs which marks the beginning of Christian art, as Buddhist architecture and sculpture came long before Nagārjuna. Even in Islam, which developed its theological and philosophical schools rapidly, even the early Muʿtazilites, not to speak of the Ashʿarites or al-Kindī and the earliest Islamic philosophers, follow upon the wake of the construction of the first Islamic mosques which were already distinctly Islamic in character. In order to breathe and function in a world, religion must remold that world not only mentally but also formally; and since most human beings are much more receptive to material forms than to ideas and material forms leave the deepest effect upon the human soul even beyond the mental plane, it is the traditional art which is first created by the tradition in question. This is especially true of sacred art which exists already at the beginning of the tradition for it is related to those liturgical and cultic practices which emanate directly from the revelation. Therefore, the first icon is painted by Saint

Luke through the inspiration of the angel, the traditional chanting of the Vedas is "revealed" with the Vedas, the Quranic psalmody originates with the Prophet himself, etc. The role of traditional art in the forging of a particular mentality and the creation of an atmosphere in which contemplation of the most profound metaphysical truths is made possible are fundamental to the understanding of both the character of traditional art and the sapiential dimension of tradition itself.

From this point of view art is seen as a veil that hides but also reveals God. There are always within every tradition those who have belittled the significance of forms of art in that they have gone beyond them, but this has always been in a world in which these forms have existed, not where they have been cast aside and destroyed. Those who have eschewed forms of art have been certain types of contemplatives who have realized the supraformal realities, those who, to use the language of Sufism, having broken the nutshell and eaten the nut inside, cast the shell aside. But obviously one cannot throw away a shell that one does not even possess. To go beyond forms is one thing and to fall below them another. To pierce beyond the phenomenal surface to the noumenal reality, hence to see God through forms and not forms as veils of the Divine is one thing and to reject forms of traditional art in the name of an imagined abstract reality above formalism is quite another. Sacred knowledge in contrast to desacralized mental activity is concerned with the supraformal Essence but is perfectly aware of the vital significance of forms in the attainment of the knowledge of that Essence. This knowledge even when speaking of the Supreme Reality above all forms does so in a chant which is in conformity with the laws of cosmic harmony and in a language which, whether prose or poetry, is itself an art form.[5] That is why the possessor of such a knowledge in its realized aspect is the first person to confirm the significance of forms of traditional art and the relation of this art to the truth and the sacred; for art reflects the truth to the extent that it is sacred, and it emanates the presence of the sacred to the extent that it is true.

It is of course pontifical or traditional man who is the maker of traditional art; therefore, his theomorphic nature is directly related to this art and its significance. Being a theomorphic creature, man is himself a work of art. The human soul when purified and dressed in the garment of spiritual virtues[6] is itself the highest kind of beauty in this world, reflecting directly the Divine Beauty. Even the human body in both its male and female forms is a perfect work of art, reflecting something of the essentiality of the human state. Moreover, there is no more striking reflection of Divine Beauty on earth than a human face in which physical and spiritual beauty are combined. Now man is a work of art because God is the Supreme Artist. That is why He is called *al-muṣawwir* in Islam, that is, He who creates forms,[7] why Śiva brought the arts down from Heaven, why in the medieval craft initiations, as in Freemasonry, God is called the Grand Architect of the Universe. But God is not only the Grand Architect or Geometer; He is also the Poet, the Painter, the Musician. This is the reason for man's ability to build, write poetry, paint, or compose music, although not all forms of art have been necessarily cultivated in all traditions—the types of art developed depending upon the spiritual and also ethnic genius of a traditional world and humanity.

Being "created in the image of God" and therefore a supreme work of art, man is also an artist who, in imitating the creative powers of his Maker, realizes his own theomorphic nature. The spiritual man, aware of his vocation, is not only the musician who plucks the lyre to create music. He is himself the lyre upon which the Divine Artist plays, creating the music which reverberates throughout the cosmos, for as Rūmī says, "We are like the lyre which thou pluckest."[8] If Promethean man creates art not in imitation but in competition with God, hence the naturalism in Promethean art which tries to imitate the outward form of nature, pontifical man creates art in full consciousness of his imitating God's creativity through not competition with but submission to the Divine Model which tradition provides for him. He therefore imitates nature not in its external forms but in its manner of operation as asserted so categorically by Saint Thomas. If in knowing God man fulfills his essential nature as *homo sapiens*, in creating art he also fulfills another aspect of that nature as *homo faber*. In creating art in conformity with cosmic laws and in imitation of realities of the archetypal world, man realizes himself, his theomorphic nature as a work of art made by the hands of God; and likewise in creating an art based on his revolt against Heaven, he separates himself even further from his own Divine Origin. The role of art in the fall of Promethean man in the modern world has been central in that this art has been both an index of the new stages of the inner fall of man from his sacred norm and a major element in the actualization of this fall, for man comes to identify himself with what he makes.

It is not at all accidental that the break up of the unity of the

Christian tradition in the West coincided with the rise of the Reformation. Nor is it accidental that the philosophical and scientific revolts against the medieval Christian world view were contemporary with the nearly complete destruction of traditional Christian art and its replacement by a Promethean and humanistic art which soon decayed into that unintelligible nightmare of baroque and rococo religious art that drove many an intelligent believer out of the church. The same phenomenon can be observed in ancient Greece and the modern Orient. When the sapiential dimension of the Greek tradition began to decay, Greek art became humanistic and this-worldly, the art which is already criticized by Plato who held the sacerdotal, traditional art of ancient Egypt in such high esteem. Likewise, in the modern East, intellectual decline has everywhere been accompanied by artistic decline. Conversely, wherever one does observe major artistic creations of a traditional character, there must be a living intellectual and sapiential tradition present even if nothing is known of it externally. Even if at least until very recently the West knew nothing of the intellectual life of Safavid Persia,[9] one could be sure that the creation of even one dome like that of the Shaykh Luṭfallāh mosque or the Shāh mosque, which are among the greatest masterpieces of traditional art and architecture, would be itself proof that such an intellectual life existed at that time. A living orthodox tradition with its sapiential dimension intact is essential and necessary for the production of major works of traditional art, especially sacred art, because of that inner nexus which exists between traditional art and sacred knowledge.

Traditional art is brought into being through such a knowledge and is able to convey and transmit this knowledge. It is the vehicle of an intellectual intuition and a sapiential message which transcends both the individual artist and the collective psyche of the world to which he belongs. On the contrary, humanistic art is able to convey only individualistic inspirations or at best something of the collective psyche to which the individual artist belongs but never an intellectual message, the sapience which is our concern. It can never become the fountain of either knowledge or grace because of its divorce from those cosmic laws and the spiritual presence which characterize traditional art.

Knowledge is transmitted by traditional art through its symbolism, its correspondence with cosmic laws, its techniques, and even the means whereby it is taught through the traditional craft guilds which in various traditional civilizations have combined technical training in the crafts with spiritual instruction. The presence of the medieval European guilds,[10] the Islamic guilds (*aṣnāf* and *futuwwāt*), some of which survive to this day,[11] the training of potters by Zen masters,[12] or of metallurgists in initiatic circles in certain primitive societies,[13] all indicate the close nexus that has existed between the teaching of the techniques of the traditional arts or crafts, which are the same as the arts in a traditional world, and the transmission of knowledge of a cosmological and sometimes metaphysical order.

But in addition to these processes for the transmission of knowledge related to the actual act of creating a work or of explaining the symbolism involved, there is an innate rapport between artistic creation in the traditional sense and sapience. This rapport is based on the nature of man himself as the reflection of the Divine Norm, and also on the inversion which exists between the principial and the manifested order. Man and the world in which he lives both reflect the archetypal world directly and inversely according to the well-known principle of inverse analogy. In the principial order God creates by externalizing. His "artistic" activity is the fashioning of His own "image" or "form." On the human plane this relation is reversed in that man's "artistic" activity in the traditional sense involves not the fashioning of an image in the cosmogonic sense but a return to his own essence in conformity with the nature of the state of being in which he lives. Therefore, the "art" of God implies an externalization and the art of man an internalization. God fashions what God makes and man is fashioned by what man makes;[14] and since this process implies a return to man's own essence, it is inalienably related to spiritual realization and the attainment of knowledge. In a sense, Promethean art is based on the neglect of this principle of inverse analogy. It seeks to create the image of Promethean man outwardly, as if man were God. Hence, the very "creative process" becomes not a means of interiorization and recollection but a further separation from the Source leading step by step to the mutilation of the image of man as *imago Dei*, to the world of subrealism—rather than surrealism—and to purely individualistic subjectivism. This subjectivism is as far removed from the theomorphic image of man as possible; the art it creates cannot in any way act as a vehicle for the transmission of knowledge or grace, although certain cosmic qualities occasionally manifest themselves even in the nontraditional forms of art, since these qualities are like the rays of the sun which finally shine through some crack or opening no matter how much one tries to shut one's living space from the illumination of the light of that Sun which is both light and heat, knowledge, love and grace.[15]

To understand the meaning of traditional art in its relation to knowledge, it is essential to grasp fully the significance of the meaning of form as used in the traditional context (as *forma, morphē, nāma, ṣūrah*, etc.). In modern thought dominated by a quantitative science, the significance of form as that which contains the reality of an object has been nearly lost. It is therefore necessary to recall the traditional meaning of form and remember the attempts made by not only traditional authors but also certain contemporary philosophers and scholars to bring out the ontological significance of form.[16] According to the profound doctrine of Aristotelian hylomorphism, which serves so well for the exposition of the metaphysics of art because it originated most likely as an intellectual intuition related to traditional art, an object is composed of form and matter in such a way that the form corresponds to that which is actual and matter to what is potential in the object in question. Form is that by which an object is what it is. Form is not accidental to the object but determines its very reality. It is in fact the essence of the object which the more metaphysical Neoplatonic commentators of Aristotle interpreted as the image or reflection of the essence rather than the essence itself, the essence belonging to the archetypal world. In any case, form is not accidental but essential to an object whether it be natural or man-made. It has an ontological reality and participates in the total economy of the cosmos according to strict laws. There is a science of forms, a science of a qualitative and not quantitative nature, which is nevertheless an exact science, or objective knowledge, exactitude not being the prerogative of the quantitative sciences alone.

From the point of view of hylomorphism, form *is* the reality of an object on the material level of existence. But it is also, as the reflection of an archetypal reality, the gate which opens inwardly and "upwardly" unto the formless Essence. From another point of view, one can say that each object possesses a form and a content which this form "contains" and conveys. As far as sacred art is concerned, this content is always the sacred or a sacred presence placed in particular forms by revelation which sanctifies certain symbols, forms, and images to enable them to become "containers" of this sacred presence and transforms them into vehicles for the journey across the stream of becoming. Moreover, thanks to those sacred forms which man is able to transcend from within, man is able to penetrate into the inner dimension of his own being and, by virtue of that process, to gain a vision of the inner dimension of all forms. The three grand revelations of the Real, or theophanies, namely, the cosmos or macrocosm, man or the microcosm, and religion, are all comprised of forms which lead to the formless, but only the third enables man to penetrate to the world beyond forms, to gain a vision of forms of both the outer world and his own soul, not as veil but as theophany. Only the sacred forms invested with the transforming power of the sacred through revelation and the Logos which is its instrument can enable man to see God everywhere.

Since man lives in the world of forms, this direct manifestation of the Logos which is revelation or religion in its origin cannot but make use of forms within which man is located. It cannot but sanctify certain forms in order to allow man to journey beyond them. To reach the formless man has need of forms. The miracle of the sacred form lies in fact in its power to aid man to transcend form itself. Traditional art is present not only to remind man of the truths of religion which it reflects in man's fundamental activity of making, as religious ethics or religious law does for man's doing, but also to serve as a support for the contemplation of the Beyond which alone gives ultimate significance to both man's making and man's doing. To denigrate forms as understood in traditional metaphysics is to misunderstand, by token of the same error, the significance of the formless Essence.

At the root of this error which mistakes form for limitation and considers "thought" or "idea" in its mental sense as being more important than form is the abuse of the terms abstract and concrete in modern thought.[17] Modern man, having lost the vision of the Platonic "ideas," confuses the concrete reality of what *scientia sacra* considers as idea with mental concept and then relegates the concrete to the material level. As a result, the physical and the material are automatically associated with the concrete, while ideas, thoughts, and all that is universal, including even the Divinity, are associated with the abstract. Metaphysically, the rapport is just the reverse. God is the concrete Reality par excellence compared to Whom everything else is an abstraction; and on a lower level the archetypal world is concrete and the world below it abstract. The same relation continues until one reaches the world of physical existence in which form is, relatively speaking, concrete and matter the most abstract entity of all.

The identification of material objects with the concrete and mental concepts with the abstract has had the effect of not only destroying the significance of form vis-à-vis matter on the physical plane itself but also obliterating the significance of the bodily and the corporeal as a source of knowledge. This tendency seems to be the reverse of the process of exteriorization and materialization of knowledge, but it is in reality the other side of the same coin. The same civilization that has produced the most materialistic type of thought has also shown the least amount of interest in the "wisdom of the body," in physical forms as a source of knowledge, and in the noncerebral aspects of the human microcosm as a whole. As mentioned already, those within the modern world who have sought to regain knowledge of a sacred order have been also those who have protested most vehemently against this overcerebral interpretation of human experience and who have sought to rediscover the "wisdom of the body," even if this has led in many cases to all kinds of excesses. One does not have to possess extraordinary perspicacity to realize that there is much more intelligence and in fact "food for thought" in the drumbeats of a traditional tribe in Africa than in many a book of modern philosophy. Nor is there any reason why a Chinese landscape painting should not bear a more direct and succinct metaphysical message than not only a philosophical treatise which is antimetaphysical but even one which favors metaphysics, but in which, as a result of a weakness of logic or presentation, the truth of metaphysical ideas is bearly discernible.

The consequence of this inversion of the rapport between the abstract and the concrete has in any case been a major impediment in the appreciation of the significance of forms in both the traditional arts and sciences and the understanding of the possibility of forms of art as vehicles for knowledge of the highest order. This mentality has also prevented many people from appreciating the traditional doctrines of art and the nonhuman and celestial origin of the forms with which traditional art is concerned.

According to the principles of traditional art, the source of the forms which are dealt with by the artist is ultimately divine. As Plato, who along with Plotinus has provided some of the most profound teachings on traditional art in the West, asserts, art is the imitation of paradigms which, whether visible or invisible, reflect ultimately the world of ideas.[18] At the heart of tradition lies the doctrine that art is the nemesis of *paradeigma,* the invisible model or exemplar. But to produce a work of art which possesses beauty and perfection the artist must gaze at the invisible for as Plato says, "The work of the creator, whenever he looks to the unchangeable and fashions the form and nature of his work after an unchangeable pattern, must necessarily be made fair and perfect, but when he looks to the created order only, and uses a created pattern, it is not fair or perfect."[19]

Likewise in India, the origin of the form later externalized by the artist in stone or bronze, on wood or paper, has always been considered to be of a supraindividual origin belonging to the level of reality which Platonism identified with the world of ideas. The appropriate art form is considered to be accessible only through contemplation and inner purification. It is only through them that the artist is able to gain that angelic vision which is the source of all traditional art for at the beginning of the tradition the first works of sacred art, including both the plastic and the sonoral, were made by the angels or *devas* themselves. In the well-known *Śukranītisāra* of Śukrācarya, for example, it is stated, "One should make use of the visual-formulae proper to the angels whose images are to be made. It is for the successful accomplishment of this practice (*yoga*) of visual-formulation that the lineaments of images are prescribed. The human-imager should be expert in this visual-contemplation, since thus, and in no other way, and verily not by direct observation, [can the end be achieved]."[20]

The same type of teachings can be found in all traditions which have produced a sacred art. If the origin of the forms used by this art were not "celestial," how could an Indian statue convey the very principle of life from within? How could we look at an icon and experience ourselves being looked upon by the gaze of eternity? How could a Chinese or Japanese butterfly capture the very essence of the state of being a butterfly? How could Islamic ornamentation reveal on the physical plane the splendor of the mathematical world considered not as abstraction but as concrete archetypal reality? How could one stand at the portal of the Chartres Cathedral and experience standing in the center of the cosmic order if the makers of that cathedral had not had a vision of that center from whose perspective they built the cathedral? Anyone who grasps the significance of traditional art will understand that the origin of the forms with which this art deals is nothing other than that immutable world of the essences or ideas which are also the source of our thoughts and knowledge. That is why the loss of sacred knowledge or gnosis and the ability to think anagogically—not only analogically—goes hand in hand with the destruction of traditional art and its hieratic formal style.[21]

The origin of forms in traditional art can perhaps be better understood if the production of works of art is compared to the constitution of natural objects. According to the Peripatetic philosophies of the medieval period, whether Islamic, Judaic, or Christian, and following Aristotle and his Neoplatonic commentators, objects are composed of form and matter which in the sublunar region undergo constant change. Hence this world is called that of generation and corruption. Whenever a new object comes into being the old form "returns" to the Tenth Intellect, which is called the "Giver of forms" (wāhib al-ṣuwar in Arabic), and a new form is cast by this Intellect upon the matter in question.[22] Therefore, the origin of forms in the natural world is the Intellect. Now, the form of art must be conceived in the same way as far as traditional art is concerned. The source of these forms is the Intellect which illuminates the mind of the artist or the original artist who is emulated by members of a particular school; the artist in turn imposes the form upon the matter in question, matter here being not the philosophical hylē but the material in question, whether it be stone, wood, or anything else which is being fashioned. In this way the artist imitates the operation of nature[23] rather than her external forms.

Moreover, the form which is wed with matter and the form which is the "idea" in the mind of the artist are from the same origin and of the same nature except on different levels of existence. The Greek eidos expresses this doctrine of correspondence perfectly since it means at once form and idea whose origin is ultimately the Logos.

Traditional art, therefore, is concerned with both knowledge and the sacred. It is concerned with the sacred in as much as it is from the domain of the sacred that issue both the tradition itself and the forms and styles which define the formal homogeneity of a particular traditional world.[24]

It is also concerned with knowledge in as much as man must know the manner of operation of nature before being able to imitate it. The traditional artist, whether he possesses direct knowledge of those cosmic laws and principles which determine that "manner of operation" or has simply an indirect knowledge which he has received through transmission, needs such a knowledge of a purely intellectual nature which only tradition can provide. Traditional art is essentially a science just as traditional science is an art. The *ars sine scientia nihil* of Saint Thomas holds true for all traditions and the *scientia* in question here is none other than the *scientia sacra* and its cosmological applications.

Anyone who has studied traditional art becomes aware of the presence of an impressive amount of science which makes such an art possible. Some of this science is of a technical character which nevertheless remains both amazing and mysterious. When one asks how Muslim or Byzantine architects created the domes they did create with the endurance that they have had, or how such perfect acoustics were developed in certain Greek amphitheatres or cathedrals, or how the various angles of the pyramids were made to correlate so exactly with astronomical configurations, or how to build a shaking minaret in Isfahan which goes into sympathetic vibration when the minaret next to it is shaken, one is already facing knowledge of an extraordinary complexity which should at least remove those who possessed it from the ranks of naive simpletons. Even on this level, however, despite all the attempts at "demystification" by positivist historians of art or science, there are amazing questions which remain unanswered. The basic one is that these feats, even if they were to be repeated today, could only be done according to physical laws and discoveries which belong to the past two or three centuries and, as far as we know, simply were not known when these structures were constructed. This fact taken in itself implies that there must be other sciences of nature upon which one can build monuments of outstanding durability and remarkable quality. This would also hold for the preparation of dyes whose colors are dazzling to the eye and which cannot be reproduced today, or steel blades, the knowledge of whose metallurgical processes has been lost.

But these are not the only sciences we have in mind. The *scientia* without which art would be nothing is not just another kind of physics which we happen to have forgotten. It is a science of cosmic harmony, of correspondences, of the multidimensional reality of forms, of sympathy between earthly forms and celestial influences, of the rapport between colors, orientations, configurations, shapes, and also sounds and smells and the soul of man. It is a science which differs from modern science not only in its approach and method but in its nature. Yet it is a science, essentially a sacred science accessible only in the cadre of tradition which alone enables the intellect in its human reflection to realize its full potentialities.[25] The difference between this science and modern science is that this science cannot be attained save through intellectual intuition, which in turn requires a certain nobility of character and the acquiring of virtues which are inseparable from knowledge in the traditional context as attested to by the very manner in which both the traditional arts and sciences are taught by the master to the disciple. There are of course exceptions but that is only because the "Spirit bloweth where it listeth."

The *scientia* with which art is concerned is therefore related to the esoteric dimension of tradition and not the exoteric. As man is a being who acts and makes things, religion must provide principles and norms for both the world of moral action and the activity of making. Usually exoterism is concerned with that world in which man must act for the good and against evil, but it is not concerned with those principles and norms which govern the correct making of things. These principles cannot but issue from the inner or esoteric dimension of the tradition. That is why the most profound expositions of the meaning of Christian art are found in the writings of such a figure as Meister Eckhart[26] or the masters of apophatic and mystical theology in the Orthodox Church.[27] That is why also Western Islamicists and historians of art have had such difficulty in finding sources for the Islamic philosophy, or rather metaphysics, of art while they have been searching in treatises of theology and jurisprudence. Besides the oral tradition which still continues in some parts of the Islamic world, as far as certain cosmological principles pertaining to art are concerned, the written sources do also exist, except that they are not usually seen for what they are. The most profound explanation of the significance of Islamic art is to be found in a work such as the *Mathnawī* of Jalāl al-Dīn Rūmī and not in books of either jurisprudence or *kalām* which, although very important, concern man's actions and religious beliefs rather than the principles of an interiorizing art which leads man back to the One. There are also treatises of an "occult" nature concerning those arts which can be comprehended only in the light of esoterism.[28]

Likewise, in Japan it is Zen which has produced the greatest masterpieces of Japanese art, from rock gardens to screen paintings, while those Sung paintings which are among the greatest master-pieces of world art are products of Taoism and not the social aspect of the Chinese tradition associated with Confucian ethics. As Wang Yu, the Chi'ing painter said, "Although painting is only one of the fine arts, it contains the Tao."[29] All art has its Tao, its principle which is related to the principles which dominate the cosmos, while painting being the traditional art par excellence in China manifests the Tao most directly. To paint according to the Tao is not to emulate the outward but the inner principles of things; hence again, the science with the aid of which the Chinese painter captures the very essence of natural forms is by definition related to the esoteric dimension of the tradition. The fruit and application of such an inward science of the cosmos is the Sung painting, the Hindu temple, the mosque or cathedral or all the other masterpieces of traditional art which are immersed in a beauty of celestial origin, while the application of an outward and externalized science of nature which rebelled against the Christian tradition once its esoteric dimension was eclipsed is the subway and the skyscraper. Even when there is some element of beauty in the works produced as a result of the applications of such a science, it is of a fragmented nature and manifests itself only here and there because beauty is an aspect of reality and cannot but manifest itself whenever and wherever there is something which possesses a degree of reality.

There is, however, another basic reason why art which deals with the material plane is related to the esoteric or most inward dimension of tradition. According to the well-known Hermetic saying, "that which is lowest symbolizes that which is highest," material existence which is the lowest level symbolizes and reflects the Intellect or the archetypal essences which represent the highest level. Through this fundamental cosmological law upon which the science of symbols is based, material form reflects the Intellect in a more direct manner than the subtle level or the pysche which is ontologically higher but which does not reflect the highest level as directly. In various tradi-tions it is taught that the revelation descends not only into the mind and soul but also into the body of the prophet or founder, not to speak of traditions in which the founder as incarnation or *avatār is* himself the message. In this case the *avatār* saves not only through his words and thoughts but also through the beauty of his body which, in the case of Buddhism, is the origin of the whole of Buddhist iconography. In Christianity also it is the blood and body of Christ that is consumed in the Eucharist and not his thoughts, which means that the revelation penetrated into his bodily form.

Even in Islam where the message is clearly distinguished from the messenger, traditional sources teach that the revelation did not only enter the mind but also the body of the Prophet to the extent that, when he received the revelation on horseback, his horse could hardly support the weight and would buckle under it. Also the night of the descent of the Quranic revelation, called "The Night of Power" (*laylat al-qadr*), is associated with the very body of the Prophet while his nocturnal ascent to Heaven (*al-miʿrāj*) is also considered to have been bodily (*al-miʿrāj al-jismānī*) according to all traditional sources. All of these instances point to the fact, fundamental for the understanding of traditional art, that the material is the direct reflection of the highest level which is the spiritual and not the intermediate psychic state and that art, although concerned with the most outward plane of existence which is the material, is related by token of this very principle of inversion to what is most inward in a tradition. That is why a canvas as icon can become the locus of Divine Presence and support for the contemplation of the formless; why the mantle of the Holy Virgin performs miracles and attracts pilgrims for centuries; why the face of the earthly beloved is the perfect mirror wherein is reflected the face of that Beloved who is above all form; why man can bow before a symbol of a material nature which has become the locus for the manifestation of an angelic or divine influence. It is also why traditional art and its principles are related to the esoteric and inward dimension of tradition and why it is through traditional art that the esoteric manifests itself upon the plane of the collectivity and makes possible an equilibrium which the exoteric alone could not maintain. It is through the channel of traditional art that a knowledge of a sacred character manifests itself, outwardly cloaked in the dress of beauty which attracts the sensibility of even those who are not able to understand its tenets intellectually, while providing an indispensible spiritual climate and contemplative support for those who do understand its veridical message and whose vocation is to follow the sapiential path.

Traditional art is of course concerned with beauty which, far from being a luxury or a subjective state, is inseparable from reality and is related to the inner dimension of the Real as such. As stated earlier, *scientia sacra* sees the Ultimate Reality as the Absolute, the Infinite and

Perfection or Goodness. Beauty is related to all these hypostases of the Real. It reflects absoluteness in its regularity and order, infinity in its sense of inwardness and mystery, and demands perfection. A masterpiece of traditional art is at once perfect, orderly, and mysterious.[30] It reflects the perfection and goodness of the Source, the harmony and order which are also reflected in the cosmos and which are the imprint of the absoluteness of the Principle in manifestation and the mystery and inwardness which open unto the Divine Infinitude Itself. In the sapiential dimension, it is this interiorizing power of beauty that is emphasized and God is seen especially in His inward "dimension" which is beauty. That is why that great masterpiece of Orthodox spirituality is entitled *Philokalia* or love of beauty and the famous *ḥadīth* asserts "God is beautiful and loves beauty."[31]

Intelligence which is the instrument and also primary concern of the sapiential path cannot be separated from beauty. Ugliness is also unintelligibility. The illuminated human intellect cannot but be intertwined with that beauty which removes from things their opacity and enables them to shine forth as transparent images and reflections which reveal rather than veil the archetypal realities that are the concern of the intellect, the Logos or Divine Intellect which is the source of the human intellect, being itself both order and mystery and in a sense, the beauty of God. That is why beauty satisfies the human intelligence and provides it with certitude and protection from doubt. There is no skepticism in beauty. The rays of its splendor evaporate all shadows of doubt and the wavering of the uncertain mind. Beauty bestows upon intelligence that highest gift which is certitude. It also melts the hardness of the human soul and brings about the taste of that union which is the fruit of gnosis. The knowledge of the sacred cannot therefore be separated from beauty. Beauty is of course both moral and intellectual. That is why man must possess moral beauty in order to be able to benefit fully from the sacramental function of intelligence. But once the moral conditions are present and beauty becomes a divine attraction rather than seduction, it is able to communicate something of the Center in the periphery, of the Substance in accidents, of the formless Essence in forms.[32] In this sense beauty not only transmits knowledge but is inseparable from knowledge of the sacred and sacred knowledge.

Beauty attracts because it is true, for as Plato said, beauty is the splendor of truth. Since beauty is ultimately related to the Infinite, it accompanies that emanation and irradiation of the Real which constitute the levels of existence down to the earthly. As *māyā* is the *shakti* of *Ātman*, beauty as the Divine *māyā* or Divine Femininity may be said to be the consort of the Real and the aura of the Absolute. All manifestations of the Ultimate Reality are accompanied by this aura which is beauty. One cannot speak of reality in the metaphysical sense without this splendor and radiance which surround it like a halo and which constitute beauty itself. That is why creation is overwhelmingly beautiful. Being and its irradiation as existence cannot but be beautiful, for ugliness, like evil,[33] is nothing but the manifestation of a relative nothingness. In the same way that goodness is more real than evil, beauty is more real than ugliness. If one meditates on the beauty of the vast heavens on a starry night and the inexhaustible beauty of the earth during a shining day, one realizes how limited is the domain of ugliness in relation to that beauty, how petty are the ugly monstrosities of human invention through the productions of the machine in comparison with the grandeur of the beauty of the cosmic order, not to speak of the transcendent beauty of the Divine Order, a glimpse of which is occasionally afforded to mortal men on those rare occasions when the beauty of a human face, a natural scene, or a work of sacred art leaves an indelible mark upon the human soul for the whole of life and melts the hard shell of the human ego. That is why beauty seen in the sapiential perspective, which always envisages beauty in its rapport with God, is a sacrament that elevates man to the realm of the sacred.

> *Oh Lord thou knowest that even now and again*
> *We never gazed except at Thy beautiful Face.*
> *The beauties of this world are all mirrors of Thy Beauty*
> *In these mirrors we only saw the Face of the King.*[34]
> AWHAD AL-DĪN KIRMĀNĪ

It is in the nature of beauty to attract spiritual presence to itself or, in the language of Neoplatonists, to receive the participation of the World Soul. From the gnostic point of view, the earthly function of beauty is therefore to guide man back to the source of this earthly beauty, that is, back to the principial domain. Beautiful forms are an occasion for the recollection of the essences in the Platonic sense.[35] They are means of remembrance (*anamnēsis*) of what man is and the celestial abode from which he has descended and which he carries still within the depth of his being. In this sense, beauty is the means of gaining knowledge; for certain human beings particularly sensitive to beauty, the central means. That is why some of the masters of the sapiential path have gone so far as to assert that a beautiful melody or poem or for that matter any creation of traditional art can crystallize a state of contemplation and bring about a degree of intuitive knowledge in a single moment that would be impossible to even conceive through long periods of study, provided of course the person in question has already purified his soul and clothed it with the beauty of spiritual virtues so as to be qualified for the appreciation of earthly beauty as the reflection of celestial beauty. That is why traditional art is a source of knowledge and grace. It makes possible a return to the world of archetypes and the paradisal abode which is the source of both principial knowledge and the sacred, for beauty is the reflection of the Immutable in the stream of becoming.

> *Consider creation as pure and crystalline water*
> *In which is reflected the Beauty of the Possessor of Majesty*
> *Although the water of this stream continues to flow*
> *The image of the moon and the stars remain reflected in it.*[36]
> RŪMĪ

The power of beauty to carry man upon its wing to the world of the essences and toward the embrace of union with the Beloved is particularly strong in those arts which are concerned with sonority and movement, arts which for that reason are also the most dangerous for those not qualified to bear the powerful attraction which they wield upon the human soul. Such arts as music and dance, which are connected with sound and movement, are like wine that can both inebriate in the spiritual sense of removing the veil of separative consciousness and cause the loss of even normal consciousness and bring about a further fall toward negligence and forgetfulness. That is why in Islam wine is forbidden in this world and reserved for paradise, while music and dancing are confined to Sufism or the esoteric dimension of the tradition, where they play an important role in the operative aspect of the path.

> *In memory of the banquet of union with Him, in yearning for His Beauty*
> *They have fallen inebriated from the wine which Thou knowest.*[37]
> RŪMĪ

Traditional music has a cosmological foundation and reflects the structure of manifested reality. It commences from silence, the un-manifested Reality and returns to silence. The musical work itself is like the cosmos which issues from the One and returns to the One, except that in music the tissues out of which the world is woven are sounds that echo the primordial silence and reflect the harmony that characterizes all that the absolute and infinite Reality manifests.[38] Music is not only the first art brought by Śiva into the world, the art through which the *asrār-i alast* or the mystery of the primordial cove-nant between man and God in that preeternal dawn of the day of cosmic manifestation is revealed;[39] but it is also the key to the under-standing of the harmony that pervades the cosmos. It is the hand-maid of wisdom itself.[40] Moreover, as described in a well-known Muslim popular tale, the soul of Adam was wooed into the temple of the body through the melody of a simple two-stringed instrument,[41] and it is through music that the soul is able to flee again from the prison of its earthly confinement. The gnostic hears in music the melodies of the paradise whose ecstasies the music brings about once again. That is why music is like the mystical wine. It cures body and soul, but above all it enables the contemplative to recollect the super-nal realities which lie within the root of the very substance of the human soul. Traditional music is a powerful spiritual instrument and, for that very reason, also one which poses a danger for those not prepared to receive its liberating grace.[42] That is why music which has turned against cosmic laws and its celestial origins cannot but be an instrument for the demonic and cannot but be the bearer of the dissolving influence of that cacophany which the modern world knows only too well.

As for dance, it, like music, is a direct vehicle for the realization of union. The sacred dance unifies man with the Divine at the meeting point of time and space at that eternal now and immutable center which is the locus of Divine Presence. From the sacred art of dance is born not only those great masterpieces of Hindu art in which Śiva performs the cosmic dance upon the body of his consort Parvati[43] but also the temple dances of Bali, the cosmic dances of the American Indians and the native Africans, and, on the highest levels, those esoteric dances connected with initiatic practices leading to union. Among these, one can mention the Sufi dance where the art of sacred dance and music are combined in bringing about recollection and placing man in a point above all time and space in the Divine Presence. In this form, traditional art complements the quintessence of spiritual practice, which is the prayer of the heart, in actualizing the Divine Light in the body of man seen as the temple of God and in placing man beyond all forms in that now which is none other than eternity.

Since beauty is the splendor of truth, the expression of truth is always accompanied by beauty. The grand expressions of metaphysics are clothed in the garment of beauty whether they be in the language of plastic forms or sounds—such as a Chinese landscape painting or a raga—or in human words such as the *Gītā* or Sufi poetry. What in fact distinguishes metaphysics and gnosis from profane philosophy is not only the question of truth but also beauty. Gnosis is the only common ground between poetry and logic, whether formal or mathematical. Wherever one discovers a doctrine which possesses at once mathematical and logical rigor and poetic beauty, it must possess a gnostic aspect. If Khayyām was at once a great poet and an outstanding mathematician, it was because he was first and foremost a gnostic.[44] It is only in gnosis or *scientia sacra* that the rigor of logic and the perfume of poetry meet, for this science is concerned with the truth. The great masterpieces of Oriental metaphysics such as the works of Śankara or Ibn ʿArabī are also literary masterpieces, a work such as the *Fuṣūṣ al-ḥikam* of Ibn ʿArabī possessing a remarkable perfection of form to complement the content.[45]

In the case of Sufism the wedding between truth and beauty is fully manifested in the numerous works which are at once outstanding expressions of sacred knowledge and masterpieces of art. The *Gulshan-i rāz* (*The Rose Garden of Divine Mysteries*) of Maḥmūd Shabistarī, written in a few days under direct inspiration of Heaven, is at once a summary of metaphysics and a poem of unparalleled beauty. The poetry of Ibn al-Fāriḍ in Arabic and the Divan of Ḥāfiẓ in Persian represent the most harmonious wedding between expression of esoteric doctrines and perfection of form with the result that this poetry is itself like the wine which inebriates and transmutes the soul. The *Mathnawī* and *Dīwān-i Shams* of Jalāl al-Dīn Rūmī are oceans of gnosis whose every wave reflects beauty of celestial origin. Its rhymes and rhythms, its rhapsodic trance uplift the soul and elevate it to that peak where alone it is able to grasp the sublime intellectual message of the great poet-saint. In the traditional world, and especially in the Orient, it has always been taken for granted that the truth descends upon the human plane with the aura of beauty which radiates from its presence and expression, like revelation itself which cannot but be beautiful whether that revelation be in the form of the Arabic Quran, Hebrew Torah, and Sanskrit Vedas, or the Buddha and Christ who are themselves considered as the message in their own traditions.

To be sensitive to the beauty of forms, whether natural or belonging to the domain of art, to see in the eye of the child, the wing of the eagle, the crystalline peaks of the mountains which touch the void, as well as in a page of Mamluk Quranic calligraphy, a Japanese Buddha image, or the rosette of the Chartres Cathedral, the signs of the Divine Hand, is to be blessed with a contemplative spirit. To remain aware of the liberating beauty of forms of traditional art as channels of grace of a particular tradition and to be open to the message of these forms is to be blessed with the possibility of reception of sacred knowledge. Traditional art is a source of this sacred knowledge and accompanies all its authentic expressions. The person who has realized sacred knowledge and who, through the path of knowledge, has reached the sacred is himself the best witness to the inextricable bond between knowledge and beauty, for such a person embodies in himself, by virtue of realized sapience, beauty and grace. Realization of sacred knowledge enables man to become himself a work of art, the supreme work of art of the Supreme Artist. To become such a work of art is to become a fountain of knowledge and grace, the prototype of all traditional art in which the artist emulates the Supreme Artisan and hence produces a work which is at once support for the realization of sacred knowledge, means for its transmission, and an externalization of the perfection which man himself can be if only he were to become what he truly is.

To behold a masterpiece of traditional art is to gain a vision of that reality which constitutes the inner nature of man as a work of the Divine Artisan, of that inner nature which man can reach through knowledge of the sacred and the realization of sacred knowledge. A great work of traditional art is a testament to the beauty of God and an exemplar of what man can be when he becomes himself, as God made him, a perfect work of art, a fountain of knowledge, and a channel of grace for the world in which he lives as the central and axial being that he is by his nature and his destiny. For man to become himself a work of art, as traditionally understood, is for him to become the pontifical man that he is and cannot ultimately cease to be.

NOTES

1. All sacred art is traditional art but not all traditional art is sacred art. Sacred art lies at the heart of traditional art and is concerned directly with the revelation and those theophanies which constitute the core of the tradition. Sacred art involves the ritual and cultic practices and practical and operative aspects of the paths of spiritual realization within the bosom of the tradition in question.

"Within the framework of traditional civilization, there is without doubt a distinction to be made between sacred art and profane art. The purpose of the first is to communicate, on the one hand, spiritual truths and, on the other hand, a celestial presence; sacerdotal art has in principle a truly sacramental function." F. Schuon, "The Degrees of Art," *Studies in Comparative Religion*, Autumn, 1976, p. 194; also in his *Esoterism as Principle and as Way*, pp. 183–97.

2. On the principle characteristics of traditional art see Schuon, *The Transcendent Unity of Religions*, pp. 66ff.

3. On the definition of traditional art see Schuon, "Concerning Forms in Art," in his *Transcendent Unity of Religions*; and idem, *Esoterism as Principle and as Way*, pt. 3, "Aesthetic and Theurgic Phenomenology," pp. 177–225; Burckhardt, *Sacred Art in East and West*, intro.; and Coomaraswamy, *Figures of Speech or Figures of Thought*; idem, *The Transformation of Nature in Art*; and idem, "The Philosophy of Medieval and Oriental Art," in *Zalmoxis* 1 (1938): 20–49.

A contemporary Japanese artist writing as a Buddhist says concerning art, "Son secret, sa raison d'être est d'aller jusqu'au fond même du néant pour en rapporter l'affirmation flamboyante qui illuminera l'univers." Taro Okawoto, "Propos sur l'art et le Bouddhisme ésotérique," *France-Asie*, no. 187 (Autumn 1966):25.

4. Coomaraswamy has dealt with this theme in many of his works esp. his well-known essays, "Why Exhibit Works of Art?" in his *Christian and Oriental Philosophy of Art*, pp. 7–22; and "What is the Use of Art, Anyway?" in *The Majority Report on Art*, John Stevens Pamphlet no. 2, Boston, 1937.

5. The work of such masters of gnosis as Śankara and Jalāl al-Dīn Rūmī belonging to two very different kinds of traditions exemplifies the wedding between knowledge of the highest order and beauty of expression.

6. It is significant to note that in Arabic *faḍl* or *faḍīlah* means at once beauty, grace, virtue, and knowledge.

7. T. Burckhardt has dealt with this theme in his various works on Islamic art.

8.

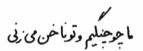

9. Until two or three decades ago, even students of Islamic thought in the West believed that the intellectual life of Islam had terminated with Ibn Rushd, or shortly thereafter, and even limited Sufism to its so-called classical expression in the sixth/twelfth and seventh/thirteenth centuries. But even in this state of unawareness of later Islamic intellectual life, a single dome of the quality and perfection of the Shāh mosque should have been intrinsic proof of the existence of such an intellectual life if only the organic and unbreachable link between sacred art and intellectuality in the sense understood in this book had been understood. Since then the research of Corbin, Āshtiyānī, and Nasr has provided the extrinsic proof of the presence of such an intellectual and spiritual life. See Corbin, "Confessions extatiques de Mîr Dâmâd," in *Mélanges Louis Massignon*, vol. 1, Paris, 1956, pp. 331–78; Corbin, *En Islam iranien*, vol. 4; Nasr, "The School of Isfahan," in M. M. Sharif (ed.), *A History of Muslim Philosophy*, vol. 2, Wiesbaden, 1966, pp. 904–32; Nasr, "Philosophy, Theology and Spiritual Movements," in *Cambridge History of Iran*, vol. 6 (in press). A decade ago when Corbin

and S. J. Āshtiyānī thought of compiling an anthology of the works of the metaphysicians and philosophers of Persia from the Safavid period to the present, they planned two or three volumes. Before Corbin's death already seven extensive volumes had been compiled of which only four have seen the light of day. The unveiling of this rich intellectual heritage, produced parallel with some of the greatest masterpieces of Islamic art, affords an excellent historical case study for the relationship between traditional art and intellectuality whose principial relationship we have outlined in this chapter.

10. It is these guilds which were at once depositories of technical and esoteric knowledge even if it were primarily of a cosmological order. Their secret organization and oral transmission made possible the preservation of a knowledge of a sacred order wed to the crafts and techniques of making and building. Only in this way can one explain the creation of cathedrals which combine art of the highest order with cosmological sciences and which display perfect unity although built by more than one generation of architects and craftsmen. Speculative Freemasonary came into being only when this esoteric knowledge became divorced from the actual practice of the arts and crafts and reduced to an occultism.

11. In Islam as in Christianity one observes a close nexus between the craft guilds and the Sufi orders, a relation which has survived to this day in certain Muslim cities such as Fez in Morocco and Yazd in Persia. The role of ʿAlī ibn Abī Ṭālib as founder of the Islamic guilds and at the same time primary representative of Islamic esoterism is very significant as far as the relation of the guilds to esoteric knowledge is concerned. On this question see Burckhardt, *The Art of Islam;* and Y. Ibish, "Economic Institutions," in R. B. Sargeant (ed.), *The Islamic City,* Paris, 1980, pp. 114–25.

12. Zen represents a perfect example of the wedding of spiritual instruction to the crafts not only in the making of pottery but also in landscape architecture, calligraphy, etc. See D. T. Suzuki, *Zen and Japanese Culture,* Princeton, 1959.

13. See M. Eliade, *The Forge and the Crucible,* chaps. 1 and 2.

14. "There is here a metaphysical inversion of relation that we have already pointed out: for God, His creature reflects an exteriorized aspect of Himself; for the artist, on the contrary, the work is a reflection of an inner reality of which he himself is only an outward aspect; God creates His own image, while man, so to speak, fashions his own essence, at least symbolically. On the principial plane, the inner manifests itself in the outer, but on the manifested plane, the outer fashions the inner, and a sufficient reason for all traditional art, no matter of what kind, is the fact that in a certain sense the work is greater than the artist himself, and brings back the latter, through the mystery of artistic creation, to the proximity of his own Divine Essence." Schuon, *The Transcendent Unity of Religions,* pp. 72–73.

15. See Schuon, "Principles and Criteria of Art," in his *Language of the Self,* pp. 102–35, where he has discussed certain works of modern painters like Van Gogh and Gaugin in which some of these qualities shine forth despite their being of a nontraditional character.

16. Among twentieth-century philosophers particularly concerned with the meaning of forms may be mentioned E. Cassirer. See *Die Philosophie der Symbolischen Formen,* 3 vols., Berlin, 1923–1929, trans. R. Manheim as *Philosophy of Symbolic Forms,* 3 vols., New Haven, 1953–1957. His appreciation of "symbolic forms" is, however, not the same as that of the traditional authors.

Traditional texts of both Western and Orthodox Christianity are replete with references to the fundamental significance of form and its effect upon the human soul. For example, St. Photios of Constantinople writes, "Just as speech is transmitted by hearing, so a form through sight is printed upon the tablets of the soul." Quoted in C. Cavarnos, *Orthodox Iconography,* Belmont, Mass., 1977, p. 30. See also the essay of L. Peter Kollar, *Form,* Sydney, 1980.

17. See Schuon, "Abuse of the Ideas of the Concrete and the Abstract," in his *Logic and Transcendence,* pp. 19–32.

18. "Art is iconography, the making of images or copies of some model (*paradeigma*)

whether visible (presented) or invisible (contemplated)." From Plato's *Republic*, 373B, trans. and quoted by Coomaraswamy in *Figures of Speech, Figures of Thought*, p. 37.

19. *Timaeus* 28A, B, trans. Jowett.

20. Quoted in Coomaraswamy, *The Transformation of Nature in Art*, p. 113.

21. "There is a highly significant connection between the loss of a sacred art and the loss of anagogy, as is shown by the Renaissance; naturalism could not kill symbolism—sacred art—without humanism killing anagogy and, with it, gnosis. This is so because these two elements, anagogical science and symbolical art are essentially related to pure intellectuality." Schuon, *Language of the Self*, p. 111.

22. On the Tenth Intellect and its emanation of forms which are not to be found in Aristotle but characterize medieval Peripatetic philosophy see chap. 4, n. 3 above.

23. St. Thomas insists that the artist must not imitate nature but must be accomplished in "imitating nature in her manner of operation." (*Summa Theologica*, quest. 117, a.I).

24. It is perhaps worthwhile to remember again the "definition" of the sacred given earlier as being related to the Immutable and the eternal Reality and Its manifestation in the world of becoming.

"It [the sacred] is the interference of the uncreated in the created, of the eternal in time, of the infinite in space, of the supraformal in forms; it is the mysterious introduction into one realm of existence of a presence which in reality contains and transcends that realm and could cause it to burst asunder in a sort of divine explosion." Schuon, *Language of the Self*, p. 106.

25. For reasons discussed already in earlier chaps.

26. His views on art are summarized by Coomaraswamy in his *Transformation of Nature in Art*, chap. 2, pp. 59–95.

27. See V. Lossky, *The Mystical Theology of the Eastern Church*, London, 1957; and L. Ouspensky and V. Lossky, *Der Sinn der Ikonen*, Bern, 1952.

28. T. Burckhardt in his *The Art of Islam* has explained for the first time in Western circles the meaning rather than just the history of Islamic art and revealed its link with Islamic esoterism whose "organizational" link to the arts was through the craft guilds which were usually associated with the Sufi orders. We have also dealt with this question in our forthcoming *The Meaning of Islamic Art*, New York, 1982.

29. G. Rowley, *Principles of Chinese Painting*, Princeton, 1947, p. 5.

30. In contrast for example to the humanistic art of late antiquity which, although possessing order and harmony, lacks the element of depth and mystery which would reflect the Infinite.

31. See F. Schuon, "Foundations for an Integral Aesthetics," *Studies in Comparative Religion*, Summer 1976, pp. 130–35.

32. Beauty possess this ambivalence, being at once means of attraction and seduction as a result of the power of *māyā* which is operative in the cosmic domain everywhere. If the exteriorizing and centrifugal tendencies associated with *māyā* in its aspect of veil and separation had not existed, tradition could rely on only beauty and not also morality, on only aesthetics and not also ethics. But the ambiguity of *māyā* requires the ascetic phase before the soul can allow itself to be attracted by the beauty of form toward the formless.

33. It is of interest to note that in Arabic beauty and goodness are both called *ḥusn* and ugliness and evil *qubḥ*.

34.

خبر در رخ خوب تو نکردیم نگاه   یا رب تو شناسی که به بیگاه و به گاه

در آینه دیدیم رخ حضرت شاه   خوبان جهان آینهٔ حسن تواند

This poem, by one of the leading Sufis who emphasized the role of beauty in spiritual realization summarizes the sacramental function of beauty. *Heart's Witness*, trans. B. M. Weischer and P. L. Wilson, Tehran, 1978, pp. 168–69.

35. "The cosmic, and more particularly the earthly function of beauty is to actualize in the intelligent and sensitive creature the recollection of essence, and thus to open the way to the luminous Night of the one and infinite Essence." Schuon, "The Degrees of Art," *Studies in Comparative Religion*, Autumn, 1976, pp. 194–207.

On the Platonic and Neoplatonic doctrine of beauty see R. Lodge, *Plato's Theory of Art*, New York, 1975; P. M. Schuhl, *Platon et l'art de son temps*, Paris, 1934; W. J. Oates, *Plato's View of Art*, New York, 1972; E. Moutsopoulos, *La Musique dans l'oeuvre de Platon*, Paris, 1959; T. Moretti-Costanzi, *L'estetica di Platone. Sua attualità*, Rome, 1948; J. G. Wary, *Greek Aesthetic Theory. A Study of Callistic and Aesthetic Concepts in the Works of Plato and Aristotle*, London, 1962; M. F. Sciacca, *Platone*, 2 vols., Milan, 1967 (with extensive annotated bibliography in vol. 2, pp. 351–427); H. Perls, *L'Art et la beauté vus par Platon*, Paris, 1938; G. Faggin, *Plotino*, 2 vols., Milan, 1962; G. A. Levi, "Il bello in Plotino," *Humanitas* 8 (1953): 233–39; F. Wehrli, "Die antike Kunsttheorie und das Schopferische," *Museum Helveticum* 14 (1957): 39–49.

36.

اندراوبید جمال ذوالجلال   خلق را جون آب دان صاف وزلال

عکس ماه وعکس اختر برقرار   شد مبدل آب این هر چند بار

37. Nicholson, *Selected Poems from the Dīvāni Shamsi Tabrīz, ī.* 177. The translation of Nicholson has been somewhat modified.

بیاد بزم وصالش در آرزوی جمالش   مُاده بنجراند زآن شراب که دانی

38. See chap. 6, n. 21 above, where the relation between traditional music and cosmology has been briefly discussed.

39. Rūmī says,

مطرب آغازید نزد ترکِ مست   در حجاب نغمۀ اسرار الست

The musician began to play before the drunken Turk
Within the veil of melody the mysteries of the eternal covenant [asrār-i alast].

See Nasr, "The Influence of Sufism on Traditional Persian Music," in Needleman (ed.), *The Sword of Gnosis*, p. 33.

40. This fundamental message of Pythagorean wisdom has now become a matter of great interest among many people in search of rediscovery of traditional knowledge as the works of H. Keyser, E. McClain, and others mentioned in chap. 3 demonstrate.

41. See Burckhardt, *Sacred Art East and West*, p. 9, where this story is recounted from the mouth of a street singer whom the author had heard in Morocco.

42. Music, esp. of the spiritual kind, which has grown out of the experience of the spiritual world and is meant to lead back to that world, can become like an opium which would replace rather than complement spiritual practice and give a false sense of

satiation of authentic spiritual thirst if it is cut off from its traditional context and heard incessantly. That is why in Islam the classical schools of music, all of which are of a completely inward and spiritual nature, are reserved for the contemplative life and closely associated with Sufism. See J. Nurbakhsh, *In the Tavern of Ruin*, New York, 1978, chap. 4, pp. 32–62; S. H. Nasr, "Islam and Music," in *Studies in Comparative Religion*, Winter 1976, pp. 37–45; idem, "The Influence of Sufism on Persian Music"; and During, op. cit.

43. On the symbolism of the dance of Śiva see A. K. Coomaraswamy, *The Dance of Śiva: Fourteen Indian Essays*, London, 1918.

44. On the relation between metaphysics, poetry, and logic see S. H. Nasr, "Metaphysics, Poetry and Logic in the Oriental Tradition," *Sophia Perennis* 3/2 (Autumn 1977): 119–28.

45. This is particularly true of the first two chaps. which contain the whole doctrine of Sufism and great beauty of expression. See Ibn al-ʿArabī, *Bezels of Wisdom*, trans. R. W. J. Austin, pp. 47–70.

CHAPTER NINE

Principial Knowledge and the Multiplicity of Sacred Forms

وَلِكُلِّ أُمَّةٍ رَّسُولٌ

Verily, to every people there has been sent a prophet.

Quran

تَفَكَّرْتُ فِي الْأَدْيَانِ جِدَّ تَحَقُّقٍ   فَأَلْفَيْتُهَا أَصْلاً شُعَباً جَمَّا

I meditated upon religions, making great effort to
   understand them,
And I came to realize that they are a unique Principle
   with numerous ramifications.

Ḥallāj

They worship me as One and as many, because they see
that all is in me.

Bhagavad Gīta

O
ne of the paradoxes of our age is that the manifestation of
religion in different worlds of form and meaning has been used
by the already desacralized type of knowledge, which has dominated
the mental outlook of Western man in recent times, to destroy further
what little remains of the sacred in the contemporary world. Modern
man is encountering the other worlds of sacred forms and meaning in
their full reality at the very moment when sacred knowledge and an
interiorizing intelligence, which would be able to penetrate into the

inner meaning of alien forms, having become so inaccessible. The result is that the multiplicity of sacred forms, which is itself the most definitive evidence of the reality of the sacred and the universality of the truth that each universe of form and meaning transmits in its own manner, has been employed, by those who deny the reality of the sacred as such, to relativize what has survived of the Christian tradition. The multiplicity of sacred forms has been used as an excuse to reject all sacred forms, as well as the *scientia sacra* which lies behind and beyond these forms. Had the West encountered other religions in a serious manner while a veritable intellectual tradition in the sense understood here still survived in its midst, the results would have been very different from the spectacle that "comparative religion" presents to the modern world.[1] For an intelligence which has been illuminated by the Intellect and a knowledge which is already blessed with the perfume of the sacred sees in the multiplicity of sacred forms, not contradictions which relativize, but a confirmation of the universality of the Truth and the infinite creative power of the Real that unfolds Its inexhaustible possibilities in worlds of meaning which, although different, all reflect the unique Truth. That is why the revival of tradition in modern times and the attempt to resacralize knowledge have been accompanied from the beginning with concern with the multiplicity of traditions and their inner unity.[2]

What is remarkable is that even in the study of the sacred, the principle that only the like can know the like has been forgotten and the secularized mind has adopted every possible path and method to study the phenomenon and reality of religion and religions, provided the nature of the sacred as sacred is not considered seriously. That is why despite all the light that the traditional perspective brings to bear upon the study of religions, it is so widely neglected. Hardly anyone in Western theological circles has made use of the keys which tradition alone provides to unlock the door of the understanding of other worlds of sacred form and meaning without destroying the absoluteness of religion; for traditional metaphysics alone is able to see each religion as *a* religion and *the* religion, "absolute" within its own universe, while reconfirming that ultimately only the Absolute is absolute. The neglect in official academic, and even theological and religious circles, in the West of traditional doctrines concerning the study of religions, either through chance or deliberately, is one of the most amazing phenomena in a world which claims objectivity for its scientific approach and manner of carrying out the study of any subject, but which usually mistakes the reduction of all reality to what can be grasped by secularized reason for objectivity resulting from the miraculous functioning of the intelligence.[3]

If one meditates upon the structure of reality, consisting of the three grand theophanies of the Principle as the cosmos, man, and revelation in the sense of religion and also tradition, it becomes clear that since manifestation implies externalization, the penetration into the meaning of external forms in all three cases is essentially an esoteric function. To go from the form to the essence, the exterior to the interior, the symbol to the reality symbolized, whether concerning the cosmos, man, or revelation, is itself an esoteric activity and is dependent upon esoteric knowledge. To carry out the study of other religions in depth, therefore, requires a penetration into the depth of one's own being and an interiorizing and penetrating intelligence which is already imbued with the sacred. Ecumenism if correctly understood must be an esoteric activity if it is to avoid becoming the instrument for simple relativization and further secularization.[4]

To be sure, in traditional worlds esoteric knowledge did not have to concern itself with other universes of meaning and alien sacred forms, except in very rare and exceptional conditions. Usually this interiorizing knowledge concerned itself with the particular religious world in which it functioned, as well as the soul of human beings and the grand phenomena of nature. Traditional sages would speak of the essence or meaning behind the form of a particular verse of their sacred scripture or religious rite. Likewise, they might explain the symbolic significance of the growth of a plant toward sunlight or certain images and states of the human soul. Rarely would a Buddhist sage provide a sapiential commentary upon the verses of the Quran or a Hindu be concerned with the specific inner meaning of a particular Christian rite, even if they would in a general way accept the universality of the Truth in alien religious worlds. The exceptions did, however, exist, as when Islam and Hinduism encountered each other in the Indian subcontinent;[5] but these cases remained more than anything else an exception and even then were not carried out in a barren desert where a living, homogeneous spiritual universe of form and meaning had ceased to exist. The full application of *scientia sacra* to the study of religions on a worldwide scale had to be preserved for modern times as both a compensation from Heaven for the secularization of human life and a cyclic event of the greatest importance, which signified the unraveling and explaining of the inner meaning of not one but all the living traditions of mankind in the light of tradition itself before the present human cycle terminates.

Strangely enough, although this traditional exposition of the various religions, their doctrines, rites, and symbols, and their relation to the Truth which they all contain inwardly and which they reflect has been neglected to a large extent in the modern world, the concern with the presence of other religions has been impossible to avoid. A sensitive and intelligent person today who is touched by those complicated sets of factors and forces which we call modernism cannot but be concerned with the multiplicity of sacred forms. And the more modernism spreads and the secularization of life increases, the more does this concern and awareness grow and even change in nature and kind.[6] A Muslim in a traditional village in northern Syria or in Isfahan is aware of the presence of Christianity in a manner which is by nature different from the concern of a college student in America or Europe for, let us say, Buddhism. Hence, the constant occupation of a large number of scholars and theologians in the West and also in modernized parts of the rest of the world with the study of other religions, which is sometimes called the history of religions, sometimes comparative religion, and sometimes by other names,[7] and the endless debate that continues about the appropriate method or methods to follow in the study of this crucial subject.[8]

From this pressing demand to have the meaning of the multiplicity of sacred forms explained, there have grown a number of approaches, most of which succeed only in debasing and trivializing even the most exalted subjects which they approach and which can explain the meaning of sacred forms provided the sacred nature of these forms has been extracted from them. In no domain, in fact, is the shortcoming of a secularized mind trying to grapple with what is really beyond its scope and power more evident than in the field of the study of religions, a shortcoming which has already had dire effects for certain schools of Christian thought and very disturbing consequences for the religious life of those who have been affected by it.

The study of "other" religions as a scientific discipline, in contrast to the kind of interest shown in Oriental doctrines as sources of knowledge to which reference has been made already, began from the background of a "scientism" which characterizes the early *Religionswissenschaft*. Religion was studied as fact belonging to various human cultures to be documented and described as one would study and catalogue the fauna of a strange land. The question of faith was of little importance; historical "facts," myths, rites, and symbols were more attractive since such aspects of religion could be made subjects for scientific study more readily than what appeared as the nebulous question of faith. It was as if music were to be studied in its purely mathematical and physical aspects and then the results were to be presented as the scientific, and thereby the only correct and legitimate study of music because the qualitative or, properly speaking, musical aspect could not be studied scientifically. This approach amassed a great deal of information about religions but rarely succeeded in providing meaning for what had been studied. A world view devoid of meaning could not possibly have provided meaning even for that which in itself was impregnated with meaning. Soon, therefore, a Western world thirsty for the meaning of religion realized the shortcoming of this approach and sought new ways and methods for arriving at understanding of its meanings. Something of this way of studying religion, however, has survived to this day and also has left a negative imprint upon the study of non-Western religions which cannot be removed so easily. This approach has provided many facts about religion but has interpreted these facts in a totally secularized manner, with the result that it has played no small role in the spread of the process of the desacralization of knowledge itself.

Parallel and often in conjunction with this "scientific" study of religion, there grew the purely historical treatment of religion based on the nineteenth-century historicism which was usually combined with evolutionism. According to this theory, all that appears in later religions is the result of historical borrowing since there is no such reality as revelation as traditionally understood. In this myopic perspective in which there is no logical nexus between cause and effect, no one bothers to ask how a person, no matter how clever, could amalgamate a few influences from Judaism and Christianity in some far away place in Arabia and create a movement which, in less than a hundred years, would spread from the Pyrenees to the borders of China, and which continues to give meaning to the lives of nearly a billion human beings today. Nor do they ask how the experience of an Indian prince sitting under a tree in northern India could change the whole life and culture in eastern Asia for the next twenty-five centuries. This complete lack of logic by those who claim to be using completely rational means of inquiry would have been understandable at least in the case of agnostics and atheists who, wanting to explain away the dazzling evidence of revelation at the origin of every tradition, took recourse to evolutionism. In this way, they hoped to explain the religious universe through purely historical causes without having to take recourse in the Transcendent in the same way that evolutionism in biology became "scientific" because it was the only way of evading the obvious evidence of the manifestation of a non-material reality or principle within the world of nature.[9]

What is more difficult to comprehend is the adoption of this point of view by many a Christian missionary or scholar who has written on occasion of the evolution of religion from the primitive level to its full development in Christianity and then has applied the historical method in its fullness to refute the authenticity of Islam as a message from Heaven.[10] It is this perspective that has caused Islam to fare worse than all other major religions in the field of the history of religions or comparative religion; it is also the reason that scholars in that field have made hardly any important contributions to the domain of Islamic studies.[11] But these scholars, who refute the authenticity of *ḥadīth* on the basis of the lack of historical evidence[12] or who consider the Quran to be merely a collection of Judeo-Christian teachings distorted because of a lack of authentic sources, hardly realize that the same arguments could be turned against Christianity itself. This has in fact been done by those who have tried to refute Christianity or some of its major tenets because of the lack of archaeological evidence, as if the Spirit needed any proof for its existence other than its own nature which intelligence can comprehend inately if it is not mutilated or veiled by extraneous factors.

The excesses of historicism, especially in the domain of the study of religion, went so far in reducing that which is itself of innate significance from the religious point of view into insignificant historical influence, that a reaction began within the circle of modern thought itself in the form of phenomenology. This school covers a rather extensive spectrum which touches at one end the traditional perspective itself[13] but which in many of its modalities falls into an error opposite to that of historicism, namely, the error of disregarding the unique reality of each manifestation of the Logos, of each revelation with the tradition, both historical and metahistorical which flows from such an opening of Heaven. In its insistence upon the value and meaning of each religious phenomenon in itself, irrespective of whatever historical origin it may have had, some phenomenologists became more or less collectors of religious ideas and symbols, as if they were going to place them in a museum, rather than interpreters of these phenomena in the light of the living tradition to which these phenomena belong. Moreover, this approach has been much less successful in dealing with an "abstract" tradition such as Islam than a mythological one. Likewise, it has not been able to distinguish between major manifestations of the Logos and less plenary ones, nor between living and thriving religions and those that have decayed.[14] Finally, for most phenomenologists of religion there has been no metaphysical basis upon which they would be able to interpret the phenomena as the phenomena of a noumenal reality. Since phenomenon means appearance, it implies even etymologically a reality of which it is the appearance.[15] But the post-Kantian skepticism of European philosophy made the knowledge of the noumena as being impossible or even absurd to pose as a possibility open to the human mind.

There have been those who have called themselves phenomenologists and who have spoken of their method as the way to unveil the outward meaning and to reach the noumenal or the inner essence of forms and phenomena and who have even called the phenomenological method the "unveiling of the hidden" (or the *kashf al-maḥjūb* of the Sufis).[16] But they have been the exception rather than the rule. By and large, phenomenology in describing religious rites, symbols, images, and ideas has avoided the error of historicism but it has fallen into another error by divorcing these elements from the particular spiritual universe in which they possess meaning. Altogether the phenomenological school of comparative religion, especially as developed in Germany and the Scandinavian countries, is the opposite but complementary pole of historicism and belongs to the same world of desacralized knowledge which gave birth to both of them.[17] In the same way that history can be used legitimately without falling into the error of historicism and that it is possible to have a historical view which is not historical in the limited sense of the term, it is possible to speak of phenomenology and use a method which is phenomenological without ending in that atmosphere of sterile fossil collecting which surrounds so many supposedly phenomenological works on religion, works which are themselves totally devoid of the sense of the sacred.

Yet another approach to the study of religions has been the one which sees in all religions the same truth, not of a transcendent order as tradition would assert but of an outward and sentimental kind which cannot but reduce religions to their least common denominator. Associated especially with certain movements which grew out of modernized Hinduism, this type of approach has characterized many of the modern syncretic and eclectic religious movements themselves, as well as various congresses and associations founded usually with the positive intention of creating understanding between religions but without the necessary intellectual perspective which would make such an understanding possible. What characterizes this type of approach is a kind of sentimentalism which opposes intellectual discernment and emphasis upon doctrine as being dogmatic and "antispiritual," together with a supposed universalism which opposes the particularity of each tradition on the level of that particularity, thereby destroying the sacred on the tangible level in the name of a vague and emotional universalism which is in fact a parody of the universalism envisaged by tradition. In its most positive form this type of approach is associated with a kind of spirituality based upon *bhakti* or love that engulfs the multiplicity of sacred forms in the warmth of its embrace without being concerned with the distinctions inherent in these forms. At worst it is feeble sentimentality which leads nowhere and which is devoid of any substance. In any case, this approach is not capable of penetrating into the meaning of sacred forms because it does not even accept the significance of these forms on their own level. In a world permeated with spirituality, such as traditional India, such a perspective could exist as a possibility but it was always complemented by the perspective based on discernment and, in any case, it was protected by the cadre of tradition itself.[18] In the modern world, it has usually served indirectly to further the process of the desacralization of knowledge and the destruction of the sacred itself by belittling the significance of both knowledge and forms even if they be of a sacred character.

Needless to say this kind of approach usually bases itself upon the mystical dimension of the religions which it studies, but its appreciation of mysticism is in the best of circumstances limited to that kind associated with love. In many cases, however, it treats that type of debased "mysticism" which is almost synonymous with incomprehension, unintelligibility, incoherence, and ambiguity and which stands at the opposite pole of the sapiential perspective which can itself be called mystical, if mysticism retains its positive character as that which is concerned with the Divine Mysteries rather than as used in its pejorative sense. It is against this oversentimentalized approach to the study of religions on the basis of a so-called universal spirituality, related to mysticism but devoid of intellectual content, that a reaction set in among many scholars of religion who began to point out the differences rather than the similarities between religions and various sacred forms, while keeping a critical distance from any claim of the existence of the unity underlying formal diversity. But these scholars have also usually been unable to distinguish between a unity which transcends forms and a supposed unity which disregards forms or rather seeks to melt them into a solution whose coagulation cannot but result in those conglomerates of religious ideas which characterize the so-called religious syntheses of the modern world. Metaphysically speaking, unity lies at the opposite pole of uniformity,[19] and the reduction of religions to a least common denominator in the name of the religious unity of mankind is no more than a parody of the "transcendent unity of religions" which characterizes the traditional point of view.

Recently, a number of scholars have turned their attention to mysticism itself to show that even mysticism is concerned with particulars of a religion and its specific and exclusive forms and not with universal ideas as claimed by the proponents of the kind of universality of religion based on mysticism already mentioned.[20] They claim that in Judaism, for example, the Kabbalists are concerned with the most detailed aspects of the Hebrew text of the Torah as are the Sufis with the Arabic text of the Quran, rather than with "abstract," universal ideas. Such authors point to the importance of sacred language and scripture as the fountainhead of mystical doctrines and teachings. They underline the essential role played by the letters, words, sounds, syntax, and other aspects of the language used in sacred texts for the mysticism of the tradition in question. In a sense, such critics reassert the significance of sacred forms; to that extent, their criticism is just and is a necessary antidote to those ideas and teachings which present mysticism as the formless without indicating the crucial significance of sacred form as the absolutely necessary means for the attainment of the formless. Where most of these critics fall short is in their lack of awareness of precisely this fact, that sacred form is not only form as particularity and limitation but also that it opens unto the Infinite and the formless. The Kabbalists do begin with the text of the Hebrew Bible and not with the Sanskrit Upanishads, but when they speak of the *En-Sof* they are dealing with that Reality which one can recognize as the same Reality with which the Advaitist school of the Vedanta is concerned. The opposition of these scholars to the sentimentalism of the syncretists is, therefore, although partly correct, a pendular reaction to the other extreme and marks one more instance in the series of actions and reactions which characterize so much of mental life and scholarly activity in the modern world.

The reductionism inherent in what can be called the sentimentalist approach toward the unity of religions has found a new expression in many of the ecumenical movements within Christianity which have come to the fore during the last few decades. This is true not only of ecumenism within the Christian religion among various churches and dimensions but also as far as the rapport of Christianity with other religions is concerned.[21] Although based often on the positive intention of creating better understanding of other religions, most of the proponents of ecumenism place mutual understanding above the total integrity of a tradition to the extent that there are now those Christian theologians who claim that Christians should stop believing in the incarnation in order to understand Muslims and have Muslims understand them.[22] One could only ask why they should then remain Christians and not embrace Islam altogether. Many ecumenists expect people of different faiths to become transformed by the very process of carrying out a religious dialogue and that, through the continuity of such a process, religions themselves will become transformed.[23] One does not, however, usually bother to ask into what they would be transformed, the assumption being that better understanding in itself is the final goal rather than understanding of another world of sacred form and meaning through the preservation of one's own tradition.

Such a perspective finally replaces divine authority by human understanding and cannot but fall into a kind of humanism which only dilutes what remains of religion. It is really another form of secularism and modernism despite the respect it has for other religions and the fact that it is carried out by men and women of religious faith.[24] That is why the stronger the hold of religion upon a human collectivity or individual, the less is there usually interest in what is now called ecumenism in that circle or for that person. Rather than the totality of the inhabited world, and hence engulfing the whole of humanity, to which ecumenism should be directed by its very meaning (*oikoumenē*), much of modern ecumenism has become like an engulfing amorphous mass which aims at dissolving all forms and removing all distinctions from several different realities by drawing them within a single or at best composite substance. One can detect in this current movement of ecumenism that same lack of distinction between the supraformal and the informal which results from the loss of an integral metaphysics in the West in modern times.

The creation of a closer relation between religions implied by ecumenism has also had its direct or camouflaged political counterpart. Numerous attempts have been made to create dialogue between two or several religions with political goals in mind.[25] This is especially true of Christianity and Islam[26] and more recently Judaism and Islam.[27] But it is also found in India as far as it concerns Hindus and Muslims and in other regions of the world as well. Despite the nobility of all attempts to create better understanding between people and the importance of realizing the significance of religious elements as underlying political and social realities, the use of religion as an instrument for political ends has caused these types of interreligious studies to end in either diplomatic and polite platitudes or false oversimplifications which have simply glided over the differences existing between different sacred forms. No amount of brotherly feeling is going to explain why Christians paint icons and Muslims do not and why each should respect the perspective of the other not through tolerance[28] but through understanding.

The result of the refusal to follow any of these paths of understanding other religions is religious disputation, exclusivism, particularism, and finally fanaticism of which the modern world does not certainly have a shortage, since these traits are not simply the characteristics of premodern men, as champions of progress would have claimed a century or two ago. What is important to note is that usually those who are exclusivist in their religious world view and who oppose other religions are usually themselves of a religious bent. Their opposition to other religions arises precisely from the fact that they do possess faith and that religion does have a meaning for them.

Those who attack this group for being prejudiced or fanatical and claim not to be so themselves because they have ceased to take religion itself seriously carry no advantage over the first group whatsoever. Nothing is easier than to be without prejudice about something which does not concern us. The problem arises precisely when one is deeply attached to a particular religion in which he has faith and within which he finds meaning in the ultimate sense. The criticism that can be made against the religious exclusivists is not that they have strong faith in their religion. They possess faith but they lack principial knowledge, that kind of knowledge which can penetrate into foreign universes of form and bring out their inner meaning.[29] There are of course those who, discouraged by what appears to them as an insurmountable obstacle to intellectual understanding, seek to emphasize the pole of faith in interreligious dialogue,[30] yet the element of knowledge remains indispensable because of the basic relation between knowledge and faith itself,[31] as well as the role which knowledge alone can play in making intelligible an alien religious world.

This rapid glance upon the landscape of religious studies today in as much as they concern the variety and diversity of religious universes reveals the shortcoming of each prevalent method from the perspective of tradition and the sapiential view which lies at its heart, although each approach may carry some positive aspect or feature. Today, one is given the choice between an exclusivism which would destroy the very meaning of Divine Justice and Mercy and a so-called universalism which would destroy precious elements of a religion that the faithful believe to have come from Heaven and which *are* of celestial origin. There is the choice between an absolutism which neglects all the manifestations of the Absolute other than one's own and a relativism which would destroy the very meaning of absoluteness. One is presented with the possibility of reducing all religious realities to historical influences or of considering them as realities to be studied in themselves without reference to the historical unfolding of a particular manifestation of the Logos. One must either accept the other politely and for the sake of convenience, or at best for the sake of charity, or contend and battle with the other as an opponent to be rebutted and even destroyed, since his view is based on error and not the truth. One is faced with the alternatives of not studying other religions at all and remaining devoutly religious within one's own tradition (although this is not a viable alternative for those touched by the truth, grace, and beauty of other religions) or of studying other religions at the expense of losing one's own faith or at best having one's faith diluted and shaken.

Modern man faces these alternatives at a time when the presence of other religions poses an existential problem for him which is very different from what his ancestors confronted. In fact, if there is one really new and significant dimension to the religious and spiritual life of man today, it is this presence of other worlds of sacred form and meaning not as archaeological or historical facts and phenomena but as religious reality. It is this necessity of living within one solar system and abiding by its laws yet knowing that there are other solar systems and even, by participation, coming to know something of their rhythms and harmonies, thereby gaining a vision of the haunting beauty of each one as a planetary system which is *the* planetary system for those living within it. It is to be illuminated by the Sun of one's own planetary system and still to come to know through the remarkable power of intelligence, to know by anticipation and without "being there," that each solar system has its own sun, which again is both a sun and *the* Sun, for how can the sun which rises every morning and illuminates our world be other than *the* Sun itself?

It is with respect to this crucial significance of the study of religions within multiple universes of sacred form that the pertinence of the traditional perspective and the principial knowledge which lies at its heart becomes clear for contemporary man faced with such a profound "existential" problem. The key provided by tradition for the understanding of the presence of different religions without relativizing religion as such is the result of one of the most timely applications of that sapience or principial knowledge which is itself timeless. Only this kind of knowledge can perform such a task because it is at once knowledge of a scared character and ultimately sacred knowledge itself.

Tradition studies religions from the point of view of *scientia sacra* which distinguishes between the Principle and manifestation, Essence and form, Substance and accident, the inward and the outward. It places absoluteness at the level of the Absolute, asserting categorically that only the Absolute is absolute. It refuses to commit the cardinal error of attributing absoluteness to the relative, the error which Hinduism and Buddhism consider as the origin and root of all ignorance. Hence every determination of the Absolute is already in the realm of relativity. The unity of religions is to be found first and foremost in this Absolute which is at once Truth and Reality and the origin of all revelations and of all truth. When the Sufis exclaim that the doctrine of Unity is unique (*al-tawhīd^u wāhid*), they are asserting this fundamental but often forgotten principle. Only at the level of the Absolute are the teachings of the religions the same. Below that level there are correspondences of the most profound order but not identity. The different religions are like so many languages speaking of that unique Truth as it manifests itself in different worlds according to its inner archetypal possibilities, but the syntax of these languages is not the same. Yet, because each religion comes from the Truth, everything in the religion in question which is revealed by the Logos is sacred and must be respected and cherished while being elucidated rather than being discarded and reduced to insignificance in the name of some kind of abstract universality.

The traditional method of studying religions, while asserting categorically the "transcendent unity of religion" and the fact that "all paths lead to the same summit," is deeply respectful of every step on each path, of every signpost which makes the journey possible and without which the single summit could never be reached. It seeks to penetrate into the meaning of rites, symbols, images, and doctrines which constitute a particular religious universe but does not try to cast aside these elements or to reduce them to anything other than what they are within that distinct universe of meaning created by God through a particular revelation of the Logos. It is thus keenly aware, as are the studies of the phenomenologists, of the value and meaning of a particular rite or symbol irrespective of its historical origin and, at the same time, is fully cognizant of the meaning of the revelation in both the temporal origin of a religion and its subsequent unfolding in history. This perspective realizes what a particular rite, idea, or symbol means in the context of a particular tradition as it has become manifested in history and not just as something by and in itself as abstracted from a particular spiritual universe. It thus avoids the error of both historicism and that kind of sterile phenomenology mentioned above which shares with historicism the unpardonable defect of studying a sacred reality by abstracting the sacred from it. It also opposes firmly every form of reductionism or the sentimental unification or even rapprochement of religions, which would do injustice to the existing differences and the unique and particular spiritual perfume and genius of each tradition willed by God, to the necessity of discernment and acceptance of all that comprises a particular religion as coming from God and therefore not to be cast aside for any reason of a human order.

A key concept in the understanding of the significance of the multiplicity of religions is that of the "relatively absolute" which, although it might appear to some as being contradictory, is impregnated with meaning of crucial importance once it is fully comprehended. As mentioned already, only the Absolute is absolute, but each manifestation of the Absolute in the form of revelation creates a world of sacred forms and meaning in which certain determinations, hypostases, Divine Persons, or the Logos, appear within that particular world as absolute without being the Absolute in itself. Within that world, that "relatively absolute" reality, whether it be the Logos itself or a particular determination of the Supreme Divinity, *is* absolute without ultimately being *the* Absolute as such. If a Christian sees God as the Trinity or Christ as the Logos and holds on to this belief in an absolute sense, this is perfectly understandable from the religious point of view while, metaphysically speaking, these are seen as the relatively absolute since only the Godhead in Its Infinitude and Oneness is above all relativity.

Principial knowledge can defend the absolute character which followers of each religion see in their beliefs and tenets, without which human beings would not follow a particular religion. Yet principial knowledge continues to assert the primordial truth that only the Absolute is absolute and hence what appears below the level of the Absolute in a particular tradition as absolute is the "relatively absolute." Thus the founder of every religion is a manifestation of the Supreme Logos and *the* Logos, its sacred book a particular manifestation of the supreme book or what Islam calls the "mother of books" (*umm al-kitāb*) and *the* sacred book, its theological and dogmatic formulation of the nature of the Divinity and the Divinity as such. It is only esoterism which can detect the trace of the Absolute in the multiple universes of sacred form and meaning and yet see the Absolute beyond these forms in the abode of the formless.

Each revelation is in fact the manifestation of an archetype which represents some aspect of the Divine Nature. Each religion manifests on earth the reflection of an archetype at whose heart resides the Divinity Itself. The total reality of each tradition, let us say Christianity or Islam, as it exists metahistorically and also as it unfolds throughout its destined historical life, is none other than what is contained in that archetype. It is the difference in these archetypes which determines the difference of character of each religion. Each archetype can be compared to a regular geometric figure like the square and the hexagon which are both regular geometric figures but which possess different characters and properties. Yet the archetypes reflect a single Center and are contained in a single all-encompassing circumference like so many regular polygons inscribed within a circle. They thus each reflect the Divine which is at once the Center and the all-comprehending circle while differing from each other in their earthly reflections.

There is, moreover, a kind of interpretation of the reflection of one archetype within the earthly reflection of another. If Christianity has a distinct archetype and Islam another, then Shīʿism appears in Islam as a purely Islamic reality, yet reflecting that type of archetypal religious reality associated with Christianity, while Lutheranism represents a Christian reality but one which, it could be said, is the result of the reflection of the Islamic archetype within the Christian world.[32] The same could be said of the *bhakti* movement in medieval Hinduism vis-à-vis Islam. In all these cases, the interpenetration of reflections of archetypal religious realities remains totally independent of historical influences which belong to a completely different order of cause and effect. It is in fact the lack of access to sapiential or sacred knowledge in modern studies of religions which makes it impossible to understand the reality of the archetypal world and of the vertical chain of cause and effect, with the result that every new phenomenon in a religious world is reduced to either historical influences or, even worse, socioeconomic causes.

This manner of seeing religions themselves as possessing archetypal realities with levels of manifestation down to the earthly and the interpenetration of the reflections of these archetypal realities within each other explains why each religion is both a religion and religion as such. Each religion contains the basic doctrine concerning the distinction between Truth and falsehood or Reality and illusion and a means of enabling man to attach himself to the Real. Moreover, although one religion may emphasize love, another knowledge, one mercy and the other self-sacrifice, all the major elements of religion must in one way or another manifest themselves in an integral tradition. Christianity as a way of love must have its path of knowledge in its Eckharts and Nicolas of Cusas. Islam which emphasizes direct access to God must have its intercession in the Shī'ite Imams. And even Buddhism which emphasizes so much man's own effort in reaching *nirvāna* through following the eightfold path must have room for mercy which appears in both Tibetan Buddhism and Amidhism.[33] It is for this reason that to have lived any religion fully is to have lived all religions and that in fact to realize all that can be realized from the religious point of view man can in practice follow only one religion and one spiritual path which are at the same time for that person *the* religion and *the* path as such.

This does not mean that at every moment of time all religions are actually in possession of all the possibilities inherent in them. Religions do not die since their archetype resides in the immutable domain and they are all possibilities in the Divine Intellect. But their earthly embodiments do have their life cycles. There are those religions of which we have historical records but which are "dead" in the sense that they can no longer be practiced. Although their forms and symbols remain, the spirit which enlivened these forms and symbols has left them and returned to the imperishable world of the Spirit, leaving behind a cadaver. There are other religions which, although still alive, are not fully and integrally alive in the sense that certain of their dimensions have become inaccessible. And there are still other religions whose ritual practices have decayed and in which the spiritual presence has given place to psychic ones. Therefore, the assertion that to have lived any religion fully is to have lived all religions does not mean that it is possible de facto to live fully every religion which happens to exist, especially as far as the esoteric dimension of tradition is concerned. As for the availability of this aspect of tradition today, surely one cannot assert that all religions can in fact be lived fully to the same extent.[34] At any event, it is only sapiential or principial knowledge that can discern the actual state of a religion as the thirst for such a knowledge can determine what religion or path a particular person will in practice seek, without this choice in any way contradicting in principle the "transcendent unity of religions" and the authenticity of all orthodox traditions as coming from the same Source and revealing messages at whose heart resides the same truth. The "theoretical" (in the original Greek sense of *theōria* as "vision") view of the universality of truth as found within the precincts of different worlds of sacred form is one thing, and the actual availability of means of gaining access to that truth in a particular moment of time and point in space quite another. In any case, from the initiatic point of view, it is in reality the way that chooses man and not man who chooses the way, whatever appearances might seem to convey from the perspective of the seeker.

The concept of the "relatively absolute" permits the traditional study of diverse religions to see the manifestation of the Logos in each religious universe as both *the* Logos and yet in its outward form as an aspect of the Logos as asserted already centuries ago by Ibn ʿArabī in his *Fuṣūṣ al-ḥikam* (*The Wisdom of the Prophets*)[35] in which each prophet is identified with an aspect of the wisdom issuing from the Logos, which Sufism naturally identifies with the Muḥammadan Reality (*al-ḥaqīqat al-muḥammadiyyah*).[36] This key concept is also able to discern within each religious universe the way in which the reality of the Logos is reflected in the founder, or a sacred book, or the feminine consort of the Divine Act, or other theophanic realities of a religion.

In contrast to outward methods of comparison which juxtapose the prophets or founders, sacred books, etc., of different religions, the traditional method realizes the different levels upon which the "relative absolute" is to be found in each world of sacred forms. It sees Christ not only in comparison with the Prophet of Islam but also with the Quran, both the Quran and Christ being the Words of God in Islam and Christianity respectively. It sees the similarity of the role played by the Virgin Mary as the ground from which the Word is born and the soul of the Prophet which received and divulged God's Word as the Quran.[37] It is able to comprehend the necessity for the presence of the feminine element of that reality which is the Logos in various traditions but in different forms and according to different degrees and levels of manifestations. It sees the presence of the Virgin in not only Christianity but also Islam as manifestation of a reality of a "relatively absolute" character in two sister religions and realizes the rapport of this reality to the feminine Kwan-Yin or the various consorts of Kṛṣna or Śiva in very different spiritual universes. It grasps the inner significance of the similarity between Śiva and Dionysius or certain aspects of Hermes and the Buddha. It might be asserted that these similarities have also been detected by scholars of religion who have in fact written much about them without any interest in, or claim of possessing, principial knowledge. This is true on the level of outward comparisons, but it is only principial knowledge or the traditional perspective that allows these comparisons to be made in depth and to be spiritually efficacious and to bring to light the relation that exists between primordial and archetypal religious types within different religious universes.

Another salient feature of much importance which needs to be repeated here is that principial or sacred knowledge of religion sees the meaning of each sacred form in the context of the spiritual universe to which it belongs, without either denying the significance of such forms on their own level or remaining bound to the world of forms as such. It sees the rites, symbols, doctrinal formulations, ethical precepts, and other aspects of a religion as part of a total economy within which alone their significance can be fully understood. Yet because at the heart of each religious universe resides the Logos which is also the root of intelligence, human intelligence is able to penetrate into these forms and comprehend their language as well as the innate significance of each and every syllable and sound of that language. It neither denies nor denigrates a single sacred symbol, rite, or practice in the name of some kind of abstract universal truth, nor does it create a simple one to one correspondence between various elements of the different religious universes.[38] At the same time, it realizes that beyond all these forms there stands the one formless Essence and that the major elements of religion as such are found in every religion despite this formal difference. The traditional method of studying religions is concerned with forms as they reveal that Essence, or with accidents which reflect the Substance. It does not negate the significance of forms on their own level of reality but considers their relativity only in the light of the Essence which shines through forms and which can be reached only through the acceptance and living of those forms.[39]

The very concept of tradition, as described already in earlier chapters, implies the character to totality as long as a tradition has been preserved in an integral manner. The great truths, which concern aspects of the Divine Nature and also the nature of the recipient of revelation, man, must manifest themselves in one way or another in each religion despite the fact that each religion is the reflection of a particular archetypal reality. There is no religion without the sense of the loss of the perfection associated with the Origin and Center and no religion without the means of regaining that perfection. There is no religion without prayer in whatever mode it might be envisaged, including of course contemplative prayer, and no religion in which prayer is not considered as the means of remolding man. There is no religion in which reality is limited to the temporal and spatial experience of this world and in which there is not a Beyond to which the soul of man journeys (including even the Buddhist doctrine of no-self which implies a state beyond that of *samsāric* existence and the possibility for man of reaching that state). There are numerous other fundamental elements of religion which manifest themselves in one way or another in all religions, although not in the same way.[40] Still, one cannot disregard in any way the fundamental differences which distinguish families of religion such as the Abrahamic, Indian, Iranian, or Shamanic from one another. But within these worlds with characteristic differences, each world possessing its own spiritual genius, the sapiential perspective is able to discern the presence of certain fundamental elements and to apply conceptual keys which concern the religious reality as such.

For example, there are three basic ways to God or relations between man and God, one based on fear, one on love, and one on knowledge, which in the practical spiritual life correspond to the three well-known mystical stations of contraction, expansion, and union.[41] In one way or another these elements are to be found in all the great traditions of mankind, although they manifest themselves in each case according to the genius of the tradition in question, and even appear in time according to the traits of the historical unfoldment of that tradition. In Judaism the perspective of fear found in the Pentateuch is followed by that of love found in the Song of Songs and the Psalms and, only many centuries later, by that of the gnosis of the Kabbalists. In Christianity the ascetic attitude of the Desert Fathers based on the perspective of fear is followed rapidly by the spirituality of love; only toward the end of the Middle Ages is it followed by the real flowering of the sapiential dimension of Christianity whose full development was truncated by the revolt against Christianity in the Renaissance. In Islam again, the same cycle is to be seen but in a more rapid order, spirituality based on knowledge appearing earlier in the tradition. With all the major differences in the manner of appearance of these basic attitudes and types of religious and spiritual life in each tradition, however, the three elements of fear, love, and knowledge have had to be present in every religion, although each religion has placed greater emphasis upon one element: Judaism upon fear; Christianity upon love; Islam upon knowledge. Nor have these elements been absent from Hinduism, where they are characterized clearly as *karma, bhakti,* and *jñāni* yoga, or Buddhism, where they are seen in different combinations and relationships in the Theravada, Vajrayana, and Mahayana schools, despite the nontheistic perspective of Buddhism.

Another example of this kind of application of metaphysical concepts as keys for the understanding of diverse religious phenomena can be found in the elements of truth and presence which characterize all religion. Every integral religion must possess both elements. It must possess a truth which delivers and saves and a presence which attracts, transforms, and serves as the means for deliverance and salvation.[42] But these fundamental components of religion are not found in the same manner in every tradition. For example, within the Abrahamic family Christianity, in a sense, emphasizes presence and Islam truth, while truth is of course indispensable to Christianity as is presence to Islam. And within the Islamic tradition Sunnism places greater accent upon truth and Shiʿism upon presence. The same two elements are to be found in Hinduism and Buddhism, where again certain schools emphasize one and certain schools the other of these fundamental components of what constitutes the reality of religion. Principial knowledge draws these keys from the "invisible treasury" of the Intellect and applies them to different worlds of sacred form in such a way as to make these worlds intelligible without either violating their particular genius or making them appear as opaque facts to be studied as either phenomena or historical influences.

It is only this type of knowledge that can take into account the amazing multiplicity of sacred forms and meaning without either becoming lost in this forest of multiplicity or reducing this multiplicity to something other than the sacred, thereby detroying its innate significance. It is also principial or sacred knowledge alone which can combine a perspective wed to the vision of a metahistorical reality with one centered upon the deployment and unfoldment of this reality in the matrix of time and history. Only this type of knowledge of religions can remain respectful of all that is discovered historically—but of course not as interpreted from the historicist point of view—without reducing that which by nature comes from the Eternal and is the call of the Eternal to that which is temporal and changing.

Needless to say, the study of other religions in this manner is essentially of an esoteric character. Man cannot penetrate into the inner meaning of a form except through inner or esoteric knowledge. Principial knowledge in fact cannot be attained save through esoterism in the sense that this term was defined and discussed earlier. One might say that only serious esoterists can carry out interreligious studies on the deepest level without sacrificing either the exoterism or the certitude and "absoluteness" associated with a particular religious world. Sages and gnostics would be perfect persons to choose for a veritable inter- and intrareligious dialogue if only they were available. One might say that total religious understanding and the complete harmony and unity of religions can be found, to quote Schuon, only in the Divine Stratosphere and not in the human atmosphere. Of course not all the faithful or scholars who study another religion are esoterists or saints and sages, but since man needs the stratosphere in order to survive in the atmosphere, it is vital today more than ever before to consider this view from the Divine Stratosphere in the question of religious dialogue or confrontation. In this as in several other domains, the presence of the esoteric dimension of a tradition is indispensable for the preservation of the equilibrium of the tradition in question, for it alone provides certain answers to questions of crucial importance, some of the most important of which in the modern world involve the multiplicity of religious universes and sacred forms.

In seeking to understand the significance of principial or sacred knowledge for the understanding of religious diversity, it is interesting to turn to those instances of religious encounter which do not belong to the modern period and which involved knowledge of a precisely sacred rather than profane character. Some of these encounters have been of a polemical, theological nature of which many examples abound especially in Jewish, Christian, and Islamic sources, there being a whole category of writings of this kind in Arabic literature.[43] With these writings and their content we are not so much concerned here, although they are also of great importance in showing to what extent the intensity of faith in a world impregnated by the presence of the sacred influences the rational faculty of veritable theologians when compared with many a secularized mind which characterizes itself as theological today. But of more immediate concern are the instances when a sage, possessing principial knowledge and participating in a sapiential tradition, has confronted another religious universe as can be found in the case of a Nicolas of Cusa, Jalāl al-Dīn Rūmī, and of course, in the Indian world, the numerous Sufis who tried to gain a direct understanding of Hinduism and vice versa. The translation of sacred texts from Sanskrit into Persian by such figures as Dārā Shukūh or commentaries written by a Muslim sage such as Mīr Findiriskī upon a basic work of Hinduism such as the *Yoga Vaiṣiṣṭha*[44] are not cultural phenomena of passing interest. They represent episodes of human history which are of great significance for contemporary men because they present cases in which, far away from the secularist context of the modern world, attempts were made by men of faith to understand other religions even across major barriers such as those which separate the Abrahamic world from the Indian. In this domain the Islamic tradition presents a particularly rich heritage which is of importance not only for contemporary Muslims, who sooner or later will become more seriously concerned than they are today with what is called comparative religion, but also for the West.[45] Such instances can help Western scholars distinguish, for the sake of their own studies of other religions, between elements which concern the innately difficult task of crossing religious frontiers and those which involve a secularized mind and a desacralized concept of knowledge with the help of which many a modern scholar is seeking to make the same journey often under more "urgent" circumstances. These cases also present examples of how an intelligence impregnated with the sense of the sacred has approached the presence of other worlds of sacred form starting from a point of departure different from that of most modern scholars of comparative religion, whether they be themselves theologians or out and out secular scholars.

Even if these overneglected instances are fully studied however, still there is no doubt that it is only in the modern world that princicial knowledge has been applied to the worlds of sacred form in detail in as much as they concern contemporary man as a religious being. Since such an undertaking would not have been necessary in normal times, it was left until the hour of the setting of the sun for tradition to decipher in principle and in detail the languages of diverse religions, which are in reality different languages speaking of the same Truth, or even dialects of the same Divine Language. Thus it prepares the ground for the rising again of the Sun which, according to the eschatological teachings of many a tradition including the

Islamic,[46] will mark the unveiling of the inner meaning of all sacred forms and their inner unity and the realization of the religious unity of mankind.

The task achieved by tradition in the study of different religions is, therefore, an indispensable element for the life of religion itself to the extent that contemporary man experiences both the secularizing influences of the modern world and other religious universes. It is only the traditional method and way of studying religions, based on the sacred conception of knowledge itself, that can go beyond both polite platitudes and fanatical contentiousness. Only through an intelligence rooted in the sacred and a knowledge which is of the principial order and attached to the sacred can the sacred be studied without desacralizing it in the process.

An immediate fruit of the resacralization of knowledge would be the expansion of the type of study of religions already carried out by the masters of traditional doctrine so that the study of various religions would not be simply a relativizing process and in itself an antireligious activity. Only a *scientia sacra* of religion, and not the science of religions as usually understood, can make available to contemporary man the unbelievable beauty and richness of other worlds of sacred form and meaning without destroying the sacred character of one's own world.

Sacred knowledge issuing from the One is able to penetrate into various worlds of multiplicity which have also issued from the One and to find therein not a negation of its own point of departure, of its own traditional foundations, but the affirmation of the transcendent Truth which shines through and across the different universes of sacred form that this Truth has created. In this manner sacred knowledge provides the most precious antidote for a world withered by the blight of the depletion of the sense of the sacred from all life and thought, an antidote which issues from the Divine Mercy itself.

NOTES

1. One could say that had such a sapiential tradition survived, the modern world would not have come about, the homogeneity of the Western tradition would not have been broken, and the presence of other religions would not have to be taken into consideration in a way at all differing from what we observe in other epochs of history. There is no doubt, in fact, that the presence of other traditions today as a reality which

concerns man in an "existential" manner is deeply related to the special predicament of modern man. Therefore, we pose this condition only theoretically in order to bring out the fundamental difference between the evaluation of the sacred by a sanctified intellect and by a secularized one.

2. The significance of this theme in the writings of the traditional authors is to be found already in the definition given of tradition which concerns eternal truth or wisdom as such. The number of articles and works by traditional authors on the study of religions and their "comparison" also attests to the centrality of this subject as far as tradition is concerned. See, for example, Guénon, *Introduction to the Study of Hindu Doctrines;* Coomaraswamy, "Paths that Lead to the Same Summit," in the *Bugbear of Literacy;* and esp. the numerous works of Schuon such as his *Transcendent Unity of Religions* and *Formes et substances dans les religions.* See alo M. Pallis, "On Crossing Religious Frontiers," in his *The Way and the Mountain,* pp. 62–78.

3. The opposition of objective knowledge to the sacred and the destruction of the sacred quality of religion on the pretext of being objective and scientific lie at the root of that error which was originally responsible for the reduction of the intellect to reason and metaphysics to a purely human form of knowledge that means ultimately the subhuman.

4. It is precisely in this sense of "esoteric ecumenism" that Schuon deals in his latest book, *Christianisme/Islam—Visions d'oeucuménisme ésotérique* (in press), with the Christian and Islamic traditions.

5. This encounter, despite its exceptional qualities, is nevertheless of great importance for the present day debates between religions of the Abrahamic family and those of India, although it has not been taken as much into consideration by those concerned with the theological and philosophical implications of the relation between religions today as one would expect.

6. One can discern this phenomenon in Europe itself where in countries such as Spain serious interest in other religions and the study of comparative religion has increased to the extent that the hold of Christianity upon the people has become weakened. Likewise, in the Islamic world the study of comparative religion has attracted most interest in those countries such as Turkey where modern educational institutions have witnessed the greatest amount of development and where there is a fairly extensive reading public which is already modernized to some degree and not strictly within the traditional Islamic framework.

7. Including the "science of religions" in the sense of the German *Religionswissenschaft.*

8. The appropriate methodology for the study of religions has been of concern to most of the leading Western scholars of comparative religion, such figures as J.Wach, M. Eliade, H. Smith, and W. C. Smith. The last has been particularly concerned with the appropriate method of studying other religions in the light of its meaning as religious activity. See, for example, W. C. Smith, *The Meaning and End of Religion: A New Approach to the Religious Traditions of Mankind,* New York, 1963; *The Faith of Other Men,* New York, 1963; and *Towards a World Theology,* Philadelphia, 1981, esp. pt. 3, which deals with the theological and "existential" significance of the study of religions from the point of view not only of Christianity but of other faiths as well.

9. The use of methods and philosophies in the study of religion in a fashion which parallels what one encounters in science is to be seen from the nineteenth century onward and the founding of the so-called science of religion which is imbued with the same positivism that characterizes the prevalent scientific philosophies of the day. The same can be said about the role of evolutionary concepts in the study of both religion and nature.

10. With the rise of evolutionary philosophy, and its application to the study of religions, many Christians thought that they could use this method to their own advantage by studying other religions as stages in the gradual perfection and growth of religion culminating in Christianity. This approach, however, left Islam as an embarrassing postscript which, according to the same logic, had to be more perfect than Christianity.

The purely historical and evolutionary approach cannot in fact be used as the means of defending any religion, including Islam, in which certain modern apologists have taken recourse to nearly the same arguments as those used by nineteenth-century Christian apologists concerning other religions. This is so because once a purely historical argument, based on the perfection of religion in time, is offered, there are those who claim that with the passage of time newer religious messages become more suitable and go "beyond" Islam or that Islam itself has to evolve into a higher form! The traditional Islamic doctrine of Islam's finality and perfection as the last religion of this cycle of humanity must not be confused with this nineteenth-century evolutionism which has infiltrated into the minds of many Muslim modernists anxious to defend Islam before the onslaught of Western orientalism or the attacks of certain Christian missionaires.

11. This subject has been already dealt with by Ch. Adams in his, "The History of Religions and the Study of Islam," *American Council of Learned Societies Newsletter*, no. 25, iii–iv (1974): 1–10.

12. There is a principle in Islamic philosophy according to which the lack of knowledge or awareness of something cannot be proof of the nonexistence of that thing (*ᶜadam al-wujdān lā yadullu ᶜalā ᶜadam al-wujūd*). Many modern scholars seem to ignore completely this principle, in fact reversing its tenet and insisting that what is not known historically could not have existed, thereby ignoring completely oral tradition and the whole question of transmission of knowledge and authority which lie at the heart of the very concept of tradition.

13. The interpretation of H. Corbin of phenomenology as the unveiling of the inner meaning of the truth (the *taʾwīl* of Islamic sources) and some of the earlier works of Eliade lie close to the traditional perspective, while there are a number of Scandinavian scholars of religion who call themselves phenomenologists but whose perspective is, to say the least, very far from that of tradition with its concern for the reality of revelation and the particular universe that each revelation brings into being.

14. This lack of discernment between plenary and minor manifestations of the Spirit and the various stages of the actual condition of various religions is to be found in the works of even such an eminent scholar as Eliade, who interestingly enough has made contributions to nearly every field of religious studies except Islam.

15. The contemporary philosopher O. Barfield has returned to this traditional theme in his *Saving the Appearances; a Study in Idolatry*, London, 1957, although treating it in an evolutionary context which destroys the permanent relationship that exists between appearances and their noumenal reality, irrespective of what Barfield calls the transformation of human consciousness from original participation to final participation. See his chap. 21.

16. Such is the characterization given by Corbin of phenomenology. See his *En Islam iranien*, vol. 1, p. xx.

17. Structuralism, which is associated with the anthropological works of C. Lévi-Strauss but which has now penetrated into the fields of philosophy, literary criticism, history, etc., is based on the tenet that all societies and cultures possess a permanent, unchanging, and common structure. Some have interpreted this view as being conducive to the traditional perspective and opposed to the antitraditional historicism that has dominated the social sciences for so long. While the latter part of this assertion is true, there is no guarantee whatsoever that structuralism leads to the traditional teachings any more than does phenomenology if the appropriate metaphysical knowledge is not available. One can say, however, that if there is such a knowledge then certain intuitions of structuralism can be integrated into the framework of that knowledge as can those of phenomenology.

18. For the Hindu *bhaktis* the tradition provided the necessary intellectual cadre and, in a sense, the tradition thought for them. It is for this reason that, once cut off from this essential framework and its protective embrace, the type of *bhakti* spirituality can lead to dangerous aberrations on the intellectual plane and finally to the kind of perversion of tradition in the name of the unity of religions which is so widespread today and which is most often identified with one movement or another of Indian origin.

19. On the fundamental distinction between unity and uniformity see R. Guénon, *The Reign of Quantity*, pp. 63–69.

20. See, for example, S. Katz, "Language, Epistemology, and Mysticism," in S. Katz (ed.), *Mysticism and Philosophical Analysis*, New York, 1978, pp. 22–74; and also idem, "Models, Modeling and Religious Traditions" (in press).

21. Although at the beginning many of those, like L. Massignon, who were concerned with ecumenism within the orbit of Christianity, were genuinely interested in the spiritual significance of other religions, soon ecumenism became identified practically with modernism within the church. In many cases during the past two decades, ecumenism has become the caricature of the concern of tradition for the transcendent unity of religions.

22. See, for example, J. Hick, "Whatever Path Men Choose is Mine," in Hick and B. Hebblethwaite (eds.), *Christianity and Other Religions*, Philadelphia, 1980, pp. 171–90.

23. L. Swidler, the editor of the *Journal of Ecumenical Studies*, one of the leading journals in America on the question of dialogue between religions, and a person earnestly interested in better understanding between religions, writes:

> By dialogue here we mean a conversation on a common subject among two or more persons with differing views. The primary goal of dialogue is for each participant to learn from the other. . . . Each partner must listen to the other as openly, sympathetically as he or she can in an attempt to understand the other's position as precisely and, as it were, from within, as possible. Such an attitude automatically includes the assumption that at any point we might find the other partner's position so persuasive that, if we would act with integrity, we would have to change our own position accordingly. That means that there is a risk in dialogue: we might have to change, and change can be disturbing. But of course that is the point of dialogue, change and growth. . . .
>
> In conclusion let me note that there are at least three phases in interreligious dialogue. In the first phase we unlearn misinformation about each other and begin to know each other as we truly are. In phase two we begin to discern values in the partner's tradition and wish to appropriate them into our own tradition. For example, in the Catholic-Protestant dialogue Catholics have learned to stress the Bible and Protestants have learned to appreciate the sacramental approach to Christian life, both values traditionally associated with the other religious community. If we are serious, persistent and sensitive enough in the dialogue we may at times enter into phase three. Here we together begin to explore new areas of reality, of meaning, of truth which neither of us had even been aware of before. We are brought face to face with this new, unknown to us, dimension of Reality only because of questions, insights, probings produced in the dialogue. We may thus dare to say that patiently pursued dialogue can become an instrument of new revelation.

From the Foreword of Swidler to P. Lapide and J. Moltmann, *Jewish Monotheism and Christian Trinitarian Doctrine*, Philadelphia, 1981, pp. 7–15.

24. We do not mean to imply that all movements for the rapprochement of religions, which in an etymological sense are ecumenical, are part of this type of ecumenism which comprises a distinct movement within both the Catholic and the Protestant churches.

25. This is not meant in a pejorative sense since it is perfectly legitimate to use every possible means to create peace among peoples provided that religious truth is not sacrificed in the process. The truth cannot be sacrificed for anything even if it be peace, for a peace based upon falsehood cannot be a worthwhile or lasting one.

26. As far as Christianity and Islam are concerned, there have been formal and official meetings and conferences involving the Catholic church, the World Council of

Churches, and individual Protestant churches outside the World Council. See, for example, the journal *Islamochristiana*, published by the Pontificio Instituto di Studi Arabi in Rome, which contains exhaustive information about Christian-Islamic conferences and dialogues as well as some articles of scholarly interest on the subject. As for the World Council of Churches, and its activities in this field, see S. Samartha and J. B. Taylor (eds.), *Christian-Muslim Dialogue*, Geneva, 1973; also *Christians Meet Muslims: Ten Years of Christian-Muslim Dialogue*, Geneva, 1977. There are many other works of concerned scholars in this domain including K. Cragg who has translated into English the *City of Wrong: A Friday in Jerusalem* by Kamel Hussein, Amsterdam, 1959, and written many works on Islamic-Christian themes including *Alive to God: Muslim and Christian Prayer*, New York, 1970; and *The Call of the Minaret*, New York, 1965; also D. Brown, *Christianity and Islam*, 5 vols., London, 1967–70; and from the Islamic side H. Askari, *Inter-Religion*, Aligarh, 1977. M. Talbi, M. Arkoun, and several other Muslim scholars have also been active in this process during the past few years, but strangely enough from both sides little use has been made of the sapiential perspective in making the inner understanding of the other religion possible.

One of the most devout Catholics and, at the same time, great scholars of Islam whose concern with Christian-Islamic understanding could have served as a beacon of light for later Catholic scholars, but who has not been as much followed as one would expect, was L. Massignon. See G. Bassetti-Sani, *Louis Massignon—Christian Ecumenist*, Chicago, 1974; also Y. Moubarak (ed.), *Verse et controverse*, Paris, 1971 (the editor, here pursuing a series of questions and responses with Muslim scholars, is a former student of Massignon and tries to reflect some of his teacher's concerns for Islamic-Christian understanding.

27. Serious religious dialogue between Islam and Judaism independent of Christianity has begun in earnest only recently because of the prevalent political conditions in the Middle East. But they are bound to be of the greatest import if taken seriously and in the context of the traditional framework of both traditions.

28. Although tolerance is better than intolerance as far as religions other than our own are concerned, it certainly is far from sufficient for it implies that the other religion is false yet tolerated. Understanding of different universes of sacred form means that we come to accept other religions not because we want to tolerate our fellow human beings but because those other religions are true and come from God. This perspective does not of course mean that one should tolerate falsehood on the pretext that someone or some group happens to believe in it.

29. In normal times when each humanity lived as a separate world, obviously such a knowledge was not necessary except in exceptional circumstances. The necessity of such a penetration into other worlds of sacred form and meaning increases to the extent that the modern world destroys the religious homogeneity of a human collectivity.

30. W. C. Smith must be mentioned esp. as one of the most notable among the academic Western scholars of religion who have emphasized the importance of faith in the study of religions. See, for example, his *Faith of Other Men; Belief and History*, Charlottesville, Va., 1977; and *Faith and Belief*.

31. On the relation between faith and knowledge see Schuon, *Stations of Wisdom*, chap. 2, "Nature and Argument of Faith," and his *Logic and Transcendence*, chap. 13, "Understanding and Believing."

32. This question is treated by Schuon in several of his recent works including *Formes et substance dans les religions*.

33. On this difficult question see M. Pallis, "Is There Room for 'Grace' in Buddhism?" in his *A Buddhist Spectrum*, chap. 4, pp. 52–71.

34. There are of course many factors which determine an act as profound as that of conversion, but from the point of view of the universality of tradition, it can be said that conversion can be perfectly legitimate for a person seeking a type of sapiential and esoteric teaching or spiritual instruction not available in his or her own tradition. In such a case the person makes the conversion without refuting the truth of the tradition

that he or she is leaving behind but in fact with the hope of coming to know even that tradition better than before. In any case, conversion from the sapiential point of view is never wed to proselytism of any kind without its denying the reality of the dynamics of religious missions, propagation, and conversion on the exoteric level.

35. See Ibn al-ʿArabī, *Bezels of Wisdom*, especially chap. 15. On his Logos doctrine see Burckhardt, *Introduction to Sufi Doctrine*, pp. 70ff., and his introduction to *De l'Homme universel* of al-Jīlī.

36. On the "Muhammadan Reality" see Ibn al-ʿArabī, op. cit., pp. 272ff.

37. Such profound morphological and metaphysical comparisons are to be found in all traditional writings on comparative religion but most of all in the works of F. Schuon, esp. his *Transcendent Unity of Religions; Dimensions of Islam;* and *Formes et substance dans les religions.*

38. For example, orientation in a sacred space is an essential part of religious rites but it does not mean that it has the same significance or even the same kind of significance let us say, in the rites of the American Indians and in the Christian Mass.

39. On this theme see Schuon, *Formes et substance dans les religions,* esp. pp. 19ff.

40. We do not of course mean that all elements are repeated in all religions or that, for example, time, creation, or even eschatological realities are the same in every religion.

41. These phases are dealt with in a general manner as far as Christian mysticism is concerned by E. Underhill in her *Mysticism, A Study in the Nature and Development of Man's Spiritual Consciousness,* New York, 1960, pt. 2.

42. See Schuon, *Islam and the Perennial Philosophy,* chap. 1, "Truth and Presence."

43. Called *al-Milal waʾ l-niḥal* in Arabic of which the work of al-Shahristānī is the most famous. *Milal* is the plural of *millah* and is used here to refer to theological views of various religious communities; and *niḥal* the plural of *niḥlah* meaning philosophical school or perspective.

44. The case of Mīr Findiriskī, who taught Avicenna's *Shifāʾ* and *Qānūn* in Isfahan, composed an important work on alchemy, was an accomplished metaphysical poet, and wrote a major commentary upon the *Yoga Vaisiśtha,* is of particular interest in the encounter between Islamic and Hindu intellectual traditions and deserves to be studied much more. On Mīr Findiriskī see Nasr, "The School of Isfahan," in *A History of Muslim Philosophy,* vol. 2, pp. 922ff. F. Mojtabāʾī undertook a most interesting Ph.D. thesis at Harvard University on Mīr Findiriskī and his commentary upon this Sanskrit work, but as far as we know, his work has never seen the light of day.

45. See S. H. Nasr, "Islam and the Encounter of Religions," in *Sufi Essays,* New York, 1975, pp. 106–34.

46. According to Islam when the Mahdī appears before the end of time, not only will he reestablish peace but he will also uplift the outward religious forms to unveil their inner meaning and their essential unity through which he will then unify all religions. Similar accounts are to be found in other traditions such as Hinduism where the eschatological events at the end of the historical cycle are also related to the unification of various religious forms.

CHAPTER TEN

Knowledge of the Sacred as Deliverance

As by a jar is meant the clay and by cloth the threads of which it is composed, so by the name of the world is denoted consciousness; negate the world and know it.

Śankara, APAROKSHANUBHUTI[1]

And ye shall know the truth, and the truth shall make you free.

Gospel of John

K nowledge of the sacred leads to freedom and deliverance from all bondage and limitation because the Sacred is none other than the limitless Infinite and the Eternal, while all bondage results from the ignorance which attributes final and irreducible reality to that which is devoid of reality in itself, reality in its ultimate sense belonging to none other than the Real as such. That is why the sapiential perspective envisages the role of knowledge as the means of deliverance and freedom, of what Hinduism calls *mokśa*. To know is to be delivered. Traditional knowledge is in fact always in quest of the rediscovery of that which has been always known but forgotten, not that which is to be discovered, for the Logos which was in the beginning possesses the principles of all knowledge and this treasury of knowledge lies hidden within the soul of man to be recovered through recollection.[2] The unknown is not out there beyond the present boundary of knowledge but at the center of man's being here and now where it has always been. And it is unknown only because of our forgetfulness of its presence. It is a sun which has not ceased to shine simply because our blindness has made us impervious to its light.

The traditional concept of knowledge is concerned with freedom and deliverance precisely because it relates principial knowledge to the Intellect, not merely to reason, and sees sacred knowledge in rapport with an ever-present Reality which is at once Being and Knowledge, not with a process of accumulation of facts and concepts through time and based on gradual growth and development. Without denying this latter type of knowledge which in fact has existed in all traditional civilizations,[3] tradition emphasizes that central knowledge of the sacred and sacred knowledge which is the royal path toward deliverance from the bondage of all limitation and ignorance, from the bondage of the outside world which limits us physically and the human psyche which imprisons the immortal soul within us.

While considering the ordinary knowing function of the mind connected with what we receive through the senses and the rational analysis of this empirical data,[4] tradition refuses to limit the role of knowledge to this level, or that of the intelligence to its analytical function. It sees the nobility of the human intellect in its being able to attain that knowledge which is beyond time and becoming, which, rather than engrossing us ever further in the accumulation of details and facts, elevates man to the level of that illimitable Being which is the source of all existents yet beyond them. To know that Being is to know in principle all that exists and hence to become free from the bondage of all limitative existence.[5] Ordinary knowledge is of properties and conditions of things that exist. Although legitimate on its own level, it does not lead to freedom and deliverance. On the contrary, when combined with passion, it can engross man in the web of *māyā* and, while leading him to ever greater knowledge of details and facts which would appear to be an expansion of his knowledge, in reality imprison him further within the limits of a particular level of cognition and also of existence. The knowledge which delivers, however, is of the root of existence itself. It is based on the fundamental distinction between *Ātman* and *māyā* and the knowledge of *māyā* in the light of *Ātman*. It is principial knowledge, the *Lā ilāha illa'Llāh*, which containing all truth and all knowledge, also delivers from all limitation. To know existence through the piercing light of intelligence is to be free from concern with the limited type of knowledge which engrosses but does not liberate the mind.

In order for knowledge to deliver, it must be realized by the whole man and engage all that constitutes the human microcosm. Intellectual intuition, although a precious gift from Heaven, is not realized knowledge. The truth held in the mind, although it is the truth and therefore of the highest value, is one thing and its realization another.[6] Realized knowledge concerns not only the intelligence which is the instrument par excellence of knowing but also the will and the psyche. It requires the acquisition of spiritual virtues which is the manner in which man participates in that truth which is itself suprahuman. Realized knowledge even affects the corporeal realm and transforms it. The physical radiance of the sage, of the one delivered through gnosis, is a reflection on the physical plane of the light of sacred knowledge itself. Realized knowledge resides in the heart, which is the principle of both the mind and the body and cannot but transform both the mind and the body. It is a light which inundates the whole being of man removing from him the veil of ignorance and clothing him in the robe of resplendent luminosity which is the substance of that knowledge itself. As the Prophet said, "Knowledge is light" (*al-ʿilmuᵘ nūrᵘⁿ*), and realized knowledge cannot but be the realization of that light which not only illuminates the mind but also beautifies the soul and irradiates the body while, from the operative point of view, realization itself requires as its necessary and preliminary condition the training of both body and soul, a training which prepares the human microcosm for the reception of the "victorial light"[7] of sacred knowledge.

Man is imprisoned by his own passions which usually prevent the intelligence within him from functioning in its "normal" fashion according to man's primordial nature, or what Islam calls *al-fiṭrah*.[8] Such infirmities as pride, pettiness, and falsehood are deformations of the soul which are obstacles that stand before the realization of knowledge. The sapiential perspective sees these evils or sins not only from a moral point of view related to man's will but also from an ontological point of view related to being and knowledge. Man should not be proud but humble because God is and we are not and the neighbor possesses certain perfections which we do not possess. The basis of humility is therefore not sentimental but intellectual.[9] The same is true of charity, truthfulness, and the other cardinal virtues whose absence or inversion marks the deformities of the soul and, theologically speaking, leads to the commitment of sin. To realize knowledge man must cultivate these virtues and embellish the soul in such a manner that it will become worthy of the visitation of the angel of knowledge. To speak of sacred knowledge without mentioning the crucial importance of the virtues as the *conditio sine qua non* for the realization of this knowledge, is to misunderstand completely the traditional sapiential perspective.[10] The virtues are so important that many a Sufi treatise which is concerned with gnosis deals most of all with the virtues rather than with pure knowledge itself,[11] thus preparing the soul for the reception of pure gnosis which is then described in terms of Unity or *tawḥīd*.

The sapiential perspective reduces all sins or deformities of the soul to ignorance of one kind or another or false attribution whose cure is knowledge, but that does not mean that the illness is not present and that the cure must not be administered. The fact that the sapiential perspective sees the root of pride in our ignorance of the truth that God is everything and we are nothing does not mean that we can continue to be proud with this theoretical knowledge in mind. That would be like reading in a book that a particular medicine is the cure for a certain illness. That knowledge in itself would not cure the illness. Somewhere along the way the medicine has to be actually swallowed no matter how bitter the taste. Likewise, man must actually cultivate the virtue of humility even after he has become aware theoretically of its intellectual rather than sentimental meaning. Only in actually becoming humble does man realize in his own being the reality which underlies and necessitates humility. The same holds true for the other virtues. Of course the emphasis upon different sets of virtues depends upon the structure of each tradition and the spiritual reality of the founder who is always emulated in one way or another as exemplar and model. But the cardinal virtues such as humility, charity, and truthfulness are present everywhere since they correspond in depth to the very reality of the human state and the stages of spiritual realization.[12]

The virtues are our way of participating in the truth. As already mentioned, the sacred demands of man all that he is. This is most of all true of sacred knowledge. Hence the necessity of the virtues which are the embellishment of the soul in conformity with the truth. Needless to say, metaphysically speaking, the attainment of supreme knowledge which delivers means the realization of the relativity of all that is relative including the soul and the virtues and the presenting of the soul as a gift to God. But this going beyond the realm of the soul is not possible save through the transformation of the soul itself, for one cannot present to God a gift not worthy of His Majesty and not reflecting His Beauty. The Sacred which is the Divine Presence itself transmutes the soul and bestows upon it beauty, power, and intelligence but then and only then does it take these gifts away to open the door to the inner chamber of the Sacred Itself wherein man receives that illuminating and unifying gnosis which melts away all otherness and separation. To overlook or belittle the significance of virtues in the name of the Supreme Identity is as much a fruit of ignorance or *avidyā* as rejecting forms on their own level in the name of the formless, as if one could ever cast aside what one does not possess or go beyond where one is not even located.

The association of realized knowledge with the spiritual virtues indicates how far removed this knowledge is from the purely mental grasp of concepts and judgments made upon them. This difference is to be seen also in the organic and inalienable nexus which exists between knowledge as here understood and love in contrast to purely mental knowledge that can and in fact does exist without any relation to love or to qualities of the person who holds such a knowledge as far as love is concerned. In the attainment of sacred knowledge there cannot but exist the element of love because the goal of this knowledge is union and it embraces the whole of man's being including the power of love within the human soul. Although the path of love and knowledge are markedly different, the gnostic, the *jñāni* or *al-ʿārif biʾ-Llāh*, cannot be devoid of what love implies although his path does not limit itself to the I-thou duality with which the spiritual way based purely on love or *bhakti* is concerned. Christian mysticism is for the most part a mysticism of love[13] but, within the Christian tradition as elsewhere, the gnostic perspective where it has existed has certainly not been devoid of the dimension of love as seen in the case of a Dionysius or Eckhart.

Furthermore, in those traditions whose spirituality is predominantly gnostic such as Islam, the element of love is constantly present as is evident in the works of an Ibn ʿArabī or Rūmī. The element of love is in fact present even in the sapiential perspective of a tradition such as Hinduism where the path of knowledge is more clearly delineated and separated from that of love. It should never be forgotten that the supreme master of Hindu gnosis, Śankara, who is the father of the Advaita Vedanta school for which only *Ātman* is ultimately real, all else being *māyā* to be pierced through by the light of knowledge and discernment, composed devotional hymns to Śiva. As for Islam, an Ibn ʿArabī, who formulated the doctrine of the Transcendent Unity of Being (*waḥdat al-wujūd*), composed works based on the language of love which were permeated with what the yearning through the power of the lover for the Beloved implies, as can be seen in his *Tarjumān al-ashwāq* (*The Interpreter of Desires*). Furthermore, he asserted that finally, after the attainment of the highest state of realization, "the Lord remains the Lord and the servant, the servant."[14] The pole of union, which is related to the realization of the One through knowledge and by virtue of passing through the gate of annihilation and nothingness, does not abrogate the other pole based upon the relation between the lover and the Beloved or the servant and the Lord, to use the expression of Ibn ʿArabī. It is only through realized knowledge that man can reach this truth and taste the actual experience of the One, which yet allows the servant to have the awareness of his own nothingness in the light of the One.[15] Only gnosis can make possible the attainment of that sacred knowledge, although pure knowledge is inseparable from love like the sun itself whose rays are at once light and heat, the Sun which both illuminates and vivifies. There is no common ground between the knowledge of Ultimate Reality of which the gnostics speak and the philosophical monism which would reduce the One to a mental concept logically opposed to the I-thou duality and all the other principial differentiations of which *scientia sacra* speaks, as there is no common ground between the realization of the Truth and mental discourse about it.

The rapport between knowledge and love and the distinction between theoretical knowledge of even a traditional character and realized knowledge are brought out in Sufism in the manner in which such masters as Rūmī, ʿAṭṭār or Najm al-Dīn Rāzī[16] speak of knowledge or "intellect" (ʿaql) and love (ʿishq). At first sight it seems that they are simply speaking about the path of love, that their concern is with a kind of mysticism based on love until we come across a verse of the *Mathnawī* such as,

> *We are non-being displaying existence;*
> *Thou art Absolute Being, our very being.*[17]

Then we realize that when such Sufis denigrate "knowledge" in the name of "love," they are trying to indicate the crucial importance of realization and the lack of common measure between theoretical and realized knowledge. For them there is the stage of theoretical knowledge, there is love, and then there is realized knowledge which includes the element of love and which they call *ʿishq* or love itself in order to distinguish it from theoretical knowledge or *ʿaql*. Their perspective, therefore, far from being opposed to the supremacy of knowledge, is based on that knowledge as it has become actualized and has consumed the totality of man's being. The whole rapport between traditional knowledge of a theoretical kind, but in the positive sense of theory as *theōria* or vision, and realized knowledge which the Sufis of this school call *ʿishq* is summarized by Ḥāfiẓ in a single verse,

The possessors of "intellect" [ʿāqilān] are the pivotal point of the compass of existence,
But love [ʿishq] knows that they are wandering in this circle in bewilderment.[18]

Traditional knowledge, even of a theoretical kind, is related to the center of existence and not to a peripheral point, but only realized knowledge is aware of the relativity of every conceptualization and every mental formulation vis-à-vis the Absolute and of that bewilderment which is not the result of ignorance but of wonder before the Divine Reality. For this bewilderment is none other than the one to which the Prophet of Islam referred when he prayed, "O Lord, increase our bewilderment in Thee."[19]

Sacred knowledge is also not opposed to action but incorporates it on the highest level as it encompasses the dimension of love. Today, contemplation is often conceived of as being opposed to action. In the modern world in which contemplation has been nearly completely sacrificed for a life of totally exteriorized action, it is often necessary to emphasize the independence and even opposition of contemplation vis-à-vis action as currently understood. Yet, there is no innate contradiction between them. The highest form of action is the invocation of the Divine Name associated with the prayer of the heart which requires the complete pariticipation of man's will and concentration of the mind and which enables man to accomplish the most perfect and powerful action possible, an action whose ultimate agent is God Himself.[20] But this action is also the source of knowledge and inseparable from contemplation.[21] On the highest level, therefore, knowledge and action meet while on the level of action itself, the gnostics and contemplatives have often produced prodigious feats of action ranging from the writing of voluminous works to the construction of great works of art, not to speak of the founding of institutions of a social and political nature. The prototype of this wedding between knowledge and action is to be found of course in those plenary manifestations of the Logos which are the great prophets and *avatārs* who have both perfect and total knowledge and transform the life of a whole humanity. The path of action, or what the Hindus call *karma yoga*, cannot embrace that of knowledge because the lesser can never comprehend the greater. But since knowledge is the highest means of spiritual attainment, it embraces the path of action as it does that of love and delivers man from the limitations of both concordant actions and reactions and the duality associated with love understood as sentiment, while incorporating unto itself all that is positive in the power of both love and action which, like knowledge, belong to that theomorphic being called man.

Having spoken of the structure and content of sacred knowledge in its relation to the totality of the human state, it is necessary to say a few words about the manner through which such knowledge is attained, although the full treatment of such a subject requires a separate extensive study of its own. How can one gain access to that knowledge which sanctifies and delivers? Based on all that has been said so far, our obvious response would be through tradition. But this answer, although necessary, is not sufficient by itself since sacred knowledge deals with matters of a veritable esoteric nature which, even in a traditional context, cannot be taught to everyone and which can even be harmful if transmitted to a person not prepared for its reception. Moreover, such a knowledge can never be divorced from ethics. The moral qualifications of the person who is to be taught must be considered, in complete contrast to the situation in the modern world where the transmission of knowledge has become divorced from considerations of the moral qualifications of the recipient of such a knowledge. The traditional view is completely otherwise, not only as far as sapience is concerned but for every kind and form of knowledge. One can see that even in the realm of the teaching of the arts and the crafts where the training of the student is ethical as well as technical. No one can be taught the knowledge associated with a particular craft without possessing the required moral qualifications and also being trained to practice certain ethical virtues along with the trade associated with the craft itself. If the teaching of the techniques of a craft is based on the moral qualifications of the pupil whom the master craftsman deems fit to instruct, how much more is this true of sciences which are ultimately of a divine character and which are not strictly speaking man's to dispense with as he wishes? Also, to teach this type of knowledge in an effective manner requires the actualization of certain potentialities and energies in the human being to which ordinary man does not have access and which can be reached only if, with the aid of certain keys, the doors to the inner recesses of the soul and the higher levels of being and of consciousness are unlocked.

All of these and many other considerations, which are in the very nature of things, have led to the necessity, within traditions which possess the possibility of providing means to attain sacred knowledge, of channeling these means through persons, orders, and organizations of an esoteric character and initiatic nature. There is the need for spiritual training, hence the master who knows and who can teach others, the master who has climbed the dangerous path of the cosmic mountain to its peak and who can instruct others to do the same. There is the indispensable need for a special power or grace which cannot but come from the source of the tradition in question and which can remain valid only if there is regularity of transmission or in any case access to the source of the tradition.[22] There is the necessity of preserving and protecting a teaching which cannot be taught to everyone and which, as mentioned, can be harmful for those who are not qualified to receive it. There is the necessity of preventing this kind of knowledge from becoming profaned. All of these considerations have necessitated within traditions belonging to the historical period, when cosmic conditions have necessitated the separation of the exoteric and esoteric views,[23] the creation within themselves of appropriated initiatic organizations, means of transmission, instruction, and the like which one can still observe in worlds as far apart as those of Japanese Zen and Moroccan Sufism.

In normal times in fact, sacred knowledge was rarely divulged in books and if it were, it appeared in a form which necessitated the traditional oral commentary to unveil its true import.[24] As Plato, himself a master of gnosis, said, serious things are not to be found in books. Over the millennia sacred knowledge survived not because the manuscripts by the masters were preserved in well-kept libraries, but because the oral transmission and a living spiritual presence continued, because in each traditional world in which such a knowledge survived the Logos continued to illuminate the minds and in fact the whole being of certain people who belonged with all their heart and soul to the religion lying at the heart of that traditional world. The realization of sacred knowledge could not but be according to a disciplined practice kept hidden to protect both that knowledge and those who, not ready to receive it, might be harmed by it as a small child might suffer mortally from the consumption of the food which constitutes the regular diet of adults.

The realization of sacred knowledge, therefore, has always been tied to the possibilities which tradition makes available. Obviously, therefore, if sacred knowledge is taken seriously both in its essence and as it has existed in human history, it cannot be separated from revelation, religion, tradition, and orthodoxy. The army of pseudo-masters who roam the earth today cannot make a plant whose roots have been severed to bloom no matter how many beautiful words or ideas they seek to draw from the inexhaustible treasury of sapience to be found in both East and West. The possibilities in the human intellect, which must be actualized in order for man to attain in a real and permanent manner sacred knowledge, cannot be actualized save by the Intellect, the Logos, and those objective manifestations of the Logos which constitute the various religions. Anyone who claims to perform such a function by himself and independent of a living tradition is in reality claiming to be himself the Logos or the manifestation of the Logos which, with what is to be observed in the current scene, is as absurd as to claim to be lightning without possessing either the light or the thunder which must accompany it. In any case, a tree is judged by the fruit which it bears. The *scientia sacra* which has issued from tradition and which is the fruit of realization is imbued with the perfume of grace and robed with forms of celestial beauty in total contrast to that type of pretentious esoterism and occultism rampant today which, even if possessing bits of traditional knowledge drawn from sundry sources, is characterized by a singular lack of that grace and beauty which liberate and which are inseparable from all authentic expressions of the Spirit.

The fact that sacred knowledge is by definition for the few does not mean either that other human beings are deprived of salvation in the religious sense or that the significance and import of such a knowledge is thereby limited to the few. All traditions are based on a way of living and dying which is for everyone in the humanity embraced by that tradition and a way which enables each human being to live a life that leads to either felicity in the hereafter or damnation, to the paradisal or infernal states. The paths of action and love are accessible to all. In religions with a Divine Law such as Islam, this Law or *Sharī'ah* knows of no exception and must be followed by everyone in his right mind from the gnostics and sages like Junayd and Ḥallāj to the simple peasant in the fields or cobbler in the bazaar. Divine Justice is therefore not denied or negated if the sapiential path remains for an intellectual elite, because there are other paths for those whose nature is not given to what the path of knowledge requires.[25]

Nor is the significance of sacred knowledge limited because only a few can follow its call. This is in fact true of all knowledge, even of the profane kind. How many physicists are there in the world and how many people can comprehend what goes on at the frontiers of physics today? Yet the effect of what those few who deal with the frontiers of physics theorize, devise, and discover has a far-reaching impact upon the life of the planet. In the 1920s and 30s, when one could fit practically all the physicists who were doing new work in physics into a single auditorium or large lecture hall, new theories and techniques were devised which soon shook the world, both figuratively and literally. In the case of sacred knowledge the rapport between the impact of the knowledge of the few and the lives of the many has always been even much greater for numerous reasons, not the least of which is that modern physics does not deal with ethics whereas sacred knowledge has been always related to the ethical foundations of the religion in which the particular form of sapience in question has flowered. Esoterism in each tradition has been the esoteric dimension of the tradition in question, not of something else. That is why the relation of the Taoist sage to the life of Chinese society as a whole or of a Clement of Alexandria to the Christian community or of a Sufi saint and gnostic like Shaykh Abu'l-Ḥasan al-Shādhilī to the Islamic world is far more profound and their influence far more extensive and enduring than that of contemporary scientists vis-à-vis modern society. One need not even speak of modern philosophers whose impact upon the world about them has become reduced to practically nil unless they become propagators of pseudoreligious ideologies such as Marxism, which would seek to replace religion itself. In the latter case we are no longer dealing with science or philosophy in the usual sense of the word but ideologies of mass appeal whose very popularity excludes their remaining of a strictly "intellectual" nature or concerned with the realm of knowledge alone.

In any case, the quantitatively limited expansion of the domain of sacred knowledge and the fact that its proponents have always been few does not at all imply any limit upon its influence within a whole world. A single lamp can illuminate a large area around it. In the same way the very existence of sacred knowledge provides not only the possibility for total liberation and deliverance for those who are able to follow its demands and pursue a path of a sapiential nature, but also makes available certain keys and answers which any religious collectivity needs in order to preserve its equilibrium. Such a knowledge makes available certain intellectual supports and props for faith and thereby helps even those who are unable to heed its call directly to live in a religious world protected from the mental doubt and skepticism which finally turn against faith itself. This knowledge alone can engage the mind in its totality and enable reason to become wed to faith rather than the mind and its rational powers becoming servile to that insatiable rationalism which devours and which like an acid burns the living tissues of the world of man and nature. The bitter experience of the modern world is categorical proof, if proof be needed, of what happens to a world in which such kind of knowledge is so eclipsed as to become practically inaccessible and, in any case, of such peripheral concern that it no longer has a role to play in either what is called the intellectual life or even the religious life of the community.

But let us return to the question of the realization of sacred knowledge itself. The goal of this knowledge is the Ultimate Reality, the Substance which is above all accidents, the Essence which is above all forms. Since man lives in the world of forms, however, even for the path of sapience which seeks the Highest Reality, forms are of great significance and as already mentioned, it is in fact only the sapiential perspective which can provide the key for the true significance of forms and symbols. The lover of God can claim indifference to forms in his state of spiritual drunkenness but the gnostic whose aim is to know cannot but pierce into the meaning of forms in order to go beyond them. That is why the metaphysics of sacred art in various traditions has been expounded by the Platos, Plotinuses, Diony-siuses, Shih-T'aos, and the like—all of whom belong to the sapiential perspective of their tradition. Metaphysically speaking, the under-standing of forms is an aspect of the intellectual journey of the gnostic toward the formless, while initiatically and operatively also forms play a crucial role as support for this journey. Whether it be a particu-lar symbol sanctified by the tradition to which the gnostic in question belongs or a particular work of sacred art or a natural feature such as a mountain, tree, or lake with which he "identifies" himself, forms play a central role in the life of those who have sung most eloquently and forcefully of the formless. Śri Ramana Maharshi who asked simply, "Who am I?" in a most direct *jñāni* manner, "identified" himself with the sacred mountain Arunachala,[26] while Ibn ʿArabī wrote one of his most powerful works on gnosis upon beholding the beautiful face of a young Persian woman circumambulating the Kaʿbah.[27] Those masters of sapience who have reached the other shore, the shore of the formless, have done so on the wing of forms of whatever nature these forms might have been. They have also been usually the type of spiritual persons most sensitive to forms and those who have created works of great beauty in their exposition of knowl-edge of the formless, as if they wanted to demonstrate in their own being to the world about them the metaphysical principle that beauty is the splendor of the Truth.

The basic form which carries the gnostic to the shore beyond all forms is of course that central theophany at the heart of revelation which constitutes prayer in its most inward and universal sense. The aspirant to sacred knowledge prays like all human beings who are aware of their human vocation. But he also performs that quintessen-tial prayer which is the prayer of the heart, the invocation of the Divine Name with its appropriate meditative and contemplative tech-niques. Although there are certainly other ways of spirtual realization based on different forms as images and symbols, the meditation upon and invocation of the Name of the Divinity, as found in the prayer of the heart of Orthodoxy, the *nimbutsu* of Jodo-Shin Bud-dhism, *japa yoga* in Hinduism, or the *dhikr* in Sufism, provides in this period of the cosmic cycle the primary path of spiritual realization and the most accessible means for the attainment of that knowledge which is sacred and which sanctifies.[28] This quintessential prayer which is the prayer of the gnostic is not in reality the prayer of man to God. Rather, God Himself "prays" in man. The invocation of the Divine Name is not by man qua man but by the Divinity who invokes His own Name in the temple of the purified body and soul of his theomorphic creature. In the same way the sacred knowledge of God is not attained by man as such. Rather, man knows God through God, he is the knower (or gnostic) by and through the Divinity and not of the Divinity (the *al-ʿārif biʾLlāh* of Islam).[29]

The great mystery of the operative aspect of the path of knowledge, as in fact of all spirituality, is the power of sacred form to enable and aid man to reach the formless, and this mystery is nowhere more directly and powerfully manifested than in the case of that supreme sacred form which is the Name of the Divinity as manifested through revelation in a particular sacred, or sometimes liturgical, language. Here, a sound system or *mantra* and a combination of letters unite in a cluster of visual and sonorous forms which, while belonging in their external aspect to the world of multiplicity and form, contain a presence which transmutes the being of man and possess a power which carries man beyond the formal order. In a sense, one can say that in His Blessed Name, God provides, amidst the very waves of the sea of forms, the vessel which enables man to pass beyond the sea of all forms and all becoming. The formless Essence "becomes" form in order for form to "become" the formless Essence. The gnostic seeks the formless but the gate to the Infinite Empyrean of the formless is sacred form at the heart of which lies the quintessential prayer associated with the invocation of the Divine Name in its proper traditional and liturgical settings.[30] The Name is both the means toward knowledge and Knowledge itself; it is the gate that opens toward the abode of the Truth in its ultimate sense and the Truth Itself. Through that inner mystery of the union of the Name and the Named, of God and His Blessed Name, the attainment of the sacred form *is* the attainment of the formless, for to live always in the Divine Name is to live in God and to see all things in Him, as they really are. Sacred form, especially the Divine Name, is thus not only the support of the seeker of sacred knowledge but also his goal. Being the direct "form of the Formless," it not only leads to the abode beyond forms but is itself in its inner infinitude the beyond here and now. In it the gnostic rediscovers his original abode toward which all creatures wander in their long cosmic journey but which only the realized human being reaches even in this life while living among men and in this world.

Precisely because of the awareness of his origin and of his home, the person in whom the fire of sacred knowledge has become inflamed and in whom the search and quest for the knowledge of the sacred has become a central concern is already a stranger to this world. He is an exile constantly in quest of that land of nowhere which is yet the ubiquitous Center and which constitutes his original homeland. The theme of the stranger or exile runs like a golden thread through the sapiential and gnostic literature of all traditions.[31] As in the Hermetic *Poimandres* or the Avicennan *Ḥayy ibn Yaqzān*, the adept in quest of knowledge encounters a luminous being, the Intellect, who recalls him to his own origin and reminds him of his own estrangement in a world which is not his own and in which he cannot but be a stranger and an exile.[32] He must therefore seek the fountain of life, led in this quest by the figure whom Islamic esoterism calls Khiḍr, the guide upon the spiritual path, the representative and symbol of the Eliatic function[33] which cannot but be always present. Having drunk of the water of immortality, which is also the elixir of Divine Knowledge, man regains his original consciousness and primordial abode. His wandering ceases and he arrives after his long cosmic journey at that home from which his true self never departed. The homeland of the gnostic is forever that spiritual country that is nowhere and everywhere, the land about which Rūmī says,

> *That homeland is not Egypt, Iraq or Syria,*
> *That homeland is the place which has no name.*[34]

For man to become an exile in this world is already a sign of spiritual awakening. To depart from the prison of limitation which this world is in comparison with the illimitable expanses of the spiritual world and finally the Divine Infinity is to be delivered through sacred knowledge.

The theme of the exile of the comtemplative and spiritual person in this world is elaborated in combination with the theme of the Orient and the Occident in the celebrated treatise *Qiṣṣat al-ghurbat al-gharbiy-*

yah (*The Story of the Occidental Exile*)[35] by Suhrawardī, the master of the School of Illumination (*al-ishrāq*) in Islam. In this remarkable initiatic narrative, the hero, who is the gnostic, hails from Yemen, the land of the right hand, hence by implication the East and the place of the rising sun or of light which is also being.[36] But he is imprisoned in a well in Qayrawān in the western extremity of the Islamic world, in the world of the setting sun and of shadows. Only when the hoopoe, the bird which symbolizes revelation, brings him news of his father, the king of Yemen, is the hero awakened to his call and he succeeds through numerous perils in reaching his original abode.

The story of the "Occidental Exile" is that of every contemplative imprisoned in the limited world of the senses and of physical forms. The soul of man and the intellect which shines at the center of his being come from the Orient of the universe, that is, from the spiritual world.[37] In this sense all men are Orientals; only the gnostic is aware of his Oriental origin and hence remains in exile in a world which is not his own, in that Occident which symbolizes the darkness of material existence in its aspect of opacity and not symbol. The Prophet of Islam has said, "The world is the prison of the faithful and the paradise of the unbeliever."[38] The sapiential interpretation of this well-known *ḥadīth* is that the person who possesses the intellectual intuition which enables him to have a vision of the supernal realities cannot but be alienated in a world characterized by material condensation, coagulation, separation, and most of all illusion. For him, knowledge is both the means of journeying from this world to the abode which corresponds to his inner reality, and which is therefore his home, and of seeing this world not as veil but as theophany, not as opacity but as transparence. Whether the gnostic speaks of journeying to the Reality beyond or living in that Reality here and now does not change the significance of the condition of the spiritual man being in exile in this world, for such a man is in exile as long as he is what he is and the world is what it is. Now, through knowledge he can either journey beyond the cosmos to that Metacosmic Reality in the light of which nothing else possesses separative existence, or he can realize here and now that the world as separation and veil did not even possess an independent reality and that the experience of the world as prison was itself a result of ignorance and false attribution. In either case the realization of sacred or principial knowledge delivers man from the bondage of that limitation which characterizes man's terrestrial existence and makes him an exile removed from his original abode and his true self.

The journey to the spiritual Orient by the person in quest of sacred knowledge is the journey to the Tree of Life, to that tree whose fruit bore for man the unitive knowledge from which he became deprived upon tasting of the fruit of the Tree of Good and Evil or separative knowledge. That is why Lurian Kabbala identifies the Orient with the Tree of Life itself.[39] To taste the fruit of this tree, which fallen man has forgotten as a result of the series of descents from the primordial perfection that mark his origin, is to experience that knowledge which is "tasted knowledge," *sapientia* (literally from the Latin root meaning "to taste"), the *ḥikmah dhawqiyyah* (the "tasted knowledge") of the Muslim sages such as Suhrawardī. To jouney to this Orient is to return to the Origin, the Orient in its metaphysical sense, being none other than the Origin.[40]

Moreover, the knowledge of this Orient is itself Oriental knowledge, that is, one based on the sacramental function of the Intellect and its illuminating power. To gain such a knowledge is to gain certitude, to be saved from the doubt that causes aberration of the mind and destroys inner peace. Sacred knowledge is based upon and leads to certitude because it is not based on conjecture or mental concepts but involves the whole of man's being. Even when such a knowledge appears as theory, it is not in the modern meaning of theory, but in its etymological sense as vision. It imposes itself with blinding clarity upon the mind of the person who has been given the possibility of such a vision through intellectual intuition. Then as the process of realization of this knowledge unfolds, it begins to encompass the whole of man and to consume him, leaving no locus wherein doubt could linger. That is why Islamic gnosis, basing itself directly upon the message and terminology of the Quran, which speaks so often of certitude (*al-yaqīn*), envisages all the stages of the acquiring of sacred knowledge as steps in the deepening of man's certitude. It speaks of the "science of certainty" (*ʿilm al-yaqīn*), "the vision of certainty" (*ʿayn al-yaqīn*), and the "truth of certainty" (*ḥaqq al-yaqīn*) which are compared to hearing about the description of fire, seeing fire, and being consumed by fire.[41] Of course only he who has been consumed by fire knows in the ultimate sense what fire is, but even the description of fire provides him with some knowledge of it which, coming from the source of traditional authority, is already combined with an element of certitude. Therefore, from the beginning of the process of acquiring knowledge of a sacred order, certitude is present.

This knowledge by its very nature encompasses all that man is and cannot exclude either love or faith which are the participation of man in what he does not know with immediacy but which he yet accepts with his mind and heart. Knowledge which removes the veil of separation does not annul this faith but comprehends it and bestows upon it a contemplative quality.[42] In any case he who has realized sacred knowledge and gained certitude participates in it with the whole of his being and with all that faith contains and implies in the religious sense. Far from being opposed to faith, sacred knowledge is both its support and its protector before that doubting mind which, cut off from both the Intellect and revelation, loses the security and peace of certitude and, in its attempt to embrace everything within the fold of its directionless agitation, turns upon faith itself.

If sacred knowledge involves the whole being of man, it also concerns the giving up of this being for its goal is union. The miracle of human existence is that man can undo the existentiating and cosmogonic process inwardly so as to cease to exist;[43] man can experience that "annihilation" (the *fanā’* of the Sufis) which enables him to experience union in the ultimate sense. Although love, as the force "that moves the heaven and the stars," plays a major role in attracting man to the "abode of the Beloved" and realized knowledge is never divorced from the warmth of its rays, it is principial knowledge alone that can say *neti neti* until the Intellect within man which is the divine spark at the center of his being realizes the Oneness of the Reality which alone is, the Reality before whose "Face" all things perish according to the Quranic verse, "All things perish save His Face."[44] This knowledge, as already stated, is strictly speaking not human. Man qua man cannot have union with God. But man can, through spiritual realization and with the aid of Heaven, participate in the lifting of that veil of separation so that the immanent Divinity within him can say "I" and the illusion of a separate self, which is the echo and reverberation upon the planes of cosmic existence of principial possibilities contained in the Source, ceases to assert itself as another and independent "I," without of course the essential reality of the person whose roots are contained in the Divine Infinitude ever being annihilated.

Between I and Thou, my "I-ness" is the source of torment.
Through Thy "I-ness" lift my "I-ness" from between us.[45]

Ḥallāj

The goal of sacred knowledge is deliverence and union, its instrument the whole being of man and its meaning the fulfillment of the end for which man and in fact the cosmos were created. During the long millennia of human history when men everywhere lived according to the dicta of tradition, this knowledge was present as an ubiquitous light in the inner dimension of various religions along with the appropriate means of realization tied, through their doctrine, symbols, formal homogeneity, and especially grace, to the source of the revelation in question. In the unfolding of the history of the world it could not but be, symbolically speaking, in the geographical West that this knowledge would be first lost, leading to the desacralization of knowledge and ultimately of all of life, including certain schools of theology. But the shadows resulting from this setting of the Sun of gnosis were to spread to the geographical Orient itself in reversal of the cosmic movement of the sun from the East to the West, weakening but not destroying the sources of such a knowledge even in those traditional worlds of the East which have survived to this day.

Before the complete setting of the Sun, however, the seed of this Tree of Life which is the spiritual Orient could not but be transplanted from the geographical Orient to the soil of the land from which the desacralization of knowledge had begun. Paradoxically enough, as those lands of the Orient, which were Oriental both geographically and symbolically, were to be covered completely by this shadow spreading from the land of the setting sun, something of that Oriental knowledge had to be reborn within the Occident itself. And as lands and areas of the East considered as sacred by various traditions became more and more desecrated in one way or another, the sacred land and spiritual homeland has had to be carried to an ever greater degree within the hearts and souls of human beings. The reinstatement of the traditional conception of knowledge as related to the sacred cannot but be a step in the rediscovery of that Orient which, although becoming ever more inaccessible as a definable geographical area, remains a blinding reality in the world of the Spirit.[46] In that sense, all those who seek such a knowledge are pilgrims to that Orient which will never cease to be, an Orient which cannot but attract more pilgrims from the Occident itself, pilgrims who, in making such a journey, resuscitate at the same time the "Oriental knowledge" or sapiential dimension of the Western tradition itself with all its depth and richness.

In this situation in which, as the shadows of a world marked by the loss of the sense of the sacred extend to lands beyond the Occident, sacred knowledge belonging to the Orient of universal existence becomes implanted in an authentic fashion and despite countless aberrations in the West and even the "Far West," the Quranic image of the Blessed Olive Tree that is neither Oriental nor Occidental becomes particularly meaningful.[47] As the Quran asserts, it is the light emanating from the oil of this celestial Olive Tree, which is neither of the East nor of the West and which is the Light of God, that illuminates all realms of existence. This Light is still accessible to man despite its apparent eclipse. The knowledge which this Light makes possible can still be realized and through it the sum of errors, which comprise modern thought and which have resulted in the unparalleled disequilibrium that characterizes the modern world, made to evaporate as the sun evaporates the morning fog. It is still possible to realize that knowledge which cannot and does not only resuscitate our minds and thoughts but which transforms our being and finally delivers us from the limitations of ourselves and of the world. Through such sacred knowledge, man ceases to be what he appears to be to become what he really is in the eternal now and what he has never ceased to be. Through this sacred knowledge man becomes aware of the purpose for which he was created and gains that illimitable spiritual freedom and liberation which alone is worthy of man if only he were to realize who he is.

Qūlū lā ilāha illaʾLlāh wa tuflihū
Say there is no divinity but the Divine and be delivered.

Ḥadīth of the Prophet of Islam

waʾLlāhᵘ aʿlam

NOTES

1. *Direct Experience of Reality*, trans. Hari Prasad Shastri, London, 1975, p. 51.
2. Principial knowledge is related to this immanent Logos in contrast to external, cumulative knowledge which is identified for the most part with science today. More-

over, the former is the root of the latter to the extent that the latter represents some degree or kind of authentic knowledge. To know the root is to know the whole in principle, if not in detail, and hence to be delivered for ever from the never ending process of the accumulation of details, of the knowledge of particulars or the various applications of principles to the indefinite reverberations of the One in the cosmic labyrinth.

3. It is important to point out that the type of knowledge that is called science today existed in traditional societies along with the, properly speaking, traditional sciences whose significance is usually misunderstood today, except that such "profane" sciences were never able to occupy the center of the intellectual stage. Nevertheless, it is only fair to add that not all the sciences cultivated in traditional civilizations were traditional and cosmological sciences with symbolic and metaphysical significance. Some were mere mental speculation or imperfect empirical knowledge corrected by more perfect observation and study in later centuries. One should not confuse the measurement of the distance between the earth and the sun by Alexandrian astronomers, which later astronomers were to refine, with the symbolic significance of geometry and arithmetic as expounded by Proclus or Nicomachus.

4. As mentioned in the first chap., even this function of the mind has a divine aspect since logic is the reflection upon the mind of the Logos and its categories are not at all arbitrary but ontological.

5. ʿUmār Khayyām who was at once a mathematician and poet and, contrary to how he is seen in the West, a gnostic rather than a hedonist, discussed various types of seekers of knowledge and modes of knowing. He came to the conclusion that the best way to know, since life is short and knowledge extensive, is to purify oneself so that the heart becomes itself the mirror of all knowledge. He writes, after describing other classes of knowers, "The Sufis do not seek knowledge by meditation or discursive thinking, but by purgation of their inner being and the purifying of their dispositions. They cleanse the rational soul of the impurities of nature and bodily form, until it becomes pure substance. It then comes face to face with the spiritual world, so that the forms of that world become truly reflected in it, without doubt or ambiguity. This is the best of all ways, because none of the perfections of God are kept away from it, and there are no obstacles or veils before it." Nasr, *Science and Civilization in Islam*, pp. 33–34. The text is from the treatise of Khayyām on being (*Risāla-yi wujūd*)—our translation.

6. "Metaphysical knowledge is one thing; its actualization in the mind quite another. All the knowledge which the brain can hold, even if it is immeasurably rich from a human point of view, is nothing in the sight of Truth." Schuon, *Spiritual Perspectives and Human Facts*, p. 9.

7. The term is drawn from the powerfully suggestive terminology of Suhrawardī who refers to the Divine Lights which illuminate the mind of man as *al-anwār al-qāhirah* (the "victorial lights") and to the soul of man himself as it is illuminated as *al-nūr al-isbahbadī* (the "signeurial light"). See Suhrawardī, *Opera metaphysica et mystica*, vol. 2, ed. by H. Corbin, Tehran-Paris, 1977, prolegomena pt. 3; and Corbin, *En Islam iranien*, vol. 2, pp. 64–65.

8. We have had occasion to refer in earlier chap. to this basic concept which constitutes the heart of the Islamic doctrine of man. The *fitrah* refers to what is essential and primordial in man and what remains permanent and immutable despite all the different veils that have covered this nature as a result of the gradual fall of man from this perfection, which he nevertheless contains within himself.

9. On the sapiential view of the virtues see Schuon, *Spiritual Perspectives and Human Facts*, pp. 171ff.

10. If in this present study more accent has not been placed upon this question, it is because our subject has been knowledge itself in its rapport with the sacred. But one should not gain the impression that this knowledge can in any way be divorced from the moral and spiritual virtues which the traditional texts never cease to emphasize.

11. A well-known example of this kind of Sufi treatise is the *Maḥāsin al-majālis* of Ibn

al-ʿĀrif. But many an early treatise such as the *Kitāb al-lumaʿ* of Abū Naṣr al-Sarrāj, the *Qūt al-qulūb* of Abū Turāb al-Makkī, and the celebrated *Risālat al-qushayriyyah* of Imām Abuʾl-Qāsim al-Qushayrī would fall into the same category.

12. Despite the many differences of technique and approach in various paths of spiritual realization, there is in every process of realization the three grand stages of purification, expansion, and union. Something in man must die, something must expand, and only then the essence of man is able to achieve that union concerning which Ḥallāj said (*Dīwān*, p. 46),

$$وفي فنائي فنا فنائي \qquad وفي فنائي وحدت انت$$

In my annihilation my annihilation was annihilated,
And in my annihilation I found Thee.

These three universal stages of spiritual realization correspond to humility, charity, and truthfulness if these virtues are understood in the metaphysical and not simply moralistic sense. See Schuon, *Spiritual Perspectives and Human Facts*, pt. 5.

13. It is the particular emphasis upon love as the central path of mysticism in Christianity that makes the term mysticism itself difficult to translate into Oriental languages, for example, Arabic, in which neither *maʿrifah* nor *taṣawwuf* means exactly mysticism; although in its most universal sense, mysticism can be understood to incorporate that reality which is *taṣawwuf*.

14. On Ibn ʿArabī's doctrine of union see Nasr, *Three Muslim Sages*, pp. 114–16; Burckhardt, *Introduction to Sufi Doctrine*, pp. 79ff; and Ibn al-ʿArabī, *Bezels of Wisdom*, esp. pp. 272ff. See also H. Corbin, *Creative Imagination in the Sufism of Ibn ʿArabī*, pt. 1, chap. 1.

15. On this difficult metaphysical question see Schuon, *Logic and Transcendence*, chap. 14, "The Servant and Union."

16. The author of the celebrated *Mirṣād al-ʿibād*, one of the masterpieces of Sufism; he is also known for his treatise *ʿAql wa ʿishq* which deals directly with the relation between love and knowledge.

17.

$$تو وجود مطلق وهستی ما \qquad ماعدم هائیم وهستی ها نما$$

18.

$$عاملان نكتهٔ پرگار وجودند ولی \qquad عشق داند كه دراین دایره سرگردانند$$

19.

$$یارب بدنا تحیراً مدّ$$

Classical Sufi treatises dealing with spiritual states and stations speak often of the state of bewilderment or *ḥayrah* which the adept experiences in more advanced stages of the path.

20. The sapiential teachings of all traditions in which the prayer of the heart or quintessential prayer is practiced insist that it is ultimately God Himself who invokes His Name within the heart of man and through his tongue.

21. On contemplation and action in their traditional context and as considered within

different religions see Y. K. Ibish and P. Wilson (eds.), *Traditional Modes of Contemplation and Action.*

22. This is especially emphasized in the Sufi orders, all of which are based on the *silsilah* or chain going back to the Prophet of Islam. See J. Spencer Trimingham, *The Sufi Orders in Islam*, Oxford, 1971, which despite a historical rather than traditional approach, contains a wealth of information on the Sufi orders and their chains. On the traditional meaning of the Sufi *silsilah* see M. Lings, *A Sufi Saint of the Twentieth Century*, Los Angeles, 1971, chap. 3, "Seen from Within."

23. The case of Christianity is quite special in that it was originally an esoteric teaching which had to externalize itself in order to become the religion of a whole civilization and thereby became an eso-exoterism. What can be more esoteric than eating the Body and Blood of the God-Man, which is what the Eucharist is for traditional Christians. This particular situation did not prevent elements of a veritable esoteric nature from becoming distinct organizations from time to time as we see in the case of the Templars, *Fedeli d'amore*, Christian Rosicrucians, Kabbalists, Hermeticists, etc. But the life of such groups was always a precarious one as the history of Christianity has born out. The esoteric dimension of course also manifested itself within the body of Christian theology and philosophy as we had occasion to point out in chap. 1.

24. In the modern world where the normal channels of transmission of esoteric knowledge are closed for many people, books play a role very different from what they did in normal situations and certain teachings, which had been preserved orally, begin to appear in writing as means of guiding those for whom there is no other means of guidance. This dispensation is a compensation for the loss of the traditional means of transmission of knowledge of the sacred, at least in its theoretical aspect, without there being any implication that even in this situation all traditional knowledge somehow appears in books in a form readily available to all.

25. It is strange how in the modern world which suffers from the stranglehold of a leveling egalitarianism, even on the intellectual level, people do not consider it against justice and equality if someone is a good mathematician or musician and another person has no gift in these fields, but as soon as it comes to metaphysics, they have a disdain for any kind of knowledge which is not comprehensible to everyone, forgetting that in the domain of knowledge, even of a profane kind, there is always a selective principle. There are simply those who know and those who do not, which does not mean that the door to the Divine Presence is not accessible for everyone born into the human state.

26. On the relationship of this great sage to the sacred mountain see A. Osborne, *Ramana Maharshi and the Path of Self-Knowledge*, London, 1970.

27. Ibn 'Arabī is said to have composed his *Tarjumān al-ashwāq* upon beholding the beauty of the face of the daughter of Abū Shajāʾ Zāhir ibn Rustam of whom he writes, "This shaikh had a virgin daughter, a slender child who captivated all who looked on her, whose presence gave luster to gatherings, who amazed all she was with and ravished the senses of all who beheld her . . . she was a sage among the sages of the Holy Places." From the *Tarjumān al-ashwāq*, quoted by E. Austin in his introd. to the *Bezels of Wisdom*, pp. 7–8.

28. In Sufism which belongs to the last religion of this human cycle, namely, Islam, the technique of *dhikr* is the central means for spiritual realization and its centrality is confirmed in many verses of the Quran and *Hadīth* as well, as in such classical treatises as *Miftāh al-falāh* of Ibn 'Atāʾallāh al-Iskandarī, while in the *Vishnu-Dharma-Uttara*, it is stated explicitly that at the end of the *Kali-Yuga* the most appropriate means of spiritual realization is invocation. The same truth is implied by certain Biblical passages. See Schuon, *The Transcendent Unity of Religions*, pp. 145–49, where many quotations from different traditions bearing on this subject have been brought together.

29. As mentioned already, *al-'ārif biʾLlāh* means literally "he who knows by God" rather than "he who knows God."

30. No Divine Name can be invoked which has not been invoked already by the Logos as founder of a religion and sanctified by the grace which issues from the

revelation in question. Likewise, the quintessential prayer cannot be practiced save under the instruction of a master and a traditional cadre which goes back ultimately to the founder of the tradition. This is a metaphysical necessity which would be obvious to anyone with a knowledge of the nature of the spiritual life and completely irrespective of whether historical records can be found of such a link of transmission in time going back to the origin of the religion in question.

31. We do not imply here by gnosticism a particular sectarian movement within early Christianity in which in fact this theme is also strongly emphasized. See H. Jonas, *Gnosis und spätantiker Geist*, 2 vols., Gottingen, 1954; and his *The Gnostic Religion: the Message of the Alien God and the Beginnings of Christianity*, Boston, 1970.

32. See Corbin, *Avicenna and the Visionary Recital*, pp. 123ff.

33. On the significance of the Eliatic function in the preservation and dissemination of sacred knowledge see L. Schaya, "The Eliatic Function," *Studies in Comparative Religion*, Winter-Spring 1979, pp. 31–40.

34.

آن وطن مصرو عراق و شام نیت   آن وطن آنجاست کانرا نام نیت

35. See Suhrawardī, *Oeuvres philosophiques et mystiques*, vol. 2 (where the Arabic text is printed), and the analysis by Corbin of the treatise in the French prolegomena; Also Corbin, *En Islam iranien*, pp. 258ff., where he discusses extensively the gnostic significance of the treatise under the title "Le récit de l'exil occidental et la geste gnostique."

36. Since in Arabic the root of the world *Yemen* is associated with the right hand, this land means symbolically the land of light, and in fact, if one stands facing the north, the right hand (*al-yamīn*) *is* the direction of the rising sun, while if one faces the sun itself the right hand points at the direction of Yemen (of course from Arabia). This obvious geographical symbolism has caused Islamic esoterism to identify Yemen symbolically with the "Orient of Light" while even historically it remained until recent times a center for the survival of the Islamic tradition and many of its most authentic and precious spiritual and artistic aspects.

37. For the symbolism of this Orient in the writings of Suhrawardī see Nasr, *Three Muslim Sages*, chap. 2; and Corbin, *En Islam iranien*, vol. 2, pt. 2 and pt. 8.

38.

الدنیا سجن المؤمن و جنة الکافر

39. This theme is treated by Ezra ben Salomon of Gerona in his *Mystery of the Tree of Knowledge* in which he identifies the Tree of Life with the Orient. See G. Scholem, *Von der mystischen Gestalt der Gottheit, Studien zu Grundlugriffen der Kabbala*, Frankfurt, 1973, pp. 59ff.

40. The root of the two words being the same.

41. This doctrine is expounded with much beauty in Abū Bakr Sirāj al-Dīn, *The Book of Certainty*, New York, 1974.

42. In Islamic sources this knowledge is often called "the theosophy based on faith (*al-hikmat al-īmāniyyah*) and contrasted with rationalistic philosophy which some sources identify with Greek rationalism (*al-hikmat al-yūnāniyyah*). Moreover, the *īmāniyyah* is often assimilated phonetically into "yemeni" (*yamāniyyah*) and identified with it.

43. In the sense of *ex-sistere*, of separation from the ground of Being.

44. Sapiential commentaries upon the Quran usually interpret the Quranic term "Face of God" (*wajhallāh*) to mean the Divine Names and Qualities, the externalization of whose reality through multiple levels of existence comprise the universe.

45.

$$فَارْفَعْ بِآنَكَ أَنِّي مِنَ الْبَيْنِ \qquad بَيْنِي وَبَيْنَكَ أَنِّي يُزَاحِمُنِي$$

See L. Massignon (ed.), *Le Dîvân d'Al-Hallâj*, Paris, 1955, p. 90.

The theme which has been echoed in the works of many Sufis including Ibn al-Fārid in his *Nazm al-sulūk* is also to be found in the famous poem of Hāfiz,

$$توخود حجاب خودی حافظ ازمیان برخیز \qquad میان عاشق ومعشوق هیچ حائل نیست$$

There is no veil between the lover and the Beloved;
Thou art thine own veil o Hāfiz remove thyself.

46. Sacred knowledge has survived to this day in the various Oriental traditions despite the vicissitudes of history which have weakened, destroyed, or mutilated the various traditional civilizations of the East. Therefore, although the Orient is obviously not the perennial traditional Orient which it has been over the millennia, even now something remains in the geographical Orient of that Orient which has to a large extent returned to the luminous empyrean from which it had descended on earth.

47. See chap. 2, n. 56.

Index

DATE DUE

HIGHSMITH   # 45220